When Worlds Converge

When Worlds Converge

What Science and Religion Tell Us about the Story of the Universe and Our Place in It

EDITED BY

CLIFFORD N. MATTHEWS, MARY EVELYN TUCKER, and PHILIP HEFNER

OPEN COURT
Chicago and La Salle, illinois

To order books from Open Court, call toll free 1-800-815-2280.

The cover image, from the Hubble Space Telescope, is used by courtesy of NASA/STScI/AURA.

The pictures on Color Plates 12–14, © Scala/Art Resource, New York, are used by permission.

Open Court Publishing Company is a division of Carus Publishing Company.

Library of Congress Cataloging-in-Publication Data

When worlds converge : what science and religion tell us about the story of the universe and our place in it / edited by Clifford N. Matthews, Mary Evelyn Tucker, and Philip Hefner.
       p. cm.
   Includes bilbliographical references and index.
   ISBN 0-8126-9451-1 (alk. paper)
   1. Religion and science. I. Matthews, Clifford N., 1921– II. Tucker, Mary Evelyn. III. Hefner, Philip J.

BL240.3 .W48 2001
291.1'75—dc21

                                                    2001133054

Contents

Preface

When we consider what religion is for mankind, and what science is,
it is no exaggeration to say that the future course of history depends
upon the decision of this generation as to the relations between them.
We have here the two strongest general forces . . . which influence
men and they seem to be set one against the other—the force of
our religious intuitions and the force of our impulse to accurate
observation and logical deduction . . . The clash is a sign that there
are wider truths and finer perspectives within which a reconciliation
of a deeper religion and a more subtle science will be found.

In the 75 years since Alfred North Whitehead issued this eloquent
challenge, we have been witness to extraordinary developments in
each of the major disciplines of science. Even more significant,
however, has been their coming together to give a coherent
story—from the Big Bang to Humankind—that makes possible
today our re-entry into Nature, here on Earth and in the Cosmos as
a whole.

Parallel to this revelation we see hopeful signs of another kind
of coming together, that of world religions, through increasing
numbers of publications, organizations, and meetings worldwide.
Perhaps, to quote Thomas Berry, it may even be that "the story of
the universe is the only thing that can bring the religions of the
world together."

A gathering of the Parliament of the World's Religions in Cape
Town, South Africa, in 1999 offered an attractive opportunity for a
dialogue involving science and religion. This took the form of a
four-day symposium with presentations by invited scientists,

science writers, and scholars of religion. Their stimulating contributions now make up the heart of this volume, *When Worlds Converge*. Rather than homogenize the chapters, we have tried to preserve much of the unique styles and approaches of each contributor.

Like the symposium out of which it developed, this book comprises three parts:

I. The Universe Story, organized by Clifford Matthews, discusses current scientific ideas on the origin and evolution of matter, life, and mind, and raises questions about cultural evolution, consciousness, and creativity.

II. The Emerging Alliance of Religion and Ecology, organized by Mary Evelyn Tucker, highlights the important role the world's religions play in constructing a moral framework for human interactions with the environment.

III. Science and Religion: Resource and Challenge for Each Other, organized by Philip Hefner, constructively examines the relation between science and religion from several different religious perspectives.

When Worlds Converge thus belongs to the rapidly developing encounter between science and religion and among the world's religious traditions, a coming together of minds which could help to bring about a peaceful, just, and sustainable future for us all.

The editors are deeply indebted to the Carus Family Foundation and the John Templeton Foundation for making it possible to bring together so many distinguished scientists and scholars. We thank Jim Kenney, Travis Rejman, Eric Carlson, Terry Deacon, and George Ellis, for their ready help with the planning of the symposium, and Rhonda Staudohar for invaluable secretarial assistance in the preparation of this book. All royalties from the sale of *When Worlds Converge* will be donated to the Council for the Parliament of the World's Religions.

PART I

The Universe Story

1
The New Story of the Cosmos

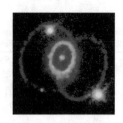

ᴇRIC ᴄARLSON

*As we leave the Earth, and journey out
beyond the solar system, we also journey
back in time, to the Big Bang, 14 billion years
ago, which generated everything we know.*

A favorite astronomy teacher of mine once said he loved to enliven his exams with this question: "If intelligent beings had been able to evolve on the planet Venus, which is perpetually shrouded in thick cloud cover, what kind of Universe would they have imagined?" Their world would shift mysteriously between diffuse light by day and utter darkness by night—with no apparent source of the light nor any evident cause for the darkness. One can only imagine what myths such hypothetical Venusians would have created to account for their world—but myths of some kind there would be in abundance, if they were anything like us humans.

Even with our easy view of the Sun and Moon and stars, during most of human existence we have all been in the position of spectators at a celestial mystery show without any program notes. We indeed made up countless stories to explain what we saw in the sky—or at least to quiet the children's questions about it—and thus took the edge off the raw mystery above us. But, despite the illogicality of many wildly different stories, the stability and predictability of celestial scenery, whatever its nature or cause, nonetheless gave us a sense of overarching comfort and security—in stark contrast to our lives on Earth amidst constant, unpredictable changes.

And so the comfort, such as it was, lasted—until with Copernicus arrived the wild idea that our Earth is not a site of fixed stability at the center of the Universe but a whirling planet traveling at high speed around the Sun. Then Galileo and his telescope revealed a sky filled with countless, formerly invisible stars. In the 1840s larger telescopes showed that stars are unimaginably far away in space—literally many trillions of miles distant—each star another sun, some bigger and brighter than our own—all part of a huge island of stars we christened the "Milky Way Galaxy." In the 1920s came the grandest revelations of all—our Galaxy is not the only one! Billions of galaxies throng a vastly larger Universe, grouped together in great superclusters of galaxies. And, even more amazing, all of the superclusters are expanding away from one another! The whole Universe is in motion. Moreover, we saw that stars and galaxies are themselves evolving in time. Stars are not eternal, our sun included, they are born, live out their lives, and end in various ways—rather too much of a parallel with human life. Like it or not, the undoing of our belief in celestial stability was complete.

This radical new picture of an open-ended developing Universe did not sit well with the stories of old, especially not where those cosmic stories had been inextricably woven together with religious beliefs. To admit that the cosmic part of religious beliefs has been in error might throw into question the validity of the other beliefs. Resistance, thus based, continues quite strongly in some quarters today—understandable at the emotional level, but also tragic, since it leaves people blind to the compelling gifts of wonder and inspiration that reside in the new and very real view of the Universe.

The New Mythos

Losing the sense of stability once found in a seemingly static or cyclic cosmos has, paradoxically, brought us an unexpected gift— a new kind of stability that is dynamic and forward moving in time—the very kind of stability, incidentally, that we experience as living beings. No longer must we see ourselves as passive spectators in the Universe. Instead, we have a new vision of ourselves as active players on a cosmic stage—part of an evolving Universe in which new levels of reality emerge over time, ourselves being one of them.

Because light travels at a finite speed, when we look at a star or galaxy we see it, not as it is now, but as it was long ago when the light, by which we now see it, left it. The farther out we look, the farther back into time we are able to see. Although we see different objects at different times in the past, we can splice these 'snapshots' of different moments in the history of the Universe together to create a realistic 'time lapse movie' of what has happened during cosmic time so far. We literally see before our telescopic eyes a cosmic drama unfolding with an unknown future yet to come—and we are part of the drama—the story of the Universe! And 'story' has always been the very essence of profound myth.

Centuries of painstaking observations, improving technologies, and complex thought have now given the human race a coherent narrative history of the Universe that presents us with a new Mythos for our time—one that is sorely needed. Generations before us have already lived through progressive dislocations and their consequent loss of 'at homeness' in the Universe. We, however, are now the fortunate first generation to experience a new kind of cosmic story that provides an exhilarating new sense of being at home in the Universe—one that is not 'just sitting there'—it's doing something! And one of the things it is doing is 'us'! We are part of the action—major players, at least locally in the Solar System. Maybe we are even early seeds of intelligent life at the beginning of its spread across our Galaxy. And we may possibly encounter other life that has arisen elsewhere.

Such new perspectives are a breath of fresh air, they inspire us, because they give us a sense of meaning and connection to the cosmic process never knowable before. At the same time, they bestow upon us the dignity of awesome responsibility, as we wrestle with the question of the fate of our own and all other species of life on Earth and confront the question of whether we are the only life in the Universe.

This new Mythos, or Cosmic Story, has another quality that fits it to the needs of our time, when change is forcing itself upon us in overwhelming quantity and speed. What we require is a cosmic story that is itself able to change as new observations and methods alter our conception of reality. No mythos that is unchanging will survive. And the magic elixir of modern science is that it can do what the others cannot, that is, change itself and its own perceptions of reality, while still providing the classic benefits of a mythos—supplying something familiar and supportive in the midst of change and challenge. Since we now perceive that we live in an endlessly evolving and emergent Universe and also see that we—and life itself—are evolving and emergent with new qualities, our new mythos must be one which is itself evolving and emergent.

The new Cosmic Story is a priceless gift to the religions of the world at a time when they are coming into close contact and often conflict with each other. As Thomas Berry puts it baldly, "The story of the Universe is the only thing that can bring the religions of the world together." But it will require of each religion the careful unwelding of teachings about the cosmos from their teachings about human nature, history, and behavior—not an easy task, yet one that is already proceeding rapidly in at least sectors of every religion today. To succeed, it also requires that the story of the Universe be told and retold as many times as possible, in as much detail as possible, and with constant careful accuracy, if it is to be believed in competition with the deeply impregnated cultural myths about the cosmos already in place in the minds of billions of people. This too is not an easy task.

The first assignment, then, is to learn the Cosmic Story in full ourselves. And, most importantly, it must also be felt and internalized at one's emotional center—which is where a new Mythos must take up residence to be effective. Think of how many pictures and tellings of the stories of competing cosmologies embedded in religious teachings have been experienced by the potential world audience for the new universe story. It is not an easy thing for people to overcome a lifetime of such experiences and separate them, with all due respect, from the hallowed cloak of religious tradition.

The universe story takes us on two vast mental journeys—one through space, the other through time. The first journey will take us outward through our Solar System, on out into the midst of our own Galaxy of stars, and ever, ever farther out into the endless ocean of galaxies (see Color Plate 1). In the second journey, we will explore what we can know about the Big Bang, then track the development of the Universe step by step forward in time—through the birth of galaxies, the birth of the higher elements in supernova explosions, the birth of our Sun and Earth, and the saga of life's development on the Earth to the present day.

Our Journey Through Space and Time Begins

As we lift off from planet Earth into our cosmic journey, for a while we gaze down in wonder at our blue planet with its oceans and white clouds, a planet some say should be called 'Water' not 'Earth'. We'll be taking our time to feel somewhat 'at home' among the planets of our Solar system, before moving much more quickly outward into stellar and galactic space.

Our nearest neighbor is, of course, the Moon. Its barren, airless and waterless expanses of rock are familiar sights to us today—thanks to the landing expeditions of astronauts. Models of its origin suggest that during the formative time of the early Solar System, a proto-planet larger than Mars collided with Earth, most of it mixing into our planet while some ejected material collected in orbit to become the Moon. Other studies show that its presence stabilizes the tilt of Earth's spin axis, preventing large changes in the tilt angle that would have greatly altered the development of life on Earth.

Now, let's head for Venus, our cloud-shrouded sister planet next closer to the Sun. Her clouds look white and friendly like Earth's water clouds, but they are not as they seem—they consist of droplets of sulfuric acid floating high up in a deep, thick atmosphere of mostly carbon dioxide. The energy of sunlight filtering through these clouds is partly trapped by a 'greenhouse' effect that has raised the ground temperature above 800 degrees Fahrenheit, without relief from pole to pole, either by day or by night. The terrible heat, along with a crushing surface air pressure 90 times Earth's, makes life unthinkable here. Radar mapping of the surface shows two sizeable upraised "continents," vast expanses of volcanic rock, and huge impact craters.

Mercury, still closer to the Sun, is much smaller than Earth or Venus. We see no air or clouds, only a barren, expanse of rock dimpled with countless impact craters, exposed to solar radiation ten times fiercer than at Earth. The ground temperature swings from above 800 degrees to minus 300 degrees Fahrenheit during super-long days and nights that last three months each.

As we draw still nearer to the Sun, we begin to sense its truly immense size. Over a hundred Earths would fit on a line through its center; more than a million Earths would fit within the Sun's huge volume. It's outer atmosphere surges with great releases of hot plasma (a gas in which all atoms are stripped of their electrons). Deep in the Sun's core, nuclei of hydrogen are colliding and fusing to become nuclei of helium—releasing in the process immense amounts of intense X-rays. These interact with particles in overlying layers of plasma, gradually transmuting their energy into the floods of gentle sunlight leaving the surface. We can estimate that over the past five billion years half the original hydrogen in the core has fused into helium, while at the same time the Sun has been slowly brightening.

As it continues to brighten, we can expect at best another one billion years before the Earth becomes unlivably hot. Then, a few billion years later, the Sun's surface will swell slowly outward as it becomes a 'red giant', enveloping and then vaporizing Mercury and Venus. It is now estimated that it will halt its outward expansion just short of the Earth's orbit, but there will be nothing to see here but hot or melted rock, the oceans and atmosphere being long gone. The outer regions of the bloated Sun will then stream away past the remaining planets into interstellar space in an expanding shell of colorful, fluorescing gases called a 'planetary nebula'. The dense helium core of the Sun, now exposed and still intensely hot, is a 'white dwarf' star hardly bigger than the Earth. It will cool gradually over many more billions of years, shining ever more feebly on its remaining planets. Any surviving intelligent life must by now have migrated farther out in the Solar System or ventured beyond it.

Farther from the Sun than Earth is Mars (see Color Plates 2A and 2B). Smaller than Earth, its entire surface is about equal to the combined areas of all Earth's dry land—a very large region indeed to explore. In its thin atmosphere of carbon dioxide float occasional clouds of ice crystals or carbon dioxide crystals. Occasional fast winds loft fine dust particles that create the orange sky we see in some pictures. A water ocean may once have covered the northern plains of the planet during its early history, and we see many signs of vast ancient flood channels. What water remains visible today is in the northern ice cap, the rest presumably locked underground. A vast canyon, Valles Marineris, stretches 3,000 miles along the equator, at points 20,000 feet deep. The rest of the terrain is a frozen, rocky desert dotted with impact craters and occasional huge volcanos. Given the recent discoveries of life forms in extreme environments on Earth, the search for life, past or present, on Mars continues enthusiastically.

It is now evident that the impacts that have left large craters on Mars, Earth, the Moon, Venus, and Mercury are capable of blasting sizable rocks and boulders off these planets and into space. Some microscopic forms of life that might exist inside such rocks could survive for long periods in space. Some of these rocks eventually collide with another planet, as we know from analyzing over a dozen meteorites on Earth that clearly came from Mars and others that came from the Moon. So there are presumably Earth-rocks on Mars and Venus, the Moon and Mercury, and similarly rocks from those bodies have landed on Earth and on each other. If life began on Earth, it could have seeded life on Mars; or it could have begun on Mars and seeded Earth, later dying out or going underground on Mars, making us all technically 'Martians'—with a few of us now hoping to return to the mother planet!

Most of the space rocks responsible for this fascinating and perhaps fruitful exchange of material in the inner Solar System are strays from a region beyond Mars called the 'asteroid zone'. In this region are countless numbers of asteroids—rocky bodies ranging in size from 600 miles down to one mile or less, about 25,000 with known orbits. The two small moons of Mars are probably captured asteroids. Some asteroids follow orbits that range even farther outside their zone and cross into the inner Solar System—one was the ten-mile-wide body that impacted Earth 65 million years ago and wiped out the dinosaurs. One important goal of space programs today is to detect any asteroids that are moving in orbits that might impact Earth in the future—and over time develop ways to divert them, and comets, from colliding with Earth.

Four large planets orbit beyond Mars—Jupiter, Saturn, Uranus, and Neptune—and they are totally different from the Sun's inner four planets. They have no rocky surfaces to explore, because they consist mainly of light gases, mostly hydrogen and some helium, compressed under strong gravity into a hot liquid state in their interiors, with cores of heavier elements that may be either liquid or 'solid' at very high temperatures. Each has rings of material orbiting it, plus a large fleet of moons. The visible colors in their atmospheres arise from the presence of small amounts of other gases floating in their high atmospheres.

Among Jupiter's 28 moons are four that are quite large—Io, Europa, Ganymede, and Callisto—originally detected by Galileo. Extreme tidal flexing of Io has heated its interior to a molten state and produces continual present-day volcanic eruptions. The outer three of these moons show some evidence that they contain oceans of saline liquid water deep below their frozen surfaces. Europa is plainly covered with a deep crust of water ice, with strong evidence of an underlying water ocean. Consequently, Europa is now a top target for exploration on a par with Mars itself, given the possibility that life might have formed in this environment. Jupiter's ring system consists of dusty material probably eroded from its innermost small moons.

Saturn's rings consist of numberless ringlets of orbiting chunks of water ice, on average the size of ordinary ice cubes. As they endlessly orbit the planet, they stick and cluster into room-size lumps, then break up in collisions. Largest among Saturn's 30 moons is Titan—a body larger than Mercury. Its atmosphere of nitrogen is thicker even than Earth's—but the temperature is minus 300 degrees Fahrenheit. The Cassini space mission arriving at Saturn in 2004 will release a probe to parachute down to the surface of Titan.

Uranus and Neptune owe their beautiful aqua and blue shades to the trace presence of the gas methane, which absorbs the warm colors of sunlight and reflects the cool colors. Both have rings of rocky debris and dust orbiting them—along with 21 moons for Uranus and 8 for Neptune. Triton, the largest moon of Neptune, compares in size with our Moon and has a trace of atmosphere. Out here the temperature is –400 degrees Fahrenheit.

Farthest from the Sun is tiny Pluto—completely different from the giant planets, yet at the same time remarkably similar to their moons of mixed ice and rock. Pluto is actually smaller than seven of the larger moons in our Solar System. Its diameter is only two-thirds that of our own Moon, and it has a moon of its own that is half its size. Pluto's orbit carries it out at times to almost twice Neptune's distance from the Sun—out into a region called the Edgeworth-Kuiper Belt. Here we are detecting hundreds of bodies much smaller than Pluto—up to several hundred miles in diameter—but much larger than the icy bodies of ice and rock we know as comets.

The cometary bodies orbiting in this region are estimated to number 200 million. Some of these at times stray closer to the Sun, where its energy evaporates their surface ices and releases gas and dust forming a surrounding cloud. As high-speed particles from the Sun strike the cloud, some of the gases are blown out into a long glowing tail, and dust particles spread away in a curving tail of reflected sunlight. As beautiful as they appear out in space, these ten-mile balls of ice and rock have collided with the planets, and a future impact on Earth could be as great a danger as an asteroid impact. Worse still, other comets continually plunge into the inner Solar System from a much more remote region known as the Oort Cloud.

Leaving the Solar System Behind

Four of our past probes to the outer planets, which left Earth in the 1970s, have now cruised far beyond Pluto, out into the inner realm of comets on their way to interstellar space, never to return. The coasting speed of the fastest probe is 37,000 miles per hour, some 70 times faster than a passenger jetliner! As fast as this seems, the space between stars is so vast that to cross the gulf between our Sun and its very nearest neighboring star traveling at this high speed would take about 80,000 years. Even at the speed of light—186,000 miles per second—it would take 4 years and 4 months.

On arrival, a radio message back to Earth would take another 4 years and 4 months. One of the interesting views at this nearest star system, named Alpha Centauri, would be the sight of two suns, both similar to our Sun, orbiting one another, with a dwarf star orbiting the pair much farther out.

Whether or not planets are present in this system we still don't know. However, we have identified over 60 Sun-like stars in our stellar neighborhood that have one or more large planets in orbit around them. In the foreseeable future we hope to detect bodies as small as the Earth and someday to analyze their light in a search for signs of an atmosphere produced by life.

The Milky Way, Our Galactic Home

Other stars lie separated from each other by similar distances in all directions from us, most of them smaller and dimmer and cooler than our own Sun, a few much bigger and brighter. All form part of the huge disk-shaped island of stars called the Milky Way Galaxy (or less formally, the Milky Way), which also includes great clouds of hydrogen gas intermixed with other gases and dust particles. Almost all of these stars and space clouds are orbiting in a common direction around the center, which includes a supermassive Black Hole containing the mass of about three million Suns. Our Sun orbits about half way between the center and the edge of the disk, requiring over 200 million years to make a complete circuit. Light leaving a star on one edge of the disk will take 100,000 years before reaching the other side. (To express cosmic distances conveniently, astronomers use the unit called a 'light-year', the distance light travels in one year, which is a little less than six trillion miles.)

Surrounding the main disk of stars is a spherical halo of faint stars extending much farther out.

The Local Supercluster

The neighboring galaxy closest to our Milky Way is the Andromeda Galaxy, about 2 million light years distant. These two, together with a few dozen small neighboring galaxies, make up what is known as the Local Group of galaxies. Several hundred other such groups are part of a Local Supercluster, which has at its center a single large cluster of galaxies known as the Virgo Cluster. The distance across our Local Supercluster is about 130 million light years.

Dark Matter

The speeds of stars in galaxies and the speeds of galaxies in clusters tell us that a large amount of invisible Dark Matter must be present to hold them in their observed orbits. No one yet knows what the Dark Matter consists of, but there seems to be about ten times as much of it as the regular matter that makes up stars and galaxies. Does the cosmic mystery ever stop deepening?

Superclusters and Cosmic Expansion

As we look farther and farther out in the Universe, we find super-cluster after supercluster, separated by huge voids between them which contain few or no galaxies. The great tangle of voids and superclusters stretches on and on through billions of light years extending in all directions—with no end in sight. But, the light from these superclusters carries an important message—it reveals that they are all separating from one another at speeds propor-tional to their distances apart. We can then compute how long the expansion could have been going on—and the answer comes out at about 14 billion years.

Recent measurements of distant supernovae indicate that the speed of expansion of the Universe is now gradually increasing. The energy driving this acceleration is unknown, but it has been given the evocative name, Dark Energy, by some cosmologists. This mys-terious energy of space itself greatly exceeds the energy embodied in all of the matter in the Universe, Dark Matter included.

All these observations tell us that, 14 billion years ago, all the matter we now see in the superclusters of galaxies, our own included, must have been commingled in a much, much smaller space—existing in a superhot superdense state. No one knows what gave rise to this incredible state, but since it appears to be the begin-ning of our expanding Universe, it was nicknamed the 'Big Bang'—even though it was certainly not an explosion in the ordinary sense.

The Beginning

Our best model for the events in the very early Universe suggests that a tiny 'seedling' of space-time erupted in some way as a mys-terious multi-dimensional reality. Some cosmologists suggest that other such 'seedlings' may also have happened, producing an ensemble of many universes, perhaps even with different laws of physics (see Chapter 2). However, at present we have no way to test the reality of this idea, so we'll stick to the story of our own 'seedling' universe.

Our bit of space-time instantly began an incredibly brief spurt of super-fast expansion called the 'inflationary epoch'. At the end of this brief spurt, most of the driving energy of the inflation transmuted into high-energy particles and high-energy photons of light, totally saturating all of space at once, while the expansion continued at a much, much slower pace.

In spite of the misleading implication of its name, the Big Bang did not begin in one place and shoot out into empty space like a modern day ordinary explosion—the birthing of particles and light took place locally, simultaneously, throughout all of space.

As space expanded, the average energy throughout the fireball dropped rapidly, and ordinary particles such as electrons and protons and neutrons formed. For a few minutes protons (hydrogen nuclei) fused into helium nuclei, until the average energy became too weak to support the process, and vast amounts of hydrogen survived to serve as fuel for the stars of the future. One of the triumphs of the Big Bang model is that it predicts a proportion of helium and hydrogen nuclei that matches the proportion we observe in the Universe.

Meanwhile, the average energy of the photons of light was dropping steadily. After about 300,000 years all of space was still a blinding fog of particles and light. But, the Universe was now at a new threshold, for electrons were able to bond with protons, and thus form ordinary atoms of hydrogen. The light, which was now largely red in color, was too weak to knock the electrons free again, as had always happened earlier in the higher energy universe. So, atoms of hydrogen and helium now formed throughout all of space—and the photons of red light began racing in all directions, no longer scattered into a fog by free electrons and protons. In a sense, this was the conclusion of the fireball youth of the Universe. The stage was set for the birth of the first darkness—and stars and galaxies to shine in it.

The Gift of Expanding Space

The expansion of space continued stretching the red light until it became infrared waves invisible to human eyes. Had we been there to watch, we would have seen a cosmic 'sunset', as the whole Universe gradually sank into utter darkness. Space continued its expandion, and the infrared light was stretched and stretched— until by now it has become harmless microwaves washing over us from all directions. We call it the Cosmic Background Radiation.

Every part of the Universe exists in a continuous bath of this cosmic energy released just 300,000 years after the Big Bang. The detection of that energy in 1965 was crucial evidence in support of the Big Bang model.

Meanwhile, back when all of space first sank into darkness, the atoms of hydrogen and helium had begun gradually pulling together under the influence of gravitational force. The closer they pulled to each other, the stronger became the gravitational attraction between them. Great clouds of hydrogen and helium gas eventually formed and contracted further. Extra-dense pockets compressed their gases to higher and higher temperatures and pressures till they began to give off light in the cosmic darkness. In their even hotter cores they began to fuse protons into helium nuclei—and the first stars were born.

A Melee of Galaxies, Black Holes, and Quasars

Vast numbers of stars were born in this way all over the Universe, forming small galaxies which pulled on one another gravitationally, often colliding and merging into larger galaxies. Massive black holes formed at the centers of many galaxies, swallowing matter and light but permitting neither to escape. In the regions just outside the black holes, swirling gases were superheated before plunging into the black holes, lighting up space like brilliant beacons—light we detect today as quasars.

As space continued to expand, most of the galaxies formed where atoms and Dark Matter were more densely distributed, and these regions developed into great superclusters. In the less dense regions of space, few galaxies formed and great voids opened and grew. And, within the galaxies, a cosmic alchemy was already at work.

Stars Begin to Explode

Most stars, then as now, had nuclear cores that produced energy at a slow rate, allowing them to survive for billions of years, like our Sun. But a few stars were unusually large, bright, and massive. Their nuclear cores used up their core hydrogen fuel at a fiercely rapid rate, after which the fusion process then began turning helium into carbon and progressively heavier elements until a core of iron nuclei accumulated. Creating still heavier elements does not release energy, but in fact uses up energy, so a core of iron nuclei cannot produce energy to support itself against gravity, and it soon reaches a point of collapse. An almost instantaneous implosion results, producing a high temperature shock wave that rebounds outward through the star, fusing even heavier nuclei as it passes. This is a 'supernova' explosion. Almost the entire star is blown violently out into space, carrying with it a precious cargo—newly minted heavier nuclei that have never previously existed in the Universe (see Color Plates 3A and 3B). The collapsed core left behind, if there is one, is an incredibly dense 'neutron star' or a black hole.

All across the early Universe in every galaxy, supernova explosions began pouring their gift of heavy nuclei into the hydrogen and helium gas clouds of their galaxies. I like to call these supernovae the 'father principle' in galaxies since they in a sense inseminate the great gas clouds, which I call the 'female principle' since it is here that new stars are gestated and born.

As the new heavier elements mixed together, they formed molecules, which sometimes collided and stuck to each other, gradually building into conglomerates of 'cosmic dust'. Great galactic clouds of cosmic dust then sheltered the birthing places for new stars, around which planets containing rich amounts of the dust could form.

Atoms for Life Are Made in Abundance

One of the great surprises in the Universe Story is that supernovae make much, much greater quantities of certain, particular elements, and these elements happen to be precisely the raw materials necessary for life! The largest quantity produced is oxygen, next largest is carbon, and fourth is nitrogen. As you read this, you are breathing in oxygen and nitrogen and exhaling carbon bonded to oxygen—all of these atoms formed long ago in a far-off supernova explosion. The water you drink, and which makes up most of your own body, is oxygen from supernovae bonded with hydrogen from the Big Bang. In your blood, the iron in the hemoglobin that carries oxygen to your cells was formed abundantly in supernovae. So was the magnesium in the chlorophyll molecule of plants. So, also, the iron and sulfur in the Earth's core, and the silicon that united with oxygen to form much of our planet's interior.

Soon after galaxies begin to form in the early Universe, supernova explosions begin to enrich their gas clouds with a profusion of these elements, the very elements necessary for life. And these enriched clouds give birth to stars with planetary systems rich in these very elements. It is a moment in cosmic history to ponder (see Color Plates 4A and 4B).

Birth of Our Solar System

Nine billion years into cosmic history, yet another star and planetary system—this one, our Solar System—began forming from a gas cloud enriched with the effluent of countless supernovae in the past, and possibly from one relatively recent supernova nearby. As a disk of enriched gas and dust swirled around the newly forming Sun, particles stuck together and accumulated into larger and larger bodies (see Color Plates 5A and 5B). In the final stages of the process huge collisions took place, in one of which proto-Earth swallowed most of a body three times the mass of Mars, while some material sprayed out into orbit to form our Moon. Another collision may have turned Uranus's spin axis on its side. Another may have split Pluto into two pieces, creating a smaller planet with a moon. Comets crashed into the early Earth adding materials—solids, water, and gases—to its developing atmosphere. Eventually, the remaining gas and dust was cleared out of interplanetary space, the outlying zones of comets had accumulated their residual material, and the great central Sun settled into a steady and reliable outpouring of energy.

Birth of Planet Earth

After half a billion years, the young Earth's crust had cooled enough to permit water to rain down and fill the ocean basins. Why was so much water available? Because supernovae had made an abundance of oxygen, which bonded with primordial hydrogen. All of the other materials needed for life were now also collected on this planet. The Moon was steadying the Earth's spin axis, keeping the pattern of seasons moderate. And massive Jupiter's gravity was diverting most incoming comets from hitting the Earth.

Life Begins

Just when and where the first primitive microscopic life forms appeared on our planet we do not know—perhaps in the darkness of ocean depths near hot vents, perhaps within the rocky subsurface of continents, perhaps in hot pools at the surface. Our oldest fossils of living things date to 3.5 billion years ago, and some may even date to 3.8 billion years ago. The significant point is that, once the cosmic conditions had produced a planet like Earth, then life sprang into being in a surprisingly short time—possibly as short as 200 million years, maybe even less. Although we do not yet discern the specifics of how life began, many fascinating outlines are already visible based on entirely natural processes.

Was Life a Miracle? Or Was It All a Miracle?

Some people wish to view the origin of life as an exception to nature—a singular miracle. If that be so, then I would have to argue that many other remarkable parts of the Cosmic Story are equally deserving of miracle status. My list would include the Big Bang itself, the expansion of space, and the elements produced by supernovae, for starters. Many more subtle aspects of the Universe are equally 'miraculous' when you consider what would or wouldn't have happened to the Universe, were they even slightly different. In a sense the whole Universal process could be seen as a miracle.

I myself prefer to view all parts of the Universe Story as natural, although ultimately why the Universe is as it is remains forever a mystery. Is life or the whole Universe natural or miraculous? I say, why not allow oneself to perceive it in both ways? The cosmic drama remains, after all, whatever it is in itself, and our perceptions do not make it one way or the other.

The Long Epoch of One-Celled Life

After life's inception on the planet, it developed in microscopic forms for about three billion years in lakes and oceans, protected by water from the ultraviolet radiation present in sunlight. During this long gestation period, some organisms developed photosynthesis—the ability to use visible sunlight as their energy supply, rather than drawing nutrients from water or rock or from eating one another. A by-product of this new process was the release of free oxygen into the atmosphere. As it slowly built up over eons, some forms of life found it poisonous, others tolerated it, and still others learned to breathe it. At the top of the atmosphere, ultraviolet sunlight broke apart the oxygen molecules, which then re-bonded as heavier ozone molecules. Eventually the ozone was dense enough to shield the Earth's surface from most of the dangerous ultraviolet sunlight, and it was at last safe for life to live in the surface waters of the ocean and venture onto the barren dry land.

The Emergence of Multicelled Life

Less than a billion years ago single-celled life forms began to join in specialized colonies, and the Earth added to itself larger and larger multicelled creatures in a fantastic variety of forms. The seas filled with fish and other aquatic life, the air sprouted flying creatures, and the land grew lush with a blanket of plants which breathed in carbon dioxide and exhaled oxygen, while animals breathed the oxygen and exhaled carbon dioxide. Many times disaster struck, when huge numbers of species were wiped out—some caused by impacts of asteroids or comets, some by vast outpourings of lava. But life each time rebounded in new ways.

New Kinds of Emergence

Very, very recently in cosmic history—some estimate about 100,000 years ago—our own species, *Homo sapiens*, appeared. Our larger brain and capacity for language and tool use introduced a new kind of evolution—'cultural evolution'—in which knowledge could pass from generation to generation, accumulate, and develop progressively (see Chapters 5–7 below).

In the last few hundred years another kind of evolution within our species—'technological evolution'—has transformed all of human life in incredible ways. Unfortunately, coupled with our human population explosion and mindless exploitation of Earth's resources, we have begun to affect the ecosystem of our whole planet—causing the progressive extinction of more and more species at an alarming rate. For the first time on our planet, an important part of our future lies in our own hands. In that sense, we have entered a time of 'conscious evolution'.

We are at a threshold comparable to the one that lay before single-celled life as it began to join into bodies with unimaginable numbers of cells. Each human body contains many trillions of cells, all co-operating in an incredible harmony most of the time. Today, we six billion humans, soon to be eleven billion or more, are communicating at the speed of light and shuttling our bodies around the planet at 500 miles per hour. We have become a compound being, a coordinated consciousness enveloping the Earth. And we have no more idea what this transition may produce in the future than a single-celled organism could have envisioned the trillion-celled beings to come.

Can we control our population? Can we create living styles that are sustainable for a world population? Can we protect the existence of the multitudes of species on Earth and our own ecosystem? These are indeed our immediate and pressing survival concerns, and our new responsibility and awareness. As we face them, the Cosmic Story gives us a new and vital perspective that grants dignity and meaning to our struggle—and gives strength to our determination.

I sometimes like to think of the Cosmic Story as a cosmic history book—a book of 14,000 pages so far, each page carrying a record of one million years. *Homo sapiens* appears only in the last two lines of this book. Our just finished millenium fits in the space of a single letter. And your and my current lifetimes fit somewhere inside a period at the end of the latest sentence. Far from dwarfing our significance, these perspectives are uplifting to me. I feel enthralled that human consciousness could arise at all, much less in such an incredibly short cosmic time. The fact that one species has, in a single lifetime, plumbed the depths of space and time and discerned the story of an entire Universe is certainly a source of greatest wonder! Where our planetary consciousness is leading us next we cannot know, although I think we are seeing the dim outlines of a next stage of evolution—the evolution of consciousness itself.

In the meantime, it is enough for me to have glimpsed the great story. My necessity is not to know the future, it is to savor the cosmic awareness that has come into being in my lifetime—and to share the awareness as far and wide as possible. At the same time, wonderful as the comprehension of the story is, there is more—so much more—in the living of it as participants in the cosmic moment. We all exist in a hundred changing awarenesses, each to be savored and shared as part of the miracle of human consciousness—in this moment—regardless of where it or we have come from or are going.

Recently I took time out from writing to attend a concert, and I sat in the front row only a few feet from 100 magnificently professional musicians. The shapes of their bodies were clearly simian, a shadow from our long past of animal evolution. Their tuxes and black dresses and skill spoke of cultural evolution. And the elaborate and exotic shapes of violins, flutes, oboes, harps, and timpani, reflected technological evolution. Then, began the ineffable beauty of Samuel Barber's Violin Concerto, and I floated into a timeless state of barely endurable beauty. Was this a living frontier of the evolution of consciousness? Who could have predicted that such an ecstasy could come into being as an end product of supernova explosions? As the music carried me on through realms indescribable, I sustained the sense of miracle with a simple unspoken thought: 'From the Big Bang—this?'

2

Life In Our
Universe
and Others

*M*ARTIN *R*EES

*Some argue that our Universe looks as if it had to be
designed so that conscious life could emerge, but if
there's a whole bunch of universes—a Multiverse—
this 'anthropic' argument for design breaks down.*

As a scientist, I feel diffident about contributing to a volume with
a religious interest. Scientists so often reveal themselves as naive in
the arena of religion. A further reason for diffidence is that—
despite my enthusiasm about the progress and prospects in cosmology—I am dubious that cosmologists have much that is new to
contribute to the dialogue between cosmology and religion.
Modern developments are clearly relevant to naive 'creationism'
and to the 'arguments from design' of nineteenth-century natural
theology. Moreover, the progress in elucidating the underlying laws
leaves less room either for vitalism, or for animist concepts of the
spirit world. But do they really have any impact on more sophisticated religious world-views?

In his brilliant book *Consilience*, E.O. Wilson regards Deism—
though not of course theism in general—as "a problem in astrophysics"! In my view, to the contrary, there has been little qualitative change in the interface between cosmology and religion since
Newton's time. Modern concepts of the scale of our universe—in
time and space—do nonetheless change our perceptions of the

likely role of terrestrial life. I shall look at these questions from a cosmological perspective. I shall also venture into more speculative territory by raising the question of whether there could, beyond our observable universe, be other domains governed by different physical laws.

The Origin of Atoms, Stars, and Planets

I'll take my text from Darwin: the famous closing words of *The Origin of Species*: "Whilst this planet has been cycling on according to the fixed law of gravity, from so simple a beginning forms most wonderful have been, and are being, evolved." Cosmologists aim to trace things back before Darwin's simple beginning—to set our Solar System in a grander cosmic context, traceable right back, we believe, to a Big Bang.

Stars and the Periodic Table

Our Sun is 4.5 billion years old, but less than half of its central hydrogen has so far been used up: it will keep shining for a further 5 billion years. It will then swell up to become a red giant, large and bright enough to engulf the inner planets, and to vaporise all life on Earth. After this red giant phase, some outer layers are blown off, leaving a white dwarf—a dense star no larger than the Earth, which will shine with a dull glow, no brighter than the full Moon today, on whatever remains of the Solar System.

To conceive these vast timespans—future as well as past—a metaphor can help. Suppose you represent the Sun's life by a walk across America, starting in New York when the Sun formed, and reaching California ten billion years later, when the Sun's about to die. To make this journey, you'd have to take one step every two thousand years. All recorded history would be just a few steps. Moreover, these steps would come just before the half-way stage—somewhere in Kansas, perhaps: not the high point of the journey. This perspective has an impact on how we should see our species. The progression towards diversity has much further to go. Even if life is now unique to the Earth, there is time for it to spread from here through the entire Galaxy, and even beyond. We may be nearer to the 'simple beginning' than to any endpoint of evolution.

Astrophysicists can compute, just as easily, the life cycle of a star that is half, twice, or ten times the mass of the Sun. Smaller stars burn their fuel more slowly. Stars ten times as heavy as the Sun—the four blue Trapezium stars in Orion, for instance—shine thousands of times more brightly, and consume their fuel more quickly. We can check our theory by observing other stars like the Sun, which are at different stages in their evolution. Having a single 'snapshot' of each star's life is not a fatal handicap if we have a large sample, born at different times, available for study.

Heavy stars expire violently, by exploding as supernovae. The nearest supernova of modern times was seen in 1987. On 23rd–24th February, a new bright 'star' appeared in the Southern Sky that had not been visible the previous night. Astronomers have studied this particular supernova, how it fades and decays. They have even found, on photographs taken before the explosion, that the precursor was a blue star of about 20 solar masses.

Supernovae fascinate astronomers, because they offer a chance to test their theories of this dramatic and complicated phase in the life of stars. These stellar explosions, occurring thousands of light years away, played a fundamental part in shaping everyone's environment: they created the mix of atoms that we, and the Earth, are made of.

When a heavy star has consumed its available hydrogen, its core contracts and heats up, until the helium can itself react. When the core helium is itself all consumed, the star contracts and heats up still more, releasing energy via a succession of reactions involving progressively heavier nuclei: carbon, oxygen, silicon, and so on. Material gets processed further up the periodic table. For stars heavier than about 8 solar masses, this continues, each step releasing further energy, until the core has been transmuted into iron. But an iron nucleus is more tightly bound than any other. The star then faces an energy crisis: it cannot draw on any further nuclear sources.

The consequences are dramatic. Once the iron core gets above a threshold size (about 1.4 solar masses) it suddenly collapses down to the size of a neutron star. This releases enough energy to blow off the overlying material in a colossal explosion—a supernova. Moreover, this material has, by then, an 'onion skin' structure: the hotter inner layers have been processed further up the periodic table. The debris thrown back into space contains the mix of elements. Oxygen is the most common, followed by carbon, nitrogen, silicon and iron. There are traces of the others. Moreover the proportions agree with those observed on Earth. At first sight, the heavier atoms might seem a problem. The iron nucleus is more tightly bound than any other, and it is only number 26 in the periodic table. It takes an input of energy to build up the still heavier nuclei. But a very hot blast wave that blows off the outer layers can produce small traces of the rest of the periodic table, right up to uranium.

The oldest stars formed about ten billion years ago from primordial material that contained only the simplest atoms—no carbon, no oxygen, and no iron. Chemistry would then have been a very dull subject. And there could certainly have been no planets around these first stars. Before our Sun even formed, 4.5 billion years ago, several generations of heavy stars could have been through their entire life cycles, transmuting pristine hydrogen into the other elements of the periodic table.

Why are carbon and oxygen atoms so common here on Earth, but gold and uranium so rare? The answer—one of the undoubted triumphs of twentieth-century astrophysics—involves stars that exploded before our Solar system formed. Our Galaxy is like a vast ecosystem, recycling gas through successive generations of stars, gradually building up the entire periodic table. Before our Sun even formed, several generations of heavy stars could have been through their entire life cycles, transmuting pristine hydrogen into the basic building blocks of life—carbon, oxygen, iron and the rest. We're literally the ashes of long-dead stars.

Planets?

One fascinating question is whether there are planets orbiting other stars. 'Catastrophist' ideas on planet formation long ago fell from favour: astronomers now suspect planetary systems to be common, because protostars, as they contract from rotating clouds, spin off around them discs of dusty gas. The dusty cloud in Orion, though denser than most of the expanses between the stars, is still very rarified—for a region in this cloud to become a star, it contracts so much that its density rises by a billion. Any slight spin would have been amplified during the collapse (a cosmic version of the well known spin-up when an ice skater pulls in her arms) until centrifugal forces prevented all the material from joining the star. Protostellar discs have been observed in Orion, and are the natural precursors of planetary systems: they are dense enough that dust particles would collide frequently with each other, sticking together to build up rocky lumps; these in turn coalesce into larger systems, which merge together to make planets (see Color Plates 5A and 5B). Our Solar System formed in this way, and there is every reason to expect many other stars to be orbited by retinues of planets.

Fully-formed planets orbiting other stars are, however, harder to detect than their precursor discs. But a real astronomical highlight of the late 1990s has been the discovery of compelling indirect evidence for planets. This evidence comes from the detection of the wobble they induce in the motion of the central star. In 1995 two Swiss astronomers found that the Doppler shift of 51 Pegasi, a nearby star resembling our Sun, was varying in a manner suggesting the presence of an orbiting planet.

Dozens more planets have by now been discovered by several astronomers. So far all are big ones—like Jupiter. They may be the largest members of other planetary systems like our own, but individual Earth-like planets would be a hundred times harder to detect. The observed 'Jupiters' are also closer to their parent stars than Jupiter is to our Sun. These other Solar Systems aren't like ours. But this also is probably a selection effect—it would need more sensitive measurements, and a longer timespan of observations, to detect the smaller amplitude and slower wobble induced by a heavy planet in an orbit like Jupiter's.

The actual layout of our Solar System is the outcome of many 'accidents'. In particular, our Moon was torn from Earth by a collision with another protoplanet. The odd spin of Uranus (around an axis in the plane of its orbit) may indicate another large collision. The craters on the Moon bear witness to the violence of Earth's early history, before the planetesimals had been depleted by impacts or coalescence. Spaceprobes that have now visited the planets, show that they (and their larger moons) are highly distinctive worlds. There is no reason to expect other solar systems to have the same configuration or number of planets.

Planets on which life could evolve, as it did here on Earth, must be rather special. Their gravity must pull strongly enough to prevent the atmosphere from evaporating into space; they must be neither too hot nor too cold, and therefore the right distance from a long-lived and stable star. There may be other special circumstances required. For example, it's been claimed that Jupiter was essential to life on Earth, because its gravity 'scoured out' the asteroids, and reduced the rate of catastrophic impacts on Earth; also, the tides induced by our large Moon may have stimulated some phases in evolution. But even if there are extra requirements, like this, planetary systems are (we believe) so common in our Galaxy that Earth-like planets would be numbered in millions.

As a foreigner, I follow the U.S. space programs with immense interest and general admiration. I'm depressed at NASA's vast commitment to the space station, but delighted that a search for Earth-like planets has become a main thrust of the space program. This is a long-range goal—it will require vast optical interferometers in space—but will stimulate much excellent science on the way. And once a candidate's been found, several things could be learnt about it. Suppose an astronomer forty light years away had detected our Earth. It would be, in Carl Sagan's phrase, a "pale blue dot," seeming very close to a star (our Sun) that outshines it by many millions. If Earth could be seen at all, its light could be analysed, and would reveal that it had been transformed (and oxygenated) by a biosphere. The shade of blue would be slightly different, depending on whether the Pacific Ocean or the Eurasian land mass was facing us. Distant astronomers could therefore, by repeated observation, infer the Earth was spinning, and learn the length of its day, and even infer something of its topography and climate.

Life On Other Planets?

What fascinates people most, of course—and what motivates NASA's interest—is whether there's life out there. In other words, even when a planet offers a propitious environment, what is the chance that 'simple' organisms emerge? Life on Earth has occupied an immense variety of niches. The ecosystems near hot sulphurous outwellings in the deep ocean bed tell us that not even sunlight is essential. We still don't know how or where terrestrial life began. Was it in Darwin's 'warm little pond', or deep underground, or even in dusty molecular clouds in space?

And what were the odds against life getting started? We still don't know whether life's emergence is 'natural', or whether it involves a chain of accidents so improbable that nothing remotely like it has happened on another planet anywhere else in our Galaxy. That's why it would be so crucial to detect life, even in simple and vestigial forms, elsewhere in our Solar System—on Mars, or under the ice of Europa. If it had emerged twice within our solar system, this would suggest that the entire Galaxy would be teeming with life. That momentous conclusion would follow provided that the two origins were indeed independent. That is an important proviso—for instance, if meteorites from Mars could impact on the Earth, maybe we are all Martians; conversely, Mars could have been seeded by a reverse traffic from the Earth. If an Earth-like planet could be detected in orbit around another star, its light could be analysed, and would reveal that it had been transformed (and oxygenated) by a biosphere.

But there's another issue, where the uncertainties are perhaps even greater. Even when simple life exists, we don't know the chances that it evolves towards intelligence.

The year 2000 marked the fourth centenary of the death of Giordano Bruno, burnt at the stake, in Rome—he was an early believer in inhabited worlds. Ever since his time, this belief has been widely shared, but there's been little firm evidence. Only in the last four years of the last millenium did we come to know for sure that 'worlds' exist in orbit around other stars. But even if innumerable planets exist, we are little closer to knowing whether any of them harbor anything alive. This question is one for biologists, not astronomers. It is much more difficult to answer, and there seems no consensus among the experts.

Systematic scans for artificial signals are a worthwhile gamble, despite the heavy odds against success, because of the philosophical import of any detection. A manifestly artificial signal—even if we couldn't make much sense of it—would convey the momentous message that 'intelligence' wasn't unique to the Earth and had evolved elsewhere, and that concepts of logic and physics weren't peculiar to the 'hardware' in human skulls. The nearest potential sites are so far away that signals would take many years in transit. For this reason alone transmission would be primarily one-way—there would be time to send a measured response, but no scope for quick repartee!

The most common idea is that contact might be achieved via radio signals. There are ongoing searches for transmissions that might be 'artificial' in origin. But this is not the only option; narrowly beamed lasers are another possibility. It is already technologically possible for us to proclaim our presence over distances of many light years by either of these techniques.

We still don't know the odds against life getting started. Even when simple life exists, we don't know the chances that it evolves towards intelligence. Intelligent life could be 'natural'; or it could have involved a chain of accidents so surpassingly rare that nothing remotely like it has happened anywhere else in our Galaxy. And even if intelligence exists elsewhere, it may be enjoying a purely contemplative life and doing nothing to reveal itself. Absence of evidence wouldn't be evidence of absence.

The odds may be stacked so heavily against life that there is none anywhere in our part of the universe. Some may find it depressing to feel alone in a vast inanimate cosmos. But I would personally react in quite the opposite way. It would in some ways be disappointing if searches for extraterrestrial signals were doomed to fail, but if our Earth were the sole abode of life in our Galaxy, we could view it in a less humble cosmic perspective than it would merit if our universe already teemed with advanced life-forms.

Back to the Beginning: Our Universe on Large Scales

EVIDENCE FOR COSMIC EVOLUTION

I've described how the atoms of the periodic table are made—that we're stardust—or, if you're less romantic, the 'nuclear waste' from the fuel that makes stars shine. But where did the original hydrogen come from? To answer this question, we must extend our horizons to the extragalactic realm. Our Milky Way, with its hundred billion stars, is just one galaxy similar to millions of others visible with large telescopes.

And we can now see vast number of galaxies, stretching to immense distances very far back. One amazing picture taken with the Hubble Space Telescope shows a small patch of sky, a thousandth of the area covered by a full Moon. It's densely covered with faint smudges of light—each a billion times fainter than any star that can be seen with the unaided eye. But each is an entire galaxy, thousands of light years across, which appears so small and faint because of its huge distance.

What is most fascinating about this picture is not the record-breaking distance in itself, but the huge span of time that separates us from these remote galaxies. They are being viewed when they have only recently formed. They have not yet settled down into steadily spinning 'pinwheels' like Andromeda. Some consist mainly of glowing diffuse gas that hasn't yet condensed into individual droplets, each destined to become a star. Their stars haven't have had time to manufacture the chemical elements. These newly formed galaxies would not yet harbour planets nor, presumably, life.

Astronomers can actually see the remote past. But what about still more remote epochs, before any galaxies had formed?

Did everything really start with a so-called 'Big Bang'? This phrase was introduced into cosmology by Fred Hoyle, as a derisive description of a theory he didn't like. Two strong lines of evidence have firmed up the case for a Big Bang (the undignified name has stuck). First, the weak microwaves which make even intergalactic space slightly warm have now been measured, at many different wavelengths to a precision of a part in 10,000. The spectrum fits a black body very precisely—the errors are smaller than the thickness of the line. This spectrum is just what you'd expect if these microwaves are indeed an 'afterglow' of a pregalactic era when the entire Universe was hot, dense, and opaque. The expansion has cooled and diluted the radiation, and stretched its wavelength. But this primordial heat is still around—it fills the Universe and has nowhere else to go!

And there is a second line of evidence. When the entire universe was squeezed hotter than a star, there would be nuclear reactions. Astrophysicists have calculated these, and found they fit with the proportions of helium and deuterium that are measured.

Astronomers can actually see the remote past and infer—via the microwave background, the helium abundance, and other evidence—what the Universe was like at still earlier stages. But how much of this should we believe? I think the extrapolation back to the stage when the Universe had been expanding for a few seconds (when the helium formed) deserve to be taken as seriously as, for instance, what geologists or paleontologists tell us about the early history of our Earth—their inferences are just as indirect (and less quantitative).

Sometimes cosmologists are asked: Is it not absurdly presumptuous to claim to know anything, with any level of confidence, about our entire Universe? My response would be that it's complexity, not sheer size, that makes things hard to understand—a star is simpler than an insect, for instance. In the primordial fireball everything must have been broken down into its simplest constituents. The early universe really could be less baffling, and more within our grasp, than the smallest living organism. It's biologists trying to understand the layer upon layer of intricate structures in an animal who face the toughest challenge. The origin of life is at least as challenging as the origin of matter.

FUTUROLOGY

In about 5 billion years the Sun will die; and the Earth with it. But will the universe go on expanding for ever? Or will the entire firmament eventually recollapse to a Big Crunch?

The answer depends on how much the cosmic expansion is being decelerated by the gravitational pull that everything in the Universe exerts on everything else. It is straightforward to calculate that the expansion can eventually be reversed if there is, on average, more than about 5 atoms in each cubic metre. That doesn't sound much. But if all the galaxies were dismantled, and their constituent stars and gas spread uniformly through space, they'd make an even emptier vacuum—1 atom in every 10 cubic metres—like one snowflake in the entire volume of the Earth.

That's 50 times less than the 'critical density', and at first sight this seems to imply perpetual expansion, by a wide margin. But it's not so straightforward. Astronomers have discovered that galaxies, and even entire clusters of galaxies, would fly apart unless they were held together by the gravitational pull of about 10 times more material than we actually see. Cosmologists denote the ratio of the actual density to the critical density by the Greek letter omega, Ω. There's almost certainly enough dark matter around galaxies to give $\Omega = 0.2$ (remember that what we see is only a fiftieth). There is almost certainly enough dark matter, mainly in galactic halos and clusters of galaxies, to contribute 20 percent of the critical density. Until recently, we couldn't rule out several times this amount—comprising the full critical density, $\Omega = 1$—in the space between clusters of galaxies. But it now seems that, in toto, dark matter doesn't contribute more than about $\Omega = 0.3$. It seems that expansion of our universe will be never-ending. Moreover, the dominant mass-energy could be in some even more exotic form than the 'dark matter'—maybe even latent in empty space. The odds now favour perpetual expansion.

EMERGENCE OF COMPLEXITY FROM A SIMPLE BIG BANG

It may at first sight seem mysterious that our universe can have started off as a hot amorphous fireball—and ended up manifestly far from equilibrium. Temperatures now range from those of the blazing surfaces of stars (and their even hotter centres) to the night sky only 3 degrees above absolute zero. This is not, however, contrary to the second law of thermodynamics: it's actually a natural outcome of cosmic expansion and the workings of gravity.

Because of the expansion, there's no time for all reactions to attain equilibrium. At high temperatures, everything tends to turn into iron, as inside a hot star. But that (fortunately) didn't happen in the early universe, because it cooled too quickly for the reactions to go to completion. Instead, the material emerged with proportions of hydrogen and helium that actually accord well with what's observed.

And, even more important, gravity renders the expanding universe unstable to the growth of structure, in the sense that even very slight initial irregularities would evolve into conspicuous density contrasts. Eventually the overdense regions stop expanding and condense into gaseous protogalaxies which fragment into stars. Ever since the beginning, gravity has been amplifying inhomogeneities, building up structures, and enhancing temperature contrasts—a prerequisite for emergence of the complexity that lies around us ten billion years later, and of which we are part.

THE INITIAL CONDITIONS

The way slight initial irregularities in the cosmic fireball evolve into galaxies is in principle as predictable as the orbits of the planets, which have been understood since Newton's time. But to Newton, some features of the Solar System were a mystery. He showed why the planets traced out ellipses; it was, however, a mystery to him why they were 'set up' with their orbits almost in the same plane, all circling the sun the same way. In his *Opticks* he writes: "blind fate could never make all the planets move one and the same way in orbits concentrick. Such a wonderful uniformity in the planetary system," he wrote, must be the effect of Providence. This coplanarity has only very recently been understood—it's a natural outcome of the Solar System's origin as a spinning protostellar disc.

Indeed, we have pushed the barrier back from the beginning of the solar system to the first second of the Big Bang.

But—and this is my reason for the flashback to Newton—conceptually we're in no better shape than Newton was. He had to specify the initial trajectories of each planet. Our calculations of cosmic structure need to specify, at some early time like 1 second, a few numbers:

  i. The cosmic expansion rate—'tuned' so that the Universe neither recollapsed very quickly, nor expanded so fast that gravity couldn't form bound structures such as galaxies;
  ii. The proportions of ordinary atoms, dark matter, and radiation in the universe;
  iii. The character of the fluctuations—large enough to evolve into structures, but not large enough to invalidate the overall uniformity;
  iv. The 'constants' of microphysics.

We've pushed the causal chain far further back than Newton did, but we still reach a stage where we're reduced to saying that 'things are as they are because they were as they were'.

Any explanation for these numbers i–iv must lie still earlier in cosmic history—not just the first second, but the first tiny fraction of a second. What's the chance, then, of pushing the barrier back still further?

THE UNCERTAIN PHYSICS OF THE FIRST MICROSECOND

I was confident in tracing back to when the Universe was a second old. The matter was no denser than air; conventional laboratory physics is applicable and is vindicated by the impressive evidence of the background radiation, helium abundance, and so forth. But for the first trillionth of a second every particle would have more energy than even CERN's new accelerator will reach. The further we extrapolate back, the less confidence we have that known physics is either adequate or applicable. So we lose our foothold in experiment.

I'm uneasy, incidentally, about how cosmology is sometimes popularised. Authors—academic cosmologists are at fault even more than professional communicators—don't always distinguish between things that are quite well established and those that are still speculative. And sometimes an unwarranted triumphalism creeps in. If cosmologists claim too often to be 'stripping the last veil from the face of God', or making discoveries that 'overthrow all previous ideas', they'll surely erode their credibility. It would be prudent, as well as seemly, to rein in the hyperbole a bit. Otherwise journalists have to become as skeptical in assessing scientific claims as they already are in assessing politicians.

The formative instants of our universe were plainly crucial, and there have been some important insights—no theories of that ultra-early time are yet, however, firm enough to have much predictive power.

The cosmic expansion rate presents a special mystery. The two eschatologies—perpetual expansion or recollapse to a 'crunch'—seem very different. But our Universe is still expanding after 10 billion years. A universe that recollapsed sooner wouldn't have allowed time for stars to evolve, or even to form. On the other hand, if the expansion were too much faster, gravity would have been overwhelmed by kinetic energy and the clouds that developed into galaxies would have been unable to condense out. In Newtonian terms the initial potential and kinetic energies were very closely matched. How did this come about? And why does the Universe have the large-scale uniformity which is a prerequisite for progress in cosmology?

The answer may lie in something remarkable that happened during the first 10^{-36} seconds, when our entire observable universe was compressed in scale by 27 powers of ten (and hotter by a similar factor). Theoretical physicists have come up with serious (though still, of course, tentative) reasons why, at the colossal densities before that time, a new kind of 'cosmical repulsion' might come into play and overwhelm 'ordinary' gravity. The expansion of the ultra-early universe would then have been exponentially accelerated, so that an embryo universe could have inflated, homogenized, and established the 'fine tuned' balance between gravitational and kinetic energy when it was only 10^{-36} seconds old.

This generic idea that our universe inflated from something microscopic is compellingly attractive. It looks like 'something for nothing', but it isn't really. That's because our present vast universe may, in a sense, have zero net energy. Every atom has an energy because of its mass—Einstein's Mc^2. But it has a negative energy due to gravity—we, for instance, are in a state of lower potential energy on the Earth's surface than if we were up in space. And if we added up the negative potential energy we possess due to the gravitational field of everything else, it could exactly balance our rest mass energy. Thus it doesn't, as it were, cost anything to expand the mass and energy in our universe.

Cosmologists sometimes loosely express such ideas by saying that the universe can essentially arise 'from nothing'. But they should watch their language, especially when talking to philosophers. The physicist's vacuum is latent with particles and forces—it's a far richer construct than the philosopher's 'nothing'. Theorists may, some day, be able to write down fundamental equations governing physical reality. But no physicist will ever tell us what 'breathes fire' into the equations, and actualises them in a real cosmos.

Possible Scope and Limits of Theory: Are There Other Universes?

I've outlined how our carbon-based biosphere has slowly evolved on a planet orbiting a stable star. It is made of atoms that were themselves transmuted from hydrogen in earlier generations of stars. The hydrogen itself emerged from a hot Big Bang about 12 billion years ago.

Our universe had to provide the galaxies that form the backdrop to the emergence of stars, planets and life. It had to possess many features—being long-lived, stable, and far from thermal equilibrium, for instance—that are prerequisites for our existence. Moreover, our emergence depended crucially on apparent 'fine tuning' of the basic physical constants: the strengths of the fundamental forces, the masses of elementary particles, and so forth.

There are various ways one can react:

The most robustly dismissive attitude is that the basic numbers defining our universe, and the physical constants, must have some values, so we have no reason to be surprised at any particular value rather than another.

A more reasonable reaction to the coincidences is to invoke a kind of 'selection effect'. Fishermen aren't surprised (to use an old metaphor of Eddington's) to catch no fish smaller than the holes in their nets. It may seem irrational to be surprised that our universe has any particular property if we wouldn't exist otherwise.

But even that doesn't seem quite enough. To say that we wouldn't be here if things were otherwise need not quench our curiosity and surprise that our universe is as it is. John Leslie has given a nice analogy. Suppose you are facing execution by a fifty-man firing squad. The bullets are fired, and you find that all have missed their target. Had they not done so, you would not survive to ponder the matter. But, realising you were alive, you would legitimately be perplexed and wonder why.

It seems noteworthy, at the very least, that the physical laws governing our universe have allowed so much interesting complexity to emerge in it, especially as we can so readily imagine still-born universes where nothing could evolve. If a 'cosmic being' turned knobs to vary the key numbers, and constructed a whole ensemble of universes, then clearly only one would be like our own, and we wouldn't feel 'at home' in most of them—that much is obvious. However, what is less trivial, and may be deeply significant, is that only a narrow range of hypothetical universes would allow any complexity to emerge.

These arguments pertain to basic physics and chemistry, and cannot be as readily discounted as those of Paley concerning the 'fitness' of animals and plants for their environment. Any complicated biological contrivance is the outcome of prolonged evolutionary selection, involving symbiosis with its surroundings; but the basic laws governing atoms, stars, and the cosmos are 'given', and nothing biological can react back on them to modify them.

A MULTIVERSE?

Some theologians would of course attribute the 'fine-tuning' to providence. John Polkinghorne, for instance, opines that the universe is not just "any old world," but it is special and finely tuned for life "because it is the creation of a Creator who wills that it should be so." But there is an alternative view: perhaps our Big Bang wasn't the only one. We may be part of an infinite and eternal Multiverse within which new domains 'sprout' into universes whose horizons never overlap. The fundamental forces—gravity, nuclear, and electromagnetic—'freeze out' as each universe cools down. The outcome of this cooling is somewhat arbitrary, like the patterns of ice on a pond, or the way a magnet behaves when cooled. So different universes would end up governed by different physics, and would evolve in distinctive ways. Other universes would be, in most versions of these ideas, completely disjoint from ours and will never come within the horizon of even our remotest descendants.

Our Big Bang would, in this perspective, be just one event in a grander structure; the entire history of our universe would be just an episode in the infinite multiverse. The multiverse could encompass all possible values of fundamental constants, as well as universes which follow lifecycles of very different durations: some, like ours, may expand for much more than 10 billion years; others may be 'stillborn' because they recollapse after a brief existence, or because the physical laws governing them aren't rich enough to permit complex consequences. In some there could be no gravity: or gravity could be overwhelmed by the repulsive effect of a cosmological constant (lambda, λ), as it would have been during the early inflation phase of our own Universe. In others, gravity could be so strong that it crushes anything large enough to evolve into a complex organism. Some could always be so dense that everything stayed close to equilibrium, with the same temperature everywhere. Some could even have different numbers of dimensions from our own.

Even a universe that was, like ours, long-lived and stable, could contain just inert particles of dark matter, either because the physics precludes ordinary atoms from ever existing, or because they all annihilate with exactly equal numbers of antiatoms. Even if protons and hydrogen atoms exist, the nuclear forces may not be strong enough to hold the nuclei of heavy elements together: there would then be no periodic table, and no chemistry.

The concept of an ensemble of universes of which ours is just one member (and not necesarily a typical one) is, needless to say, not yet in sharp theoretical focus. But it helps to explain basic—and previously mysterious—features of our universe, such as why it is so big, and why it is expanding. In the broader perspective of a 'multiverse', anthropic reasoning could acquire genuine explanatory force.

Let me add a semantic note about the definition of 'universe'. The proper definition of 'universe' is of course 'everything there is'. I am arguing here that the entity traditionally called 'the Universe'—what astronomers study, or the aftermath of our Big Bang—may be just one of a whole ensemble, each one maybe starting with its own Big Bang. Pedants might prefer to redefine the whole ensemble as 'the Universe'. But I think it is less confusing, especially while the concept is so tentative and provisional, to leave the term 'universe' for what it has traditionally connoted, even though this then demands a new word, 'multiverse', for the entire ensemble of 'universes'.

Most universes would be less propitious for complex evolution than ours, but not necessarily all. We cannot conceive what structures might emerge in the distant future of our universe. Still less, therefore, can we envisage what might happen in a universe where the forces differentiated into more than the four we are familiar with, or where the number of dimensions was larger. Our universe could be 'impoverished' compared to some others, which could harbour vastly richer structures, and potentialities beyond our imaginings.

The status and scope of such concepts, in the long run, will depend on the character of the (still quite unknown) physical laws at the very deepest level. If the physical constants were indeed uniquely fixed by a 'final theory', it would then be a brute fact that these universal numbers happened to lie in the narrowly restricted range that permitted complexity and consciousness to emerge. The potentialities implicit in the fundamental equations—all the intricate structures in our universe—may astonish us, but this reaction would be akin to the surprise mathematicians must sometimes feel when vastly elaborate deductions follow from innocuous-looking axioms or postulates.

Simple algorithms generally have dull outcomes, but a few do not. Consider, for instance, the Mandelbrot set. The instructions for drawing this astonishing pattern can be written in just a few lines, but it discloses layer upon layer of varied structure however much we magnify it. Similarly, latent in the succinct equations of a 'final theory' could be everything that has emerged in our universe, as it cooled from the initial Big Bang to the diffuse low energy world we inhabit.

But what we call the fundamental constants—the numbers that matter to physicists—may be secondary consequences of the 'final theory', rather than direct manifestations of its deepest and most fundamental level. The multiverse may be governed by some unified theory, but each universe may cool down in a fashion that has 'accidental' features, ending up governed by different 'bylaws' (and with different physical constants) from other members of the ensemble. Anthropic arguments can properly be deployed to account for the physical constants in our universe—indeed this would be the only way to understand why these numbers didn't have values that were very different.

Any final theory is still such a distant goal that we cannot yet assess how far our universe can be explained anthropically. However, we may be able to fathom the nature of the final theory even before we know its specific details.[1]

An Unending Quest

The frontiers of science are the very small, the very large and, most of all, the very complex. Cosmology involves them all.

Theorists must elucidate the exotic physics of the very early stages, which entails a new synthesis between the cosmos and the microworld, and might tell us whether there is a basis for the multiverse, and for 'selection' of physical constants. (Such a theory may 'explain' some aspects of the particles and forces governing which are so far 'fed in' from experiment. If so, it would gain enough credibility that we would take seriously its predictions about how inflation occurred, and whether our Big Bang would be the only one,

---

1. See Chapter 15 of my book *Before the Beginning* (Perseus, 1997)), and its successor, *Just Six Numbers* (Perseus, 2000).

and whether the other universes would be governed by different physics.)

But cosmology is also the grandest of the environmental sciences, and its second aim is to understand how at least one Big Bang evolved, over 10 billion years, into the complex cosmic habitat we find around us—so that on at least one planet around at least one star, creatures evolved able to wonder about it all. And that's an unending quest that's barely begun.

By mapping and exploring our universe, using all the techniques of astronomy, we are coming to understand—to a degree that even a decade ago would have seemed impossible—our cosmic habitat, the laws that govern it, and how it evolved from its formative initial instants. But, even more remarkably, we have intimations of other universes, and can deduce something about them. We can infer the scope and limits of a final theory even if we are still far from reaching it—even if, indeed, it eludes our intellectual grasp forever.

3

Cosmochemistry and the Origin of Life

CLIFFORD N. MATTHEWS

Ancestral molecules of life form readily from hydrogen cyanide and water, simple compounds abundant in our solar system and beyond.

How did life begin on planet Earth? In seeking answers to this age-old question, we make use of two of the most far-reaching generalizations of modern science: the unity of biochemistry and the unity of cosmochemistry.

The unity of biochemistry tells us that essential to all life are certain classes of organic compounds, in particular the macromolecular structures known as proteins, nucleic acids, fats, and sugars, familiar to each of us as daily dietary requirements. Each of these structures are polymers, chains of particular monomer units. Fats and sugars—homopolymers with identical repeating units—are primarily suppliers of energy for chemical reactions, whereas the complex heteropolymer structures of proteins (enzymes) and nucleic acids (DNA and RNA) enable them to act as sources of information within living cells, the whole ensemble of these and other compounds giving rise to the characteristic activities of living systems we refer to as metabolism and reproduction. Within the enveloping framework of evolution—all living forms are interrelated by common descent—we draw the inescapable conclusion that all life must have had a common chemical origin.

41

The unity of cosmochemistry also arises from a kind of metabolism, this time involving the myriad stars we see out there in galaxies, as well as our parent star Sol, which brightens, and indeed is responsible for, our daily existence. As described in the first two chapters, it seems that some 14 billion years ago there was a Big Bang that in a matter of minutes gave rise to the fundamental particles of matter that eventually became the hydrogen and helium atoms that essentially constitute our expanding universe. Gravitational forces cause some of these atoms to clump together as massive conglomerates—stars—within which heavier elements soon appeared because of the intense compression. A star can thus be regarded as a factory for the stepwise production of elements from hydrogen, with the concomitant release of enormous amounts of energy we perceive as radiations of various wavelengths including heat and light. In 1967, when Hans Bethe received a Nobel Prize in Physics for first proposing these ideas, he ended his acceptance speech with the following words: "If all this is true, stars have a life cycle much like animals. They are born, they grow, they go through a definite internal development and finally die, to give back the material of which they are made so that new stars may live." The outcome of this process of stellar evolution is that interstellar atoms and molecules are widely distributed throughout the universe, giving rise not only to new stars but also to accompanying planets, possible abodes of life. As the geologist Preston Cloud put it, extending Hans Bethe's original statement: "Stars have died so that we may live."

Table 3.1 lists the relative numbers of atoms of different elements existing within and between the stars of our galaxy, the Milky Way. Only the most common elements are represented, their abundance expressed on a percentage scale. Most striking is the fact that in this hydrogen-rich environment the next most common elements (other than the inert gases helium, neon, and argon) are oxygen, carbon, and nitrogen, which readily form compounds with hydrogen that we know as water (H_2O), methane (CH_4), and ammonia (NH_3). These are among the many molecules so far detected in dense molecular clouds between stars and surrounding some of them, formed by photochemical reactions around interstellar grains possessing inorganic and organic components. The same four elements—H, O, C, and N—are also the major compo-

TABLE 3.1

Cosmic abundances of most abundant elements (percentages of atoms).

Hydrogen	87.0	Magnesium	0.003
Helium	12.9	Silicon	0.002
Oxygen	0.025	Iron	0.001
Nitrogen	0.02	Sulfer	0.001
Carbon	0.01	Others	0.038

nents of living organisms, constituting 99.5 percent of the biosphere. Why this amazing coincidence? The answer came in 1953 from a revealing experiment which showed dramatically how the unity of cosmochemistry could be related to that of biochemistry.

Considering the question of Earth's origin with Table 1 in mind, Harold Urey had concluded that the aggregation of abundant atoms such as H, C, O, and N around the developing Sun would cause planets to form with atmospheres consisting mainly of the hydrogen-rich compounds methane (CH_4), ammonia (NH_3), and water (H_2O) as well as molecular hydrogen (H_2). On Earth, no hydrogen would have settled, but the other gases present—methane, ammonia, water—would eventually have been converted to today's oxidizing mixture (O_2, N_2, and CO_2) due to the presence of life itself following prebiotic chemical reactions in the atmosphere and oceans. How did this come about? What happened to the methane and ammonia?

It was questions such as these that intrigued a new graduate student, Stanley Miller, after he heard Urey lecture on these ideas at a departmental seminar at the University of Chicago. Together they carried out the now-famous Miller-Urey experiment, in which the postulated components of Earth's primitive atmosphere were subjected to an electric discharge that brought about the ready synthesis of a number of organic compounds known to take part in today's biochemistry (Figure 3.1). Most significant was the detection of four of the twenty amino acids that are the building blocks of today's proteins. Later spark studies by Miller and others showed the presence of even more of these important monomers. Cyril Ponnamperuma and his co-workers in the Laboratory of Chemical

FIGURE 3.1

The Miller-Urey apparatus (all glass) for subjecting a mixture of methane, ammonia, and water to a high-energy electrical discharge, simulating atmospheric reactions on the primitive Earth.

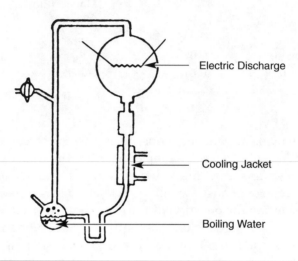

— Electric Discharge

— Cooling Jacket

— Boiling Water

Evolution at the University of Maryland were able to detect adenine (a key component of DNA, RNA, and other important biomolecules). Adenine had previously been obtained by John Oró from aqueous reactions of hydrogen cyanide (HCN) and ammonia which had also led to the synthesis of glycine and other amino acids. Further extensions of this HCN chemistry by James Ferris and Leslie Orgel enabled more nitrogen-containing heterocyclic compounds to be formed. By now it seems well established from a variety of experiments that many of the very compounds needed for biochemistry, components of the essential macromolecules of life, would have been readily formed in reducing environments. How they might have gotten together to form the necessary polymers, however, remains problematic. Indeed, this uncertainty has led to an impasse in current thinking about chemical evolution and the origin of life, raising questions that need to be addressed.

Let us look at the situation more closely. A widely held belief is that the prebiotic formation of primitive proteins, for example, occurred in two steps: the synthesis of α-amino acids brought about by the action of natural high energy sources on the components of a reducing atmosphere, follwed by their linking together by splitting off water—condensation—to form polypeptides on the surface of planet Earth. The pioneering demonstration by Miller and Urey that α-amino acids are readily obtained from methane, ammonia, and water subjected to electric discharges, taken together with subsequent apparently successful syntheses of polypeptides from amino acids by dehydration reactions (by Sydney Fox and others), seems to be in accord with this view. When I look more critically at the evidence for condensation, however, I find that the specific conditions chosen—anhydrous, high temperature, acidic, for example—are not necessarily characteristic of a young, developing planet. Troubling questions also arise concerning the concentration, purification, and interaction of the initial products, a host of organic compounds constituting a dilute soup. Even if complex α-amino acids were present, could they have joined together selectively to form long chains in amounts sufficient for life's beginnings? How plausible are these attempted simulations as models of prebiotic chemistry? To me, and to many others, they almost suggest that life could not have started here on Earth!

How, then, did this polymerization come about? I propose that a key step was the synthesis of polyaminomalononitrile (see Figure 3.2), a key polyamidine that can be formally derived by addition reactions from aminomalononitrile, $H_2NCH(CN)_2$, itself a trimer of hydrogen cyanide. Figure 3.3 shows how the polyamidine structure of polyaminomalononitrile, made up entirely of HCN molecules, can be transformed to the polyamide (or polypeptide) structure of proteins by treatment with cold water, since as a rule, amidine groups —C—NH— are readily converted by water to amides
$$\underset{\text{NH}}{\overset{\|}{}}$$
—C—NH—. Further, the nitrile groups ($-C \equiv N$) in each
$$\underset{\text{O}}{\overset{\|}{}}$$
repeating unit are so reactive that cumulative addition of more HCN (as well as acetylene, H_2S, etc.) can convert them to side chains, denoted here by R´, to give heteropolyamidines (that is, polyamidines with side chains that are diverse, not merely repeated). When this modified cyanide polymer meets water, the amidine groups become amides and R´ becomes R, where R represents the side chains of today's proteins. What is so intriguing about the

FIGURE 3.2

Structures of hydrogen cyanide polymers. A sample of HCN polymer may possess any or all of these structures including hybrids (multimers).

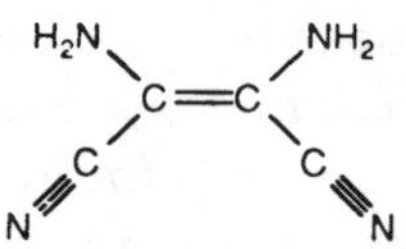

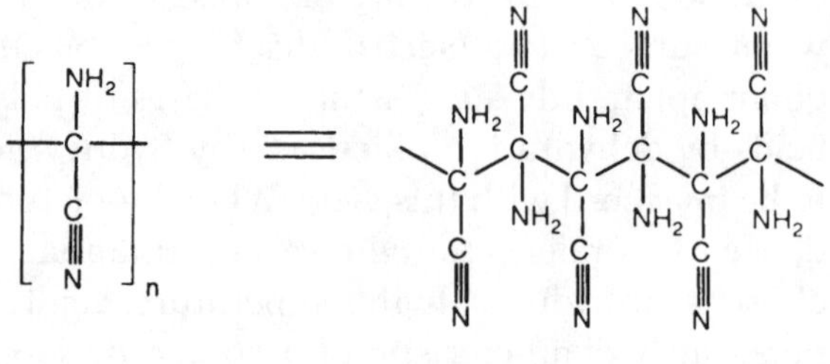

DIAMINOMALEONITRILE
A

POLYAMINOCYANOMETHYLENE
B

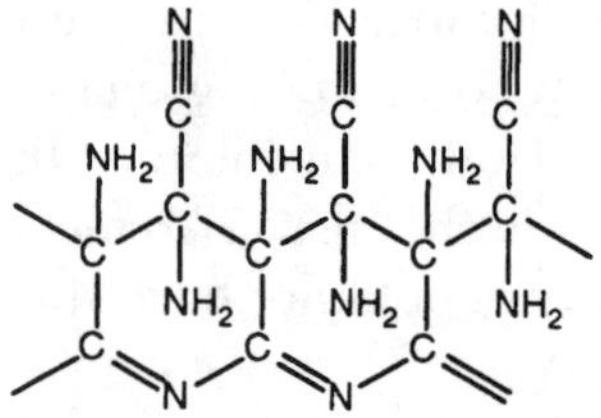

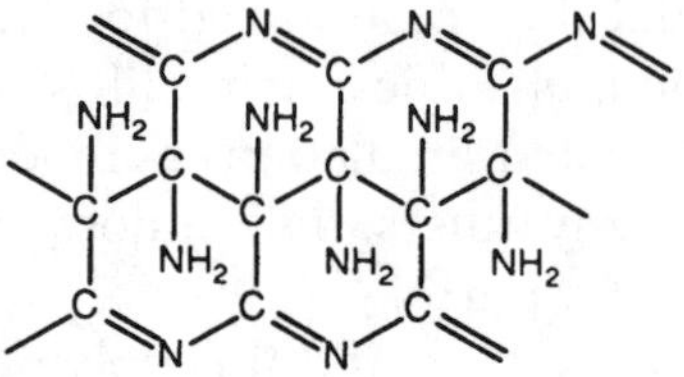

BLACK HCN POLYMERS (AZULMIC ACID)

C   D

HCN polymers (ladder structures) formally derived from HCN tetramer
(diaminomaleonitrile) (Völker, 1960)

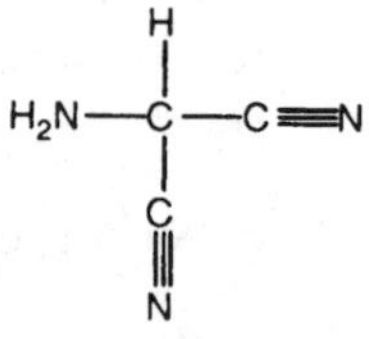

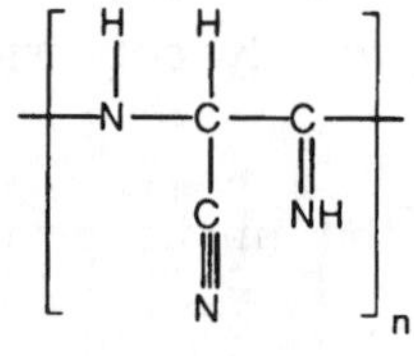

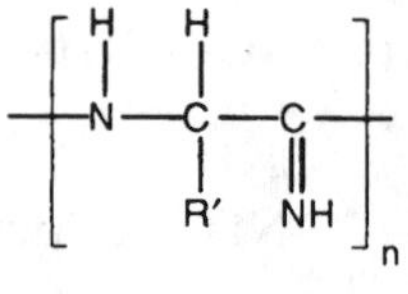

AMINOMALONONITRILE
E

POLYAMINOMALONONITRILE
F

HETEROPOLYAMIDINES
G

HCN polymers (polyamidine structures) formally derived from HCN trimer
(aminomalononitrile) (Matthews, 1966)

FIGURE 3.3

Polypeptides from polyamidines. Cumulative reactions of HCN on poly-aminomalononitrile yield heteropolyamidines (with side chains R) which are converted stepwise in water to heteropolypeptides (with side chains R).

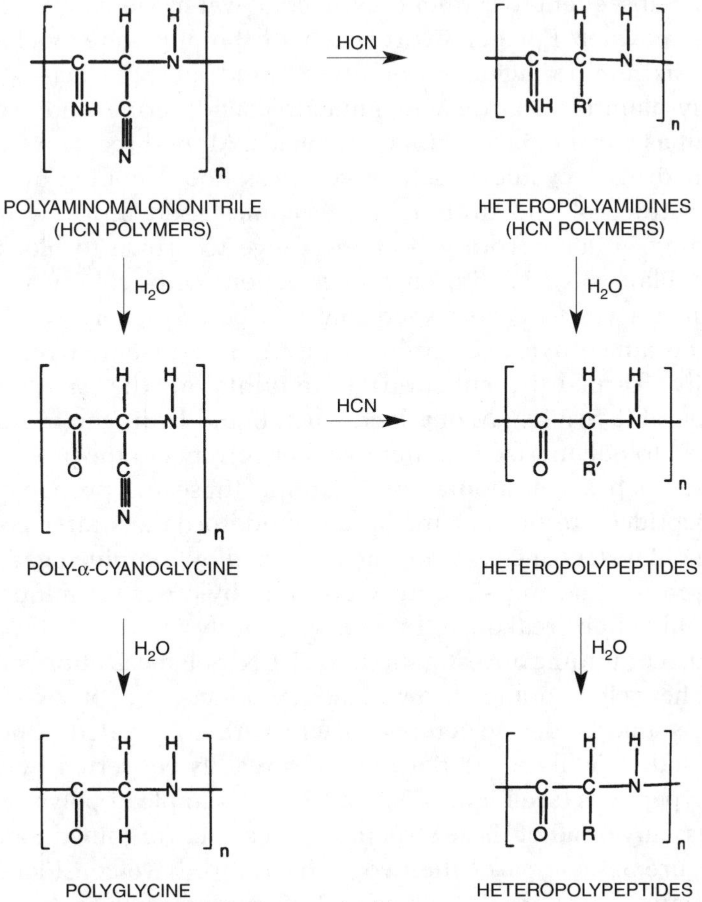

POLYAMINOMALONONITRILE
(HCN POLYMERS)

HETEROPOLYAMIDINES
(HCN POLYMERS)

POLY-α-CYANOGLYCINE

HETEROPOLYPEPTIDES

POLYGLYCINE

HETEROPOLYPEPTIDES

parent polymer, polyaminomalononitrile, is that it can be converted by more HCN and, finally, water to heteropolypeptides possessing both the backbone and the side chains of proteins. In principle, then, two of the simplest and most common molecules in the universe, HCN and H_2O, can give rise to a variety of primitive proteins!

What kind of experiments can we perform to obtain evidence for this hypothesis? First, a variation of Miller's. We sparked a mixture of methane and ammonia (without water) and obtained a sticky brown-black solid that covered the inside of the reaction flask. Subsequent treatment with cold water yielded a yellow-brown powder. Further hydrolysis with boiling water yielded at least six amino acids commonly found in proteins—glycine mainly, alanine, aspartic acid, gluatamic acid, serine, and valine— as well as some non-protein amino acids. More directly, we found that hydrogen cyanide itself (a colorless liquid boiling at 25°C), with a trace of added ammonia, becomes solid in a few hours, changing in color from yellow to orange to brown to black (see Color Plate 6A). Again, after extraction with cold water we obtained a yellow-brown solid that can be further hydrolyzed to give the same mixture of amino acids. A black insoluble residue is usually formed in substantial amounts at the same time. Comparable results are obtained when liquid hydrogen cyanide is allowed to polymerize in water or other solvents in the presence of a base such as ammonia or an amine. It seems probable that polypeptides are present in these cyanide products after contact with cold water, since amino acids detected by combined gas chromatography and mass spectrometry and by other techniques are seen only after breakdown by drastic hydrolysis.

Our continuing investigations of HCN polymerization suggest that the yellow-orange-brown-black products are of two main types: stable ladder structures (black) with conjugated bonds, as proposed by Völker, and polyamidines readily converted by water to polypeptides (see Figures 3.2 and 3.3). A sample of polymer may possess any or all of these structures, separately or joined together.

Figure 3.4 compares the two pathways we have considered for the origin of proteins. Which came first, amino acids or their polymers? On the left is shown the dilute soup model whereby amino acids formed by the Miller-Urey route are assumed to have somehow got together to give primitive proteins. On the right is the cyanide model not requiring water in the atmosphere, where methane and ammonia give HCN polymers directly, which become heteropolypeptides after settling in the oceans. I have argued against the first view and will now explain what I think really happened in the Miller-Urey experiment.

FIGURE 3.4

Two opposing models for the origin of proteins. Which came first, amino acids of their polymers? The left pathway shows α-amino acids somehow condensing in a dilute soup to form polypeptides. The pathway on the right shows clouds of HCN polymerizing in the atmosphere to form heteropolyamidines which settle in the oceans and become hydrolyzed to heteropolypeptides (primitive proteins).

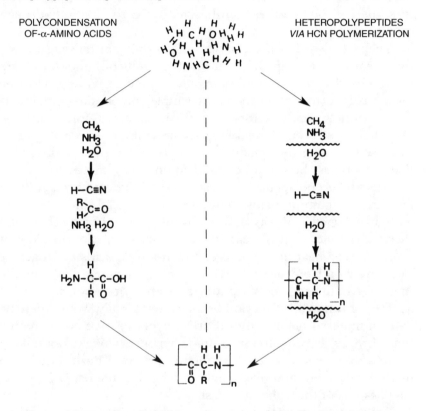

It seems clear to me from our reinvestigations that the primary products were not α-amino acids, as claimed, but rather HCN polymers, the HCN being formed from methane and ammonia by electric discharge reactions and by elimination from intermediates such as the trimer of HCN and its tetramer, diaminomaleonitrile. The polymers then became hydrolyzed to amino acids, either during reflux in the reaction flask or later during the working-up procedure. The same conclusion, I believe, applies to virtually all reported experiments simulating primitive atmospheric chemistry, as well as to studies of aqueous cyanide reactions by James Ferris and others based on the original work of John Oró. I believe these investigations ostensibly yielding α-amino acids actually supply evidence for the abundant prebiotic existence of protein ancestors—heteropolypeptides synthesized directly from hydrogen cyanide and water.

I believe also that the cyanide model answers the questions I raised earlier arising from the dramatic results of Miller and Urey. First, why do complex molecules like amino acids appear to be more easily formed than the many simple compounds—hydrocarbons, alcohols, acids, ketones, aldehydes, amines, for example—expected from reactions of methane, ammonia, and water? Because the major intermediate, by far, is hydrogen cyanide, which then undergoes the rapid polymerization we discussed to eventually yield heteropolypeptides, some of which become broken down by water to α-amino acids. What we have here is kinetic control, with a preferred pathway defined by HCN chemistry, rather than thermodynamic control leading to a statistical distribution of products. The next question asks how α-amino acids got together to form primitive proteins. My answer, of course, is that initially they didn't. Instead, polypeptides appeared first, not via amino acids but from hydrogen cyanide and water. Finally, would there be enough material deposited on Earth for life to have come about? Indeed, yes, according to this cyanide hypothesis. We're not talking about a dilute soup. Instead we picture primeval Earth knee-deep in HCN polymers and, eventually, primitive proteins. Our model supplies lots of the right stuff, fast.

The ready conversion by water of polyamidines to polypeptides demonstrated by our investigations suggests that the polyamidines—HCN polymers—might have played a further essential role in chemical evolution. In the absence of water—on land—they could have been the original condensing agents of prebiotic chemistry giving rise to essential polymeric structures. Their reactive amidine groups, eager to become amides, would have brought about the stepwise formation of nucleosides, nucleotides, and polynucleotides from available sugars, phosphates, and nitrogen bases by a series of dehydration reactions. Most significant would

FIGURE 3.5

HCN polymers on land and sea, giving rise to life on Earth.

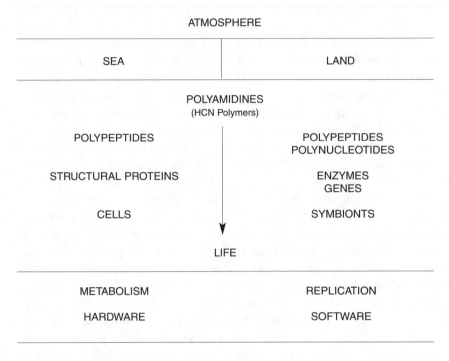

have been the parallel synthesis of polypeptides and polynucleotides arising from the dehydrating action of polyamidines on nucleotides (see Figure 3.5):

polyamidines + nucleotides → polypeptides + polynucleotides

Optimum conditions might well have existed on a primitive Earth where photochemical synthesis of organic molecules proceeded in the atmosphere in three overlapping stages defined by the relative volatility of methane, ammonia, and water. As I see it, hydrocarbon chains formed first from methane in the upper layers of the atmosphere, formed by way of acetylene intermediates. Then, as ammonia became more involved, hydrogen cyanide and cyanoacetylene became major reactants leading to the synthesis of nitriles and their hydrolysis products, carboxylic acids. Polymeric peptide precursors were formed as described above together with nitrogen heterocycles possessing the basic skeletons of purines, pyrimidines, and pyridines. Such compounds, adenine especially, are being obtained from HCN polymers by my collaborators Shirley Liebman and Bob Minard, using state-of-the-art pyrolysis techniques. When most of the ammonia had been used up, photolysis of water vapor that had been confined to lower levels became possible, leading to the third stage when oxygen-containing molecules such as formaldehyde and sugars—carbohydrates—were synthesized, as well as phosphates from phosphine, making possible the synthesis of nucleic acids (DNA and RNA) and energy-supplying compounds such as adenosine triphosphate (ATP). Unlike the prevailing dilute soup picture of chemical evolution, this atmospheric model supplies the necessary prebiotic compounds in sequence, in the right place at the right time. As Earth's surface became covered with this organic shower, potential membrane material—carboxylic acids, carbohydrates, polypeptides—accumulated in lakes and oceans, rapidly becoming cellular, while on land the simultaneous synthesis of polypeptides and polynucleotides, potential genetic material, was promoted by cyanide polymers, perhaps assisted by clays. Interaction on beaches of this potential 'software' with the metabolic 'hardware' in protocells produced elementary replicating systems that become increasingly efficient (see Figure 3.5). On our dynamic planet this polypeptide-polynucleotide symbiosis mediated by polyamidines may have set the pattern for the evolution of protein-nucleic acid systems, controlled by enzymes, so characteristic of life today (see Figure 3.6).

Underlying much of past thinking about the origin of life has been the question: Which came first, proteins (enzymes) or nucleic acids (genes)? A popular view today is that RNA was in at the beginning, before DNA and proteins, since it has recently been shown that some RNA can act both as a catalyst and as a carrier of information. This RNA world, it is assumed, would eventually have evolved into today's world with its genetic code connecting nucleic acids to proteins. But how did the first RNA come about? And how did it lead to DNA and proteins? By contrast, in the HCN world described above, HCN polymer came first, giving rise simultaneously to polypeptides and polynucleotides, precursors of proteins (enzymes) and nucleic acids (both DNA and RNA). This is an argu-

FIGURE 3.6

On our dynamic planet, this polypeptide-polynucleotide symbiosis mediated by polyamidines may have set the pattern of protein/nucleic acid systems controlled by enzymes, the mode characteristic of life today.

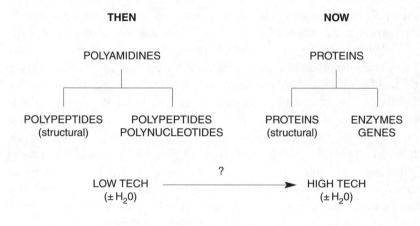

ment from abundance, given the ease of formation both of HCN and its polymers in the solar system and beyond.

So let us consider next some of the extraterrestrial implications of the cyanide model. In our solar system we know that the four small, warm terrestrial planets are oxidizing in character whereas the cold, giant outer planets have reducing environments. They are the ones we're most interested in, because they still resemble primitive Earth in some important respects. For example, methane, ammonia, and water are present in Jupiter's hydrogen-rich atmosphere, as Urey predicted. What chemistry then is producing those yellow-orange-brown-red streaks shown so clearly by the Pioneer and Voyager missions? I suggest—surprise!—HCN polymerization, since these are the very colors we see in our reaction flasks. Saturn, too, could be colored with cyanide polymers, as well as Titan, its giant moon, which has an orange haze that has been shown to be polymeric. Laboratory simulations by Bishun Khare and Carl Sagan of Jupiter and Titan chemistry—reactions of methane, ammonia (or nitrogen), and water subjected to high energy sources—have yielded so-called tholins, dark materials of undefined structure which can be hydrolyzed to α-amino acids and other compounds. We have shown by many analytical techniques that the tholins consist largely of HCN polymers together with some hydrocarbon materials. We'll know more about this situation when various ongoing missions, in particular Galileo (for Jupiter) and Cassini-Huyghens (for Titan), send back analyses obtained by instruments parachuted into these colorful atmospheric layers.

Cyril Ponnamperuma, John Cronin, and other researchers have found amino acids and nitrogen-containing organic compounds in carbonaceous meteorites. Again, I believe these are hydrolysis (or pyrolysis) products of cyanide polymers. We have been able to extract from the Murchison meteorite the same kind of yellow-brown powders that we obtain from HCN. They yield α-amino acids following drastic hydrolysis. Similar cyanide chemistry would be expected on asteroids (the dark parent bodies of mete-orites) and on comets (with their frozen surfaces rich in methane, ammonia, and water). The black crust covering the nucleus of Halley's Comet very likely consists largely of cyanide polymers (see Color Plate 6B), a conclusion supported by the detection in its coma of free hydrogen cyanide, lots of cyanide radicals (CN), and solid particles consisting only of H, C, and N. Most intriguing will be the analysis of cometary material brought to Earth around the year 2005 by the ongoing Stardust mission. I predict that HCN polymers and related compounds will be major components. It seems, then, that primitive Earth may well have been covered with HCN polymers as well as other organic compounds through bolide bombardment and/or by photochemical reactions in the atmos-phere. In an aqueous reducing environment, life emerged from this vital dust, woven out of air by light.

In sum, laboratory and extraterrestrial studies suggest that hydrogen cyanide polymerization is a truly universal process that accounts not only for the past synthesis of protein ancestors on Earth but also for chemistry proceeding today elsewhere in our solar system, on planetary bodies and satellites around other stars, and in the dusty molecular clouds of spiral galaxies. This preferred pathway surely points to the existence of widespread life in the uni-verse—protein-dominated life based on Earth-like planets possess-ing liquid water.

Why does the cyanide theory remain so controversial? Certainly it touches on, and challenges, much of today's research on chemical evolution. So there is a technical opposition—Show me!—which of course is very welcome since it leads to further research and additional results, pro and con. In the words of the influential philosopher of science Karl Popper: "The way in which knowledge progresses, and especially our scientific knowledge, is by unjustified anticipations, by guesses, by tentative solutions to our problems, by *conjectures*. These conjectures are controlled by criticisms; that is, by attempted *refutations*, which include severely critical tests. . . . What is important about a theory is its explanatory power, and whether it stands up to criticism and to tests."

But there is also a more profound objection, which I can best illustrate by using comments of my friend the late Cyril Ponnamperuma when he was Director of the Laboratory of Chemical Evolution at the University of Maryland. In an article in *Science News* reporting some of our results, Cyril was quoted as finding the Matthews hypothesis "an interesting suggestion but probably one that is much too complicated." This surprises me, since if anything I would consider simplicity to be its main strength, simplicity of a type that generates complexity. Cyril went on to suggest that the logical approach is to build up more complicated structures like proteins from simple building blocks like amino acids; philosophically it seems more likely that the simple structures came before the complicated ones. Yes, but . . . The fallacy here lies in the assumption that amino acids were the original building blocks, as they are today. I am arguing instead that the reverse is true—the buildings came before the blocks. In the beginning—at all beginnings—things were necessarily different. According to this model, then, proteins in all their diversity arose essentially from HCN polymers, a conclusion surprising in many ways, especially since today we are accustomed to thinking of hydrogen cyanide as leading to death rather than to life. But in those early times there was no oxygen-dependent life to be poisoned! Indeed, the original poison on Earth was oxygen, which can transform—oxidize—other compounds all too easily. Our metabolism today involves handling this poison through controlled, rather than random, oxidation reactions.[1]

---

1. This chapter draws on Chapter 3 of Lynn Margulis, Clifford N. Matthews, and Aaron Haselton, *Environmental Evolution*, Second edition (Boston: MIT Press, 2000)

The following poem, *Blue Beginning*, is Part 4 of a longer poem written in 1983 by George Drury, an undergraduate English major at the University of Illinois at Chicago, while taking a course for non-science majors taught by myself entitled *Chemistry and Life*. The Blue in the title refers to the Latin word *cyan*, as in *cyanide*— so named, I hear, because of the blue color brought on by asphyxiation resulting from breathing HCN. The poem is introduced by these lines from George Herbert's *Providence*:

Ev'n poysons praise thee. Should a thing be lost? Should creatures want for want of heed their due? Since where are poysons, antidotes are most: The help stands close and keeps the fear in view.

BLUE BEGINNING
George Drury

Hands covered with
crimson chalk dust
Professor Matthews

shakes a beaker
of bright,
plastic beads

and talks
about his work.
Hydrogen Cyanide

and proteins.
A blue beginning.
A building defining

its bricks.
Not only
an incremental build

but a universe
in conversation—
searching

in all directions
in definition
of its instances.

The larger
into
the smaller.

Peace there
to be found
perhaps, but

only in
the finding.
Language needing
words.

Think of it—
from that deadly
substance,
life.

Recommended Reading

Brack, A., ed. 1998. *The Molecular Origins of Life: Assembling Pieces of the Puzzle*. New York: Cambridge University Press.

Deamer, D.W., and G.R. Fleischaker, eds. 1994. *Origins of Life: The Central Concepts*. Boston: Jones and Bartlett.

de Duve, C. 1995. *Vital Dust: Life as a Cosmic Imperative*. New York: Basic Books.

Delsemme, A. 1998. *Our Cosmic Origins: From the Big Bang to the Emergence of Life and Intelligence*. New York: Cambridge University Press.

Dyson, F. 1999. *Origins of Life*. Second edition. New York: Cambridge University Press.

Fry, I. 2000. *The Emergence of Life on Earth: A Historical and Scientific Overview*. New Brunswick: Rutgers University Press.

Morowitz, H.J. 1992. *Beginnings of Cellular Life: Metabolism Recapitulates Biogenesis*. New Haven: Yale University Press.

Schopf, J.W. 1999. *Cradle of Life: The Discovery of Earth's Earliest Fossils*. Princeton: Princeton University Press.

Shapiro, R. 1999. *Planetary Dreams: The Quest to Discover Life Beyond Earth*. New York: Wiley.

Wills, C., and J. Bada. 2000. The Spark of Life: Darwin and the Primeval Soup. Cambridge, MA: Perseus.

References

Ferris, J. 1979. HCN Did Not Condense to Give Heteropolypeptides on the Primitive Earth. *Science* 203, pp. 1135–37.

Liebman, S.A., R.A. Pesce-Rodriguez, and C.N. Matthews. 1995. Organic Analysis of Hydrogen Cyanide Polymers: Prebiotic and Extraterrestrial Chemistry. *Advances in Space Research* 15, no. 3, pp. 71–80.

Matthews, C.N. 1992. Dark Matter in the Solar System: Hydrogen Cyanide Polymers. *Origins of Life* 21, pp. 421–434.

———. 1997. Hydrogen Cyanide Polymers from the Impact of Comet P/Shoemaker-Levy 9 on Jupiter. *Advances in Space Research* 19, no. 7, pp. 1087–091.

Matthews, C.N., and R.E. Moser. 1967. Peptide Synthesis from Hydrogen Cyanide and Water. *Nature* 215, pp. 1230–34.

Minard, R.D., P.G. Hatcher, R.C. Gourley, and C.N. Matthews. 1998. Structural Investigations of Hydrogen Cyanide Polymers: New Insights Using TMAH Thermochemolysis/GC-MS. *Origins of Life* 28, pp. 461–473.

4

The Conscious Universe

ℰLISABET 𝒮AHTOURIS

*New findings are overturning the prejudice
that consciousness came late to the cosmos.
Living systems display purposive intelligence,
and evolving human technology recapitulates
the history of simpler organisms.*

We are members of a vast cosmic orchestra,
in which each living instrument is essential to the
complementary and harmonious playing of the
whole.

> J. Allen Boone

As an evolutionary biologist, my work and passion are looking at
the evolving patterns of biological living systems over time in order
to make sense of our present human affairs in a broad evolutionary context. One might say that I'm a 'pastist' looking for perspective that will help me be a good 'futurist'. But I have an even deeper
passion, which is to understand myself, my world and the entire
Cosmos in which we exist locally.

Within this broader mission I have long sought to undo the artificial barriers we have erected between Science and Spirit for historical reasons, to reveal a richer worldview or 'cosmovision'.

I especially like the latter term, *cosmovision*, for its breadth and depth to the farthest reaches of what we can know through experience. The word *cosmos* is Greek, and in Greek it means people, world, or cosmos in the English sense, depending on context. So cosmovision is a very inclusive term.

Every culture present and past has, or has had, its worldview or cosmovision. Western science has evolved a cosmovision very different from all other human cultures, though it has now become the one most influential in all the world. Its most obvious divergences from other cosmovisions lie in its seeing life and consciousness only in Earth's biological creatures, and in its narrowing of 'reality' to what can be tested and measured scientifically. This excludes from its reality gods, soul, spirit, dream experience, thoughts, feelings, values, passions, enlightenment experiences, and many other aspects of consciousness beyond their physiological correlates.

Given that no one, neither scientist nor anyone else, has ever had any experience outside of consciousness, these omissions seem gravely limiting and unrealistic.

Nevertheless, Western science has defined the universe as an array of non-living matter and non-conscious energy—a universe in which changes over time are due to random or accidental processes that assemble material particles, atoms and molecules into patterns within the constraints of a few physical laws. Thus random events account for life, which is seen as arising from non-life on the surface of one non-living planet, and possibly on others yet undiscovered, evolving by Darwinian random mutations and 'blind' natural selection. The origin of the universe is seen as a 'Big Bang' and its end envisioned as the gradual wearing out of the Big Bang's spreading energy in 'heat death'—the ultimate coldness in which no further change takes place.

One way to sum up the essential difference between this western scientific cosmovision and all other human cultural cosmovisions is to see it portraying a universe in which things happen by accident rather than by intelligent design.

The cosmovision which is the framework in which we attempt to understand the patterns of biological evolution is enormously important. If evolution proceeds by accident, rather than by intelligent intent, the same evidence for evolution, the same observations of it, will be seen very differently. Context gives perspective, determining perception, meaning and interpretation. And cosmovision, or worldview, is context. Humans, for example, will be seen very differently from a religious, economic, cultural, or scientific perspective.

While the western scientific worldview as described gives a satisfying picture and interpretation of nature to many scientists and persuades many others influenced by it, and while its adherents can feel awe at nature's complexity and beauty, ever larger numbers of people either cannot accept it or feel impelled to revise and expand it. These numbers include many scientists dissatisfied with its limitations. In fact, they are changing western science very rapidly now, toward an understanding of nature as alive, self-organizing, intelligent, conscious, or sentient and participatory at all levels from subatomic particles and molecules to entire living planets, galaxies, and the whole cosmos, from local human consciousness to Cosmic Consciousness.

The reductionist pursuit of matter to its tiniest particles broke us through to seeing all matter as disturbances of a great energy field, now called the Zero Point Energy (ZPE) field, in which everything is as dynamically interconnected as in Shiva's Dance or Indra's Net. Furthermore, physics is now demonstrating non-locality in this ZPE, meaning that information from any spatial point in the universe is accessible at any other point, and that all events taking place in the universe at any time are accessible at any other time.

Non-locality thus implies a non-physical, non-timespace ground of being—deeper and more essential than our mundane timespace reality—in which everything exists as potential to be played out in our physical world and whatever other worlds exist. I am reminded of the Kogi Indians of Colombia, saying of Aluna, their Creatrix, symbolized by water: "Through great mental anguish She lived all possible worlds before creating them; thus she is called Memory and Possibility." And I am reminded of the Mayoruna—the 'Cat People' of the Amazon—thought to be extinct until well-known explorer and *National Geographic* photographer Loren MacIntyre stumbled on them while lost in the rainforest. While living with them, MacIntyre not only learned to communicate their way—by the telepathy he called "Amazon beaming"—but discovered that they easily handled two concepts of time—the eternal Now of non-timespace and linear time as we understand it. That Now is also the Dreamtime of the Australian aborigines, the Akashic records of the esoterics, and has been made accessible through ritual and meditation in many human cultures: indigenous, religious, and other.

Microbial Civilization

Looking closely for the first time at intact bacterial microcities, scientists are amazed to see them packed as tightly as our own urban centers, but with a decidedly futuristic look. Towers of spheres and cone- or mushroom-shaped skyscrapers soar 100 to 200 micrometers upward from a base of dense sticky sugars, other big molecules, and water, all collectively produced by the bacterial inhabitants. In these cities, different strains of bacteria with different enzymes help each other exploit food supplies that no one strain can break down alone, and all of them together build the city's infrastructure. The cities are laced with intricate channels connecting the buildings to circulate water, nutrients, enzymes, oxygen, and recyclable wastes. Their diverse inhabitants live in different microneighborhoods and glide, motor, or swim along roadways and canals. The more food is available, the denser the populations become. Researcher Bill Keevil in England, making videos of these cityscapes, says of one, "It looks like Manhattan when you fly over it."

Microbiologist Bill Costerton in Montana observes: "All of a sudden, instead of individual organisms, you have communication, cell co-operation, cell specialization, and a basic circulatory system, as in plants or animals . . . It's a big intellectual break." Researchers are now coming to see colonial bacteria or even all bacteria as multicelled creatures despite their separate bodies.

In addition to rearranging Earth's crust, creating an atmosphere, devising urban lifestyles and creating the first worldwide web, bacteria invented other amazing technologies. Some produced polyester, though biodegradable; others harnessed solar energy as photosynthesis, permitting the making of food when it became scarce; still others invented the electric motor for locomotion—a disk with flagellum attached, rotating in a magnetic field, complete with ball bearings, not to mention the atomic pile, probably to raise local temperatures. Seeing these startling parallels to human lifestyles and inventions makes us see evolution fractally. In fact, when I fly over human cities, I see them as cells spread over a substrate, or as bacterial colonies.

Some bacterial colonies, as we know, cause diseases and deteriorate our teeth, our buildings, and bridges. But most bacterial co-operatives are harmless or indeed co-operative with other creatures, many living inside their guts, as in termites and cows, helping with digestion. They maintain our worldwide habitats by renewing and chemically balancing atmosphere, seas, and soils; they work for our health by the billions in our guts and have evolved into the organelles inside our cells.

We use bacteria in our original biotechnologies of making cheese, yogurt, beer, wine, bread, soy sauce, and other foods. We harness them for newer biotechnologies: to remove contaminants from water in sewage treatment plants, to clean up our oil spills and other pollution, to refine oil, mine ores and even to make that biodegradable polyester they were making long before we were. All our genetic engineering efforts depend on them as they do much of the work of DNA recombination in our laboratories.

The Conscious Universe

Most cultures understand the universe as conscious, and this cosmic consciousness, by various names, as the source of Creation. Now science itself is coming close to these views, through some quantum physicists' recognition that consciousness is essential to reality and somehow a deep feature of the ZPE field or an even deeper non-timespace.

Thus, our scientific cosmovision is shifting 180 degrees from the view of consciousness as a late product of material and biological evolution to the view of consciousness as the very source of material and biological evolution, as I and many of my scientific colleagues have shifted it for ourselves.

In molecular genetic biology this shift is supported by fifty years of research evidence that DNA reorganizes itself intelligently when organisms are environmentally stressed, and that the required information transfer often seems to obey some form of nonlocality rather than slower chemical or electromagnetic transmission.

Rather than being the sources of variation and evolution, errors known to occur in DNA during reproduction and by cosmic radiation or other accidents are recognized at the molecular level and fixed by repair genes. Thus we see intelligence at work not only in higher brains, but in the lowliest of bacteria and cellular components. We are thus moving toward a post-Darwinian era in evolutionary biology.

The earliest creatures of Earth, Archean bacteria, invented complex and diverse lifestyles, rearranged the planet's crust to produce patches of oxides (rusted earth) and pure streams of metals we mine today, including copper and uranium. They created an entirely new atmosphere from their waste gases, especially oxygen, and built up huge continental shelf formations. By evolving ways to exchange DNA information among themselves around the world, we can rightly say they invented the first worldwide web of information exchange. The importance of this astoundingly flexible gene pool, which exists to this day, cannot be underestimated. It is still as active as in Archean times and is related, for example, to rapid bacterial resistance to our antibiotics.

Information exchange gave bacteria close relationships that facilitated both competition and co-operation in communal living. We have known of their communal lives for some time, but only now are we able to investigate their amazing urban complexes in real detail and understand how surprisingly like our own their history has been.

Life's Creative Self-Organization

In what seems to us the almost unthinkably ancient past, the first half of Earth's four and a half billion year life, when bacteria still had the world to themselves, they not only discovered the advantages of communal living but even evolved sophisticated cityscapes. We can see their huge urban complexes today as slimy films—in wetlands, in dank closets, in the stomachs of cows, in kitchen drains. Scientists call them biofilms or mucilages, as they look like slimy brown or greenish patches to the unaided eye. Only now can we discover their inner structure and functions with the newest microscopy techniques that magnify them sufficiently without destroying them (for example, confocal scanning laser microscopy).

Most astonishing to investigators, communal bacteria turn on a different set of genes than their genetically identical relatives roaming independently outside of biofilms. This gives the urban dwellers a very different biochemical makeup. A special bacterial chemical, homoserine lactone, signals incoming bacteria to turn into city dwellers. All bacteria constantly discharge low levels of this chemical. Large concentrations of it, in urban environments, trigger the urbanizing genetic changes, no matter what strain the bacteria are.

These changes include those that make bacteria most resistant to antibiotics. Costerton estimates that more than 99 percent of all bacteria live in biofilm communities, and finds that such communities, pooling their resources, can be up to 1,500 times more resistant to antibiotics than a single colony. Under today's siege by antibiotics, bacteria respond with ever-new genetic immunity. Our fifth generation of antibiotics failed in 1996.

Researcher Eshel Ben-Jacob also finds bacteria trading genes and discovers complex interactions between individuals and their communities. The genomes of individuals—defined as their full set of structural and regulatory genes—can and do alter their patterns in the interests of the bacterial community as a whole. He observes that bacteria signal each other chemically, calculate their own numbers in relation to food supplies, make decisions on how to behave accordingly to maximize community well being and collectively change their environments to their communal benefit.

Bacterial communities thus create complex genetic and behavioral patterns specific to different environmental conditions. The genomes of individual bacteria alter their composition, arrangement, and the pattern of which genes are turned on, in response to changes in the environment or communal circumstances. This important information is coming from various research laboratories. Both Ben-Jacob and Costerton see individual bacteria gaining the benefits of group living by putting group interests ahead of their own. Ben-Jacob concludes that colonies form a kind of supermind genomic web of intelligent individual genomes. Such webs are capable of creative responses to the environment that bring about "co-operative self-improvement or co-operative evolution."

The Omnipresence of Purpose

Einstein's worldview was shaken when some quantum physicists suggested that electrons intentionally leap orbits. Microbiologists are beginning to see similar intentional activity at systemic, cellular and molecular DNA levels. These discoveries of genomic changes in response to an organism's environment, in the context of a holistic systems view of evolution, are changing our story of how evolution proceeds in very significant ways. We are discovering that the fundamental life forms from which all other organisms evolve are capable of both self-organization in community and self-improvement through environmental challenge.

Genomic changes in response to an organism's environment have actually been known since the 1950s, but they challenged the accepted theories of the time, so it has taken half a century to amass sufficient data to warrant changing our scientific picture of evolution accordingly.

Barbara McClintock, who did much of her work on corn plants, pioneered this research showing that DNA sequences move about to new locations and that this genetic activity increases when the plants are stressed. She also found closed-loop molecular bits of self-reproducing DNA called plasmids moving about among the normal DNA and exchanged from cell to cell. Plasmids were invented by ancient bacteria and persist in multicelled creatures. They are used a great deal in genetic engineering as they can be inserted into new genomes.

McClintock's work on transposable genetic elements was verified and elaborated by many researchers until it became clear that DNA reorganizes itself and trades genes with other cells, even with other creatures. The trading process sometimes involves virus-like elements known as transposons. Some are retrotransposons and retroviruses that transcribe their RNA into DNA—opposite to the usual order and not thought possible before their discovery. Some theorists now believe that bacteria may have invented viruses as well as plasmids.

Phillip Sharp and Richard Roberts, 1993 Nobel Laureates, discovered that RNA is arranged in modules that can be reshuffled by spliceosomes, referred to as a cell's 'editors'. Other researchers have shown that bacteria naturally retool themselves genetically and can correct defects created by human genetic engineers. Ancient bacteria had already evolved the ability to repair genes damaged by UV radiation.

Further research shows that bacteria not only alter genomes very specifically in response to specific environmental pressures, but also transfer the mutations to other bacteria. Many of these genetic transfers appear to be evolutionarily related to 'free living viruses', according to Temin and Engels in England. Retroviruses are known to infect across species and enter the host's germline DNA.

We are still in the early stages of understanding the extent to which DNA is freely traded in the world of microbes to benefit both individuals and their communities. And we are just beginning to see these processes of genetic alteration at cellular levels as intelligent responses to changing environmental conditions in multi-celled creatures. We know viruses and plasmids carry bits of DNA from whales to seagulls, from monkeys to cats, and so on, but it remains to be understood whether all this transfer is random or whether it is meaningful.

Most research in this area is still confined to microbes, in which these matters are easier to study. As yet we do not know to what extent DNA trading occurs in creatures larger than microbes, nor to what extent it facilitates specific responses to environmental conditions. For that matter, we still do not know what the vast proportion of multicellular creature DNA does at all. Depending on the particular plant or animal species, only 1 to 5 or 10 percent (in humans) codes for proteins. The remaining 90 to 99 percent remains a mystery! So our stories are far from complete, but it seems reasonable to hazard the guess that nature would not have evolved an evolutionary strategy as sophisticated as gene trading to facilitate evolution billions of years ago only to abandon it in evolving larger creatures.

When we see that genomes respond to stress in many different species, from microbes to plants and animals, with the changes passed on to succeeding generations, as Jeffrey Pollard in England has reported, we are closer to the much-discredited Lamarck than to Darwin. Pollard tells us we are seeing "dramatic alterations of developmental plans independent of natural selection," which itself may "play a minor role in evolutionary change, perhaps honing up the fit between the organism and its environment."

Multidimensional Being

This growing body of evidence suggests that evolution may proceed much faster under stress than was thought possible. It also reveals how the worldwide web of DNA information exchange invented by ancient bacteria still functions today, not only among bacteria as always, but also within multicelled creatures and among species. As Lynn Margulis puts it: "Evolution is no linear family tree, but change in the single multidimensional being that has grown to cover the entire surface of Earth."

Margulis meant the multidimensional being of an interwoven biological network. But let's look at this concept of multidimensional being in an even broader sense. Physicists discovered an astounding interconnectivity and interdependence among all the particles of our material universe, with each particle actually created by the others, just as Buddhist monk Thich Nhat Hanh tells us that a sheet of paper is everything that it is not, showing us how we can trace the paper to its source in factory and forest, the workers and woodcutters, their families, and so on to all things interconnected. Now biologists are showing us the same interconnectedness among bacteria and larger organisms, in ecosystems and in the Earth as a whole living entity. Earth continually recycles its matter into new organisms through the great recycling system of erupting magma cooling into rock, transforming into creatures, eventually into sediment and back into rock and molten magma as tectonic plates slide beneath each other and back into the Earth's fiery depths below the continents.

My co-author Willis Harman once said, "If consciousness is anywhere in the universe, it must be everywhere." The easiest way to understand this is to see that consciousness is a fundamental property of the source of all being, as more and more physicists believe it to be. This consciousness is a vital dimension of being, more fundamental than energy or matter.

I like to think of creaturehood as life music played on a keyboard, with consciousness or spirit represented by the high keys, electromagnetic energy as the mid-range and matter as the low keys. With this metaphor, we see that Einstein showed us how to transpose the music of the mid-range to the low range and back, with his simple equation $e = mc^2$. Now we are seeking the key to transposing from the high keys into the world of matter, via electromagnetic energy, through the ZPE field, formerly called the plenum by the Greeks, the ether by Europeans, and the Implicate Order by physicist David Bohm. I participate in many different discussion groups on this subject, mostly with other scientists, all of us asking: "If consciousness is the source of creation, just how does it transmute into our measurable electromagnetic energy? What are the properties of electromagnetic energy that we do not yet understand? What keys lie in the ZPE range?"

I said earlier that western science is changing very rapidly now, toward an understanding of nature as alive, self-organizing, intelligent, conscious or sentient and participatory at all levels from subatomic particles and molecules to entire living planets, galaxies and the whole Cosmos, from local human consciousness to Cosmic Consciousness.

In this newer framework or cosmovision, biological evolution is holistic, intelligent and purposeful. Notions such as entropy in a non-living universe, running down to its death, no longer apply. Rather we see a living universe, with a metabolism like that in our bodies, with its continual creation from the ZPE as anabolism, while entropy can now be seen as catabolism—continual dissolution for purposes of recycling. In this version entropy does not lead to the death of the universe because the universe is capable of replenishing itself continually.

Evolution from the perspective of linear time displays cycles that move ever upward, reflecting the complex spiraling paths of planets and stars and galaxies. Each cycle begins with some form of unity dividing into diversity, leading to conflict, which then moves into negotiations and resolution in a higher lever of co-operative unity.

The ancient bacteria diversified from the unity of a new planet's crustal mixture of elements, moving them about as they invented new forms and lifestyles. They competed with each other for resources as they caused major planetwide problems such as starvation and global pollution. They invented new technologies to solve them, but finally had to negotiate and learn to co-operate in communities and in the ultimate symbiotic bacterial community which became the first 'multi-creatured cell'—the nucleated cell—a new unity at a higher level of complexity.

From this nucleated cell, new diversity emerged as many kinds of single cells competed, negotiated and finally co-operated as multicelled creatures. From this new level of unity, all other creatures diversified, competed and negotiated their way into harmonious ecosystems. The best life insurance for any species in an ecosystem is to contribute usefully to sustaining the lives of other species, a lesson we are only beginning to learn as humans.

Human History Recapitulates the History of Life

Today we humans are repeating this process in amazing detail, in what we have come to recognize as *globalization*. Human history repeats evolutionary history, with all its problems and technological solutions—diversification from the unity of the earliest human family, all the old patterns of competition and negotiation played out in wars, conquests and assimilations for the thousands of years in which we have built the empires of individual rulers, then of nations and now of corporations. Finally we recognize that we need a co-operative world—unity at a higher level, a new multi-creatured cell the size of our entire planet. And gradually we see that just as our beautifully evolved body cannot be healthy if one or more organs are ill, so our global economy can thrive only if all local economies are healthy as well. Thus we become concerned with the ecosystems we have damaged and with the economic inequities we must solve.

How fascinating that just as we evolve this pattern of globalization in recognition of our need for harmony with each other and with other species, we also awaken to our 'full keyboard' selves, to our identity as spirit having a human experience, striving to understand the ultimate unity from which we sprang! What ancient mystics and religious prophets and saints taught is now becoming widespread. Thus, our new negotiations toward co-operation are not only reflected in economic globalization and our own worldwide web—the Internet—but in many efforts to globalize friendly conversation among the world's religions. In this process we move from religious conflicts to co-operation, in part by recognizing that ultimate unity, that cosmic consciousness, that ground of being, as the source of all 'God' concepts.

The barriers between science and spirit are dissolving as scientists find cosmic consciousness in a non-local, non-time energy field that transmutes itself into electromagnetic energy, and, in turn, matter, in the creation of universes such as ours, as we have seen. Presumably it can also create itself—self-organize—into other pure energy patterns in a myriad ways, including angelic realms, for example, and all the 'worlds' we may exist in between lives, and eternally.

This Creative Source has been called 'I Am' from the perspective of the local consciousness in beings such as you and me, when we practice meditation to expand our little consciousnesses into the Cosmic Consciousness of which they are part. In this state we not only perceive union with God, we may even transcend our local selves such that we recognize ourselves as God.

From a linear time perspective, our universe appears to be a learning universe. I like to say its basic principle is 'Anything that can happen, will happen', and so it learns what works well and what doesn't. Evolution can thus be seen as an improvisational dance, keeping the steps that work and changing those that don't. God-as-Cosmic-Consciousness becomes Cosmic Consciousness transmuting into material universes. Perhaps we could say that in this process even God learns to know the nature of Self by exploring all possible forms and states of being and reflecting on those 'selves', just as we, God's human reflections, learn to do.

Cosmic Consciousness, then, begins as Unity and divides into Complexity a stage at a time as it embodies itself in such vast varieties of energetic and material forms as we see in biological evolution, for example, from our human perspective of linear time. In its non-timespace Source, which some physicists now identify as the more fundamental nature of the universe, all these possibilities exist together in complexity inconceivable to us humans.

I believe each life comes with the freedom to choose a path through these endless possibilities at a myriad choice points along its way, just as every particle weaves its trajectory through timespace. Every organism composed of and playing on its full keyboard from pure consciousness to matter, can theoretically be led in its development by its ultimate goal. The acorn can know the oak tree it will become, as we can know the higher selves toward which we evolve.

All nature is thus conscious, in my worldview or cosmovision, and all of it has access to non-timespace; all of it is an aspect of God. Only we humans of western culture have played the game of cutting ourselves off from the Great Conversation that our very cells can still hear! I have come to believe, like many of my indigenous teachers, that soils, waters, organisms, ecosystems, Earth, even DNA itself, all know themselves in relation to the whole play of universal evolution as our cells know each other and our whole bodies in evolution, behaving intelligently to maintain themselves and that whole. Only this way can I understand how my own body, in its tremendous complexity, functions and preserves its health.

Perhaps God, through western technological culture, is trying out the most dangerous game of all—the game of truly forgetting our nature. A great risk, but it had to be done to try all possibilities! It seems our human task now is to wake up and recognize ourselves as parts or aspects of God-as-Nature and behave accordingly. All are One, all harm harms each of us, all blessings bless each of us. What a guideline for choice!

Suppose we remind ourselves occasionally to see ourselves as *the creative edge of God* (a phrase I learned from a dear friend)—as God looking out through our eyes, acting through our hands, walking on our feet, in exploration of the new—and to observe how that changed things for us.

This is the scientific worldview, as I see it, when the barriers are removed, expanding it to include the larger cosmovision traditionally relegated to religions. It is the view that makes sense to me at this point in my lifetime of exploration. We have only our stories to go by, and each must necessarily be at least somewhat, if not radically, different—for God/Cosmic Consciousness has become very complex, though always an eternal Unity.

I pray that all the religions will recognize the importance of the uniqueness in each story and the unity of All That Is. I pray that scientists, who have been given the role of 'official' priesthood, with the mandate to tell us 'how things are', will soon officially recognize that there is one alive, intelligent universe in which spirit and matter are not separable and in which creation is continuous. I pray that the indigenous people who never separated science and spirituality will be honored for that. It is time for the true communion which alone can save our species and all others, which alone can bring about the perfectly possible world we all dream of—a world expressing this understanding of ourselves as the creative edge of God!

5

The Probability
of Human Origins

Matt Cartmill

*The emergence of humankind was not a
sure thing but neither was it a miraculous
billion-to-one long shot. Thirteen key
innovations were required to produce*
Homo sapiens—*they all have parallels in
the evolution of other species.*

I'm going to summarize the story of human evolution and then
analyze that story in terms of what it takes to make us feel at home
in the universe.

The first thing we need to notice here is that what makes one
person feel comfortable may give another person the creeps. Take,
for example, the people one encounters at a gathering of
strangers—say, at a party, or at an international parliament of
world religions. Some people at these gatherings are trying to fit in,
while others are trying to stand out. The fitters-in want to be
accepted as part of the community. The standers-out want to be
noticed as different.

What applies to parties and parliaments applies equally to the
universe. Some want to fit into it. Others want to stand out in it.

People of the former sort feel comfortable when they can see
themselves and the rest of the human race as fitting into the big
picture, as part and parcel of the system of natural laws and
processes. Let's call these people *integrators*. They like to think of

themselves as part of nature: objects among their fellow objects, animals among their fellow animals. They don't believe that there is a sharp boundary between people and other creatures, or that human life has a peculiar kind of sanctity, or that human souls have a unique supernatural existence or destiny. They tend to think that human mental and spiritual properties have at least some sort of rudimentary presence in other animals. They want to believe that the human species came into existence naturally, and that it was exactly the sort of thing that you might have expected to happen.

Other people, by contrast, prefer to stand out from the universe. Let's call these people *isolators*. They like to see themselves and their fellow men and women as radically different from the stones and trees and beasts. They regard humans as splendidly set apart from the rest of the material world: unique in intellect, unique in moral perception, unique in conceptual thought—maybe even unique in being conscious of the world at all. They regard the creation of the human species as something of a miracle, or at least a billion-to-one coincidence. They tend to see the human mind and spirit as unique, and human interests and wishes as having a transcendent importance that utterly outweighs the interests and wishes of nonhuman creatures. They are seldom ethical vegetarians.

Of course, these are polar stereotypes, and most of us fall somewhere in the middle in our feelings about the place of humanity in the universe. Still, I think that most people tend to fall closer to one extreme or the other.

In the following pages, I propose to sketch a very brief outline of the history of life that we see in the fossil record, or at least of those events that are especially important for explaining human origins. Then I'm going to lay out two alternative ways of looking at that history. The first is an isolator's view, which portrays the major events in the human evolutionary career as unpredictable accidents, and sees the emergence of human beings as a unique and highly unlikely happenstance. The second, which is the way I myself prefer to look at things, views those events as the sort of things that might have been expected to happen sooner or later. I intend to argue that the emergence of intelligent life on this planet was chancy but not wildly improbable, and that it has in fact happened more than once. I also propose to argue that this way of looking at things helps us to feel more at home in the universe.

A Brief History of Human Origins

Multicellular life first shows up in the fossil record around 570 million years ago, in the so-called Precambrian period. All living things on Earth at this time lived in the sea—as we might expect, because life originated in the sea, and it took it a long time to work out ways of moving onto the land.

Most organisms back then were microscopic, just as most organisms are today. But the multicellular life of the Precambrian doesn't look much like anything we find in our modern oceans. Most of the large Precambrian organisms are built on a body plan unlike anything known from the present. They were flattened mats of pasted-together tubes, spreading outward from a central core or axis. In cross-section, these things looked like an inflatable swim-mat or air-mattress. One theory about these creatures holds that the hollow tubes acted like greenhouses, in which photosynthetic bacteria grew in a protected environment and provided their tube-making host with food and oxygen.

What did the bacteria need to be protected from? We don't know for sure. But other Precambrian deposits yield fossils that can be described as worm tracks in mud—traces left by animals moving in or along the surface layer of the ocean floor. Whatever left these Precambrian tracks was probably grazing on the thin mat of tiny one-celled organisms that covered the bottoms of the shallow Precambrian seas. The hollow tubes of the larger Precambrian creatures may have sheltered their internal micro-organisms from these grazers.

This collection of creatures is sometimes called the Ediacaran fauna, after the type locality in Australia. Mark and Dianna McMenamin (1990) have called this phase in the history of life the "Garden of Ediacara." And here at the dawn of terrestrial life, there does appear to have been something rather like a Peaceable Kingdom. There is no evidence of Precambrian predation, no multicellular organisms eating each other: just microscopic plants and bacteria living directly or indirectly by photosynthesis, and a few larger organisms living off the bacteria, either by slurping them up from the sea floor or by culturing them internally and digesting their byproducts. There are no jaws or teeth in this world. As a corollary, there are no defensive structures—no shells or carapaces or spines or spikes—preserved in the fossil record. We can assume that the chase and the arms race between predator and prey had not yet begun. This was a world without weapons or armor; and therefore it was a world without speed, and a world without brains.

Shells make their first appearance around 550 million years ago. At the end of the Precambrian, there is an abrupt change in the fossil record. Quite suddenly, in the space of a few million years of transition, hundreds of genera of armored animals appear in the rocks, covered with shells and carapaces and spikes and plates. This change marks the beginning of the Cambrian period.

Among the most common and familiar of these Cambrian newcomers are the trilobites, which vaguely resemble armored seagoing centipedes. These creatures, once wildly successful but now extinct, represent a major group (phylum) of animals called arthropods: segmented animals with external skeletons of chitin and many jointed legs. Other arthropods are still wildly successful today. They include centipedes, spiders, scorpions, and all the innumerable hosts of insects on the land and crustaceans in the sea. Most of the other major groups of living animals are represented in the Cambrian, including mollusks and echinoderms and various groups of worms, as well as a lot of strange-looking creatures of uncertain relationships. One of the strangest of these—whose name, for obvious reasons, is *Hallucigenia*—is shown in Figure 5.1, in two reconstructions. The experts on Cambrian animals now believe that the first reconstruction (Figure 5.1, A) is upside down. The spikes running along the animal's body aren't walking legs, but defensive spines on the back (Figure 5.1, B). Presumably, these spines would have made this bizarre creature less attractive to predators.

This sort of defensive armor is one of three important themes or motifs that occur over and over again in many of these diverse Cambrian groups. The second of these Cambrian themes is bilateral symmetry. *Hallucigenia* has a head end and a tail end and left and right sides. That tells us that it's specialized for moving in one particular direction. In this particular case, we aren't sure which end is which. But in most other cases, it's pretty clear, because the head end has sense receptors and jaws and prey-catching organs. This fact illustrates the third Cambrian theme—predation. These Cambrian creatures are true animals: they live by eating other organisms, biting chunks out of them and killing them and con-

FIGURE 5.1

The enigmatic Cambrian invertebrate Hallucigenia. *Originally reconstructed as walking on its pointed spines (A), it was later reconstructed the
other way up (B) when a second row of tentacles was discovered.*

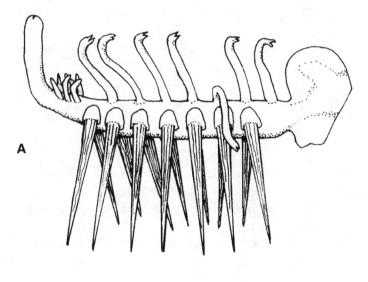

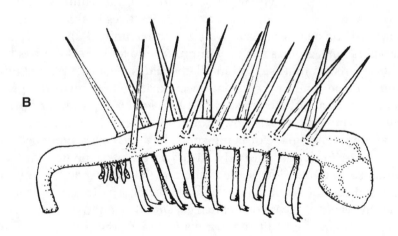

suming their tissues—as we all do ourselves. The Garden of
Ediacara is closed; and the harmless air-mattress creatures of the
Precambrian have abruptly vanished from history.

FIGURE 5.2

A simplified drawing of a midline slice through the primitive chordate
Branchiostoma, *showing some of the characteristic chordate features.*

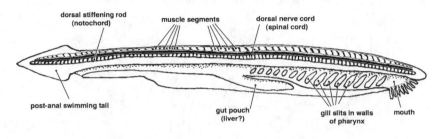

In several Cambrian localities around the world, fine-grained shales deposited in deep water have preserved soft-bodied animals in great detail. And in one of these, the Middle Cambrian Burgess Shale in Canada, we find something close to the beginning of the human story. This wormlike creature is *Pikaia*. It is the first generally accepted representative of our own phylum, the Chordata or chordates.

A similar, still surviving representative of the primitive chordate stock is the lancelet, *Branchiostoma*, which lives in shallow sea bottoms off the coasts of Asia. It's a wormlike animal about five centimeters long, and it's not very impressive to look at. But it has four characteristics that we find in all chordates (Figure 5.2), including you and me. The first chordate peculiarity, which gives the group its name, is a stiffening rod called the *notochord*, a kind of primitive backbone that runs down the back of the animal. The second is another cord, made of nerve cells: the *spinal cord*, lying between the notochord and the skin. The third is segmented muscles attached to either side of the notochord. These wiggle the animal's tail and send it scooting through the water. The fourth is holes in the side walls of the throat, called *gill slits*. The animal breathes and feeds at once, by squirting sea water out through these slits and swallowing any solid leftovers. Human embryos still retain the notochord and gill slits. The segmented muscles and spinal cord are evident in human adults.

The Cambrian fossil *Pikaia* had the muscle blocks, the swimming tail, and the notochord that we see in a modern lancelet. It had begun the development of a long series of key evolutionary inventions that were crucial for the eventual appearance of humankind. The first was a predatory habit of life—using other organisms for food. The second was the invention of bilateral symmetry, with a head and a tail end. I've already mentioned that both of these innovations are general themes of Cambrian life. A third novelty was the invention of a rudimentary internal skeleton—the notochord. We don't see this in most other Cambrian animals, who wear their hard parts on the outside for protection. A fourth was the invention of a centralized nervous system: a nerve cord running down the back, which could take in sensory stimuli, process them, and produce appropriate motor responses, like wiggling the tail to swim or burrowing into the mud to hide.

The lancelet is a chordate, but not a vertebrate. It has no jaws, no brain, no eyes or other sense organs at the front end—just gill slits and a ring of tentacles surrounding the mouth. Vertebrates added two more key inventions to the chordate list. The first was a true head with eyes and brain, more or less just pasted onto the front end of the animal in front of the notochord. (Certain rudiments of this new add-on were already present in the Cambrian chordate *Pikaia*.) The second vertebrate innovation was an internal skeleton of bone or cartilage, with a brainbox surrounding the brain and a string of vertebral elements forming a primitive backbone around the notochord.

The early vertebrates appear to have been something like living lampreys, which are found today in rivers and lakes and seas all around the world. Lampreys have no jaws; they attack their prey with a rasping sucker surrounding the mouth opening. But they have eyes of the standard vertebrate sort, and a sort of tongue, and a skull and backbone of cartilage, and a small but clearly vertebrate brain elaborated out of the front end of the spinal cord.

The first true vertebrates appeared about 430 million years ago, in the period after the Cambrian, the Ordovician. Because they had skeletons made of bone, these primitive fish had a much better chance of fossilizing than a soft-bodied animal like *Pikaia* or a lamprey. Most of their bones were worn right underneath the skin, forming a sort of dermal armor plating. Their armor presumably helped ward off attacks from predators. We still preserve some pieces of this dermal armor in our skulls and collarbones.

Most of these early fish had small, stiff, toothless mouths. They were probably bottom-feeders and worm eaters like modern catfish. More aggressive predation on larger prey had to wait on the next major invention in the human lineage: namely, jaws that could cut and kill other big animals and tear them up into pieces small enough to swallow.

Vertebrate jaws evolved from the bones of the gill arches, the columns of tissue in between the gill slits. The first vertebrates with jaws appeared about 400 million years ago. In most of these early-jawed fish, the body was no longer covered with bony armor. It wore a sort of flexible chain-mail coat made of small bony scales, coated with hard enamel. The scales inside the mouth were pointed, with sharp tips to help hold and tear prey. We still have a set of these enamel-coated scales in our own mouths: our teeth.

The scales on the bodies of most modern fish have degenerated into delicate little translucent chips of bone, but we're descended from a group that hung on to the big primitive scales for quite a while. These fish manifested another invention that was crucial for the emergence of humankind: two pairs of fins, a front pair just behind the head and a hind pair back near the anus. These fish are called sarcopterygians, from the Greek for 'fleshy fins', because their fins were thick and muscular. It was lucky for us that they were, because this made it easier for those fins to function as arms and legs when some of these fish began coming out of the water. The larger bones inside some sarcopterygians' fins can be matched up, bone for bone, with the major bones in our own arms and legs.

The first land vertebrates show up in the fossil record in the late Devonian, around 370 million years ago (Figure 5.3). Apart from their arms and legs, they still looked quite a bit like big fleshy-finned fish. Some of the very early ones even had a fin on the tail. These vertebrates weren't the first creatures to colonize the land. If they had been, there wouldn't have been anything for them to eat when they got there. Plants had preceded the vertebrates onto land by some 30 or 40 million years, and various invertebrate groups, including the ancestors of insects, followed the plants onto the land not long afterward.

The spread of land plants may have altered the Earth's atmosphere. Changes in the chemistry of the sedimentary rocks suggest that oxygen levels began to rise some 380 to 400 million years ago

FIGURE 5.3

Fluctuating levels of atmospheric oxygen from the Devonian to the Triassic, as inferred from the chemistry of the rocks (after Graham et al. 1997).

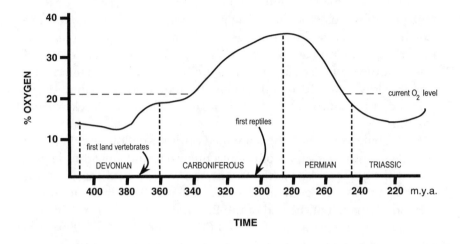

(Figure 5.3), at about the same time that plants were colonizing the continents. During this period, great forested swamps spread across the continental lowlands, and land plants underwent an evolutionary radiation. Much of our coal today is mined from deposits laid down in these swamps, which is why this period is called the Carboniferous. The air's oxygen content rose to a peak 280 million years ago in the early part of the next period, the Permian. It plunged back down again during the Permian to its earlier level, and then rose more slowly up to an intermediate level like that of the present.

Some biologists think that these changes in the atmosphere were driving the evolution of animals as well. They contend that the rise in oxygen during the Late Devonian period would have made it easier to live by breathing air, and that the oxygen-rich air allowed animals to move out of the water onto the land. Some argue that the high oxygen levels in the Carboniferous—and the high metabolic rates that must have gone with them—allowed insects to take to the air as well. The Carboniferous witnessed the evolution of giant insects, looking like dragonflies with a wingspread a meter across, which probably couldn't have survived in today's less oxygenated air.

During the Permian and the period that followed it, the Triassic, the swamps of the Carboniferous tended to be replaced by deserts. One possible cause for this is the movement of the continents. The Earth's continents float on the slowly moving liquid rock that underlies them, and are borne around by its currents like islands of scum on the surface of a simmering pot of soup. The Permian continents slowly drifted together near the equator to form a single Triassic supercontinent, called 'Pangaea', which is Greek for 'all earth'.

The coalescence of Pangaea wiped out the shallow seas between the continents. The supercontinent's huge size and low latitude promoted the spread of deserts. And as the world's land masses grew drier and merged together, plant life suffered. The diversity of fossil land plants fell at the end of the Permian—the only time this has ever happened in geological history (Tiffney and Niklas, 1990). It is probably not a coincidence that oxygen in the Earth's atmosphere dropped throughout the Permian and bottomed out with the Triassic consolidation of Pangaea (Figure 5.3).

This drying-out of the continents contributed to the success of the next great invention by our ancestors—the development of an egg that could be laid on land. The Carboniferous land vertebrates had needed to lay their jelly-covered eggs in fresh water, just as frogs and salamanders do today. But the new eggs were covered with a tough shell, stiff enough to keep the egg from flattening out and tough enough and tight enough to keep bacteria out and water in. This allowed vertebrates to move away from the water and adapt to a new sort of life in the dryer uplands. Reptiles, birds, and a few mammals today continue to lay eggs of this sort.

The new eggs were a marvel of economy. They had sealed-in supplies of food and water, complete with toilet facilities to store the wastes of the developing embryo. While the shell was strong and watertight, it was also porous enough to let oxygen in and carbon dioxide out so that the embryo could breathe. This is a tricky set of conflicting demands for an eggshell to try to juggle. Some scientists claim that the high oxygen levels of the late Carboniferous atmosphere were the only thing that made the evolution of this new egg possible.

The animals that were laying these eggs were the early reptiles, which appeared near the end of the Carboniferous. We can trace the separate lineages of birds and mammals all the way back to this time period. The very first reptiles (Figure 5.4, A) had a solid bony skull roof, like that of the primitive land vertebrates. But most later reptiles evolved openings in the sides of the dermal armor of the skull. There were two main groups of these reptiles—a group with one hole on each side, and another group sporting two holes (Figure 5.4, B and C). The one-hole group contained the ancestors of the mammals, including human beings. You can still trace the remnants of that single hole in your own head; it's the soft area full of muscles on the side of the braincase, between the crown of the head and the cheekbone.

The one-hole reptiles were the dominant land animals of the Permian, but their rule was short-lived. The end of the Permian saw perhaps the greatest mass extinction in the history of life on this planet. We aren't sure why this happened. The coming together of Pangaea may have had something to do with it. Another theory holds that massive volcanic eruptions at this time altered the atmosphere, kicking already-stressed animal populations over the line into extinction. For whatever reason, most animal species disappeared. It has been estimated that 95 percent of all multicellular organisms may have become extinct at this time—including most of the one-holed reptiles.

The ecological roles that they vacated were snapped up by the two-hole reptiles. This group included the ancestors of the dinosaurs. The first dinosaurs made their appearance around 200 million years ago, in the late Triassic. The old-fashioned view of dinosaurs is that they were slow, cold-blooded, stupid, lumbering creatures who died out because they couldn't adapt to changing times. The current fashion is to see dinosaurs as active, nervous, birdlike creatures with warm blood and feathers. And if birds are surviving small dinosaurs, as the consensus has it nowadays, then at least some dinosaurs must have been warm-blooded and birdlike.

By the end of the Triassic, the dinosaurs and their relatives had replaced the one-hole reptiles as the dominant land animals. But one small group of the losers had figured out a way to survive in the shadow of the dinosaurs. They became tiny, nocturnal, and warm-

FIGURE 5.4

A variety of early reptile skulls (top views) from the later part of the Carboniferous period. A. Paleothyris, *illustrating the primitive (anapsid) condition, with no temporal openings in the skull roof. B. The primitive two-holed reptile* Petrolacosaurus, *with two skull openings (shown in gray) on each side. C. The primitive one-holed reptile* Archaeothylis, *with one opening (gray). The black opening in the midline (p) is the socket for the third or pineal eye, lost in most later reptiles but still retained by some living lizards (after Carroll 1988).*

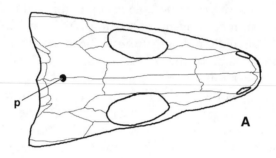

A

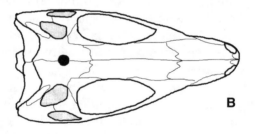

B

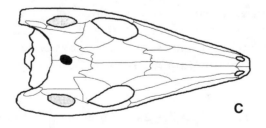

C

blooded, scurrying around in the darkness under the roots and leaves of the forest floor, protected against the chill of the night by a coat of insulating bristles. They were fierce predators—on beetles and worms and such—and they were also fiercely protective mothers, guarding and incubating their eggs, and feeding their hatchlings on fatty secretions from modified sweat glands on their bellies.

These were the early mammals, from which we are descended. The suite of innovations that made their way of life possible included a lot of the key inventions in the human lineage. The list of these mammalian innovations is long, but they can all be summed up in two phrases: small size and a constantly high metabolic rate. All the details of the teeth and jaws and fur and lungs and skin and reproductive system that are peculiar to mammals are corollaries of these two items.

The mammals stayed small and inconspicuous for the next 135 million years. Of course, they made some improvements during that period. Their teeth became more complicated and efficient at grinding and slicing food. Some of them evolved keener senses of smell or hearing. Others began eating plants. One group of early mammals, from which we are descended, stopped putting shells around their eggs and just let the embryos develop inside the warmth and safety of the mother's abdomen until they were ready to come out into the world and drink milk. But despite these innovations, mammals retained their nocturnal habits and their small size, from a few grams up to no more than four or five kilograms. They didn't grow big or presume to compete with the dinosaurs. It took an astronomical collision to bring them out into the sunshine and raise them into prominence as the dominant land animals.

The collision involved a medium-sized asteroid, a rocky piece of space debris some 10 to 15 kilometers in diameter. It struck the earth 65 million years ago near what is now the northern coastline of Yucatan, in Mexico. We can still trace the faint outlines of that impact, which left a crater around 200 kilometers across. Sedimentary rocks all around the world from this time horizon carry debris thrown up by the impact—dust with enriched levels of the metal iridium, tiny spheres of molten glass, amino acids not found in terrestrial sources, and so on.

In the rocks overlying this thin layer of debris, no one has ever found an undisputed fossil of a dinosaur. The conclusion seems inescapable. In one way or another, the asteroid impact was responsible for yet another great mass extinction, marking the boundary between the Mesozoic Age of Reptiles and the Cenozoic Age of Mammals.

Within ten million years, most of the niches that had been occupied by dinosaurs had been filled by big furry upstarts. This evolutionary explosion of the mammals also struck out into some new ways of life that hadn't been explored by members of the dinosaur group. One group of mammals stayed small and nocturnal, but took to climbing around in trees to feed on fruit and insects. They developed soft, moist, prehensile hands and feet for grasping the thin twigs they crept around on, and they enlarged their eyes and moved them around to the front of the head so that they became more useful for detecting prey. These were the earliest representatives of our own mammalian order, the Primates.

Several lineages of these tiny primitive primates soon began experimenting with larger body size and plant-eating habits, feeding on the leaves and fruits of the trees they lived in. These large arboreal plant-eaters included the ancestors of modern monkeys and apes—and humans. This group, the so-called higher primates, has tended to evolve habits of daytime activity, nimble hands, and big brains.

The higher primates underwent a modest evolutionary diversification of their own. Several different groups are known from the fossil record and from modern fauna. The one to which we belong, the Hominoidea or apes, was a diverse and successful group 10 million years ago. But since then, the apes have been largely pushed aside in the tropical forests of the Old World by monkeys that have more efficient teeth and guts than the apes have. The surviving apes—gibbons, chimpanzees, orangutans, and so on—share some peculiar features of their arms and shoulders that allow them to feed while hanging *underneath* branches, instead of running along the tops of branches on all fours. Our own ancestors came from this arm-swinging group. We retain their specializations in our arms and shoulders, and we can still swing by our arms if we have to, though we're not nearly as good at it as a chimpanzee or orangutan.

In Africa around five million years ago, some of these arm-swinging apes started coming to the ground and walking on their hind legs. They are the earliest representatives of our own peculiar lineage. These so-called man-apes, the australopithecines, have no living descendants except ourselves. They looked something like chimpanzees with human legs and feet. You can read about them in more detail in the next chapter of this book, written by Ron Clarke, who is one of the world's leading experts on these creatures. I'll just point out here that we know that the man-apes were bipeds—partly because of the evidence of their limb bones, but also because we are lucky enough to have some actual fossil footprints, laid down around 3.6 million years ago in a fresh fall of volcanic ash in Tanzania.

It isn't clear why the ancestral man-apes took to walking around on their hind legs, and scientists debate how much their locomotion resembled ours. Some think that these early hominids had an essentially human form of terrestrial bipedalism. Others, including Dr. Clarke, think that they were still spending a lot of time up in the trees, and that their locomotor habits were quite a bit different from ours. But there is general agreement that bipedalism had been perfected by around two million years ago, when the first fossils of our own genus, *Homo*, show up in the rocks of Africa and Java.

These early species of *Homo* were still subhuman; but their bodies were essentially like ours from the neck down, their brains were far larger than any modern ape's, and they made and used simple stone tools. The rest of the story of human evolution is mainly a matter of the enlargement of the brain, culminating some 50,000 years ago in the appearance of people indistinguishable from ourselves, with fully human language and culture, capable of making the celebrated cave art of France and Spain or the rock art of Africa and Australia.

The Probability of Humankind

I've summed up the story of 500 million years of human evolution in just under 4,000 words. That works out to around 125,000 years per word. I've skimped on the details. But I think we have enough facts at hand to address the question I started with—namely, was the emergence of humankind something that could have been expected, or was it a miraculous billion-to-one long shot?

Some of the scientists who study this 500-million-year-long story would call our species a billion-to-one shot. And we can see why if we look at a list of what I've been calling the key inventions in human evolution. There are at least 13 of them:

1. Heterotrophy (eating other organisms);
2. Bilateral symmetry;
3. Internal skeleton;
4. A head with special sense organs and nerve centers;
5. Jaws and predation on large prey;
6. Paired fins/limbs;
7. Reptile-type eggs, laid on land;
8. Small size plus high metabolism (implying insulation, maternal care, and so forth);
9. Arboreal visual predation;
10. Monkeylike brains and social intelligence;
11. Large size (and suspensory habits);
12. Bipedality;
13. Large brains, technology, and language.

For an intelligent, upright, and bipedal vertebrate to emerge from the long, complicated history of this planet, all of these things had to happen in the right order—and at just the right time to take advantage of environmental opportunities, like surges in atmospheric oxygen or asteroid impacts.

Let's assume, for the sake of argument, that the chances of each of these 13 events happening were fairly high. Say the odds against each event were no more than ten to one. That means that the probability of the whole series is one in 10 to the 13th power. The chances against our evolutionary emergence would be ten trillion to one.

It would follow that the emergence of intelligent life on this planet must have been either staggeringly improbable or driven by an external Providence. So it might seem—and so many people have argued.

I doubt it, because I doubt the numbers.

It's always hard to make statistical arguments about the history of life, because we have a sample size of one—namely, life on this planet. But what we can do is to see whether any of these events have happened more than once in that history. If we can find multiple occurrences of these events—what are called evolutionary parallels—then we can assume that the story of human evolution reflects patterned regularities in the evolutionary process. If so, then something like this series of events would have been likely to have happened sooner or later—or at any rate, more likely than one chance in ten-to-the-thirteenth.

Let's take a look at the parallels for these 13 innovations in animal lineages other than our own. We've already noted that the first two items—heterotrophy and bilateral symmetry—are general themes of the Cambrian radiation. I would go further and say that anywhere in the universe where life evolves, some organisms are eventually going to stumble upon the cheap and dirty strategy of eating other organisms. Once this happens, the chase is on. And that makes it inevitable that some organisms will develop preferred directions of movement, and therefore have a head end and tail end and bilateral symmetry. So for the first two items on this list, we have a probability of 100 percent in the long run—not of 1 percent, as our original calculations suggested.

Innovation #3, the internal skeleton, seems chancier. Most nonchordates don't have one, and the ones that do, like starfish and sea urchins, don't look very much like plausible human ancestors. But there is one invertebrate group that has evolved its own sort of backbone along with a very fishlike way of life—namely, squids. The octopus-squid group of mollusks evolved from animals with a coiled external shell, like that of the surviving chambered nautilus. Squids have reduced that shell to an internal rod that serves as a stiffening axial skeleton, doing much the same job as a notochord or vertebral column. For jaws, squids have a parrot-like beak and a rasping tongue. They have big image-forming eyes very much like a vertebrate's, attached to a well-developed brain (Innovation #4). They have added on some other bits of skeleton, including cartilage in their steering fins and a skull-like box of cartilage surrounding the brain.

In short, squids are pretty convincing fake fish (Figure 5.5). They are poised to take over if fish suddenly become extinct. They give us some reason to think that the evolution of fish-like fast-swimming predators, with eyes and brains and spines and skulls, was not a billion-to-one improbability.

FIGURE 5.5

Convergent structural similarities between a schematic fish (top) and squid (bottom).

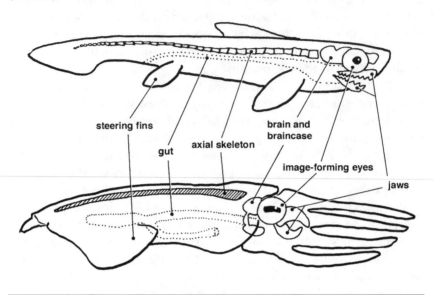

Jaws and predatory habits, the fifth item on our list of key inno-vations, are another sure bet in the evolutionary lottery. Similar organs and habits have emerged in dozens of invertebrate lineages. We have already noted the birdlike beaks of squids and octopuses among the mollusks. Other sorts of grabbing, piercing, cutting, and shredding apparatus around the mouth have been evolved in other phyla, including annelids, arrow worms, rotifers, and many groups of arthropods, culminating in the enormous variety of complicated mouthparts found among insects.

Our next item—the conquest of land, and the evolution of eggs that could be laid on land—was also a sure bet. Once plants learned how to survive on land, animals were bound to follow. At least eight different lines of animals, including vertebrates, mollusks, three phyla of worms, and several arthropod groups, crawled onto land and started laying eggs there. And this story isn't over. There are creatures around today—crabs, walking catfish, mud skippers, and so on—that are even now in the process of learning to breathe air and compete for a place on dry land.

The next key innovation in our list was warm blood and small size, and the maternal care of helpless offspring that goes with these things. This complex of traits isn't a sure bet. But we know it wasn't wildly improbable, either, because birds evolved the same complex.

Some people have suggested that the worldwide dip in atmospheric oxygen in the Triassic (Figure 5.3) caused the evolution of adaptations for warmbloodedness—fur, feathers, four-chambered hearts, and so on—in the ancestors of mammals and birds, as these animals struggled to maintain their high Permian metabolic rates despite the increasing scarcity of oxygen. If so, then the appearance of these adaptations might have been an unpredictable event, driven by the happenstances of climate change. Maybe it was. But I doubt it, because the birds and their relatives probably didn't evolve warm blood and feathers until near the end of the Triassic, by which time oxygen levels were back up to about what they are today.

Primate origins—that is, the shift of small mammals into a life of visually-directed predation in the trees—were also a good bet. First of all, trees themselves are a sure thing. Anywhere in the universe where there are photosynthetic plants whose growth is limited by the available sunlight, we can expect to find them competing by casting shadows on each other. A tree is a plant adapted to casting shadows on its shorter neighbors. So trees and forests were an inevitable outcome of the plants' conquest of land. And where there are trees, there will eventually be small herbivores climbing in them and eating off them; and so we can expect that small arboreal predators will eventually evolve to eat the herbivores. And in fact, this has happened more than once on this planet. Several groups of marsupials have evolved primate-like visually-directed predatory habits and grasping extremities. So have chameleons among the lizards.

How about the evolution of big brains in the higher primates (Innovation #10)? Again, we see lots of parallels. As Loring Brace pointed out long ago (Brace 1976), parrots are something like avian monkeys—noisy, bright-colored, gregarious, diurnal fruit-eaters living up in the trees in the tropics. It probably isn't a coincidence that parrots include some of the most intelligent of all birds. And if we step back and look at the bigger picture, we see that all sorts of mammalian brains have been slowly getting larger ever since the dinosaurs went away—not just among higher primates, but in many other lines as well.

Figure 5.6 compares the skull and brain of a modern lemur from Madagascar with those of a 40-million-year-old fossil relative of about the same size. You can see what a difference 40 million years has made in brain size, even in these primitive primates. And parallel changes have gone on in many other lineages of mammals—for example, among whales, hoofed creatures, carnivores, rodents, and elephants (Jerison 1973). We're not sure why so many mammals (and also birds) have been gradually getting smarter. Apparently, intelligence is advantageous in a great many different ways of life. Brain enlargement isn't inevitable, but it clearly isn't an unlikely chance event restricted to the human lineage. There seem to be selection pressures driving it in many other lines of warm-blooded vertebrates.

The pendulous arboreality of the living apes (Innovation #11) also has its parallels in other lines of mammals. There aren't very many big tree-dwelling animals, because big animals are more likely to get hurt or killed if they fall out of a tree than small animals are. But those few tree-dwellers that do grow big tend to move cautiously through the trees, hanging underneath branches for greater security. These sorts of suspensory habits and correlated anatomical features have evolved in at least four different lineages of medium- to large-sized primates (apes, spider monkeys, and two extinct groups). Among non-primates, the tree sloths of South and Central America (which get about as big as spider monkeys) have evolved a similar hanging-and-feeding adaptation.

What about human bipedality (Innovation #12)? Here we find no real parallels among other primates, or indeed any other mammals. But other bipeds have evolved. Striding bipedalism was one of the key adaptations underlying the whole radiation of dinosaurs—including their modem representatives or close cousins, the birds. Who knows what might have emerged after an additional sixty million years of evolution of warm-blooded dinosaurs with functional, grasping forelimbs? If it hadn't been for that asteroid, the world today might have been populated by intelligent bipeds—covered with feathers, no doubt, and attending learned meetings to argue about why no large mammals ever evolved.

FIGURE 5.6

Outlines of the skulls of a living lemur from Madagascar (A. Eulemur
mongoz)*, and a similar-sized Eocene primate (B.* Adapis parisiensis)*, seen
from the left side with a gray silhouette of the brain superimposed on each
(after Martin 1973).*

A

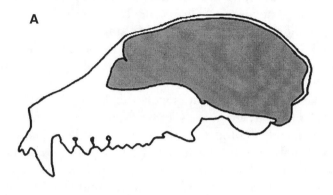

B

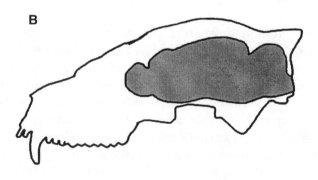

But this is fantasy, and that Cretaceous asteroid impact is a fact.
And you might argue, as many people have argued, that without
that asteroid, human beings would never have come into being. For
Stephen Gould (1989) and many others who champion the unpre-
dictability of history, the impact event at the end of the Age of

Reptiles has become something of an icon, demonstrating beyond any shadow of doubt that the race is not always to the swift, nor the battle to the strong, and that the course of evolution is governed by a kind of ontological randomness that pervades the history of the world. Who could have known that the asteroid would strike? And without that knowledge, who could have predicted that human beings would step forth on the world's stage?

This is a seductive argument, but I think it is philosophically mistaken. And in this particular case, I think it is grounded in a misleading habit of thought about large body size.

We like to say that dinosaurs were the dominant land animals of the Mesozoic. Why do we say that? Well, because they were big. Mammals couldn't compete with dinosaurs at large body size. The poor mammals crept about under the feet of the dinosaurs, trembling at the thunder of their footsteps, and occasionally getting snapped up and eaten. Doesn't that mean that the dinosaurs were dominant? Isn't that what we mean by domination?

Well, it does if we think about individuals—about big guys and little guys getting into fights in bars. But this is a mistaken analogy. The important fact here, in terms of ultimate survival, is that the dinosaurs couldn't compete with mammals at the other end of the size spectrum.

It's true that there were no very large mammals at the end of the Cretaceous. But there were also no very small dinosaurs. The smallest dinosaur known is the Jurassic *Compsognathus*, about the size of a house cat or a large chicken. Compared to more familiar dinosaurs like *Stegosaurus* or *Tyrannosaurus*, it was a tiny creature. But it was huge by comparison with the average mammal of the period, which was fifty or a hundred times smaller.

Large size is ultimately not a survival trait. In the long run, small size makes for survival and large size makes for extinction. Large animals are fragile. They're physically fragile, because of the square-cube law—that is, for the same reason that big cartons of books break open more easily than small cartons. But large animals are also ecologically fragile. It is a reliable rule throughout the history of life that whenever there is an environmental catastrophe, most or all of the big animals—what we call the megafauna—will disappear.

Why are large animals ecologically fragile? For two reasons: 1. they have fewer individuals per square mile than small animals, and therefore 2. they have fewer species. If a catastrophe wipes out 95 percent of the individuals in a species, or 95 of every 100 species, mice are far more likely to survive than elephants are.

In the long run, the small things are the ones that survive. And so a wise Martian who came to Earth in the Jurassic would have looked around at all the tiny, trembling mammals—and noted the absence of tiny, trembling dinosaurs—and said, 'Well, that's it, then; the dinosaurs have lost. It's just a matter of waiting for the next asteroid.'

If a similar asteroid hit the Earth tomorrow, elephants and lions and giraffes would probably vanish away. But mice would survive, if any mammals did. Would the human species survive? I don't know. I'd like to think so. But if we didn't, and if subsequent evolution brought forth another species capable of writing symphonies and equations, I would venture to predict that the composers and mathematicians of that successor species would have very large front teeth. Among today's mammals, the rodents are clearly the ones that have achieved the dominion of the Kingdom of the Small—which is what makes for survival in the long run.

And what about that last trait on the list—human intelligence? Why hasn't that evolved in parallel? Here again, our preconceptions are blinding us to the facts. Minds surprisingly like our own, though stupider, have evolved in parallel in several lineages of other animals. I'm not thinking here about apes. To be sure, the minds of apes are surprisingly humanlike in some ways. Chimpanzees can be taught language-like signing systems, and even pick up a fair amount of spoken English on their own (Savage-Rumbaugh and Lewin 1994). But the psychological similarities between people and chimpanzees might represent a shared inheritance from our last common ancestor. We can't be sure that chimpanzees evolved those traits independently.

No, I am thinking here of other, non-mammalian lineages—parrots, for example. The last common ancestor of people and parrots was a primitive anapsid reptile that lived back in the Carboniferous (Figure 5.4). It looked like a giant salamander with scales. It had no more social skills or intelligence than a frog has. And yet 300 million years later, the minds of people and parrots have undergone so much convergent evolution that the two can be friends. They can enjoy each other's company, and groom and pet each other, and understand and respond appropriately to each other's emotions. Parrots even possess rudimentary language abilities. Properly trained parrots can use human words meaningfully, and understand what we mean when we say them (Pepperberg 1999). Similar convergent evolution of mind, social intelligence, and protolanguage has gone on in many non-primate mammals as well. There are even glimmerings of mind in the squid-and-octopus group of mollusks (Wells 1962).

I don't want to leave you with the impression that I think there is some sort of Bergsonian life force behind the history of life, pushing it in a human direction. Life pushes in all available directions at once. But some directions are more available than others. The sequence of key innovations that led to the emergence of humanity follows some well-worn pathways, each of which has been traced in parallel by more than one evolving lineage. The appearance of an animal something like ourselves was not a sure thing—humans are not as inevitable as trees—but it was *natural*. Something like us had a decent chance of coming into existence on this planet.

To an integrator like myself, this is a pleasing thought. It makes me feel more at home in the universe to know that creatures like us might be expected to emerge from the evolutionary process given the right circumstances. And this also pleases me as a scientist seeking to understand the workings of the world. The supposed uniqueness of the human condition, which some people think gives human life its significance, seems to me to be just another word for unintelligibility. If anything is truly unique it is inexplicable, because explaining something means showing that it isn't unique but fits some recurring pattern. One of the peculiar gifts of our species is that we are better at discerning such patterns than the other animals are. The singular glory of humanity is not our isolation from the order of nature, but our ever-growing comprehension of how we fit into it.

References

Brace, C.L. 1976. Monkey Business and Bird Brains. In E. Giles and J.S. Friedlaender, eds., *The Measures of Man* (Cambridge, Massachusetts: Peabody Museum Press), pp. 54–71.

Carroll, R.L. 1988. *Vertebrate Paleontology and Evolution.* New York: Freeman.

Conway Morris, Simon. 1977. A New Metazoan from the Cambrian Burgess Shale, British Columbia. *Palaeontology* 20, pp. 623–640.

———. 1998. *The Crucible of Creation: The Burgess Shale and the Rise of Animals.* Oxford: Oxford University Press.

Gould, S.J. 1989. *Wonderful Life.* New York: Norton.

Graham, J.B., N. Aguilar, R. Dudley, and C. Gans. 1997. The Late Paleozoic Atmosphere and the Ecological and Evolutionary Physiology of Tetrapods. In S.S. Sumida and K.L.M. Martin, eds., *Amniote Origins: Completing the Transition to Land* (San Diego: Academic Press), pp. 141–167.

Jerison, H.J. 1973. Evolution of the Brain and Intelligence. New York: Academic Press.

Martin, R.D. 1973. Comparative Anatomy and Primate Systematics. *Symp. Zool. Soc. London* 33, pp. 301–337.

McMenamin, M.A.S., and D.L.S. McMenamin. 1990. *The Emergence of Animals: The Cambrian Breakthrough.* New York: Columbia University Press.

Pepperberg, I. 1999. *The Alex Studies: Cognitive and Communicative Abilities of Grey Parrots.* Cambridge, Massachusetts: Harvard University Press.

Savage-Rumbaugh, S., and R. Lewin. 1994. *Kanzi: The Age at the Brink of the Human Mind.* New York: Wiley.

Tiffney, B.H., and K.J. Niklas. 1990. Continental Area, Dispersion, Latitudinal Distribution, and Topographic Variety: A Test of Correlation with Terrestrial Plant Diversity. In R.M. Ross and W.D. Allmon, eds., *Causes of Evolution: A Paleontological Perspective* (Chicago: University of Chicago Press), pp. 76–102.

Wells, M.J. 1962. *Brain and Behaviour in Cephalopods.* London: Heinemann.

6

From Ape-Man to Wise-Man

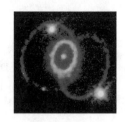

*R*ONALD *J. C*LARKE

Fossils show that our ancestor the ape-man lived in a forest fringe environment populated by many carnivores. Trees have always been crucial to human development.

Humans, known scientifically as *Homo sapiens*, or 'wise man', are biologically animals and yet have set themselves apart from the animal kingdom by virtue of their development of culture. This encompasses not only material culture in the form of items that we manufacture but also types of behavior that are not necessary for the basic animal requirements of eating, shelter, defense, territoriality, sleeping, and procreation. Examples can be seen in the elaborate behavior and rituals associated with meal times, such as sitting evenly spaced around a table with cutlery correctly placed on table mats and perhaps with candlesticks or a vase of flowers in the center.

Although many animals and birds demonstrate behavior that some might class as culture, it's related only to basic needs and is never complex. For example, swifts build well-designed nests of mud that could be likened to a mud hut of a human, but unlike humans, they do not create a fireplace inside for warmth and cooking and they do not store artifacts inside. Thrushes use stone anvils to break snail shells, Egyptian vultures drop stones onto ostrich eggs, and chimpanzees use stones to crack nuts. None of these basic tool uses, however, has developed into anything more elaborate, despite the probability that they have been customary for those birds and mammals since before the origins of human tool-making.

Humans have not only greatly elaborated their tool kits, but they have also enhanced the five senses of vision, hearing, taste, smell, and touch beyond the essential into the esthetic. Thus we have visual arts, music, culinary art, perfumes, and flower gardens, and a variety of man-made textiles and surfaces designed for tactile enjoyment.

Another uniquely human cultural attribute is religion, which is based on belief in a spiritual existence and life after death. Associated with religions are non-tangible gods or holy beings, which may be represented in tangible effigy, and ancestral spirits that are revered. Thus there is a behavioral similarity between the New Guinea inhabitant who reveres the decorated skull of an ancestor and the devout Catholic who reveres the corporal relic of a saint. There is similarity also between the so-called pagan who worships wooden effigies and the devout Catholic who prays in front of an effigy of the Virgin Mary or Jesus. Those Christian missionaries who condemned the 'pagan' worship of idols were displaying extraordinary hypocrisy.

Most of us are fascinated by our past. We like to look at old photographs and to read books on aspects of history or early exploration where there are old paintings or drawings of events and culture long past. As we go further back in time, we have to rely on buried archeological artifacts to tell us something about the way of life of the people of prehistory. Prehistoric tombs and cave burials provide information on religious practices, and yet earlier Stone Age cave paintings are testimony to the artistic skill and sometimes to the apparent existence of spiritual beliefs. As we look back through the mists of time beyond 100,000 years ago, the story of human physical and cultural evolution becomes more sparse and fragmented, back to the probable time of origin of ape-like human ancestors at 5 to 6 million years ago.

We do not know when humans first began to think about their origins but we do know that the earliest written records of such thoughts are in the form of creation myths, like that of Adam and Eve. It was natural that in those days, before the advent of zoological and biological research, people should seek to explain their obvious differences from the animals in terms of special creation. There is no longer any excuse for such beliefs, as anatomical and genetic research has demonstrated our kinship to other animals, particularly to the apes. For example, we have a coccyx (a vestigial tail) and we have a separate premaxillary bone, which holds the upper incisor teeth, visible in the embryo but fused to the maxilla in adults. The apes display a separate premaxillary bone in the adult, as do some *Australopithecus* fossils (ancestors of humans). It is thus apparent that during the course of evolution, the incisors became reduced in size and the separate premaxilla in which they were rooted also reduced its size to the extent that it was overgrown in the embryo by thin plates of the maxillary bone. If humans had been specially created, there would be no need for a vestigial premaxilla or tail.

Ancient and medieval writers recorded the existence of monstrous human forms in remote regions, such as the Sciapod that had one large foot used as a sun shade or the Blemyae that had their faces in their chests. They also wrote of wild men covered in hair and it is probable that these were based on travellers either sighting or being informed of apes in Asia. By the eighteenth century, the existence of apes had been established in Asia and Africa but depictions of them were often confused and inaccurate, so that they appeared more like strange hairy forms of humans.

The African Cradle

In 1774 the Scottish writer James Burnett, Lord Monboddo, wrote in his treatise on *The Origin and Progress of Language* the following prophetic statement: "From the South Sea, I will come back again to Africa, a country of very great extent; in which, if it were well searched, I am persuaded that all the several types of human progression might be traced, and perhaps all the varieties of the species discovered." He further averred that he considered the chimpanzee (which he called orang utan) to be a degenerate human.

Although the first recognition of archaic forms of man were the Neanderthal in Germany in 1856 and *Pithecanthropus (Homo erectus)* in Java in 1891, they were relatively far along the scale of human evolution. Monboddo proved correct in predicting that the most ancient forms of human ancestry would be traced in Africa. In 1924 a fossilized skull of a four-year-old child, from Taung in South Africa, came into the hands of Professor Raymond Dart. He cleaned it and identified it as an ape that was on the way to becoming human. He named it *Australopithecus africanus*. Because it has both ape and human characteristics it is popularly known as an ape-man (see Color Plate 8).

In 1936 Robert Broom discovered the first adult *Australopithecus* in the concrete-like filling of the dolomite caves of Sterkfontein, South Africa. Although its brain was not much larger than that of a chimpanzee and its facial structure was also ape-like, it had teeth which were remarkably human in form, albeit of larger size. Further work at Sterkfontein by Broom, later assisted by John Robinson, uncovered many fossils of *Austalopithecus*, including a vertebral column and complete pelvis in 1947. That pelvis also confirmed the man-like status of *Australopithecus* as it was more like that of modern humans than like that of apes, though there are some minor ape-like characteristics in the pelvis. This find indicated that *Australopithecus* walked upright, though not in the manner of modern humans.

These ape-men lived between 2.6 and 2.8 million years ago. The environment in which *Australopithecus* lived was at least partly forested, as we know from 300 fragments of fossil wood from Sterkfontein. These were identified by Dr. Marion Bamford as mainly belonging to a vine of the species *Dichapetalum mombuttense,* which now only occurs in tropical forests of Central and West Africa. She also identified two shrubs that currently occur in more tropical environments.

In addition, the occurrence of several species of large fossil monkeys, including *colobus* (which currently occupies forests in Asia and Central and East Africa) is an indicator that there was forest at Sterkfontein. Fossils of *Makapania* (a large hoofed animal related to the present-day takin of the Himalayas and musk-ox of the Arctic) and a *Chalicothere* (a clawed animal somewhat resembling a horse) are also likely indications of woodland or forest.

It was by no means a tranquil environment for *Australopithecus*. Fossils from Sterkfontein show that many large carnivores were present. In addition to lion, leopard, cheetah and spotted hyaena, there were also saber-toothed cats in the form of *Megantereon*, *Homotherium*, and *Dinofelis*, and there were long-legged hunting hyenas which have been named *Chasmoporthetes*. The safest place for the ape-men would have been in the trees, particularly for sleeping at night and, as we will see later, recent fossil discoveries of foot, arm, and hand bones show that *Australopithecus* was adept at tree climbing. *Australopithecus* did not possess the large canines of other apes and baboons which can put up a spirited defence against carnivores. The best defense for the ape-man was avoidance.

By 2.5 million years ago, the climate at Sterkfontein and at other fossil sites in South and East Africa had become drier and more grassland had opened up. This we know from the appearance of fossils of horse, ostrich, and springhare. Stone tools also appeared for the first time, together with fossils of a flat-faced, large-toothed ape-man called *Paranthropus* and fossils of our own direct ancestor in the form of the genus *Homo*, larger brained than *Australopithecus* or *Paranthropus*. These earliest known members of the genus *Homo* are generally placed into the species *Homo habilis*, meaning the human with ability for tool-making. They are believed to be the makers of the stone tool industry known as the Oldowan. These crude tools consist of cores, flakes, and choppers. The Oldowan was named after Olduvai Gorge in the Serengetti of Tanzania, where it was first recognised as an early and crude stone tool industry by Louis and Mary Leakey. In higher and younger strata at Olduvai were found the earliest crude handaxes and cleavers of what is known as the early Acheulean (after the site of St. Acheul in France where handaxes occur in abundance). These date to about 1.7 million years ago and from contemporary strata at East Lake Turkana in Kenya and at Swartkrans and Sterkfontein in South Africa have been recovered fossil crania and lower jaws of a species named *Homo ergaster* (meaning the human that worked). This species had prominent brow ridges and a somewhat larger brain than *Homo habilis*. Its jaws and teeth were relatively small and in the structure of its skull it seems to represent a good direct ancestor of *Homo sapiens*. Although the fossil record for human ancestors after this time is sparse, there are some fossils which seem to fill the evolutionary gap between *Homo ergaster* and modern humans. Examples of such skulls are the 1-million-year-old

Buia cranium from the Danakil Depression of Eritrea, the Ndutu cranium from Tanzania at about 400,000 years ago, the Djebel Ighoud cranium from Morocco and the Qafzeh and Skhul skulls from Israel, at around 100,000 years ago.

On the Trail of Our Ancestors

When we look to the other end of the evolutionary scale, for the earliest ancestral members of the family of man, fossils are rare and fragmentary. A piece of mandible with one first molar tooth found in Bryan Patterson's Harvard Expedition at Lothagam in Kenya is considered to be the oldest known hominid fossil at 5.5 million years old. This is followed by very ape-like mandible fragment and skeletal parts dated to 4.4 million years ago found by Tim White's team in Ethiopia and named *Ardipithecus ramidus*. From 4.2-million-year-old deposits at Kanapoi in Kenya, Meave Leakey's team has recovered a well-preserved mandible and maxilla that are very ape-like hominids. These are classed as *Australopithecus anamensis*.

Part of the famous Olduvai Gorge in Tanzania runs close by an extinct eroded volcano called Sadiman. On the far side of that mountain is an area known as Laetoli or Garusi, where ape-like hominid jaw fossils were found by Mary Leakey's team between 1974 and 1979 in 3.6-million-year-old volcanic tuffs. These have been grouped together with fossil hominids from Hadar in Ethiopia as *Australopithecus afarensis*.

One of the most exciting discoveries relating to our ancestry was made at Laetoli by Paul Abell, a chemistry professor, in 1978. As the geologist Dick Hay was about to knock off a sample of volcanic tuff, Paul noticed what looked like a human heel impression in that 3.6 million year old layer. Subsequent excavation by Tim White revealed the footprints of two upright walking hominids and the following year I, Mwongela Muoka, and Mary Leakey continued to excavate and uncovered a long footprint trail of those two individuals. Although they walked upright, side-by-side their footprints are not fully human in form. I and Yvette Deloison noted ape-like characters, such as a big toe slightly separated and divergent from the others and an ape-like bulge of the abductor muscle on the inner side of the foot. That muscle controls the sideways movement of the big toe in apes and this grasping big toe helps them in tree climbing. Another strange feature was that for each footprint there was only a single wide indentation to represent all four small toes. Yvette Deloison has suggested that this is because the small toes were curled underneath as with the orang utan when it walks upright.

These hominid footprints have been attributed to *Australopithecus afarensis* individuals who walked over a volcanic eruption of carbonatite tuff that had been moistened by rain and that was also indented with other animal footprints. There was a succession of such volcanic eruptions interspersed with rain showers which reacted with the carbonatite tuff to transform it into a kind of soft cement. Thus is preserved a succession of layers that contained footprints of many types of animals and birds, as well as raindrop impressions.

Coincidentally, in 1978, the very year that Paul Abell discovered the Laetoli hominid footprints, footbones from the kind of *Australopithecus* foot that could have made the footprints were being lifted in blocks of matrix from the Sterkfontein Caves in South Africa. These and other fossil animal bones had been blasted out of a lower cave infill in the 1920s or early 1930s by lime miners quarrying layers of thick stalagmite. The fossil-containing rock was left on the cave floor until it was winched to the surface by Alun Hughes and his excavation crew in 1978. The footbones were cleaned from the rock by one of the excavation crew in 1980 but were not recognised as hominid and were variously classified as monkey, bovid, and miscellaneous. Then in 1994, in a box of those bones at Sterkfontein, I chanced upon and recognized the ankle bone and three adjacent bones leading toward the big toe. These showed ape-like characters, including a certain amount of mobility and divergence of the big toe.

In 1997 in another box in the Department of Anatomy in Johannesburg, I found more bones of the same left foot and lower leg and part of a lower shin bone of the right leg. This led me to search in more bags of animal bones from the same locality at Sterkfontein and I discovered the lower shin bone and part of a heel bone of the left leg and a fragment of another footbone from the right leg. I then concluded that the whole skeleton must be still embedded in the ancient infill of the lower Cave (the Silberberg

Grotto) at Sterkfontein. I gave a cast of the lower right shin bone to two assistants, Stephen Motsumi and Nkwane Molefe, and asked them to search the deep, dark cave for a matching cross-section of bone exposed in the concrete-like cave infill. After one and a half days of searching, they located the bone and our subsequent excavation has so far uncovered the lower legs, a complete skull and a complete left arm and hand of this ape-man (see Color Plate 7).

Palaeomagnetic dating of several layers of stalagmite from above and below the skeleton has given this *Australopithecus* an age of 3.33 million years, a quarter of a million years younger than the 3.6 million years of the Laetoli footprints. This Sterkfontein skeleton is the first *Australopithecus* ever discovered with a complete skull and a complete arm and hand, and all indications are that the rest of the skeleton, apart from many missing footbones that disappeared after the lime mining, will be uncovered by the excavation.

The anatomy of this skeleton, as well as the footprints from Laetoli, suggest that these early forms of *Australopithecus* spent much time in the trees and undoubtedly slept in trees at night, a necessary survival behavior in an environment populated by many species of saber-toothed cats and long-legged hunting hyenas.

The fossil hand of the Sterkfontein ape-man is similar to that of modern humans with a relatively short palm and fingers when compared to those of apes. The hand of this ape-man with its long, powerful thumb was ideally suited for firmly grasping branches. Humans use their hands in similar fashion to hold vertical supports or overhead handgrips for stability on buses and underground trains. Gymnasts and circus performers also make good use of this ability to powerfully grasp bars and supports. This type of hand, with a thumb that could be rotated to oppose the fingers, eventually proved to be uniquely pre-adapted for the efficient manufacture and use of tools.

Our Family Tree in the Forest

All indications are that our early ancestry was in the forests and that trees provided our ancestors with food sources and a safe refuge during the day—but especially at night. The types of forest that nurtured our ancestors provide for us still today and also provide homes for a host of wildlife. We benefit from food resources and from the medicines that derive from trees, and for centuries we have used wood to construct houses, ships, and furniture. Without trees our world would be a physical and cultural desert and thus it is in the best interests of all human beings to value and protect the forests that are left. What is the use of being religiously devout in the hope of an afterlife when we cannot look after the world and this life that was provided for us?

Thus the allegory of Adam and Eve has a special meaning. The eating of the fruit of the tree of knowledge of good and evil supposedly set humans apart from the animals. Humans alone know right from wrong and, to put it simply, it is right to create and wrong to destroy, whether it be destruction of life and well-being, property, or environment. Throughout the long process of evolution of human beings, our brains have so developed that by the mid-eighteenth century Linnaeus classified humans as *Homo sapiens*. Humankind's accumulated and ever-expanding wisdom concerning the world we live in, and the universe beyond our world, is extraordinary. Yet this wisdom has been and still is marred by destructive actions which are the very antithesis of wisdom and are rather indicative of a perverted use of human knowledge for the personal gain or power of a few. Such actions include warfare in pursuit of dominance or greed for territory and material wealth, mental and physical cruelty usually in the name of political or religious dogma, destruction of wildlife and forests, and pollution of air and water and landscape. Something is radically wrong with the so-called wise man, and if religions are to play a meaningful and positive role, they should eschew all harmful dogma from the inadequately enlightened past and rather help to eradicate destructive behaviour and promote the evolution of wisdom.

Recommended Reading

Johanson, D., L. Johanson, and B. Edgar. 1994. *Ancestors*. New York: Willard Books.

Johanson, D. and B. Edgar 1996. *From Lucy to Language*. New York: Simon and Schuster.

Leakey, M.D. 1979. *Olduvai Gorge: My Search for Early Man*. London: William Collins.

Schwartz, J. 1987. *The Red Ape.* London: Elm Tree.

Tattersall, I. 1993. *The Human Odyssey.* New York: Prentice Hall.

———. 1995a. *The Last Neanderthal.* New York: Macmillan.

———. 1995b. *The Fossil Trail.* Oxford: Oxford University Press.

7

A Century of Surprises in Human Evolution

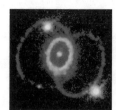

Phillip V. Tobias

The last 100 years have witnessed revolutionary changes in the understanding of our origins: humans originated in Africa, not Asia, and large brain size came late, not early. Unresolved issues remain: how to classify hominids, the beginning of spoken language, and catastrophic interventions from space.

When I was born, there were not quite two billion people on earth: today, there are six billion. That is revolution, not evolution! When I was born, less than one quarter of humanity lived in towns and cities; today that figure is just over 50 percent. That is another revolution.

When I was born, scientists believed that the family of mankind had arisen in Asia; today, it is almost universally accepted that the hominids first appeared in Africa and only much later reached the Far East. That is another kind of revolution—a clean sweep in thinking.

Anyone who writes marking a special moment in time—be it a commemoration of an historical episode, the end of a century or of an epoch—has a duty to look back, to appraise the present, and to peer into the future. I have to look back a long, long way, but I do not have a long, long time in which to do this. To cover the time of humans on Earth, I should have to condense every one hundred thousand years of their sojourn on the planet into a single minute! At that rate, I could cover five million years of human evolution in a fifty-minute presentation.

Let me start by taking stock at the beginning of the twenty-first century. The last hundred years may be divided conveniently into quarters.

The First Quarter, 1901–1925

In the first quarter of the century it was widely believed that Asia had been the cradle of humanity. This was partly because of what Java had yielded: the remains of a creature known as Java Man, considered today to belong to a species known as *Homo erectus*. It had been found late in the nineteenth century and many scientists accepted it as an ancestor of modern humans. Then a few isolated teeth from China had given warning that there, too, had been an ancient form of mankind. But additionally, as Peter Bowler has stressed, there was a pro-Asia sentiment and an anti-Africa bias: nobody wanted to believe that anything important had come out of Africa.

The Second Quarter, 1926–1950

The onset of the second quarter of the twentieth century was heralded by the discovery of the Taung child skull. It was found in the Buxton Limeworks near Taung, about 100 km north of Kimberley, North-West Province, South Africa. In late 1924 the skull was brought to Raymond Dart, a young man who had been appointed professor of anatomy at the new University of the Witwatersrand Medical School (see Color Plate 8). From a hurried study of the skull, Dart made the startling claim that it had belonged to a hitherto unknown kind of primate which he dubbed *Australopithecus africanus*. It was, he said, basically an African ape but one that showed a number of human-like features. The species it represented had apparently developed in a human direction and Dart claimed that it could be regarded as a 'missing link' (an effete concept based on a putative Chain of Being, of which all links were supposedly known save for that between humans and non-human animals).

In the world of science, an international reputation and, indeed, world fame may sometimes rest on a single momentous discovery. In other cases lifelong achievements add up to a distinguished record, even though no single breakthrough has been of such brilliance as to bring global recognition on its own. Raymond Dart falls into the first category, for his revelation and interpretation of the Taung skull brought deathless renown to the man, to his institution, the Anatomy Department of the University of the Witwatersrand, and to South Africa. In one blinding moment the roots of the human tree were plucked from Asia, where they had previously been thought to lie, and transplanted to Africa, where no finds bearing on human origins had ever come to light. Not only did Dart's view of the Taung child ultimately effect a geographical revolution in our thinking about human origins, but it compelled a re-think about the kind of creature which filled the role of a 'missing link'.

Robert Broom, a distinguished palaeontologist who was working in South Africa, supported Dart's theory. He later went even further when he proposed in 1933 that the child should be admitted to the ranks of the human family, then called the hominids.

Up to the outbreak of World War II and for several years after its end, Dart's claims for the Taung child were generally rejected. Most scholars said it had no bearing on human origins. Dart's critics asserted that the Taung child was in the wrong continent; it was too young for scholars to be sure what kind of adult it would have grown up into; it was held (on insubstantial grounds) to be geologically far too recent for it to have been an ancestor of humans; the name *Australopithecus* was a hybrid of Latin (*australis*) and Greek (*pithekos*) and this was unacceptable to some savants; Dart was too young and inexperienced, and too liable to challenge the established authorities in anatomical science, for his claims to be taken seriously.

What was more, the Taung skull was curiously commingled of an apish small brain, human-like upright posture and small canine teeth (see Figure 7.1). This blend was diametrically at variance with the kind of ancestral anatomy that many theoreticians had envisaged—namely, one in which the brain was thought to have enlarged early in human emergence, whilst the posture and teeth were suposedly humanised late. This prevailing image was strongly held, even although there were no fossilized remains showing the com-

FIGURE 7.1

The oblique quadrupedal posture of an anthropoid ape such as the gorilla (left), contrasted with that of the upright standing and walking modern human. In the ape the weight-line falls between the fore-limbs and the hind-limbs. In the bipedal human being, the axis of the body mass ('center of gravity') passes from the occipital condyles of the cranial base, close to the vertebral column, through the hip-joints on either side, and so to the tripodial feet. Although various forms of bipedalism may be encountered in primates other than man, the peculiarly human sustained and habitual bipedalism is a distinctive adaptation acquired early in the process of hominidization. It was R.A. Dart who first found evidence that Australopithecus *carried its body nearly upright.*

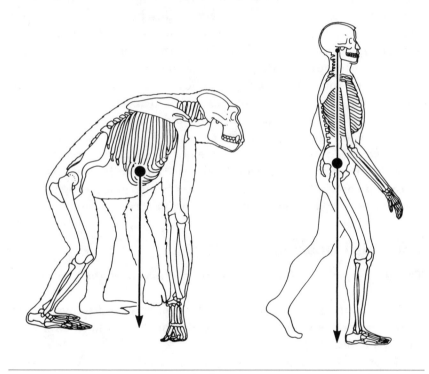

bination of traits that that theory predicted—so strongly indeed that an attempt was made to fabricate just such a combination. In the notorious Piltdown forgery from East Sussex, England, a recent human cranium with a large-sized brain and an apish lower jaw (of an orang-utan) were doctored, stained and salted into a gravel pit at Piltdown in 1911–12. Those who strongly supported the ancestral place of the Piltdown skull were most forcefully opposed to Dart's view of the place of *Australopithecus*! They could not both be human ancestors.

The tide of rejection began to turn about the middle of the century. It was found in 1953–55 that the skull from Piltdown was a forgery. It had been a serious deterrent to the acceptance of Dart's and Broom's claims. Other reasons for the world's change of mind were that a number of similar ape-man specimens had been found in limestone caves in South Africa; scientists came to learn more about the living great apes, such as the chimpanzee and gorilla— for it was important to know what was an ape and what was not; Broom drew together all that was known about the various South African ape-man fossils in an important book put out by the Transvaal Museum in 1946, while Sir Wilfrid LeGros Clark, the Professor of Anatomy at Oxford, carried out independent studies of the anatomy and affinities of the ape-man fossils which showed indisputably that they were hominids and not apes.

There was a groundswell of acceptance of *Australopithecus*. The world was becoming used to the idea of an African rather than an Asian origin of mankind. And the theory that brain size must have increased early in human evolution was being replaced by the new view that marked enlargement of the brain arrived late.

The Third Quarter, 1951–1975

The third quarter of the twentieth century brought changes of many kinds.

First, many more South African hominids were discovered, and there were now six sites that had yielded australopithecine remains (see Color Plate 9A).

Secondly, the scene of African discoveries, hitherto confined to South Africa, extended to East Africa. There was a remarkable series of finds from Tanzania, Kenya, and Ethiopia.

Thirdly, new and revealing data were being amassed about the anatomy and behavior of the living great apes, the chimpanzee and gorilla of Africa and the orang-utan of Asia.

Fourthly, a new approach to the probing of the past arose: molecular evolution. It was to play a major role in a field previously dominated by bones and stones.

Fifthly, the dating of fossils was transformed when new methods were introduced, such as the use of radio-isotopes. The new era dawned with dating by the potassium-argon technique of the very robust hominid cranium which Mary Leakey found in the Olduvai Gorge, Tanzania, in July 1959: its date of 1.75 million years ago came as a shock. It sparked a search for other and older datable hominid fossils.

Sixthly, Willi Hennig of Germany introduced a new approach to the analysis of fossils and their relationships to one another: it was called cladistics and it made a rapid impact upon paleontological studies.

Seventhly, the new field of taphonomy emerged. It was stimulated by Dart's hypothesis that the ape-men from Makapansgat in the Northern Province, South Africa, shaped and used tools made of the bones, teeth and horns of mammals they had supposedly eaten. Dart's fanciful and original posit was that a Bone, Tooth, and Horn Culture had preceded the Stone Age. His forceful advocacy of this notion led scholars to find out how other mammals alter and accumulate bones—and also the effects on bones of physical agencies like water, ice, the sun's radiation, burial and exposure. Among those who were moved to make such studies was C.K. Brain of the Transvaal Museum, Pretoria. He showed that it was very probable that carnivores had accumulated the hundreds of thousands of bones at the apeman sites. As by- products of their bone-chewing activities, they had churned out the Makapansgat broken bones which had sparked Dart's fertile imagination. So Dart's 'bone age' conjecture turned out to be an example of what the nineteenth-century evolutionist, Thomas Henry Huxley, had called, in another context, "The great tragedy of science—the slaying of a beautiful theory by an ugly fact" (1870, Presidential Address to the British Association).

The Final Quarter, 1976–2000

In the last 25 years of the twentieth century, new dating, new cladistics and new molecular data re-modelled the approach and methods of paleo-anthropology. Emphasis was laid on ecology, taphonomy, demography, and better statistical methods with which to analyze bone and tooth measurements. Novel techniques like CAT-

FIGURE 7.2

One recently devised family tree of the hominids. In this simplified human pedigree, a minimalist approach to the number of species is adopted. The question marks indicate uncertainties of the lineages between earlier and later hominids. In this chart, the last common ancestor between chimpanzee (Pan) and the hominids in the strict sense is set at about 6 million years ago, while the oldest fossil hominids known to date are close to 5 million years ago. Somewhere in the no-man's-land between these two dates, the last common ancestral population of chimpanzees and hominids split into two lineages, one leading to today's chimpanzees and one to the hominids. A = Australopithecus. H = Homo.

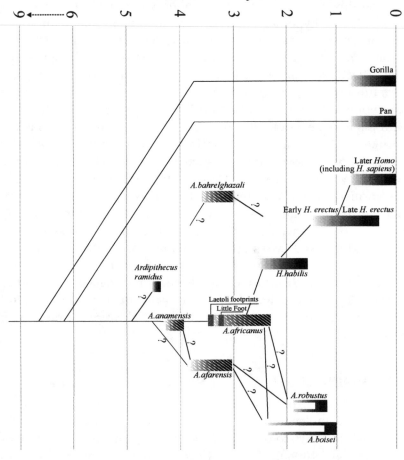

scanning were applied to old bones. At ground level, the search for more fossil hominids continued unabated. Bigger samples were needed, in order to compare the features of young and old and male and female within a species. This was necessary in order to draw a line between variations within a species and those between different species (see Figure 7.2). Incessantly, too, there was the driving quest for ever older remains to take us nearer to the alpha point when the last common ancestors of apes and hominids had split into two (or more) lineages. One resulting line led to the hominids and the other to chimpanzees and bonobos.

More Sites, More Samples

In South Africa, only four early hominid sites were known before World War II. They were Taung (1924), Sterkfontein (from 1936 onwards), Kromdraai (from 1938), and Cooper's B (from 1938). Two more hominid sites were added in the years immediately after the Second World War: Makapansgat (from 1947) and Swartkrans (from 1948). Two of these six sites have proved so fruitful that they have continued to be excavated—Sterkfontein (until the present) and Swartkrans (until 1989), while excavations have been resumed at Kromdraai, Makapansgat, Taung, and Cooper's B (Color Plate 10).

In the 1990s, three new early hominid-bearing sites in South Africa were revealed: Gladysvale (from 1992), Drimolen (since 1993) and Gondolin (from 1997). In the quantity of hominid fossils, Sterkfontein is the richest of the nine South African sites. Indeed, one of the six strata that make up the filling of the Sterkfontein cave, Member 4, has given us the most extensive population of any single early hominid species—the one named *Australopithecus africanus*. The second richest of the nine South African sites, Swartkrans, on the opposite side of the stream to Sterkfontein, has given up a trove of specimens of another kind of ape-man, known as *Australopithecus (Paranthropus) robustus*. In addition to australopithecines or ape-men, both Sterkfontein and Swartkrans have remains of early *Homo*, who lived as a contemporary of the later ape-men.

The most exciting of the newer sites of the 1990s, is certainly Drimolen. In the hands of Dr. Andre Keyser, it is proving to be exceptionally rich in robust australopithecines, with signs of contemporary early *Homo*.

At several of these sites, the later deposits—less than 2 million years old—contain stone tools. In Member 5 of Sterkfontein, for instance, Kathy Kuman has shown that two different stone industries are present (see Color Plate 9B). One is called Oldowan (a name given by Louis and Mary Leakey to similar tools from Olduvai Gorge in northern Tanzania). Many archaeologists believe that this is the oldest stone industry on the planet and in parts of East Africa some examples are as old as 2.5 million years. The second industry in Sterkfontein Member 5 is known as the African Acheulian and it has been widely found from Stellenbosch to Algeria. The name of the industry stems from St. Acheul in France, where numerous handaxes have been found. The Acheulian is found also in the Middle East and at least as far to the east as India and south-east Asia. Sterkfontein is the only place in the world where the two industries, Oldowan and Acheulian, are preserved in a stratified sequence in a sealed cave deposit.

The early *Homo* fossils and stone tools in South Africa, as well as the robust australopithecines, are dated to less than 2 million years ago. On the other hand, *A. africanus* is dated from about 3 million years ago (at Makapansgat) to about 2.5 million years ago (at Taung).

Foot-bones as Clues to a Major Discovery

Member 2 in the Sterkfontein Formation is about 10 meters deeper than Member 4 with its wealth of *A. africanus* fossils. In a sequence like this, the deeper the stratum, the older. In 1973, I took the first steps towards beginning an excavation of the very ancient Member 2. By 1978, Alun Hughes and I were provided by Randfontein Estates Mine with the means to winch to the surface bone-bearing breccia from the floor of what we called Silberberg Grotto. In 1980, working through some of these fragments from Member 2, David Molepole found and extracted four foot-bones. These were put in a box along with remains of monkeys and small antelopes. Molepole recovered a further eight foot- and leg- bones and Hughes brought these to the Anatomy Department at the Witwatersrand University. Like the four in the Sterkfontein store, these languished unidentified for fourteen years.

The four foot-bones were re-discovered in the box by Ronald Clarke in 1994. He and I studied the remains of what we called

'Little Foot' and published an account of them in 1995. We pointed out some most unexpected features of the foot. It combined the hallmarks of a two-legged, ground-dwelling creature with those of a tree-climbing primate, whose foot could grasp a branch as a hand can do. Ron Clarke went on, in 1997, to re-discover the other eight bones, some from the same left foot and leg, and a few from the opposite leg. Clarke was now presented with matching left and right feet and legs. He was convinced that there must be a skeleton in the rock. In the Member 2 breccia, two of our Sterkfontein team, Stephen Motsumi and Nkwane Molefe, managed to find the broken end of the shaft of a shin-bone or tibia, on to which one of Molepole's broken fragments of 1980 fitted perfectly. As this piece of tibia was still embedded in undisturbed cave earth of Member 2, Clarke now had the proof that 'Little Foot' stemmed from Member 2.

To prove Clarke's hunch about the rest of the skeleton, he and Motsumi and Molefe chipped away at the *in situ* breccia, through most of 1997, 1998, and 1999. They laid bare much of the rest of a virtually complete skeleton in the Member 2 deposit.

The skeleton lies in breccia sandwiched between layers of calcified flowstone. Happily, Tim Partridge of the University of the Witwatersrand and John Shaw and David Heslop of the University of Liverpool, England, discovered that clearcut palaeomagnetic signatures are imprinted in the layers of flowstone. This led them to place the skeleton, with great confidence, between 3.22 and 3.58 million years ago. Further analysis enabled them to reduce this range of time to 3.30–3.33 million years ago. This figure of three-and-a-third million years ago is the best estimate of the skeleton's age.

These are the oldest fossil hominid bones ever found in South Africa. Moreover, this is the oldest hominid skeleton, with skull, ever discovered. It is indeed the first ever discovery of such a complete *Australopithecus* skull and skeleton. It seems justified to claim that in its completeness, morphology, and antiquity, the new Sterkfontein skeleton is the most important ancient hominid skeleton yet discovered. When I started working towards the excavation of Member 2 in the 1970s, I knew that a hominid would be found in that ancient stratum and said so at the time. Not in my wildest flights of fancy, however, could I foresee what a magnificent specimen Clarke and his assistants would present to the world from that layer.

There are two flowstones and layers of intercalated and subjacent breccia deeper than the new skeleton. As Partridge, Shaw, and Heslop have shown, these layers are deep within a phase of Reversed Geomagnetic Polarity known as the Gilbert. Down there we would be grovelling in the depths of time, close to, or even older than, 4 million years ago! I am convinced that hominid bones and teeth are waiting in the deepest parts of the Sterkfontein Formation, for the unerring instincts and skills of Ron Clarke, coupled with the superb powers of observation and dedicated patience of Stephen Motsumi and Nkwane Molefe, to reveal in the new century.

Neat Symmetry

There is a nice symmetry about the earliest and the latest discoveries made in South Africa. The finding of the Taung skull in 1924 wrought a revolution in hominid evolutionary studies. As Robert Broom said, it was "one of the greatest discoveries in the world's history . . . that may yet rank in importance with Darwin's *Origin of Species*." Seventy-five years later, after the ongoing dig I conducted from 1966 to 1996 had brought to light over 600 early hominid fossils from Sterkfontein, the Member 2 skeleton appears set to close an important gap between the South African and East African australopithecines. It provides, for the first time, faithful linkages between an identifiable skull and the rest of the skeleton (when some remaining bones have been brought to light). At the risk of sounding chauvinistic, the 75-year-symmetry applies also to the institution concerned. Both the 1924 and the 1998 discoveries were made by scientists in the Anatomy Department of the Witwatersrand University Medical School. This University and its Anatomy Department have verified anew their claim to being one of the world's greatest centers for research and instruction in human evolution. I am free to say this now that I am no longer head of the Anatomy Department.

Tropical Tales

Michel Brunet of Poitiers, France, has shown that ancient hominids lived between 3 and 3.5 million years ago in the Saharan part of Africa. He and his colleagues have named the Chadian ape-man *Australopithecus bahrelghazali* after the name of the site. It lies 2,500 km west of Africa's great Rift Valley. This discovery furnishes support for a view that I have long propagated, namely that the spawning of humankind was a pan-African phenomenon. In years to come, as exploration is extended to north and west Africa, we may confidently expect that the pan-Africanism of human origins will be proved as a fact of the history of higher primate life.

Late in the century, Tim Bromage of New York and Friedemann Schrenk of Darmstadt, Germany, extended the digging fields to Malawi. They found hominid remains at Uraha and Malema close to Lake Malawi (formerly Lake Nyasa) in conditions similar to those of the East African Rift Valley sites.

From Kanapoi and Allia Bay near Lake Turkana in northern Kenya, Meave Leakey and her colleagues five years ago presented the world with a new species of hominid. They called it *Australopithecus anamensis*. It is dated to between 3.9 and 4.2 million years ago. This is about the same age as the deepest parts of the Sterkfontein deposit.

At the same time in the 1990s, Tim White of Berkeley, California, with Berhane Asfaw of Addis Ababa, Ethiopia, and Gen Suwa of Tokyo, Japan, pushed back the temporal frontier of known humanity to 4.5 million years ago. Their dramatic finds at Aramis and elsewhere in the Middle Awash area of Ethiopia yielded a hominoid which they at first called *Australopithecus ramidus*. When further fossils came to light, they changed its name to *Ardipithecus*, a new genus, for these most ancient claimants to hominid status.

The depths are now being plumbed down to the six-million-year mark! With hominids now found at that level, the search is at a defining moment of the human story. The period between 7 and 5 million years ago has been calculated by molecular evolutionists to be the most probable time at which a key split occurred among the last common ancestors of apes and humans. It was a parting of the ways, that separated the human lineage from that of its nearest relatives, the chimpanzees. Hominoid fossils at these time depths pose nerve-wracking difficulties of classification. The anthropologists of tomorrow will agonize over the criteria by which to distinguish the earliest hominids from the earliest proto-chimpanzees and both from their last common ancestors. The scholars of the new century will need self-control so as not to assign names wantonly on too little evidence. They will needs be blessed with the patience of Job.

Here are some other critical problem areas which we of the outgoing century bequeath to those of the new century. First, let me refer to the problem of making names and creating species.

Too Many Species? Too Few Species?

Human evolutionary studies have recently been bedevilled by a spate of new and revived names for hominids. Anyone interested in the field is likely to be frightened off by the confusing welter of names. On one recent count, there were as many as twenty hominid species grouped into at least 4 or 5 genera. In addition, two or more alternative names are available for many of these. Some defend this situation by saying that the hominids are underclassified and all of these species are needed. Others, including myself, stress that this classification of the hominids takes too little account of variation within species.

Forceful attempts have been made to separate the Asian and African representatives of *Homo erectus* into two or three different species. There is much well-informed opposition to this. An old idea that the Neandertals were a separate species from modern *Homo sapiens* has recently been revived and is strongly supported by some heavyweights. Other scholars have squared up against this idea. Some have sought to classify the earliest *Homo* of Kenya in a different species from *Homo habilis* of Tanzania, and even to revert to a belief held by some in the 1960s that *H. habilis* belonged not to the genus *Homo* but to *Australopithecus*.

When fossils are few, "we are more likely to indulge in typological reasoning. Additional material allows us to appreciate [a hominid species] as a variable population in time and space." Neither my colleagues nor I were the first to point this out. In *The Descent of Man*, 128 years ago, Charles Darwin wrote:

> If we consider all the races of [living] man as forming a single species, his range is enormous; but some separate races, as the Americans and Polynesians, have very wide ranges. It is a well-known law that widely-

ranging species are much more variable than species with restricted ranges; and the variability of man may with more truth be compared with that of widely-ranging species, than with that of domesticated animals.

There is another schism—between those who base classifications and family trees on old bones, and those who base them on the DNA of living forms. By comparing DNA of living species, they judge how closely related genetically two or three groups are to one another. The molecular excavators are even able to calculate when related living creatures probably diverged from their last common ancestors.

Many of the scientists who work with fossils create more and more species and even genera of hominids. They are known as 'splitters'. On the other hand, the molecular evolutionists have been zealously 'lumping' species and genera into fewer and fewer units.

There was a time when it was held that humans stood on their own private pedestal in the universe. Today the exalted family of the hominids is no longer the special preserve of humans and their ancestors; it has been widened to let in the great apes. The lumping process has gone further recently and it has been argued by some that not only *Australopithecus* but even the apes should be placed in the genus *Homo*!

We cannot here resolve this thorny problem: but it was imperative to draw attention to these two opposing trends. The splitters make ever more genera and species, while the lumpers favour fewer categories. Neither the fossil fellows nor the molecular mortals have a monopoly of the truth. As long ago as 1975 some of us started working towards a reconciliation between the two schools of thought. The quest continues but the situation has not yet been tidied up sufficiently. This is one rather messy area that the twentieth century has handed on to the twenty-first.

Even the way in which we classify animals and plants needs to be looked at again. Our system is based on one devised by that arch-classifier of everything, Linnaeus, the great Swedish naturalist. Loren Eiseley of Philadelphia described him as "a phenomenon rather than a man." His was a nature replete with "a Whitmanesque love of the incredible variety of life . . . He was the naming genius *par excellence*, a new Adam in the world's great garden, drunk with the utter wonder of creation." We often forget that Linnaeus devised his System of Nature to classify *living* plants and animals. It is when we try to apply the same system of naming names to fossil populations that we run into trouble. A new method called Numerical Taxonomy has been offered like a thread of Ariadne to guide us through the Labyrinth, but even it has not helped us to escape the Minotaur. It is not surprising that the first human evolution meeting of the year 2000 grappled anew with Hominid Classification.

The Origin of Modern Humans

This subject was for long a quiet backwater of palaeo-anthropology. It became a mainstream issue in the 1980s and remains a matter of high contention. In the 1970s and early 1980s several scholars—especially Peter Beaumont of South Africa, Reiner Protsch of Frankfurt, and Günter Brauer of Hamburg—found evidence that modern human skull features had first emerged in Africa. Then from 1987 came supporting evidence from the molecular biologists. From studies on the DNA of living human populations, they concluded that Africa was the source of modern humans. One could of course be chauvinistic and say, 'We are proud to have in Africa not only the world's first hominids and first stone tools but also the first modern humans'. But there's no place for blatant prejudice in scientific research: we need a more critical approach. The molecular methods are rigorous and seem to be sound, but it's of some concern that, in different laboratories, the same data base yields dates for the movement of modern humans out of Africa which vary from under one hundred thousand years to over six hundred thousand years. Our molecular colleagues are needful of standardized methods and definitions, as are those who work at the seemingly cruder level of bone and tooth morphology.

The Origin of Spoken Language

When speech began is another vexed question. Quite serious scholars have been arguing about whether the Neandertals could speak. Others consider that spoken language must have emerged together with what they see as a recent flowering of human culture. Twenty-

FIGURE 7.3

*The left cerebral hemisphere of a modern human seen from the left side,
showing the major lobes of the cerebrum, two important fissures and the
positions of the three cortical areas for the control of speech. Of these three
areas, Broca's and Wernicke's are detectable on the surface of the brain in
modern man—and corresponding protuberances occur on the surface of the
endocranial casts of* H. habilis.

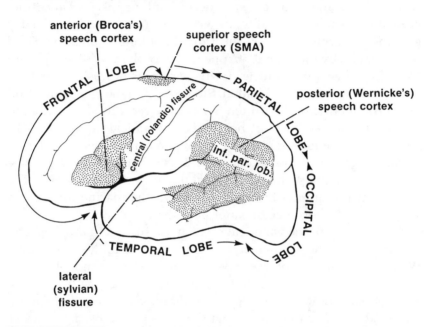

five years ago I threw a spanner in the works. At the height of the
argument about how speechless Neandertal people were a mere
forty thousand years ago, I found evidence to suggest that *Homo
habilis* had the capacity for spoken language nearly two million
years ago (see Figure 7.3). At first I stood alone. Gradually, in the
1980s and especially the 1990s, a groundswell of support arose
from such scholars as Dean Falk, Sir John Eccles, P. Lieberman,
Terry Deacon, W.K. Wilkins, J. Wakefield, and others. One cannot
yet claim that the last word has been spoken on the subject of the
first word. In the coming millennium, there will be much speaking
about speaking, parleys about the differences between the verbal
behaviour of apes and the thoughtful linguistic behaviour of
humans, and cognitive verbal intercourse about verbal intercourse.

Water and Human Evolution

A gently flowing theme in the new century will undoubtedly be the all-pervading role of water in the stream of human evolution. For too long our thinking has been earth-bound: we have seen humans as terrestrial primates *par excellence*. They are that, to be sure, but without water there could be no survival of humans. Our ancestors needed water to drink and to keep cool. So do we. And the need is growing. A recent study by the United Nations Population Fund predicts that, by the year 2050, one fourth of the world's people are likely to be living in countries facing shortages of fresh water.

Michael Crawford of London, Stephen Cunnane of Toronto, and Leigh Broadhurst of the United States have recently shown that, to develop the large brains of hominids, a chemical known as DHA (Docosa Hexa-enoic Acid) is necessary. Where do we find DHA? There is a lack of it in savanna food. It is the marine food chain—plants and animals—that has an abundant supply of DHA. The claim that the human brain depended on the marine food chain supports the importance of water in human evolution.

Then there are the waterways which are so vital in the dispersal of humans around the planet, especially since 2 million years ago. Waterways were peopleways. What may seem formidable water barriers today were less forbidding obstacles when sea-levels were lower. At such times the Strait of Gibraltar boasted stepping-stones, an island and a peninsula, so that the maximum crossing of water to travel from Tangier and Ceuta in North Africa to Iberia (in Europe) would have been a mere 5 km. It should not surprise us that there are signs of hominid culture and perhaps hominid bones in south-eastern Spain, dated possibly to 1.5 million years ago.

Another route for the movement of hominids out of Africa was from Tunisia to Sardinia and Corsica, and from Tunisia to Peninsular Italy by way of such stepping stones as the islands of Pantelleria, Lampedusa, Malta, and Sicily to the Calabrian toe of Italy.

The importance of coastal settlements in the pattern of human dispersal has gained new emphasis from the archaeological findings of Hilary Deacon on the southern Cape coast of South Africa and of Robert Walter and his colleagues on the Red Sea coast of Eritrea. From both ends of Africa there is evidence that, by 125,000 years ago, human society had adapted to a coastal marine environment and were likely to have been subsisting on coastal marine food resources.

In the Indonesian archipelago, close on 1 million years ago, humans crossed the Wallace Line, moving from Malaysia, Sumatra, and Java to Flores. This necessitated the crossing of a body of water which, at its narrowest, was 13 km across. Japan is a series of off-shore islands of mainland Asia. It was peopled from Sakhalin Peninsula to Hokkaido and from the Korean Peninsula to Kyushu and Honshu. The whole of America is an offshore island of Asia. Its earliest peopling was across a land connection called Beringia from Siberia to Alaska. That migration probably occurred on several occasions when the land connection was available, over at least the last 100,000 years.

So the waterways of the Earth and their many-changing faces provided sustenance, support, and new horizons through most of the Pleistocene Epoch. Since water is no less crucial to the survival of humanity today, anthropologists and archaeologists may be able to help regional planners by providing a deep time dimension.

An elegant example is to be found in Robert Raikes's *Water, Weather, and Prehistory*. Raikes was not a trained archaeologist but a hydrologist. He worked on water-related matters in Baluchistan in 1955, and also in the Mediterranean, especially the Middle East. When I visited him in Rome nearly 40 years ago, he told me he had been able to distinguish between ancient and recent springs by the presence or absence of archaic stone tools on their margins. This is an example of applied archaeology. Who would have thought that archaeology could be of potential value in areas of the world stricken by water-shortages?

Neo-Catastrophism

For years I have been thinking of the past and its message for the present and the future. I tried drawing graphs out of the past, up to the present, and I tentatively extrapolated them into the future (see Color Plate 11). But the smoothness of these graphs worried me. Let me take you back briefly to Charles Darwin.

The Darwinian picture of evolution has been much modified in the 140 years since *The Origin of Species* was published. In early editions of *The Origin* the emphasis was on continuous change.

Most people have remembered only this early stage of Darwinism. Yet in later editions, we find the expression of an idea suggested to Darwin by the palaeontologist, botanist, and physician, Hugh Falconer. Darwin now supposed that there had been long periods of stability and then fairly sudden bursts of new species formation. These outbreaks of speciation, Darwin reasoned, would have coincided with environmental changes. Many scholars overlook the fact that Darwin recognized such an episodic pattern of evolution. Niles Eldredge and Stephen Jay Gould gave a name to this kind of pattern—Punctuated Equilibrium—and under the new name, in the last quarter of the twentieth century, the idea became popular.

So we have sudden spurts in the history of life on Earth, and we also have waves of extinctions. This picture has lately focussed my mind on the role of catastrophes in the archives of life. I have suggested the revival of the word 'catastrophism', or better, the introduction of a new one, 'neo-catastrophism'.

Catastrophism was very much in the minds of geologists in the nineteenth century. The term was coined in 1832 by the British philosopher, William Whewell, in his review of Sir Charles Lyell's *Principles of Geology*. In the same review, Whewell coined the term Uniformitarianism, connoting the belief that the same physical laws had operated as causes in the past as were operating today.

Other nineteenth-century geologists were opposed to this view. They were catastrophists: for them, events of the past had been different from those of the present—in degree and quality. For example, vulcanicity of yesteryear was held to be much severer than that observable in recent times. For some there was an attempt to reconcile past cataclysmic events with Judaeo-Christian beliefs. Among the really telling catastrophes of the past were deemed to be the creation of life, the creation of humans, and the biblical flood.

Inevitably catastrophism became associated in many people's minds with an attempted scientific verification of Creation and the Flood. So, it was seen as a major deterrent to the acceptance of Darwinism. In reviving the word catastrophism, I do not seek to revive this theological aspect. My use of it refers to the occurrence of unexpected, one-of-a-kind events on a large scale. Catastrophes are not necessarily negative in their effects. Catastrophe is not a synonym of disaster, although in everyday usage we tend loosely to equate the adjective 'catastrophic' with 'disastrous'. But they have different shades of meaning. For the version of the concept I am adopting here, I should use the term neo-catastrophism.

Evidence has been uncovered that there are few or no smooth curves in the history of life. It has been a pathway punctuated by often quite violent derailments on to new and different tracks. Some are mega-catastrophes and some micro-catastrophes, such as the extinction of only a single species.

First there are catastrophes of terrestrial origin, what we may call 'catastrophes of the geosphere'. One example is the fragmentation of Gondwanaland about 130 million years ago, with its massive impact on the history of life (see Figure 7.4). Another is the formation of the great Rift Valley. It extends from Mozambique and perhaps Botswana in the south to Syria and Lebanon in the north. Then there are volcanic eruptions such as Krakatoa in 1883, Kilimanjaro, and Ngorongoro (23km in diameter, the world's second biggest volcanic crater). Some of these geospheric catastrophes had localized and temporary effects on living things, such as deforestation around Mount St. Helens. Others created conditions which were felt far and wide over a longer period, such as river reversals. In 1783, there were heavy volcanic eruptions in Calabria, Italy, and in Iceland. Records reveal that Europe was covered by a toxic fog, composed of volcanic gases and aerosols, and it caused respiratory illness, crop damage, panic and extreme weather.

Second, there are catastrophes of extra-terrestrial origin, 'catastrophes of the cosmosphere'. Here are two major examples, one well known, the other not yet widely known. The impact of an asteroid or comet at Yucatan, Mexico, some 65 million years ago produced the great impact crater of Chicxulub, about 180 km in diameter. Chicxulub is credited with wiping out most of the dinosaurs, though some questions do remain. If this account is correct, this was a gigantic catastrophe in the history of life on Earth. From an evolutionary perspective, as I have said, not all impacts that are catastrophic are necessarily disasters. Even the Chicxulub impact, although apparently calamitous to the unfortunate dinosaurs, gave a marvellous opportunity to those most opportunistic of animals, the mammals!

The less well-known instance is the Vredefort Impact Structure in South Africa. This strange feature, with its center at Vredefort,

FIGURE 7.4

The fragmentation of the Gondwanaland supercontinent about 130 million years ago. A rotated Australia lies to the south-east; just west of it is the Indian subcontinent, while East Antarctica lies due west of Australia. The concordance between the West African shoreline and that of South America is striking. The living creatures of the derived land masses thereafter evolved relatively independently of one another.

was formerly thought to be of volcanic origin. Uwe Reimold and his group in the Geology Department at the University of the Witwatersrand, with their colleagues at the University of Potchefstroom, have recently shown that the Vredefort structure was caused by the impact of an extra-terrestrial projectile, such as an asteroid or comet. It has a reconstructed diameter of 300 km or more and is thus the largest impact structure yet identified on planet Earth. It exceeds even the Sudbury crater in Ontario, Canada, which is about 200 km in diameter. Not only is the Vredefort crater the biggest so far identified, but it is the oldest! It has been dated to 2.1 billion years.

The Vredefort crater is of interest not only to students of meteoritics, but to students of the history of life. The Vredefort impact coincided with two major events. The first was the charging of the Earth's atmosphere with oxygen. Prior to about 2 billion years ago (according to William Schopf of Los Angeles) the amount of oxygen in the Earth's atmosphere must have been kept at a low, more or less anaerobic level. Thereafter, we find evidence that the atmosphere became charged with oxygen. Secondly, the date of 2.1 billion years coincides with the first appearance on Earth of the *eukaryotes*. These are organisms whose cells contain a nucleus. They include all animals and all plants. The appearance of the eukaryotes must be rated as one of the most momentous events in the history of life on Earth.

Was this concurrence of three mega-events coincidence, a kind of Jungian synchronicity, or were they causally linked? It seems very likely that it was not a coincidence, but that there was a causal connection. Like Chicxulub, Vredefort may well have been a major catastrophe whose world-wide consequences had an enormous impact on the history of life on Earth. All complete eukaryotes are aerobes; they need oxygen, hence the correlation of the first signs of appreciable oxygen in the atmosphere with the earliest appearance of eukaryotes is easy to accept. Both events could, in turn, have been an amazing, catastrophic outcome of the Vredefort impact! We don't yet have a theory as to how an impact like Vredefort could have released huge quantities of oxygen into the atmosphere: that's a problem for the twenty-first century.

There have been several other great extinctions in the history of life—the causes are unknown. Were other extra-terrestrial events responsible or at least contributory? Maybe impacts of projectiles from space have played a far more important role in the history of life on Earth than Charles Darwin or any other early evolutionist ever dared to imagine. A single Chicxulub impact might have wrought more change on life forms than millions of years of evolution.

Another possible catastrophe from the cosmosphere may be mentioned in passing. This is an alternative theory of the origin and evolution of life on our planet. Some scholars of distinction have questioned whether there has been enough time for the evolution of life on Earth by the processes of genetic mutation and selection. They have expressed the view that it was mathematically out of the question in the time available within the confines of planet Earth. They have sought to resolve the problem by looking outside of

Earth. Life on Earth they hold is the result of the insemination of our planet by living forms from other planets which are not necessarily even part of our solar system. This account has been called the 'Guided Panspermia' theory and has been considered by such luminaries as Francis Crick, Enrico Fermi, Leo Szilard, Albert Szent-Györgyi, Fred Hoyle, Carl Sagan, and C. Wickramasinghe. The theory has not been proven, but it is easy to understand now why every new meteorite recovered from Earth or other planets is frenziedly examined for signs of fossilized life. If this theory is ever confirmed, the whole story of the mathematics of life on Earth will have to be transformed. While we should keep a corner of our mind open for this hypothesis, it remains at present only a possible catastrophe.

The Urban Revolution

The picture of human evolution has undergone major metamorphoses in the last 15,000 years. At first there was the development of pastoral pursuits and agriculture resulting in the first population explosion. Later, came the rise of towns and cities—what Gordon Childe called the Urban Revolution. For the last five thousand years a new kind of creeping growth has appeared on the surface of the planet: we call this new excrescence *urbanism!* Although towns and cities appeared less than ten thousand years ago, this new, man-made ecology is today a home to 50 percent of our species *Homo sapiens.* Direct hits by asteroids or other projectiles from space may, under these circumstances, produce very different effects from those which resulted when the whole of the world's surface was rural. This is true also of earthquakes such as the urban disasters at Kobe in Japan in 1995, at Izmit in Turkey, in Greece and in Taiwan in 1999.

Any new Chicxulub-like impact, if it fell on or near a city, would wipe out millions of people on a mega-Hiroshima scale. This would not be selective elimination: it would kill indiscriminately, strong and weak, healthy and sickly, young and old, the only natural bounds being geographical.

There's another reason why I refer to the urban revolution. Cities were once considered to be the highest form of human ecology. Aristotle said that people came to live in cities 'to live a good life'. When we look at what has happened to cities, we may well wonder whether Aristotle's words are still correct. Even back in 1757, Jean Jacques Rousseau wrote in a letter to Denis Diderot: "You philosophers amuse me when you consider the inhabitants of cities [to be] the only people with whom you are in duty bound to concern yourselves. It is in the country that one learns to love and serve humanity; in the cities all one learns is to despise it." A text book of urban pathology—if anyone has had the percipience to write one—would reveal that in cities there are more homicides, suicides, assaults, accidents, deaths from violence, major and minor nervous manifestations—such as talking to oneself and biting one's nails—than among our country cousins.

Most cities are no longer people-friendly. In an age of vehicles, cities have become machine-friendly. When a road has to be widened or re-routed, dwellings, street-trees, gardens and other open spaces are wantonly sacrificed. No wonder books are written with titles like *The Lonely Crowd* and *The Human Zoo*.

Human evolutionists should give their perspective to town-planners and architects. Above all anthropologists have a duty to uphold the place of the human animal in cities. During the next century, the percentage of town- and city-dwellers will rise from 50 to 80 percent. The figure of 80 percent has already been reached and surpassed in heavily industrialized countries.

In crowded cities, mind-sets are spawned which may generate catastrophes of the sociosphere. One such mind-set is color prejudice and racism, which may lead to catastrophes that *are* disasters—like genocide, the Holocaust, ethnic cleansing, pogroms, purges, and apartheid. Other prejudices relate to gender, language and accent, nationality, class, religion, and sexual preference. As an interested party, I hesitate to mention *ageism*! Religious persecution, racial murders, xenophobia, are not historical aberrations of the Middle Ages only: they are still with us. They are worse in urban concentrations of people.

From Printed Books to the Internet

Books have played a great part in the recent evolution of human culture. They enshrine and preserve the legacy of past wisdom and record present knowledge and experience. We should thus see them as a potent means for the dissemination of yesterday's truths, today's images, and tomorrow's visions. Books have been part of humanity's evolution, at least since the clay tablets of Mesopotamia and the papyrus rolls of Egypt. These early traces of what we may call books go back for five thousand years. There are even earlier traces of written documents in China.

Have brains developed functional areas specialized for writing in such a brief, recent period? We know that the birth of spoken language was made possible by the development of specialized areas—those of Paul Broca and the Supplementary Motor Cortex for carrying out speech, and that of Carl Wernicke for receiving and interpreting spoken language. We have yet to learn whether the onset of writing was accompanied by any changes in our brains.

In the test-tube of the past we may find out what went before writing. Its earliest fertile expression and subsequent embryonic development are to be found in those wonderful rock paintings on the walls of thousands of caves in the Drakensberg and the Malutis, and in the glorious folded mountains of the Eastern and Western Cape Provinces. South Africa's heritage of rock art is the richest in the world, and I have been told by Professor David Lewis-Williams that we have over 20,000 prehistoric art sites.

After such a lengthy and honorable history, how tragic it would be if our generation were to pave the way for books to become extinct. We are so good at wiping out biological diversity—by carelessly or deliberately extinguishing scores of living species of plants and animals. Is our misspent skill in wiping out biodiversity going to be paralleled by the systematic slaughter of cultural diversity? It is sad to confess what a fiendishly excellent start we have made during the past five hundred years. Books are a vital part of cultural diversity: all of us should solemnly swear that we shall not do anything to hasten the extinction of printed books.

Some people in the developed countries are beginning to speak of the imminent death of the book in its present printed form. They foresee the replacement of the printed book by 'virtual books' available on the Internet, and the supplanting of libraries by 'virtual libraries'. These exciting new developments have been made possible by the extraordinary advances of technology. That they will play an increasingly important role in the developed parts of the mod-

ern world is inevitable. Will books survive? When we consider electronic substitutes for books, we should realise that such developments are possible (at least at present) only among those sectors of
the world's population where electricity and the appropriate hardware are freely available. This probably means, at the beginning of
the twenty-first century, only about a third of the 6 billion peoples
on earth. What of the rest of humanity? Dare we leave them out in
the cold and the nuclear darkness? They, I believe, will continue to
seek knowledge and enlightenment through books in languages
they can understand. This is another big reason why books should
survive.

Let me refer to telecommunications, computers, the Internet,
the quest for 'artificial intelligence'. When I was carrying out
research for my PhD project just over 50 years ago, I used a borrowed manual calculator. It is hard for younger scientists today,
and even schoolchildren, to imagine what it was like to carry out
research in the pre-computer age. Not long before that, wartime
Britain had pioneered something called Operational Research. In
the U.S. a similar development was known as Operations Research.
Scientists were called upon (in World War II) to use their own
brains to solve problems—as though they were electronic brains or
computers. Men like Zuckerman, Waddington, Nabarro, and others
were taken out of their laboratories and put into small quiet spaces:
that's when the phrase, 'back room boys' began—*The Small Back
Room*, in Nigel Balchin's novel of that name. They were asked to
apply their faculty of scientific analysis to the solving of war problems such as the saturation bombing of Germany, the invasion of
Italy and of Occupied France. With hindsight, we may say that
these scientists were being used as human computers.

Look where we stand today. Consider the products of any of the
great computer companies. If such a revolution has been wrought
in a mere half-century, what staggering horizons must lie before us
in the next fifty years, let alone the next hundred—or the next thousand!

The birth and lusty infancy of the computer age has been one of
the greatest steps in human evolution: I regard it as the most significant leap since humans first acquired the capacity for spoken
language some 2 million years ago. It was cognitive speech, I
believe, that effected a revolution in the evolution of humans: it

converted hominids that were basically animals into human hominids.

The infancy and the childhood of the Computer Age are not without problems. What will the Computer Age do to the use of speech? Educational programmes and goals? The writing and publishing of books? Even the reading of books? Our systems of governance, controls of society, medical diagnosis and practice, belief systems? If the qualities and capacities that have made humans human are attenuated and perhaps even forfeited, how human will the humans of the day be?

Another thought crosses my mind: all of the planning and projecting of the future is being made by the most technologically advanced and the most affluent peoples on Earth. Yet large segments of the world's population still live in the pre-computer age. For example: Africa, with an area one quarter of the habitable land surface of the world, and with 750 million people—possesses 14 million telephones. There are more phones in Manhattan than in the entire African continent.

My plea is not to abort the computer revolution (even if such a thing were possible), but to feed into the equation for the future the quiet desperation of Africa and of other parts of the world whose people survive without electricity. Let us plan the electronics and telecommunications of the future in such a way that we do not widen the gulf between the technologized minority and the pretechnologized or undertechnologized peoples of the Earth (which is another way of saying the gap between the 'haves' and the 'have-nots'). I am not a Cassandra prophesying disaster on the shores of the Hellespont! I believe that it would be possible to find the will and the money to bring the pre-tech part of the world's population gradually into an increasingly technological world. I am sure that most people of goodwill will fervently desire that. Can it be achieved? Is there the will to work in this direction? After a fairly long and moderately difficult life, I remain an optimist.

I have tried to stress that anthropologists have a duty not only to unravel the past, but also to direct their attention to the problems of *Homo sapiens* of the present and to help in the planning of the future. As they have a five million years' perspective on the place and potential of humanity, is it claiming too much to suggest that anthropologists should be able to see a little further into the future? We have a responsibility to impart that perspective to national and international leaders and planners. We cannot sit back passively and allow the future to just happen to us. We must help to forecast and to shape it.[1]

1. I thank the Standard Bank Foundation for inviting me to deliver the Millennium Lecture on which this chapter is based. I express my appreciation to the Foundation for its generous support in the past and, especially its invaluable help to the Dual Congress held in South Africa in 1998. On behalf of myself and my fellow South African paleo-anthropologists, let me also express heartfelt gratitude for the Standard Bank Foundation's decision to pledge magnanimous aid to the advancement of the discipline in South Africa. A special word of thanks is due to the PAST Fund (Palaeo-Anthropology Scientific Trust Fund). Its arrival on the scene in 1993 was a life-jacket to myself and my team which were then faced with the prospect of being disestablished. Their most generous financial support kept my Research Unit going and thus, indirectly, made possible the discovery of 'Little Foot' and the rest of its skeleton. My new Sterkfontein Research Unit, for which I share the responsibility with Ronald Clarke, continues to benefit from the faith and support of the PAST Fund. My gratitude is extended to the University of the Witwatersrand and the National Research Foundation of South Africa (and its predecessors, the Council for Scientific and Industrial Research and the Foundation for Research and Development), which have munificently supported my research for over half a century. Valued aid has been received from the Ford Foundation, the Wenner-Gren Foundation for Anthropological Research, the L.S.B. Leakey Foundation, the Department of Arts, Culture, Science and Technology, Pretoria, the National Science Foundation (Washington, D.C.), the National Geographic Society, and the Boise Fund (Oxford). I am grateful for help from Heather White, Francis Thackeray, Ron Clarke and many others.

8

How I Gave Up the Ghost and Learned to Love Evolution

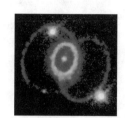

Terrence W. Deacon

By providing an alternative to prior design and preformation, an evolutionary emergent account of natural 'design' locates the creative force in the world rather than outside it. An emergent spiritualism is consistent with an evolutionary world view.

Do we move ourselves, or are we moved by an unseen hand?

—Alfred Lord Tennyson

I believe we stand on the threshold—or perhaps the precipice—of the last and potentially the most humbling Copernican revolution. In the half-millennium since Copernicus first suggested that terra firma might not be located in the center of the cosmos, most of the remaining vestiges of human specialness have come into doubt.

Among those precious illusions of chosen birthright were the essence of life (which turned out to be just a complicated series of chemical processes), our place in the animal kingdom (which turned out not to be at some apex of creation but amidst the African apes), our place in the cosmos (which turned out to be near a not too atypical second-generation star among millions in a not too atypical galaxy among billions more), and our place in cosmic creation (which appears to be as a very minor byproduct of 14 billion or so years of cooling following the mother of all cosmic explosions). What more of human dignity is there to be lost to the reducing furnace of science?

Why, our souls, of course. I believe that the final Copernican revolution will be completed within the next century, with the explanation of how the electrical-chemical processes in our brains produce the experience of being persons, of how certain variants of these processes produce the few special characteristics of human cognition that distinguish us from our very close animal cousins, and by the manufacture of devices that experience themselves in the world much as only we and our flesh and blood cousins do today. With this discovery we might well be plunged into spiritual cataclysm, if we are not prepared.

There are many from the world's spiritual traditions who think that science can never ever really address these issues and that a core ineffable essence will remain forever outside the purview of scientific inquiry. Even among scientists and philosophers who otherwise assume that consciousness is just a difficult conceptual problem, many still imagine that this final step will remain forever beyond the capacity of human minds to grasp, due to human limitations. Others doubt that we will ever have a way of determining the difference between mindful and mindless things, even if we were able to simulate computing devices rivalling the sophistication of brains. And still others believe that the 'folk psychology' suggesting the existence of a phenomenal experience of self, however compelling and heuristically useful it may be, is itself ultimately illusory. They believe that the final victory of reason will involve abandoning the questionably useful fiction of consciousness altogether for a more parsimonious account involving only physical-chemical reactions and the neural computations they perform.

But I have little doubt that, so long as the current pace of intellectual exploration continues unabated, a full working understanding of the essential details of conscious physical processes could become available surprisingly sooner than we might have guessed. Even if you refuse to believe this is possible, however, I submit that it may be prudent—even morally imperative—to assume that this day will come and to consider how we might want to respond when it does. To pretend that this is not in the cards of human endeavor, is to fail to be prepared for the greatest challenge to human values ever posed. The news may arrive in scientifically and philosophically incremental stages, but it will probably infect the population of the Earth, ready or not over the course of no more than a generation or two, on the wings of mass media and mass-produced devices. The way it will affect human relationships and human institutions depends both on the nature of the resulting explanation and on how this knowledge becomes translated into personal experience and practical consequences. But it will also depend on our readiness to let loose our embrace of a view of human spirituality that it must inevitably undermine—a view I call 'spiritual essentialism'—and on our ability to articulate a more consistent, and yet not ethically bereft replacement.

I maintain that both the key to this discovery and the key to understanding its spiritual significance lies in understanding the emergent character of evolutionary processes. The evolutionary paradigm is relevant to the explanation of far more than just the phylogenetic history of life. Evolution-like processes are now recognized to play a significant role in processes at all levels of life, including cognition, as well as in processes that are not, strictly speaking, biological, such as the formation and spread of cultural information. There are even cosmological theories that borrow significantly from evolutionary selection logic to explain the basis for the physical constants and the anthropic principle, though these are considerably more speculative than their biological counterparts. Of course, many important theological speculations (such as those of Teilhard de Chardin) and spiritual movements have been animated by evolutionary theories. The power of the evolutionary paradigm is that it promises an account of design and function in the world that is emergentist and creative rather than reductionist and eliminative.

In scientific description the substantial world is treated as passive and blindly mechanistic. The clockwork universe of Descartes and Newton leaves no room for novelty or creative processes, and thus no room for personhood, free will, or subjective experience. Indeed, this worldview can provide no account of the origins of the world itself. Creation of this dead world, the animation of its clockwork mechanisms, and the determination of its principles of operation are details that appear to be outside of descriptions of physical processes themselves. As a result, all these processes of creation and mentation tend to be relegated to discussions of metaphysics, not physics. The clockwork world is a world analogous to a logical deductive system in which all the complexity of its details and all future permutations of their expression are implicit and fully preformed in its antecedent axioms, its initially 'given' conditions. This view is reinforced by the miraculous and precise pre-established correspondence of the world of mathematical expression to formalized descriptions of physical processes. That apparent marriage of formal and physical clockwork has recently been extended into the realm of cognition by modelling processes carried out by brains as algorithmic computations. Such a world view has been the foundation underlying the last three centuries of unprecedented scientific progress, and as we cross over into a new millennium it appears as an almost unimpeachable axiom and the instrument of an unstoppable self-vivisection.

But one class of physical theories—evolutionary theories—provides an alternative to the paradigms of prior design and preformation. Evolutionary explanations are unlike other physical accounts in that they do not specify a procedure for tracing and describing precise cause-effect relationships. Moreover, evolutionary accounts do not have as their subject merely material objects and forces. By this I mean that evolutionary accounts are instead directed to matters of function and natural 'design'. These are not, strictly speaking material objects or forces but relationships that have a kind of meaning or significance. Biology is not merely a physical science; it is a semiotic science. Concepts like function and adaptation make no sense in a purely physical context, such as in geology or chemistry. So in this sense evolutionary explanations are not like explanations in physics or chemistry, even if they apply to materials which could also be described in physical and chemical terms as well. In this regard, evolutionary explanations inevitably involve accounting for a source of information, and information, unlike the 'stuff' of the world, can be created or destroyed. New information can 'emerge' from old configurations of matter because it is a relational entity, and although a strict Leibnizian determinist might be tempted to argue that newly evolved biological configurations were in some way virtually present antecedently, to the extent that there is true quantum chaos underlying everything, this interpretation must be rejected since the basis of evolutionary processes is ultimately the selective amplification of certain highly rare microchaotic events to the point that they become highly regular large-scale structural features of the world. Though the concept of emergence is problematic in many uses (for example, in calling liquidity an 'emergent property' of large ensembles of water molecules), its application to the evolutionary appearance of new classes of biological functions, such as oxidative metabolism or symbolically mediated cognition, is far more difficult to deny.

The important point for considering the relationship between spiritual traditions and scientific knowledge is that an evolutionary emergence paradigm for the origins of functional pattern and meaning in the world locates the creative force in the world rather than outside of it. I believe that the apparent paradox of creative intelligent processes embedded within blind mechanistic clockworks, that has long driven dualistic accounts of mental and physical processes, is due in large part to the misapplication of physicalistic accounts to realms where evolutionary accounts are required: that is, realms of information and function.

Most recently, parallel confusions are beginning to enter into discussions of cognition and mental experience, as computationalist analyses are increasingly used to describe mental phenomena, with similar eliminative consequences. The confusion of levels of explanation is more subtle and more deeply woven into the terms of this analysis, because although the language of computationalism appears on the surface to reflect the manipulation of information, the implementation of functions, and operations involving the transformation of meanings, that's ultimately only a gloss for an account which is, at base, a theory of mechanistic, not semiotic, relationships. What I hope to show is that an evolutionary emergent account of the neural processes underlying phenomenal experience offers a way to understand human experience and the origins of meaning and value as self-creative phenomena, rather than as passively inherited mental content.

As I will try to show, this can be seen as a confirmatory insight with respect to the intuitions of many spiritual and mystical traditions, so long as we carefully distinguish this approach from the still-dominant eliminative materialist paradigm that ultimately denies the possibility of true evolutionary emergence. But let me also begin with a caveat to this suggestion of consonance. Approaching the mental world from an emergentist perspective doesn't mean that some major aspects of traditional spiritualistic views aren't at risk of elimination. The evolutionary world-view is at odds with two conceptual paradigms often entangled in the world's various spiritual traditions. Though I believe they are not essential to the core insights of these traditions, giving them up may be quite difficult. I believe the spiritual benefits ultimately outweigh the costs.

Two deeply ingrained notions that must be sacrificed I call 'spiritual essentialism' and 'spiritual preformationism'. Spiritual essentialism is the conception of a materially transcendent noncorporeal soul, a self-essence that persists independent of any physical embodiment and is typically modelled on the folk-psychological conception of an individual subjective self. Spiritual preformationism is the conception that there must be a prior intentional design causing or at least guiding the complex orderliness of the world, especially of the living and mental worlds. This latter view grows out of an incredulity, a conviction that the intelligence of the world, so to speak, for example its anthropic orderliness, could not have come into being spontaneously. A sort of deductive logic arises in which worldly consequences depend on their form already being nascent and complete in the antecedent axioms of creation, in the mind of a creator or some other kind of prior intelligence.

Spiritual Essentialism

What I call spiritual essentialism is a variant of vitalism, its now deceased older sibling. It is the view that mental experience is only contingently correlated with the physical processes of a body, or, to put it differently, it assumes that there can be no explanation for the subjective experience of being a person that can be phrased in physical terms because this experience is of a different kind, something added on top of—or outside of—the world of matter, energy, and the patterns of matter and energy we use to convey information. In this view, human conscious experience is deemed to be something apart from a human body. Both its individuality and its persistence are imagined to not depend on bodily processes, though correlations may exist.

This view leads to two metaphysical consequences, with very real influences over human action.

First, a living body is treated as a sort of vehicle. Birth, death, and other bodily changes are thought to affect it only externally and transiently. Ultimately, with death of the body, some essential part is imagined to be uncoupled from the body, and still persistent, a belief made explicit in theories of resurrection and reincarnation, and captured by the oxymoronish phrase 'life after death', which also exemplifies an explicit confounding of life and consciousness that is a nearly universal cultural concept.

Second, this quasi-independence view suggests that although the content of consciousness may enter into experience as a direct consequence of physical causality, the essence of experience itself is something apart from this, and is thus beyond the grasp of empirical explanations. But not only does that view allow one to imagine not being wholly subject to the base vagaries of material things, its detachment also brings with it an implicit nonidentification with the world, which can foster a complacency about misuse of our own and others' bodies and of the physical environment, especially in service of spiritual ends, because material entities are presumably more base and dispensable than the spiritual ones they are transiently correlated with. Our bodies and the world they inhabit are thus essentially treated as dead stuff. No wonder, then, that scientific news suggesting that our minds are just the clockwork output of neural computers is spiritually threatening, as was Darwin's suggestion that we are merely another species of African ape.

Spiritual Preformationism

Spiritual essentialism has a corollary, spiritualistic preformationism, that can also trace its roots to traditional beliefs in almost every human society. From the assumed malevolent magical designs of sorcerers who take—or are assigned—responsibility for unfortunate accidents visited on others, to the many stories offering accounts of where persons reside before birth and after death, to traditions that accord personal status to the objects or forces that shape momentous natural events, there appears to be a human predisposition to understand causality on the analogy of human action. Wherever we encounter spontaneous orderly activity, complex pattern formation, and notable coincidence in the world we are predisposed to see it as the actions of an 'unseen hand'.

Spiritual preformationism is a bit like its historically defunct biological counterpart, preformationism in development. In this view it was supposed that bodies developed from tiny homunculi, miniature human forms constituting the human 'seeds' (perhaps curled up on the head of the sperm). The idea of epigenesis, that complex and finely designed bodies could develop from an initially undifferentiated cell by some sort of self-organizing process seemed to challenge credulity. The form had to be there in some manner from the beginning. Where else could it come from? Today, this argument is seen as totally without basis, but in my opinion there are numerous cryptic parallels still around. My favorite example comes from the world of linguistics: the notion that human language abilities are traceable to our possession of an innate language of thought dubbed Mentalese, that possesses all the structural and functional qualities of spoken languages and more. Indeed, linguists have often described the acquisition of a first native language as learning to translate, say, French into Mentalese. This of course does not explain how this complex kind of structure arose, why it has the features it has, nor how it works. It merely replaces one mystery, language learning, with another, the biological evolution of Mentalese.

In some ways, the popular view of development is merely a coded version of preformationism: the blueprint for building the body is there in the DNA of the fertilized egg, and merely gets implemented during development. However, developmental biologists have long been aware that much of the 'information' incorporated into the dynamics and structures of developing bodies is derived from self-organizing processes that emerge within and among cells as genes are expressed and their products interact. This is what makes developmental biology such a challenging field. The blueprint metaphor—as indeed also the developmental 'program' metaphor—implicitly ignores the essential dysanalogy between engineered artifacts (for which we need to fashion extrinsic design and assembly instructions as well as extrinsic tools) and organisms which must self-assemble in most respects. Taking a hint from one of the primary functions of gene products—catalytic activity—we can reformulate this metaphor. Genes are not so much instructions (program codes) and blueprints (icons) as they are biases of spontaneous molecular-cellular processes that predispose certain self-organizing patterns of activity. Much of the 'information' for building bodies and brains is recruited in this process from topological and temporal and environmental regularities that are the context of gene expression.

One of the things recommending preformationist analyses to our intuition is its affinity to deductive argumentation and proof. Ever since Euclid demonstrated how much implicit complexity could be unfolded from a very few basic axioms and postulates in the formulation of a geometry, we have been fascinated by this as a metaphor for the derivation of order in the world, as well as for its reduction to a few basic principles.

Whence Essentialism?

In my book, *The Symbolic Species*[1] I suggest that this predisposition for viewing the world may reflect an adaptation of human brains to ease the difficulties of learning to communicate with and ultimately to think with the aid of symbolic reference. I argue that each person's discovery of the symbolic use of signs depends on an unusual human learning strategy. In order to learn new symbolic relationships (recall for example your own discovery of the underlying 'meaning' behind the rules for manipulating mathematical signs), one first must learn to recognize and use superficial correspondences between signs and their referents, often in a sort of rote fashion. But in order to get beyond this somewhat mindless 'how to' knowledge to a true symbolic understanding we must 'see' the hidden logic behind these patterns, and ultimately abandon the rote knowledge in favor of guiding thought and communications with these otherwise cryptic patterns of logical relationships

---

1. Terrence Deacon, *The Symbolic Species: The Coevolution of Language and the Brain.* New York: Norton, 1997.

between the signs. These higher-order more abstract systematic relationships between signs by which symbols are given meaning provide the ground for the very much more flexible virtual reference system. This is what words and sentences provide, which more hardwired and simply correlated communicative sounds like laughter and sobbing do not.

Thus in order to be facile at discovering symbolic relationships we humans have evolved predispositions to seek and appreciate attentional and mnemonic figure-background shifts, to 'look for' patterns and correspondences 'behind' more obvious ones, in ways that no other species exhibit. As a consequence of this special evolutionary past, we implicitly expect there to be cryptic patterns, hidden meanings, and unrecognized purposes behind the superficial appearances of things. We are in this sense like the autistic savant who obsessively sees the world through one idiosyncratically enhanced capacity. And so, like the savant who may reflexively calculate the number of cars in a parking lot, we reflexively view the patterns and coincidences displayed in the natural world as though they were the cryptic symbols produced by an unseen communicator yet to be understood. Throughout the ages, people the world over have demonstrated this irrepressible urge to read meaning into processes that arose without it and to assume that physical processes in general are not sufficient unto themselves, nor able to account for the mentality exhibited by our physical bodies.

Coupled with a predisposition to see the world instrumentally, as filled with potential tools (which may also have been fostered by our special evolutionary past), we are handed an almost unavoidable implicit paradox—a dead world shaped through and through by meaning and intelligence from without. Again, no wonder the scientific view that this clockwork world needs no watchmaker, and merely self-organizes through blind chance and the statistics of biased reproduction, seems like a move to eliminate meaning and intelligence from things altogether. Add to this the suggestion by many evolutionary psychologists (aka sociobiologists), such as E.O. Wilson, Matt Ridley, Robert Wright, and others that ethical principles, moral value, and even esthetic taste may also be derivative of our species' particular evolutionary history and you have the promise of a thoroughly contingent eliminative paradigm.

Symbolic abilities may thus be the *raison d'être* for our mean-ing-seeking tendencies and our insatiable appetite for finding higher purpose behind worldly events, and may also provide the motivation for personalizing this sense of overarching guiding intelligence. This is because symbolic abilities evolved in response to communicative demands. This makes symbols and symbolic knowledge inextricably social. For the most part, for any social species, the major source for hidden intentionality typically is located in others' minds. Symbols don't just allow us to express the otherwise occulted contents of our mental activities, they also serve as our major window of access into the world of others' minds. Using the intrinsically extrapersonal vehicle of symbolic communi-cation and reasoning, we can imagine ourselves as observed objects as well.

To collapse a complex argument (too extensive to unpack here) into a few words: I think that this decentering capacity of symbolic thought is the key that transformed social instincts into contents for ethical and moral reasoning, that predisposes us to personalize the source of order and meaning behind things, and which ulti-mately allows us to entertain the self-contradictory view that our own experience might be an illusion, reducible to mere electrical-chemical clockwork. Against this background, evolutionary emer-gent accounts seem awkward and alien in all ways, even though the alternatives—dualism versus a world without meaning or experi-ence—appear equally absurd.

Is Darwinism Eliminative?

What might be called the modern 'crisis of spirituality' has arisen in parallel with the growing recognition that most of the sponta-neous actions of things around us, as well as the fittedness of the patterns that arise, can be explained without assuming prior design or cosmic intentionality. This recognition, served up to us by the successes of scientific investigations, hints that this may also be the fate of apparent human intentionality as well. The demonstration by Darwin and his intellectual progeny that the 'blind' statistics of molecular damage and spontaneous selective breeding—natural selection theory—were probably sufficient to account for the ori-gins of the exquisitely adaptive complexity of organisms, has particularly fostered this suspicion. Not surprisingly, adherents of the essentialist traditions find the Darwinian perspective most threatening. As well they should. This is because it not only threatens the view of things in the world as designed and intrinsically meaningful; it offers a slippery slope down which we can see all conceptions of intentionality—even that which we know we experience—falling. Scientists and philosophers are, of course, adepts at thinking impossible thoughts—just think of the behaviorists' contention that minds could be ignored as epiphenomenal—and so this will hardly be an impediment to 'progress' in this area. A growing schism seems inevitable.

But the evolutionary account of how complex activity that is 'fitted' to the world can arise spontaneously, does not ultimately have eliminative implications. Only when collapsed into a mechanistic reductionistic metaphysics does this happen. And the same can be said of cognitive science. An evolutionary emergent account of human intentionality, intelligence, and symbolic ability has a very different spiritual implication. This view forces us to abandon a vision of the world in which the essence of personhood is independent of any physical mechanism; in which meaning and value are givens, irrespective of human action or reflection; and in which subjective experience remains an immutable, eternal, and ineffable essence. Instead, it urges us to accept a vision of the world in which the orderliness and fittedness of things comes about spontaneously; in which meaning, purpose and value are *post hoc* undesigned features of things; and in which conscious experience is an emergent quality of an evolutionary process of a specific kind that may not be limited to brains. If we are willing to make this trade, we may be able to have our materialism and experience it too.

Spiritual Cataclysm Or . . . ?

The crisis of spirituality is already implicit in the enterprise of scientific investigations as we enter the twenty-first century. Even if we still lack fully worked-out hypotheses and currently have only vague suspicions of a possible outcome of scientific research and its philosophical analysis, I believe that these nagging thoughts about the potential elimination of mind and meaning are fueling many of the nihilistic turns of thought and fostering some of the

thoroughly relativistic ethical perspectives that have been characteristic of the industrial and post-industrial age. But what will be
the consequence of answering these still open questions. Spiritual
essentialism has at least been protected by the absence of a complete theory of cognition and mental experience, and the fact that
engineers have yet to even come close to making actual thinking
devices. But what if blind trial and error engineering or neuroscience succeeds in the near future, as I think they will? This will
pull away the curtain of mysteriousness behind which we have protected the faith in spiritual essentialism. If the uproar caused by the
previous Copernican revelations are any indication of what we can
expect, we should not imagine that this news will be accepted easily, especially since this time it will appear to be about the 'soul'
itself. It's one thing to be told that you are not standing at the center of God's world. It's another to be told that there is no you standing there!

Not to worry yet. I think we are still far from having a detailed
understanding of the logic that organizes global brain functions,
and yet we may not be so far from knowledge that is of sufficient
detail to approach some of the more general questions and indicate
where the search appears to be leading. In many ways these clues
hint at an answer that is both uncharitable to spiritual essentialism
and preformationism and yet do not force us to the opposed claims
of cold clockwork mechanism and meaninglessness.

This is because the evidence points unmistakably toward an
evolutionary emergent account of consciousness as well as of life.
By this I do not merely mean the view that consciousness evolved,
but rather that it is itself a form of evolutionary emergent process
in some interesting sense. Far from eliminating meaning and value
from the world, I think this product of science will transform our
understanding of its true origin. This is a grandiose claim that I will
not be able to flesh out, but I think it is possible to at least provide
some indication of how I think this scientific claim is linked to the
spiritual problem.

Evolutionary Emergence versus Computation

I have become convinced that mental processes demand an evolutionary and emergent explanation, in part, because of the very suc-

cesses of computer models of cognitive processes. These have done a wonderful job of helping us to ask explicit questions about what can and cannot be accomplished by determinate processes (for instance, machines whose actions embody algorithms), and at the same time help to mark the boundary between the mindless and the mindful.

The point of computational design is this: if a symbol-manipulative task can be specified precisely (either by explicit instructions or by the implicit structure of a device, such as a neural net), it can thereby be carried out automatically—in other words mindlessly—by constructing (programming) a mechanism that manipulates symbol tokens according to this same pattern. The implication isn't that symbol manipulation is mindless, or that thought is 'mere' mechanism of the same sort, but rather that this particular aspect of thought, what might be called its syntactic aspect, could be carried out mindlessly. The more critical and less obvious implication, however, is that what can be described as a computation is then precisely not the mindful aspect of mental functions.

Perhaps, then, it would be better to think of computation as constituting much of the unconscious business that brains engage in. Indeed, this is precisely our experience. Take for example the learning of some skill, typing on a computer keyboard or driving an automobile. We experience this process as one that begins with very conscious intentionally directed patterns of action and perception, carefully regulated by assessing the effects of these actions, and after extensive training and experience eventually becomes relatively automatic and unconscious. The same is true of perceptual processes alone. We quickly habituate to incessant stimuli, except for those that are quite aversive, and stop noticing them altogether. Even the categorical perceptual skills we develop, like recognizing traffic lights or pencils or birds, begin to recede into automatism as we become familiar with them, except when we need to intercede to inhibit or redirect these entrenched tendencies. In this way we might be justified in suggesting that much of the work of minds is dedicated to creating computational architectures in order to free up conscious resources for tasks as yet unable to be matched to an appropriate computation. To put this more succinctly, it appears that one of the points of consciousness is to create computers. The purpose is to eliminate consciousness when possible.

But if computation is in some sense the converse of conscious-ness, how can we describe what is left, after setting aside compu-tation, that is the ground of our experiencing? Again a hint at the answer comes from distinguishing features of computation from other sorts of processes. In this case, we can turn to the hardware of mental processes—brains and neurons and their connections—and try to distinguish the computational from the non-computa-tional aspects of its architecture. One way to do this is to ask, what kind of computations does the architecture of brains suggest that they are best suited to perform? So let's take a superficial look at neural 'design features'.

The first thing we notice about the brain from a computational point of view is that '. . . it's made of meat'! Or so an incredulous alien android reports to his superior (in Terry Bisson's oft-quoted story[2]) when asked about the device that humans think with. The significance of this should not be minimized, because implicit in this are a number of factors that, as the android intimates, should render this a rather poor choice for a computing device. Brains are made of cells that are only superficially modified from the standard animal cellular plan. As cells, neurons need to synthesize their own molecular building blocks, burn oxygen and glucose for energy, transduce and transmit signals along surface membranes using ionic gradients sustained by molecular 'pumps', and so on. All of which contributes to slow inefficient signal processing, exemplify-ing the fact that neurons are cells first and signal processors sec-ond. But these limitations are merely impediments to computation, since noisiness might be controllable. There are, however, other attributes of brains that may be equally troublesome.

In addition to intrinsic noisiness of signal processing within neurons, the circuits they are embedded in have other messy and troublesome attributes. First they are highly interconnected nets. Second, the major fraction of synapses appear to be excitatory (at least in the cerebral cortex) and so together these attributes mean that noise will tend to get rapidly distributed and even amplified by recurrent connectivity. Third, in a modestly large brain (for exam-

2. This imaginary conversation is found in a story fragment by science fiction writer Terry Bisson, from *Omni* magazine (April 1991), widely circulated in the early daysof AI.

1. HUBBLE DEEP FIELD SOUTH

In this image of deep space taken by the Hubble Space Telescope we see galaxies at many different distances—larger, brighter images are closer galaxies, while the faintest, smallest images are galaxies perhaps 12 billion light years away. The further away a galaxy lies, the longer its light has had to travel to reach us, so the most distant images in this scene give us glimpses of the Universe as it looked soon after the Big Bang. This image was acquired by a series of exposures totaling ten full days (240 hours) of telescope time.

2A. ROVER ON MARS

The Mars rover Sojourner is seen crossing a small dune about six feet long running from upper left to lower right.

2B. PLANET MARS

The huge split in the Martian crust called Valles Marineris cuts across much of this hemisphere of the planet. The valley is 3,000 miles long and in places 20,000 feet deep. Although not carved by a river, certain locations show signs of ancient lakebeds.

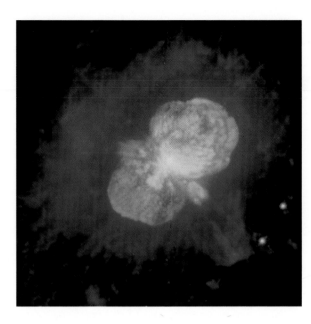

3A. ETA CARINAE

This is a supergiant star on the verge of exploding as a supernova, already dramatically surrounded by clouds of gas and dust from earlier expulsions. The star itself is hidden by the clouds. Its distance of 9,000 light years ensures that the eventual explosion will not endanger the Earth. Its mass is estimated at 150 times the mass of our sun and its luminosity at four million times greater than our sun's.

3B. CASSIOPEIA A

The aftermath of a supernova explosion is revealed by radio waves emanating from this still-expanding shell of gases—located about 9,100 light years away.

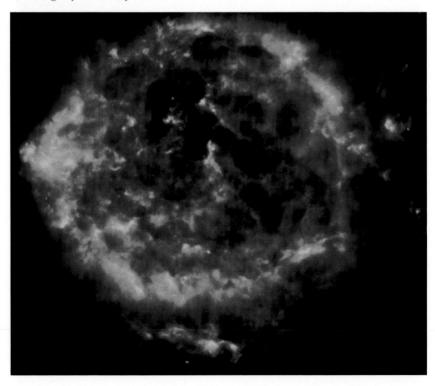

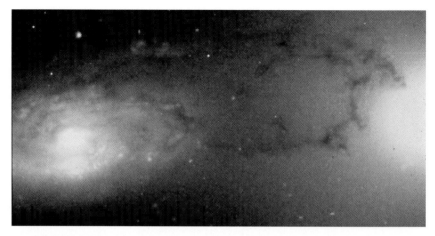

4A. COSMIC DUST

Cosmic dust in a distant galaxy is dramatically silhouetted against the light of another galaxy behind it. Much of the dust is formed from atoms forged during earlier supernova explosions.

4B. EAGLE NEBULA

These huge columns of cosmic dust and gas—one of them a trillion miles tall—are birthing new stars. A nearby brilliant star, out of view, is slowly evaporating the clouds.

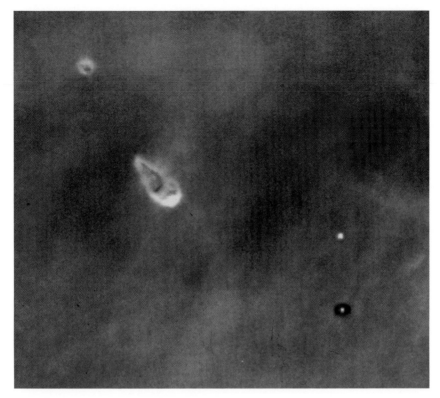

5A. PROPLYDS IN THE ORION NEBULA

Proplyds—young, low-mass stars with surrounding disk of material—are seen here in the Orion Nebula. Radiation and a wind of particles from nearby stars are distorting some of the disks into comet-like shapes.

5B. PROPLYDS SEEN EDGE-ON.

Planets may be forming in these disks.

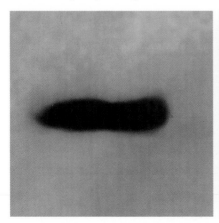

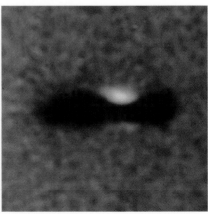

6A. HYDROGEN CYANIDE POLYMERS

Hydrogen cyanide (HCN) is a colorless liquid at room temperature. Addition of a trace of ammonia to the liquid (or to HCN dissolved in water or other solvent) brings about a rapid color change to yellow to orange to black, with increasing thickening as the cyanide molecules join together to form long polymer chains from which amino acids and nitrogen heterocycles can be extracted.

6B. COMET HALLEY

Halley's black nucleus, upper left, was photographed on 14th March, 1986, during the Giotto fly-by from a distance of 8,200 miles. Could the black crust covering Halley's rocky core (about 15 × 10 km in size) consist of polymers arising from the HCN formed from methane and ammonia known to be frozen on the comet surface?

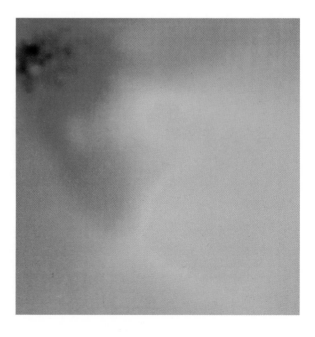

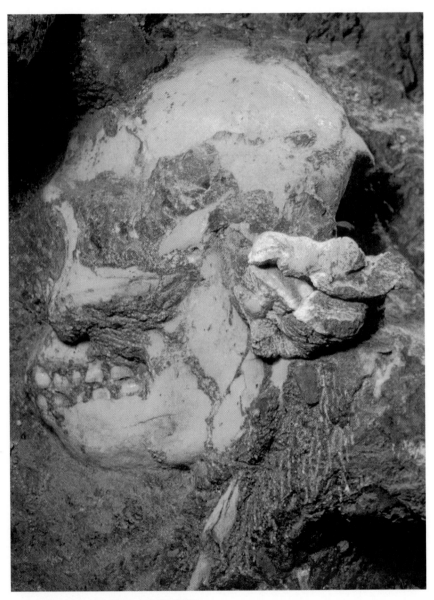

7. A PROFILE OF OUR ANCESTOR

The skull and upper arm bone of the 3.3 million-year-old skeleton of Australopithecus from Sterkfontein discovered in 1998 by Ronald Clarke and co-workers Stephen Motsumi and Nkwane Molefe.

8. FACIAL VIEW OF THE TAUNG SKULL.

This skull of Australopithecus africanus, *the first of Africa's ape-man fossils to be found, was discovered in the Buxton Limeworks at Taung late in 1924. Dart's recognition of its hominid features in 1925 is one of the most important events in the history of paleo-anthropology. The individual to whom the skull belonged would have been between 3 and 4 years of age at death.*

9A. FOSSIL HOMINIDS FROM STERKFONTEIN

Eriam Maubane demonstrates some of the six hundred hominid specimens from the Sterkfontein Formation, Members 4 and 5. These specimens are in the Sterkfontein Research Unit of the School of Anatomical Sciences at the Witwatersrand University Medical School in Johannesburg.

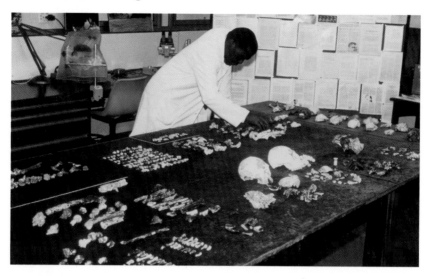

9B. STONE TOOLS FROM MEMBER 5 OF THE STERKFONTEIN FORMATION

Kathy Kuman has shown that two distinct Stone Age industries are represented in Member 5, namely the Oldowan (as shown below), similar to those recovered by Mary Leakey at Olduvai Gorge, and a more advanced industry, the African Acheulian. These are the oldest stone tools (just under 2 million years) yet found in a sealed cave deposit.

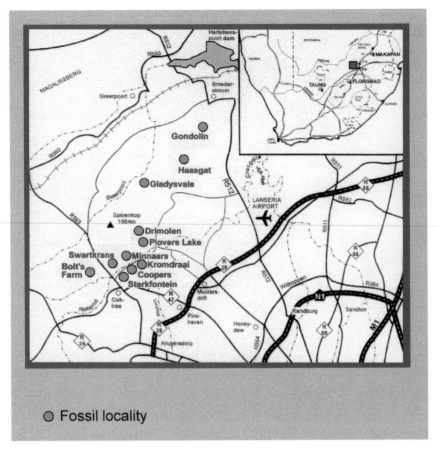

○ Fossil locality

10. SOUTH AFRICAN HOMINID SITES

Fossil sites in the newly proclaimed World Heritage Site, not far to the north-west of Johannesburg. Of the eleven sites pin-pointed, seven—Gondolin, Gladysvale, Drimolen, Kromdraai, Swartkrans, Coopers, and Sterkfontein—have been shown to contain hominid fossils. The three richest caves are Sterkfontein, Swartkrans, and Drimolen. The area shown above has the greatest concentration of hominid-bearing cave sites in the world. (After an original by Andre Kayser.)

11. HUMANITY'S PATTERN OF EVOLUTION OVER THREE MILLION YEARS

Fossil evidence shows that human-style walking on two legs came long before human-style big brains. These graphs, which portray the development of various hominid traits, approach the top line—representing 100 percent hominization, or the attainment of modern human structure—at varying rates and at varying times.

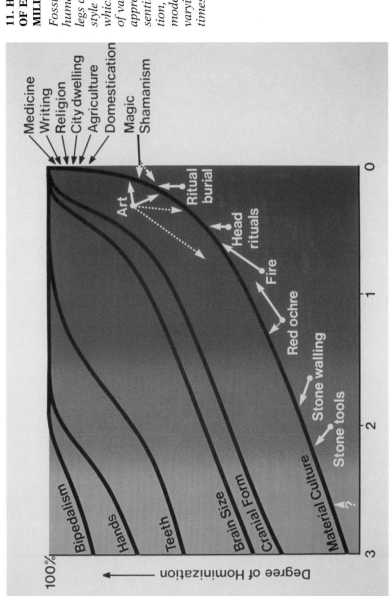

12. GIOTTO, *THE LAST JUDGMENT*. THE ARENA CHAPEL, PADUA.

The cycle of frescoes by Giotto (1303–1306) covering the walls of the Arena Chapel in Padua depict the life of Mary's parents (Joachim and Anna), the Virgin and Christ, the Passion and the Pentecost in a remarkably flowing, story-telling manner arising from a deep humility of spirit, the scale being in all respects human.

13A. GIOTTO, *ANGEL OF THE ANNUNCIATION*. THE ARENA CHAPEL, PADUA.

13B. GIOTTO, *THE ANNUNCIATION*. THE ARENA CHAPEL, PADUA.

14. RAPHAEL, *THE SCHOOL OF ATHENS* (1510–1511). THE VATICAN PALACE, ROME.

This all-embracing fresco on Philosophy, commissioned by Pope Julius II for his library together with other frescoes concerning Theology, Law, and the Arts, celebrates the glory of classical thought with its assembly of ancient philosophers and scientists centered around Plato (holding his Timaeus) and Aristotle (with his Ethics). Included are, on the bottom left, Pythagoras (reading intently) and Heraclitus (thinking hard at a marble desk). On the bottom right are Euclid the geometer and Ptolemy the astronomer (holding a starry globe). Contemporary Renaissance artists are also present (extreme right, bottom) in the person of Raphael himself (black cap) and his teacher Perugino (white cap). Leonardo may have been the model for Plato, while the model for Heraclitus may have been Michelangelo who was working next door on his Sistine Chapel ceiling.

15. A MANDALA FOR CONSCIOUSNESS

Three fundamental symbols—yin-yang, DNA, and ouroboros—representing creativity, history, and mystery, underlying aspects of art, science, and religion, are incorporated in this mandala for human consciousness.

16. WELCOME!

His Holiness the Dalai Lama and President Nelson Mandela at the Parliament of the World's Religions in Cape Town. Its logo is shown below.

ple of a typical mammal) the vast majority of neurons are not sensors or effectors and so the vast fraction of signals introduced into this network will be from intrinsic sources, and as we have seen there is good reason to believe that much of this is spontaneous and uncorrelated with any external pattern or internal need.

One final troublesome attribute that makes brains unsuitable as computers is that in even modestly large brains (such as in even small vertebrates), connectional patterns are quite degenerate. There is not precise control of connectivity during development. Surprisingly there is only minimal genetic specification of connectivity provided during embryogenesis and from a remarkably limited number of molecular signals, when compared with the astronomical number of precise connections in need of specification. In fact, contrary to what might be expected, large mammalian brains (such as our own brains) do not appear to use significantly more genetic information for their construction than do the smallest mammalian brains (such as mouse brains), even though the numbers of connections must differ by many orders of magnitude. This is yet a further humbling realization.

So our brains are not wired up in point-to-point detail from the start. Not even close! We could hardly expect neuronal connection patterns to be the biological equivalent of logic gates or even signal processing chips found in digital computers. In fact, most of the details that generate the complex functional maps in the brain are generated *post hoc* by a kind of mini-Darwinian process in which neurons compete with one another for a limited number of connection sites, and are eliminated or selectively retained by virtue of how the signals they carry interact with signals from other neurons with converging competing connections For a much more detailed account and many examples I direct the reader to my book *The Symbolic Species*, especially the chapter titled 'A Darwinian Electrician'.

Brains are not made of signal processing and circuitry components that are even vaguely well-suited to fill the requirements for computations in the normal sense of this word. In this kind of network computing would be pointless. There is, I believe, only one alternative: all this noisiness must be a feature, not a bug.

There's another approach in which noise is a feature. It's suggested by the very facts that make the computational approach appear so ill-fitted to brains. It is also reflected in the way brains use their own intrinsic signal processing in a kind of mini-Darwinian competition to generate the fine details of functional circuitry during development. Indeed, this developmental logic can be seen as the physical expression of this underlying signal processing logic, which merely decreases in the extent of its cellular level consequent with maturity

The approach is to think of neural signal processing as a variant of an evolutionary process. Evolution is the epitome of a noisy non-linear ampliative process, that, although unpredictable in its details, doesn't produce messy results, and in fact has produced some truly elegant and complex forms and functions, well fitted to the unique and idiosyncratic contexts in which they arise.

In summary, I believe we have good evidence for thinking that the adaptive complexity of mental action emerges moment to moment, like novel evolutionary adaptations—unprecedented and yet conditioned by what has come before—from the interactions of intrinsically noisy neurons, arranged into chaos-producing complex networks, and shaped by the competition and selection among signals that results. Like all evolutionary processes, then, we can understand cognition as what I call an originative process. It is at base chaotic and unpredictable, and yet produces 'fitted' and highly structured consequences spontaneously; biased perhaps by the accumulated constraints of an evolutionary and experiential past but still without being prefigured or preformed in that past. This is a self-creative dynamic, unlike the products of design processes. Such intentionality as might be described from this perspective, is ultimately *post hoc*. It is a product, not a cause. In this view our self-experience is self-generated, not given and immutable from without and before, but it is also free and open in some sense as well.

This, then, is the starting point for the argument for evolutionary emergence as the basis of conscious experience. From this perspective life and consciousness can be seen to be deeply interrelated, not just because consciousness has evolved in living things, but because they are each manifestations of a common underlying creative dynamic. Life and this one of its rare and special functional attributes, consciousness, are not just products of biological evolution, but are at many levels evolutionary emergent processes in action. To reiterate this astonishing hypothesis in very simple and unambiguous terms: I believe that the experience of being alive and sentient is what it feels like to *be* evolution.

In a world that is chaotic at base and in which orderliness and the semblance of fittedness just happen to 'fall out' of the statistics of entropy with replication (evolution in its broadest sense), there is no essential intentionality or purpose. That sense of it which we experience ourselves to be part of must be seen as *post hoc* in nature and not *a priori*. But does this commit us to a world in which spirituality is a fiction and value is ungrounded? Are human ethical predispositions merely, as some would suggest, contingent on the social predispositions evolved in our paleolithic ancestors? Only, I think, if we restrict our understandings of these as requiring a priori existence rather than emergent existence.

Post hoc-ness is the rub, but it is also the unrecognized promise in the demise of essentialism. Indeed, I think that the trade is a good one. A universe that we imagine requiring prior intentionality, prior design, and prior meaningfulness, implies that we must conceive of a spirituality that is also prefigured, in which my efforts to create meaningfulness are ultimately derivative, in which my intuition that I am the source of myself and the mover of my thoughts is an illusion. A universe that we imagine to arise spontaneously, in which fittedness, intentionality, and purpose are *post hoc* attributes that evolve and emerge *de novo* from prior chaos, is also a universe in which spirituality is emergent as well, in which the experience of self, of being an evolutionary process, is not prefigured, but is truly originative, something out of nothing.

Spiritual Emergence

This is the trade that I think science is about to offer us. Emergentism in exchange for essentialism. It could be a bleak trade, if we persist in thinking in essentialistic terms, because it suggests that all spirituality and value will dissolve into dead, blind mechanism. But there is another possible interpretation. It means giving up the independence of self experience from the physical world, giving up the persistence of self irrespective of the entropy of physical bodies, giving up preformed intelligence, values, and meaning, and accepting suffering and pointlessness along with a view that the harshness of the world may not have a purpose in some divine imagination. It means an identification with the physical and an abandonment of simple notions of transcendental spirit. It means embracing the transience and post hoc character of evolutionary emergence as the essence of experience and spirit. It means accepting that value and meaning are not prefigured either divinely or in our genes, but are attributes that have evolved symbolically, and so can be created from whole cloth and can be destroyed. It means that evolutionary information processing in some form is the physical correlate to subjective experience and is therefore (wherever it is found) its embodiment, subject to considerations of value. In an emergent view, value is a new order of fittedness in the world, that cannot be taken for granted but must be shepherded so as to grow and possibly give rise to yet new considerations of value, hitherto unrecognized. In a world where everything is emergent, nothing is intrinsically meaningful and valuable, but as a result meaning and value become more rare and more fragile.

So, in answer to Tennyson's eternal question: It does indeed appear as though we move ourselves! And we do so by the same logic as the whole of creation moves itself toward orderliness and meaningfulness: by the spontaneous self-emergent hand of evolution. As without, so within. Perhaps, in looking back on this way of reconceiving the world from a timeless perspective, we can still say that from this imagined God's eye view, the world is meaning and mind, because experience is incessantly created within its turning. The view from evolution is not, then, just a new narrative for explaining the emergence of order and purpose in the world and how we fit into it. It may also offer a new story about the everyday miraculous emergence of spirit—a vision of why there is experience rather than nothing.[3]

---

3. This chapter is a much-expanded reworking of my 'Giving up the Ghost: The Epic of Spiritual Emergence'. *Science and Spirit* 10: 2, pp 16–17 (1999).

9

How Close Is Science to Understanding Consciousness?

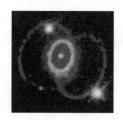

George Johnson

For all the efforts of psychologists, neuroscientists, and philosophers, the puzzle of consciousness remains intractable. Is it possible that our modern civilization is no closer to the answer than were the ancient Anasazi?

I don't believe in ghosts. But standing inside the fallen stone walls of the ruins of Yapashi, I can almost feel the presence of the hundreds of souls who once inhabited this abandoned plateau. Their disappearance left the pueblo—isolated deep inside the Bandelier wilderness in northern New Mexico—one of the loneliest places on Earth. About the only sound, other than wind blowing through ponderosa pines in the canyon below, is the ringing of blood rushing through the vessels in my eardrums, the buzzing of a brain contemplating the weird feeling of being alive.

Halfway through this millennium, Yapashi teemed with human life—a way station, archeologists believe, for the Anasazi, ancestors of the Pueblo Indians who now live east of here along the Rio Grande. All around where I am walking, people once cooked rabbits, made pottery, danced to appease their invisible gods. Spirits seem to hover everywhere. Just beyond the edge of the pueblo, you can still see two stone mountain lions crouching on the ground, symbols of an old religion in which everything—rocks, rivers, mountains, thunder and lightning—was aware and alive.

What were these people thinking as they looked out at the distant mountains and up at the stars? What was it like to see the world through their eyes? These questions preoccupy me every time I take the six-mile hike to Yapashi, up and down the sides of the intervening canyons, across the pine-covered mesa tops. When I arrive, all that remains of the ancient ponderings are material clues, bits of inanimate matter carefully shaped by conscious minds.

Consciousness—the undeniable presence at the core of our being—may be more a mystery now than it was to the Yapashi. This year marks the end of what was grandiosely christened the Decade of the Brain. In the last ten years, scientists have used new scanning techniques to see which parts of the brain light up when you listen to music, read a book, or recall a buried memory. They have even uncovered neuronal circuits involved in mathematical computation. But all this has only served to deepen the mystery. The brain indeed appears to be a biological computer. So where in the neurological wiring is the source of consciousness? How does a three-pound glob of cerebral flesh exude thoughts and know that it is alive?

At the edge of a kiva, an underground ceremonial chamber whose rock walls collapsed long ago, I spot a broken shard of white-glazed pottery deliberately emblazoned with precise black lines. Turning it over with my fingers, I marvel at the pleasing geometric pattern. What made the potter decide to use this particular design? So little is known about the people of Yapashi or the meaning of their markings, but staring at the potsherd you immediately feel a sense of kinship, a connection across the centuries with a mind at play—the existence long ago of a contemplative individual. A self.

The potter's artistic inventiveness would seem, on the surface, to confer no real advantage in the Darwinian struggle for survival. Learning to make vessels to store food and carry water would give a tribe an edge in the game of life. But why expend the energy to decorate them? And what use was served by the spirals and zigzags the Anasazi carved into the sides of the volcanic cliffs throughout this region? What is it that drives us—both ancient artists and modern scientists—to dwell so intently on the abstract rhythms called patterns?

Turning my head eastward, I can barely see on the horizon a radio telescope pointing its white steel dish at the sky, a reminder that this isolated world is only a few miles from Los Alamos National Laboratory, where cosmology and theoretical physics are now pursued as avidly as weapons research. From etching patterns on rocks, people have gone to contemplating patterns in the sky and in the particles that make up the universe. But the patterns that fascinate us most are the ones inside our heads, in the land of the inner self.

Materialists versus New Mysterians

Throughout much of the century, speculating about the nature of consciousness was a sure way for a scientist to be labeled an eccentric or a crank. But as the picture we've drawn of the universe becomes more and more refined, this vacuum in our understanding only looms larger, begging to be filled. Since the mid-1990s, psychologists, philosophers, neuroscientists, physicists, mathematicians, and other academics have flocked to interdisciplinary jamborees with titles like *Toward a Science of Consciousness*, and have issued one book after another laying out their conflicting visions.

On one side are materialists of various stripes, sure that the inner light can, like everything else, be explained scientifically—in terms of matter, energy, and information. On the other side are the 'New Mysterians', named by their opponents in honor of the 1960s rock band Question Mark and the Mysterians. They believe that consciousness is so far outside the domain of conventional science that it may be the one pattern we never understand.

For those who hope that, in time, science will answer every question, the rallying cry of the materialists is reassuring: the mind is what the brain does. As the trillion brain cells called neurons communicate with electrochemical signals, intelligence, awareness and all the mysterious inner feelings emerge like a simulation run on a biological computer. Francis Crick, co-discoverer of the double-helical structure of DNA, has starkly described this view in his book entitled *The Astonishing Hypothesis: The Scientific Search for the Soul:* "You, your joys and your sense of personal identity and free will, are in fact no more than the behavior of a vast assembly of nerve cells and their associated molecules."

In fact, to many neuroscientists, there is nothing astonishing about the hypothesis at all. Explaining consciousness, they assume, will turn out to be no more of a philosophical problem than explaining life—as interlocking whorls of chemistry. What really would floor them would be to find that the mind could not be entirely explained in terms of neuronal circuitry.

It's not too difficult to imagine how billions of brain cells trading signals process the information people need to survive. There are circuits for detecting patterns in the light that falls on the retina, circuits for teasing the phonemes of language from vibrations of sound. From this information the brain builds models of the world. So why not models of one's own behavior? Could this crude sense of self-awareness be what we mean by consciousness?

In his *tour de force, Consciousness Explained,* the philosopher Daniel Dennett showed how neuronal machinery might even give rise to the stream of consciousness, the inner voice that plays constantly in our heads. The brain, in this view, is a sense-making machine, engaged in a constant internal debate. Is that a herd of elk grazing over in the valley, or a cluster of pinyon trees? And over there: is that a huge snowcapped mountain or a low-hanging cumulus cloud? In Dennett's theory, competing teams of neurons silently weigh and discard the possibilities: it can't be a mountain because the whole thing just moved.

The Zombie Problem

From the pandemonium, bubbling just below the surface of awareness, a single narrative emerges—the voice of the inner 'I' conducting its running story about what seems to be going on in the world. Consciousness, then, is a tale-spinning computer, what Dennett calls "the Joycean machine." The implication is that there is no reason a properly programmed digital computer couldn't be made equally aware. And that is where Dennett's opponents rise up with their objections. One can imagine a robot that is aware of its surroundings and even aware of its place in its surroundings. But could these rudimentary cogitations ever be accompanied by the profound feeling of inhabiting vast mental spaces?

Of course, the robot could operate perfectly well without agonizing over its own existence. But so, it seems, could we. Philosophers call this 'the zombie problem'. If the point of life were simple survival, creatures could conceivably have evolved that performed all the functions people do—building houses, villages, civilizations—but without the sensation of being alive. What purpose does the feeling of consciousness, of inner experience, really serve?

In the mid-1970s, the psychologist Julian Jaynes created a sensation with an intimidatingly titled book, *The Origin of Consciousness in the Breakdown of the Bicameral Mind*. People, he declared, indeed used to be zombies, with no more feeling of I-ness than the living dead. For centuries they were steered through life by persistent inner voices, as controlling circuits in the right side of the brain sent signals to the left side. Modern people experience these thoughts as the sound of the inner self. But in the beginning, Jaynes says, they were interpreted as the voices of gods. "There were no private ambitions, no private grudges, no private frustrations, no private anything." As the world grew more complicated, this 'bicameral mind' broke down. The two sides of the brain became more closely intertwined and consciousness, the sense of being a self, was born. The spirits were replaced by the ego, the I.

From studying ancient texts like the *Iliad* and the *Odyssey*, Jaynes concluded that in Europe and Asia consciousness arose around 3,000 years ago. When the Asiatic tribes believed to be the ancestors of all Native Americans crossed the Bering land bridge at least 12,000 years ago, could they still have been Jaynesian robots haunted by inner voices? Had consciousness dawned by the late thirteenth century when the Anasazi abandoned their empire on the Colorado Plateau, dispersing to places like Yapashi, and eventually settling in the pueblos along the Rio Grande?

We have no way of knowing. Science can study the signs of self-awareness: drawings on rock walls and pottery, written words, facial expressions. But the only consciousness anyone has access to is the private world inside oneself. In trying to map this unique geography, the scientific method of separating subject and object breaks down. The subject is the object, and in thinking about thinking we get caught in dizzying regresses of introspection.

No wonder archeologists have habitually regarded ancient peoples as automatons, moved around like pawns by geographical forces. Why did the southwest pueblo cultures so often build on mesa tops, like Yapashi, when the source of water and the best farmland was down below on the canyon floors? The common textbook explanation is that the villagers were defending themselves against enemies. But maybe they were just enjoying the view.

One can always find a reductive answer. When the Anasazi scratched their patterns on the rocks, maybe they were just instinctively marking territory like ancient gangs. Even the curiosity that drives modern astronomers to explore the night sky could be no more than an outgrowth of the primitive need to watch for invaders.

It all seems so logical, and so unsatisfying. I pick up a shard of glassy black obsidian, wondering it it's a flake left by the maker of an arrowhead or by the insentient weathering of nature. My visual sensors register black and shiny. My tactile sensors register the sharpness of the edge. But I also experience the feeling, both subtle and intense, of seeing and holding the rock: the sharpness of the sharp, the blackness of the black.

The immediacy of subjective experience is so overwhelming that the New Mysterians believe conventional science will never explain it. Their predecessors, the Old Mysterians, were dualists, who saw mind as a spiritual essence separate from matter. Members of the new wave assume that consciousness is a natural feature of the brain matter.

The Return of Panpsychism

The problem, as Colin McGinn argues in *The Mysterious Flame*, is that people simply haven't evolved enough to understand it, and probably never will. The most provocative of these skeptics, David Chalmers, offers a strange kind of hope: he believes that the impenetrability of consciousness is a clue that science needs to start over again from scratch and carve up the world in a whole new way.

"The physical structure of the world—the exact distribution of particles, fields, and forces in space-time—is logically consistent with the absence of consciousness," he recently wrote, "so the presence of consciousness is a further fact about our world." Science has been treating consciousness as something secondary, to be explained in terms of existing concepts. Chalmers believes it will be necessary to admit consciousness into science as an irreducible thing-in-itself, along with matter, energy, space, and time. Then perhaps we will truly understand the universe.

It seems absurd to think that this newfound quality would happen to reside only in human heads. So Chalmers has joined a handful of philosophers who reluctantly entertain the possibility that what we call consciousness might somehow pervade the material world. This notion, panpsychism ('mind everywhere'), is not so different from what the Anasazi believed—that everything is full of spirits. And so we return, full circle, to the philosophy of Yapashi.

The idea seems crazy. But so, a century ago, did the notion that a lump of seemingly inert matter holds vast amounts of energy—the discovery that put Los Alamos on the map and almost erased Hiroshima.

The modern Pueblo Indians, who trace their ancestry to Yapashi and other nearby ruins, teach that northern New Mexico is the center of the universe. Four sacred mountains, one for each direction, mark the boundaries of this mythological world. But the cosmologists, at Los Alamos and elsewhere, say there is no center. The universe, as Freeman Dyson put it, is infinite in all directions.

As I look one last time at the mountainous panorama, it's easy to understand the Pueblo view. The center is right here where I am standing, at the focus of my awareness. In trying to make sense of the world, we fight to overcome such parochial feelings. But future archeologists—if they are able to decipher the scratchings we leave in our books and on our computer disks—will probably understand, and maybe even improve upon our confusion.[1]

---

1. This chapter first appeared as 'Terra Incognita' in the *New York Times Magazine* (17 October 1999), pp. 132–34.

References

Chalmers, David. 1996. *The Conscious Mind: In Search of a Fundamental Theory.* New York: Oxford University Press.

Crick, Francis. 1994. *The Astonishing Hypothesis: The Scientific Search for the Soul.* New York: Scribners.

Dennett, Daniel C. 1991. *Consciousness Explained.* Boston: Little, Brown.

Dyson, Freeman. 1988. *Infinite in All Directions.* New York: Harper and Row.

Jaynes, Julian. 1976. *The Origin of Consciousness in the Breakdown of the Bicameral Mind.* Boston: Houghton Mifflin.

Johnson, George. 1995. *Fire in the Mind: Science, Faith, and the Search for Order.* New York: Knopf.

McGinn, Colin. 1999. *The Mysterious Flame: Conscious Minds in a Material World.* New York: Basic Books.

10

Cosmology and Religion

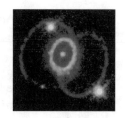

𝒢EORGE 𝒻.ℛ. 𝓔LLIS

There are issues that science will never be able to settle. Science and religion explore different aspects of reality using some of the same methods. Intimations of transcendence in our daily life point to the existence of a beneficent Creator.

I approach this topic as a scientist who has already devoted some time and energy to thinking about issues broadly in this area. My underlying position is that while individual commitment and practice are fundamentally important to a spiritual life, they need to be underpinned by or at least related to a viable world view, otherwise they will in the end wither away—and may indeed ultimately turn out to be based on self-deception or delusion. Developing a viable intellectual position in this area is important to me, not as a substitute for personal commitment or action, but as a necessary concomitant.

When we compare science and religion, one viable view (Ellis 1993b; Murphy and Ellis 1996; Barbour 1997) is that they explore different aspects of the same underlying reality, together enabling us to attain a reasonably comprehensive understanding of the fundamental nature of things that is both consistent and viable. Either science or religion is incomplete without the other, for providing an adequate worldview. Each in turn must be supplemented by experience and understanding in practical arts and methods in order to allow a satisfactory overall approach to life.

Both science and spirituality, properly understood, rely on the same broad methods of intellectual understanding, but these are applied in somewhat different ways to different data. Science attains near-certainty by limiting itself to very specific quantifiable issues, but consequently cannot look at many issues of vital importance to human beings. Theology—the attempt to put religious issues on a rational basis—uses broader classes of data which deal with much wider issues—of major significance to everyday life— and so where much less certainty is attainable.

Both rely on judgment and discernment in their practice; both in effect use authorities and scriptures to proclaim the current canon; both test their views in relation to data, but theology relies much more on personal data while science depends more on public data. In principle science relies solely on public data; in practice it is not possible to describe everything about even the simplest experiment. The language of description is a shorthand that may or may not give a complete description of all significant aspects of the actions and experience of the experimenter. A myriad of minor details, decisions and judgments are omitted from the publicly available description.

However, if properly pursued, both science and theology allow a very similar attitude of questioning and a process of testing, which in the long term leads to a continually improving representation and understanding of reality. In both cases this testing process needs to inform and be informed by experiential methods of learning which ensure that theory and practice are closely related and properly integrated.

By its rigorous method of mathematical modelling and testing, science attains great certainty in limited domains of understanding of how the physical world functions, and this is what underlies the technological revolutions that have transformed our lives. By contrast, theology is able to attain much less certainty, indeed there is no widely accepted canon of theological belief across all cultures (such as there is in the case of science), even though people of faith may be able to live lives based on an unshakeable belief that is grounded in their own experiences.

Curiously, each touches deeply on some fundamentals of the other and on important underlying attitudes, yet neither deeply touches the practice of the other, provided one has already in both cases adopted a mature, open, and enquiring attitude—which is in any case fundamental to pursuing either enterprise with integrity. Given that the practice of science per se has long been independent of overt religious influence and has developed a mature, open approach—by and large—the point here then is that most of the religious viewpoints that are excluded by science are in fact immature religious viewpoints, being also excluded on purely religious grounds if one adopts a 'right' attitude.

What I have just said needs to be defended: what religious attitudes am I rejecting here, and on what grounds?

Many, perhaps most, of those religious attitudes that are rejected by scientists as immature or objectionable (Sagan 1997) can also be rejected from the religious side if one adopts a coherent approach to religion that is not only in tune with the present age but also with millennia-old spiritual traditions that have always been aware of the major pitfalls in religious attitudes and practice. This approach is in essence epitomized in the attitudes of my own present spiritual home, the Quaker tradition (Gorman 1986; Hubbard 1976)—which claim means that my approach to religious viewpoints would be self-serving and empty, were it not that I have consciously chosen this tradition rather than being born into it or having drifted into it unthinkingly. Historically this tradition has been sympathetic to and had strong links with science—as for example in the life of Arthur Stanley Eddington, one of the foremost astrophysicists and relativists of the twentieth century. Furthermore there is evidence that this broad approach occurs in almost all major religious traditions, albeit emerging in a variety of ways with very different surface structure (Butler and Butler 1996; Edwards 1983; Paden 1992).

I will now look at the following issues: 1. The limits of science, something worth considering given the power of science and the omnicompetence claimed for it by some. My discussion locates the religious themes pursued here as not being related to a 'God of the gaps' but rather as being essential in consideration of boundary issues that science by its very nature will never be able to answer. 2. The possible basis for a comprehensive worldview that, as well as taking science seriously, consistently includes a spiritual element that relates to the Transcendent. Fleshing this out depends on finding some viable view on: 3. The nature of

Transcendence. Here is where some religious traditions are accepted and others excluded. If such a viewpoint is to be held in a way that is compatible with modern scientific understanding, there must be some kind of evidence for it; I will develop that evidence by pointing out a variety of: 4. Intimations of Transcendence. With this basis set up, the main science-religion relation is already defined in broad terms. I can then review the theme of: 5. Physical cosmology and spiritual issues: what are the relations between them?

A traditional religious view is viable and appropriate, provided one avoids some of the monarchical trends in religious approach, rather adopting a kenotic worldview (Ellis 1994). Substantial support for such a view comes from consideration of the broad sweep of evidence. I don't claim any significant originality in what is presented below; much of what is stated here has been known by many people, perhaps for thousands of years. However the particular integration of these ideas given here may be useful at the present time.

The Limits of Science

The fundamental issue here is that as the achievements of science accumulate and our understanding of what it is able to achieve increases, we are in a position to start delimiting what science cannot do. We can then identify some of the boundaries beyond which science will never be able to go because of its very nature. Specifically, I mention three areas (Ellis 1993b; Murphy and Ellis 1996):

Science cannot deal with aesthetic issues, because there can be no scientific criteria for 'beautiful' or 'ugly'; no experimental apparatus can scientifically prove a greater aesthetic value in one painting than in another. Art lies outside the domain of science.

Science cannot tackle moral issues, because there can be no scientific criteria for 'good' or 'bad'; no experimental test can prove that some action ought not to have been taken, because 'ought' is not a scientific category. Thus ethics lies outside the domain of science.

Science cannot deal with metaphysical issues, including those that underlie science; specifically, it cannot answer any of the fundamental cosmological questions (Ellis 1999): *Why are there any regularities in nature that can be described by physical laws? Why do these regular behaviors have the form they do? That is, why do the laws of physics have the specific form we determine by scientific investigation? Why is there a universe? Why does anything exist?*

There are various philosophical possibilities here but science cannot choose among them, for there is no experimental way to investigate these questions. We can investigate the implications of various options, but ambiguity will remain: a variety of consistent possibilities is available. Making a choice between metaphysical options lies outside the domain of science.

Various writings explicitly or implicitly claim that science can resolve some or all of these issues; but these all of necessity proceed on the basis of some *a priori* philosophical assumption that is untestable and chosen on the basis of individual experience and prejudice. Thus the challenge to scientists who wish to extend their theorizing beyond the limits of empirical science into issues regarding the deeper meaning of our lives is to be open to all the possibilities, and to pay proper attention to metaphysical and other philosophical issues which underlie science and in particular underlie physical cosmology. These are seldom dealt with adequately; indeed a simplistic technocratic approach ('there are only technical issues involved here') is often taken as a substitute for properly thinking the issues through.

This problem becomes acute in relation to the very existence and nature of the laws of physics, for example when authors either assume that various fundamental physical principles were in some sense valid and held sway when the universe did not exist, even before the beginning of space and time (and hence can causally give rise to the universe), or when they claim that they can arise out of pure chaos. The first is difficult to make sense of unless one adopts a more or less theological position—it's an implicit recognition of a transcendent reality; and the second is very problematic; can one really create order out of total chaos or pure chance? In the end this is an incoherent idea; order (laws of physics, the nature of matter) can only emerge out of a substratum of previous order, for otherwise there is no foundation from which it can develop. Again, 'chance' is not a cause, as is often assumed in scientific discourse—it is rather a statement that we do not know the cause. Furthermore, the fundamental problem of initial conditions for the universe cannot be resolved by science, despite valiant efforts, because science cannot conclusively treat unique events; it is designed to handle classes of similar events (Ellis 1999b).

In all these cases, the point is that these are not 'gaps' in present day science that will some day be filled; they are boundaries beyond which science cannot go. They define some of the limits of science. Anyone who claims that science by itself can deal adequately with these issues (in the sense of providing a properly testable theory that can reach scientifically based valid conclusions) is in fact knowingly or unknowingly transgressing the bounds of science. This may occur through wishful thinking, or perhaps through trying to use the prestige of science to claim certainty in buttressing some form of personal prejudice or strongly held philosophical opinion; neither is legitimate. However this often happens (Ellis 1998; Bowker 1995).

While much attention has been given recently to the problem of postmodern interpretations of science and the denial that science says anything about reality—a denial that no working scientist with experimental experience will assent to—much less attention has been given to the tendency to claim for science more that it can in fact achieve, which is also a real problem. In particular, this arises with religious issues (Ellis 1998). Science can neither prove nor disprove the correctness of a sensible religious stance towards metaphysical issues; neither science nor philosophy can give a conclusive answer as to the existence of God. Any claims to the contrary—either way—should be resisted as illegitimate.

The problem lies in claims of certainty, which is unattainable with respect to ultimate reality (Ellis 1998; Priest 1995). Neither science nor religion can attain intellectual certainty about ultimate issues. This does not prevent us from having deep convictions which may amount to personal certainty, but that's not the same as scientific or philosophic proof. Most of the errors on both sides come from trying to claim certainty where it is not achievable. The illusion of certainty is usually achieved by excluding yourself from the same criticism that you apply to other people's analysis [6,24]. The necessity is acknowledging the cultural and intellectual limitations of each approach to knowledge, including the 'scientific' approaches, and the way they restrict the nature of the conclusions attained.

The Possible Basis for a Comprehensive Worldview

In relating science to spirituality, there is a need for a coherent approach to Cosmology in the broad sense (Ellis 1993b; Swimme 1996), relating daily life, the world, and the universe. This requires an integration of scientific and everyday views of life: it enables the scientist to be a coherent believer, and can arrive at a position in which a traditional spiritual approach is essentially vindicated— provided one takes a strong view of religion as well as of science, and adopts a pre-power play view of religious reality, kenotic rather than monarchic, implying the 'emptying' of the self rather than self-aggrandisement. This standpoint will be explained further in the next section; it can form the basis of a consistent transcendent worldview.

We now have three issues to consider: 1. How broad or narrow is the focus of cosmology? Once a decision has been made on that, we can turn to: 2. What is the appropriate range of data to take into account, to address such a viewpoint? Finally there is an issue of congruence of approaches: 3. How can the full range of issues be developed in a broadly compatible way, without obvious areas of disagreement?

MICROPHYSICS => COSMOLOGY

This is the standard line of argument (Ellis 1993b; Bondi 1962; Harrison 1983; Silk 1998). We use astronomical data to support the model of the universe expanding from a hot Big Bang, where densities and temperatures were indefinitely high. As the universe expanded and cooled, a series of well-understood interactions took place: nucleosynthesis of light elements out of elementary particles; growth of large density inhomogeneities and oscillation of smaller ones due to the competition between gravitational and pressure forces; decoupling of matter and radiation after electrons and nuclei combined to form atoms; growth of structure from the perturbations at last scattering through the force of gravitational attraction, leading to formation of stars, galaxies, and clusters of galaxies.

COSMOLOGY => MICROPHYSICS

However it's also possible to some degree that the nature of the universe in turn affects the nature of microphysics, for example the strength of the gravitational coupling constant or the direction of the arrow of time. Indeed writers such as Bondi and Sciama emphasize the unity and interconnectedness of the universe, so that if you study any one detail long enough, you should be able to tell about it all—a train ticket, for example, implies the expansion of the universe.

The former approach now dominates, but some thoughtful books (such as Ellis 1998b and Harrison 1983) still consider the latter. The usual anthropic principle arguments (Barrow and Tipler 1986) are examples, studying why the universe has the remarkable property of being such as to allow the existence of human life. However they are too narrowly focused—they don't relate to humanity specifically, despite the name; rather they relate to the possibility of existence of any complex physical structure. We need to take into account truly human issues such as ethical or moral ones to take the argument seriously in regard to humanity (Ellis 1998b; Murphy and Ellis 1996). So the essential claim here is that we also need to take these kinds of issues seriously if we want to talk about Cosmology in the broad sense—the relation of the universe to humanity—rather than simply cosmology—the physical evolution of the universe but not its philosophical implications.

DATA AND DISCERNMENT

It follows that when we approach the cosmology-spirituality interface we must take the relevant data into account too. We can legitimately study cosmology (small 'c') without this data, then this is a complete study at its own level of the hierarchy of the sciences, disconnected from the more fundamental issues; but then we must not start to make pronouncements on such issues. If we want to do so legitimately, we must take into account the relevant (higher-level) data, and insist that our world view or theory accommodate this.

There is still a major problem to be faced here: namely the issue of discernment: What is reliable and what is unreliable data? What is the essential (or 'guiding') data as opposed to the misleading (secondary) data?

This is already a problem in science, but is much more acute in the broad area of claimed religious or spiritual experience. Hence a key element is developing tests of discernment of what is valid and what is not valid data. However this has indeed been a long-standing concern in the area of spirituality; there is much experience to go on in developing such tests. The approach of scientism is to assume that none of this data has any validity. However that stance—which is conceivably correct—cannot be developed adequately without indeed looking at the data seriously. If that stance is held without serious consideration of the full range of data, open-mindedly considering whether it can reflect reality or not, then the conclusions arrived at will be determined by this choice of a subset of data, and will simply reflect whatever prejudice was used in selecting that data.

As to the third question, the congruence of approaches: this is firstly based in using a suitable epistemological approach (Murphy and Ellis 1996; Murphy 1990), a key part of which is an awareness of the nature of knowledge representation, by use of models of whatever kind, and the limitations of their use (Priest 1995; Soskice 1992). In particular, we must avoid approaches that confuse models with reality. We need an awareness of the partial nature of representation of reality by models, and the limits of use of each one we employ. This is particularly relevant when we consider models of the transcendent, which by its very definition cannot be fully captured by any description or analysis based on our experience.

Secondly it is based in ensuring no specific unacceptable anomalies between the different approaches to the different areas when one tries to integrate them. Paradox is often a central feature of spirituality (Elliott 1987; Palmer 1980), particularly because our partial view of the transcendent whole may be misleading. Thus one must be very careful not to reject a theory by mistaking a genuine paradox in an acceptable approach for an anomaly that should lead to the rejection of the approach. They may be hard to distinguish.

Finally the congruence is based on a general consonance of approach that is partly a matter of taste. While science can raise metaphysical questions but not determine a philosophical view, it can perhaps support some philosophical positions as being more in consonance with the scientific method than others, for example in terms of openness and readiness to explore alternatives; and in particular in terms of looking for testable causal reasons for what happens rather than explanations in terms of undetectable demons and spirits (Sagan 1997). But when any such claim is used to reject a worldview, this has to be treated with the greatest care: it can easily turn out to be just a way of supporting previously adopted prejudice. The vital question here is whether all philosophic positions consonant with a scientific view have been considered, or whether some have been refused consideration on emotional or political grounds, or simply because of personal prejudice.

The specific need is to distinguish between well-considered religious positions that may be consonant with science, and superstition. The problem of course is that some religious positions are indeed superstitious. However a trained intellect should be able to distinguish these from those that are not—just as we are able to distinguish pseudo-science from science. We do not claim that astronomy does not make sense because some people believe in astrology; similarly it is not sensible to claim no religious positions are compatible with science because there are some that are not. Thus an openness of approach is required that will take all the alternatives seriously. This is indeed in principle the scientific way; however this courtesy is not always extended to approaches used in looking at the broader area considered here (Ellis 1998; Bowker 1995). It remains an essential ingredient in an open approach to knowledge.

The Nature of Transcendence

Transcendence is to a weak extent captured by the religious traditions; it is deeply encountered in some religious experience and practice. However the point now is that, properly interpreted, it profoundly underlies all everyday experience—it is not to be specifically found in way-out esoteric phenomena but rather in the properly understood nature of the ordinary (see for instance Berger 1990; Hubbard 1976)—which in fact is remarkable but we have come to take it for granted. If seen properly it becomes extraordinary for it is all sacramental. The transcendent is immanent in every time and place. Thus the view I support is that, based on a broad variety of data discussed below, we can indeed consistently and logically propose a view of God as creator and transcendent and also as active in the universe in an immanent kenotic way. This view can be evidenced by a mass of data, not of 'way out' experiences, but of experiences from everyday life.

However this position is not consistent with all views of the nature of God. Rather it is specific to a kenotic-theological-ethical view as a consistent world picture that validates all levels in the hierarchy of sciences in a coherent way and that accepts an evolving universe and the evolution of life. Hence I see a kenotic understanding and love as the overall key to understanding the deep nature of creation: kenosis (or letting go)—a joyous, kind, loving attitude that is generous and creative, and—if needed—willing to give up selfish desires and to sacrifice on behalf of others, but in a humble way, avoiding the pitfall of pride, doing this all in the light of the love of god and gift of grace. Kenosis (Vanstone 1977; Cronin 1996) is seen as the key to understanding morality, God, and thence the created universe (for a detailed exposition see Ellis 1993a; Ellis 1994; Murphy and Ellis 1996).

The evidence comes from a great variety of experience. The basis for why this should be so is theological: this is an essential part of the nature of God. It is here that I reject the many religious traditions that are militant, monarchical, or tyrannical, and accept at least provisionally those that are genuinely loving, freedom-based, and with a strong element of self-sacrifice as an essential ingredient. This includes, but is not restricted to, a major strand of the Christian tradition. It informs the nature of ethical behavior, which should be along these lines in order to be consonant with the nature of reality. The implication is that moral commitment is a real way of interacting with spiritual reality. However it is not the only way: it happens to be the one that is most real to many people at the present time.

What is the evidence for this higher-level vision? It is based on discernment: the gift of seeing what is truly there, which may be obvious yet hidden, or may not be obvious (this is an essential part of the hidden nature of the universe).

Evidence: Intimations of Transcendence

To make a strong case, we need the full range of data: we can see, as channels of transcendence, daily life as well as scientific data. We now consider the different channels of such evidence. The basic common theme I will use is not merely that the evidence exists, at least to some degree, in each case: the essential point will be that in each case, there is more there than is needed. There is a superfluity of abundance in what is achieved by the physical universe. This is the sign of grace.

SCIENTIFIC => METAPHYSICAL ISSUES

The scientifically based support comes from contemplation of the existence of a universe leading to the origin of intelligent life (the anthropic issues, as so often discussed): the required fine-tuning has a metaphysical base, and the creator-designer hypothesis is as persuasive as any—it's fascinating how non-religious cosmologists so often feel compelled to use the image of the creator-God in their discussions. While this has an intellectual base and can be comprehended and argued that way (see Ellis 1993a; Murphy and Ellis 1996), it also has a strong intuitive and experiential component.

The natural world commonly leads to wonder, even awe, in the spectator, particularly when confronted by the miracle of life. What it is that touches each person will be individual and different: it may be birds and butterflies, blue disas, sunset at Noordhoek. This wonder is a legitimate reaction to the self-creative nature of creation. It suggests a beneficent creator God. This is not a logically necessary conclusion: but it is a credible reaction to what we see around us. Given that any physical universe existed, it was not necessary that it lead to this kind of complex structure and function. This is much more than is needed if one simply contemplates the requirements for the existence of a physically realized universe. So the point here is the extraordinary order in nature: it is at a fundamental level expressible as mathematical laws, allowing self-organization properties and emergent order to arise, and results in an intelligible universe giving rise to self-conscious beings who can contemplate that order. The question is what underlies this form of nature, however creation is construed: what is the metaphysical underpinning of cosmology. Some choice has been made somehow amongst all contingent possibilities; that which has occurred allows this extraordinary capacity for structure and life. Thus this—essentially the ages-old design issue—can be seen as an intimation of transcendence: an expression of the creativity of God. It is expressed admirably in the following quotation:

> I like to walk alone on country paths, rice plants and wild grasses on both sides, putting each foot down on the earth in mindfulness, knowing that I walk on the wondrous earth. In such moments, existence is a miraculous and mysterious reality. People usually consider walking on water or in thin air a miracle. But I think the real miracle is not to walk on water or in thin air, but on earth. Every day we are engaged in a miracle which we don't even recognise: a blue sky, white clouds, green leaves, the black, curious eyes of a child—our own two eyes. All is miracle. (Hanh 1991)

MORAL => ETHICAL ISSUES

Given the existence of intelligent life, the question of meaning in the individual's life arises. This relates to ethics which embodies the idea of Telos or purpose. Now to some degree one can put together explanations of generous behavior on the basis of sociobiology arguments. However that is not in any way an adequate explanation of morality: rather it is an exercise in explaining morality away. My view is firstly that morality is real, and secondly that it is based on the nature of God (Murphy and Ellis 1996). This provides a basis for the reality and meaning of concepts such as justice and sympathy, generosity and giving.

True morality goes way beyond anything that sociobiology can accomplish: it entails sacrifice and self-giving love that is incomprehensible in terms of evolutionary mechanisms alone, but makes solid sense when seen as a consequence of the existence of 'that of God' in everyone. It entails the sacrificial reaction based on the potential for change and for good even in the enemy, the attempt to change the hardened heart instead of annihilating the enemy, thus imitating the kenotic and willing suffering of God on behalf of His creation, as specifically revealed to us in the life of Christ. Its reality is made clear in many examples: Mother Teresa, Gandhi, Martin

Luther King, Christ, and Christ's disciples. What we see is more than is needed for the biological functioning of life. It is an intimation of and response to the transcendent nature of God. It is the foundation of an ethics of persuasion and sacrifice instead of coercion and punishment (Ellis 1994; Murphy and Ellis 1996), and hence serves as a criterion of authenticity: any truly valid religion must mirror this quality.

CREATIVITY

One of the characteristics of God is creativity: and one of our possibilities is to mirror that creativity in our own lives, to become "co-creators with God," as Philip Hefner has expressed it. We see this creativity in daily life, in economic achievements, in artistic endeavors, in sport, in education; we see it in scientific discovery and in technical achievement. Again the point is that the time and effort put into this, and the joy that is got out of it, is more than the necessary minimum. Our creation of technology and beauty is much more than is needed to sustain life. It can be regarded as a reflection of the creative nature of God, another intimation of transcendence. One of the hallmarks of real creativity is the giving up of the creator's power in the face of the reality of the created object: a truly creative act requires the creator to acknowledge and respond to the nature and integrity of that which is created, which develops its own inner logic and autonomy (Vanstone 1977). This can be seen in great art and literature.

A specific aspect that has been developed by Peter Berger (1990) is the way that the creativity of humor is a sign of transcendence. A confusion of inside and outside views of human life leads to exposure of the pathos of the human condition, as in the *Peanuts* cartoon strip. The incongruence at the center of humor hints at something beyond, at the greater reality lying behind the appearances of this world, of a larger framework of meaning and life when the limits of this one are stripped away.

AESTHETIC BEAUTY => BEAUTY AS REVELATION

While a created artifact or theory may have functional or technical excellence, it may also have beauty, and again here we see much more than is necessary in the dedication people put into the creation of beauty, and into its appreciation. This is of quite a different character than is simply required to live one's life at a materially satisfactory level. Furthermore the beauty of natural creation is far in excess of what is required by the fact of material existence, or even by the possibility of life; and the human response to this beauty mirrors that fact. Neither in any way demands beauty of the order we see in the world around us, or that we see created lovingly with enormous dedication by men and women. This may again be seen as an indication of transcendence, as intimations of the beauty of the underlying nature of God, calling forth a corresponding response in men and women.

This theme can be developed in depth by referring to the variety of art, its depth and the devotion given to it: in painting (Rembrandt), sculpture, music (Bach, Debussy, Ravel), ballet, plays (Shakespeare), novels (Dostoyevsky, Hugo, Saint-Exupéry), architecture (Gaudi, the Mendel church), photography (Walker Evans), films, handicraft (pottery, weaving, baskets, clothes) to mention just a few. They all provide astonishing evidence of creative capacity and dedication of the kind alluded to above—as well as in other cases providing evidence of self-indulgence and lack of ability; but that is precisely where the issue of discernment arises. This leads to a further theme: the distinction between art that points beyond itself, as opposed to that which points to itself or to the artist. It leads again to the issue of artists and kenosis: the requirement of giving in to the vision. Pursuing this would take us too far off course; the point here is that again we see much more than the necessary minimum: we see a kind of achievement that can indeed evoke awareness of and response to transcendence, in those whose minds are open to it.

LOVE AND JOY

Next, as emphasized by Berger (1990; 1993) and C.S. Lewis (1960), is all the evidence from love and joy: the evidence of the value of the individual seen in both the unreserved love of the mother and baby, and of the lover and loved. While a sociobiological explanation will be valid as far as it goes, it will be a very partial explanation: what we see evidenced around us is more than is needed for the human race's survival. The deeper meaning is seeing this as an intimation of transcendence, indeed of the nature of God, as made explicit in the line from Hugo's *Les Miserables*: "To love another person is to see the face of God." This fits in strongly with the Quaker concept that there is 'that of God' in everyone (Gorman 1986; Hubbard 1976)—we each are both images of and realizations of divine love—which then becomes a guiding feature in how we treat each other. It affirms the value and mysteriousness of the individual. This is beautifully expressed in the following quotation:

> I say to myself as I watch the niece, who is very beautiful: in her this bread is transmuted into melancholy grace. Into modesty, into a gentleness without words. . . . Sensing my gaze, she raised her eyes towards mine, and seemed to smile . . . A mere breath on the delicate face of the waters, but an affecting vision. I sense the mysterious presence of the soul that is unique to this place. It fills me with peace, and my mind with the words: 'This is the peace of silent realms'. I have seen the shining light that is born of the wheat. (Saint-Exupéry 1995)

SPECIFICALLY SPIRITUAL => INTERPRETATIONAL KEYS

Finally there are the specifically spiritual visions and intimations of various kinds, which may sometimes be delusion, but sometimes may be what they claim to be: Visions of transcendence, intimations of the presence and nature of God.

This may take many forms: preconceptual experience of God (Edwards 1983), an awareness of the immanent presence or of a gathered Quaker meeting (Butler and Butler 1996), leading to prayer and contemplation, and the practice of the presence of God; or a sense of transcendence, sometimes a gradual hardening of perception until a definite intimation of what should be done is present as something given to one, rather than representing one's own will (Hubbard 1976).

The sense of divine presence, often within the community of the Church, can be a vehicle for and make a reality of a kenotic Christian vision in accord with centuries-old traditions and patterns of revelation. Many issues arise: how to withdraw one's own will and center down so as to be accessible to this inner voice; how to test for self-delusion and self-interest; how to decide what action to take, however painful or difficult, in response to a felt calling from God; above all, the fundamental issue of pride and humility—remembering the contrast between the Creator and the Created, the finite and the infinite, and so avoiding the temptation to seek to be God, as opposed to being like God. However many centuries of experience with such issues is available, for example in the writings of the saints and mystics of old, these writings must be sharply contrasted with much of what is called 'spirituality' today, which does not have the hallmarks of true spirituality, namely a relation to the transcendent that seriously deals with the above issues; without those concerns being properly met, this is simply self-indulgence or superstition.

In summary, the avenues for intimations of transcendence mentioned above can be represented as shown in Figure 10.1. As mentioned above, the point is not just the existence of these features—

FIGURE 10.1

Different dimensions of experience that give some intimation of a transcendent underlying nature.

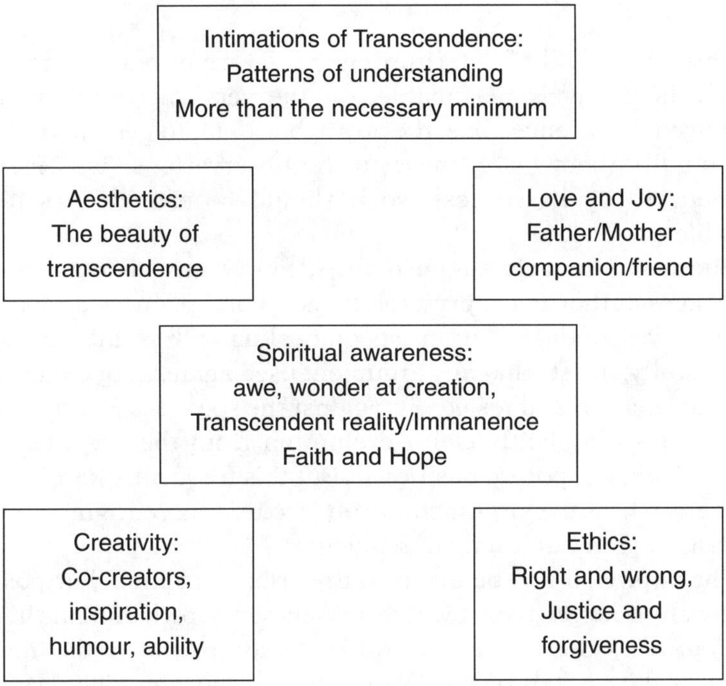

it is the unreasonable joy and illumination they provide, and correspondingly the unreasonable amount of effort that people are prepared to put into them, for example devoting their whole lives to art or music. This is an illustration of the importance of what Berger calls "ecstasy": visions that illuminate and transcend our daily lives, giving us an understanding of a much greater reality that is present but hidden in our daily lives. None of the above gives a logical proof of the reality of what is experienced: rather it exhibits a pattern that you either recognize or don't recognize.

Cosmology and Spiritual Issues: What Are the Relations?

Given this understanding of the nature of transcendence, what are the implications for the science-religion issue?

SCIENTIFIC METHOD AS A BROAD METHOD OF UNDERSTANDING

The broad method of determining the nature of reality should be based, as far as is reasonable, on the very successful method employed in science: use the available data to test hypotheses and modify them in response to the observations. This method is endorsed by its success, so it should be extended as far as possible.

Such an approach: supports the idea of transcendental reality; challenges authority (in principle); insists on openness to data and seriously responding to it; insists on dealing with counter-evidence successfully; insists that any argument used against opposing views be also deployed and tested out against the speaker's position—it is untenable to implicitly claim exemption from the argument you use to dismiss opposing positions. (But this frequently happens, for example when the argument from evolutionary origins is used against religion but not against science.)

The approach can be taken to underlie a skeptical but positive approach to larger issues which is well developed and can handle theological issues in an appropriate way, provided the needed realm of data is taken fully into account (Murphy 1990; Murphy and Ellis 1996).

SCIENTIFIC DISCOVERIES AS BACKGROUND FOR VIABLE THEOLOGY

The nature of the world as determined by science, particularly cosmology, is the background in which we live and make our moral decisions. It excludes certain visions of the universe, for example an unchanging universe or one where we are at the center. It also requires an overall assent to a causally-based universe where physical laws underlie what happens, so superstition is replaced by laws of nature.

Viable theology cannot ignore this; it excludes simplistic conceptions of God acting in the world—for example, it undermines special creation, and calls into doubt the idea of God causing rain to fall in answer to prayer (although, curiously, this is not impossible in terms of physical law: quantum uncertainty combined with chaos theory makes this technically feasible!). However most of these simplistic models were not theologically viable anyhow.

The key issues that arise are not the nature of creation of the universe or the mechanism of evolution, both of which are largely theologically neutral, nor the alleged ability of genes or culture to control completely what we are, which clearly ignores major causal factors; rather the key issues are whether free will is real or not, and whether there is any possibility of some channel of revelation to the human mind, allowing the spiritual experiences claimed in the great religious traditions to be authentic.

Thus there is an important relation between neurology, consciousness, and the transcendental. We do not understand these issues. My view will be that we have sufficient data here that we can require of a viable theory that it accept this data as real and needing to be explained; we will reject a theory of the mind that cannot explain them—just as we will reject a theory of the mind that cannot explain or at least accommodate consciousness, in contrast to those theorists which in essence explain away consciousness rather than accepting its reality.

Apart from these specific issues, one would like a broad consonance between the world seen by science and the theological stance that one wishes to incorporate into a larger coherent worldview. This is true to a considerable degree if one takes a kenotic view of the nature of the universe (Murphy and Ellis 1996). The consonance is one reason why each of the two areas does not significantly influence the practice of the other.

SCIENCE ILLUMINATES ONE SIDE OF THE MIND OF GOD

One can see something of the way God thinks by the way he/she has chosen to create by self-organizing principles enabling existence of moral beings. Thus one can pursue a natural theology along these lines, firstly by finding overall agreement in spirit: there is the nature of divine action as non-coercive and self-creative, and as models of kenosis, there are supernovae dying to give birth to new stars, and animals giving off life to evoke new life.

There is a broad consonance, and lack of definite disjunction; hence science provides models of aspects of theology. This is also true of the epistemology of religion: relativity theory and many viewpoints on religion both illustrate how a variety of different views can be had of some invariant reality—but with these different views strictly constrained and related.

The scientific approach of selecting data to construct a model and then later dealing with the counter-data (broken symmetries) can be seen as a way of approaching the theological issue of good and evil, and particularly the counter-evidence provided by the behaviour of some churches and self-proclaimed believers.

But perhaps most fascinating is the contemplation of God as the supreme technologist: decoding the way nature works is indeed a way of seeing the Mind of God. This used to be the spirit in which scientists such as Newton undertook their work. Most religions do not emphasize thinking of God as a technologist, super-expert in mathematics, physics, chemistry, biochemistry, astronomy, and so on: but this is a viable and fascinating thing to do!

METAPHYSICS PROVIDED BY THEOLOGY AS GROUND FOR SCIENCE

I have emphasized that theology can answer metaphysical questions science cannot tackle, linking them in to larger picture, as for example in the case of creation of the universe and the anthropic issue (Ellis 1993a; Murphy and Ellis 1996). Theology can provide a consilience, in E.O. Wilson's term, linking these metaphysical issues in cosmology to the issue of the foundation of ethics, for example.

Thus we can provide a metaphysical base for science that is otherwise missing or thin by conceiving of an ultimate transcendent reality who creates. Some of the current quantum creation ideas come close to this concept of a creative transcendent reality that precedes the universe: indeed, as has been pointed out by Davies, the way some scientists refer to the laws of physics confers on them many of the properties normally associated with God!

Our metaphysical base does not affect the way science is carried out in practice, except perhaps when it tries to touch issues such as the creation of the universe. Our theological metaphysics insists on recognizing the uncertainties and limitations of science and the ultimate mystery that remains after science has determined all it can, and the metaphysics must be consonant with both the proposed theology and established science, serving as a unified base for both.

ETHICS AND LIFE EXPERIENCE PROVIDE DATA FOR SCIENCE

As has been emphasized above, data from life is valid as a source of understanding of cosmology. Science must be compatible with, for example, the existence of consciousness and free will.

ETHICS PROVIDES THE CONTEXT FOR THE PRACTICE OF SCIENCE

Finally the scientist, even as a scientist, has to make personal choices of an ethical nature—how to spend one's time as well as how to use science. The view put forward here insists on identifying humans as moral agents and denies the possibility of doing science in a moral vacuum: thus one must consider why is it worth doing science, spending resources on it, and devoting one's life to it.

Ethics is based on theology: so this is the real basis (*telos*) for all activity including science. Man being created in the image of God is the ultimate rationale for doing science—we are 'created co-creators'. We have a possibility of understanding reality and the mind of God by being creative ourselves—which involves kenosis in terms of giving up preconceptions in order to see what is there. In the end this activity is part of the worship of God and enables a deeper relationship with God. It also can be viewed simply as giving fulfillment to ourselves as human beings, and as opening up access to technology which has the possibility of greatly improving human life—and also of destroying life and the environment.

So wherever science relates to practical applications it brings with it an obligation to consider its uses and the benefits and dangers of those uses. This is one of the areas where science has been weakest in the past: by insisting on a divorce from issues such as ethics, science has been unable to tackle the ethical issues that inevitably arise in its practice. As a result, it has been able to be used for mass destruction. A holistic view will insist that scientists get some education in ethics—and hence become fuller human beings as they practice their craft, as well as being more responsible in relation to the rest of humanity.

PARTS OF A WHOLE

Both science and theology illuminate an ultimate transcendental reality that cannot be captured by any of the words or models we attempt to use to understand it—they each provide only a very partial illumination: each models part of the whole. Each needs the other for a broad understanding that starts to capture the full dimensions of the reality of the universe.

We can allow a reality to its moral and ethical nature as also to its physical nature, and try to see how they relate to each other; this will inevitably end up considering spiritual and theological aspects. That in turn will allow consideration of a whole range of data on these matters that convey real information on the nature of the universe. The whole will be much more complete and satisfying than the parts, and help us become whole human beings. In the end science cannot dispel the ultimate mystery of creation, nor should it be allowed to diminish our sense of awe at the universe and life. Rather science should help us to understand better the remarkable nature of creation and its mechanisms; spiritual experience and practice can help us understand why it is the way it is. Consonance is possible.

References

Barbour, Ian G. 1997. *Religion and Science: Historical and Contemporary Issues*. New York: Harper.

Barrow, J., and F Tipler. 1986. *The Anthropic Cosmological Principle*. New York: Oxford University Press.

Berger, Peter L. 1990. *A Rumor of Angels*. New York: Anchor.

———. 1993. *A Far Glory*. New York: Anchor.

Bondi, H. 1960. *Cosmology*. New York: Cambridge University Press.

Bowker, J. 1995. *Is God a Virus? Genes, Culture, and Religion*. London: SPCK.

Butler, Barbara, and Tom Butler. 1996. *Just Spirituality in a World of Faiths*. London: Mowbray.

Cronin, K.M. 1996. *Kenosis*. New York: Continuum.

Edwards, Denis. 1983. *Human Experience of God*. New York: Paulist Press.

Elliott, Charles. 1987. *Praying through Paradox*. London: Collins 1987.

Ellis, G.F.R. 1993a. The Theology of the Anthropic Principle. In R.J. Russell, N. Murphy, and C.J. Isham, eds., *Quantum Cosmology and the Laws of Nature* (Vatican Observatory), pp. 367–406.

———. 1993b. *Before the Beginning*. London: Bowerdean Press/Marion Boyers. [A semi-popular book on cosmology that describes the achievements of science as well as its limits, and then considers the larger issues of meaning and ethics.]

———. 1994. God and the Universe: Kenosis as the Foundation of Being. *Bulletin of the CTNS* 14, pp. 1–14.

———. 1995. Ordinary and Extraordinary Divine Action: The Nexus of Intervention. In R.J. Russell, N. Murphy and A. Peacocke, eds., *Chaos and Complexity: Scientific Perspectives on Divine Action* (Vatican Observatory/ Center for Theology and The Natural Sciences), pp. 359–395.

———. 1998. The Thinking Underlying the New 'Scientific' World-views. In R.J. Rusell et al., eds., *Evolutionary and Molecular Biology* (Vatican Observatory/CTNS), pp. 251–280.

———. 1999a. The Different Nature of Cosmology. *Astronomy and Geophysics* 40: 4 (1999).

———. 1999b. Before the Beginning: Emerging Questions and Uncertainties. In D. Block, I. Puerari, A. Stockton, and D. Ferreira, eds., *Toward a New Millenium in Galaxy Morphology* (Dordrecht: Kluwer).

Gorman, George. 1986. *The Amazing Fact of Quaker Worship*. London: Quaker Home Service.

Hanh, Thich Nhat. 1991 [1987]. *The Miracle of Mindfulness*. New York: Rider/Random House.

Harrison, E.R. 1983. *Cosmology*. New York: Cambridge University Press.

Hubbard, Geoffrey. 1976. *Quaker by Convincement*. London: Penguin.

Lewis, C.S. 1960. *Mere Christianity*. London: Collier.

Murphy, Nancey. 1990. *Theology in an Age of Scientific Reasoning*. Ithaca: Cornell University Press.

Murphy, Nancey, and G.F.R. Ellis. 1996. *On The Moral Nature of the Universe: Cosmology, Theology, and Ethics*. Minneapolis: Fortress. [A systematic philosophical and theological attempt at a synthesis of these three areas, claiming that each is incomplete without the other two. The approach adopted is developed in a specifically Christian setting in order to give it solidity and depth.]

Paden, W.E. 1992. *Interpreting the Sacred*. Boston: Beacon Press.

Palmer, Parker J. 1980. *The Promise of Paradox: A Celebration of the Contradictions in the Christian Life*. Notre Dame: Ave Maria Press.

Priest, G. 1995. *Beyond the Limits of Thought*. Cambridge: Cambridge University Press.

Sagan, Carl. 1997. *The Demon Haunted World: Science as a Candle in the Dark*. New York: Random House.

Saint-Exupéry, Antoine de. 1995. *Flight to Arras*. New York: Penguin.

Sciama, D.W. 1962. *The Unity of the Universe*. New York: Doubleday.

Silk, J. 1998. *A Brief History of the Universe*. New York: Scientific American/Freeman.

Soskice, J. 1992. *Metaphor and Religious Language*. New York: Oxford University Press.

Swimme, Brian. 1996. *The Hidden Heart of the Cosmos*. New York: Orbis.

Vanstone, W.H. 1977. *Love's Endeavour, Love's Expense*. Darton, Longman, and Todd.

11

Space and Spirit

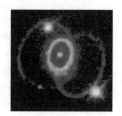

ᴍᴀʀɢᴀʀᴇᴛ ᴡᴇʀᴛʜᴇɪᴍ

*Our changing conceptions of space shape
our views of who we are as human beings.
The modern concept of space, from Nicholas
of Cusa to hyperspace, has been extremely
successful, but in this purely physical
account of reality there is no place for a
soul.*

My subject here is the nature of space, and how our conceptions
of space have shaped our conceptions of who and what we are as
human beings. I want in particular to deal with the evolution of the
modern scientific view of space and to consider some of the ways
in which this view has impacted on Western perceptions of ourselves as spiritual beings.

It may at first seem that space is a rather esoteric subject for
discussion in a science and religion forum, but for much of
Western history our thinking about space has been deeply influenced by religious ideas. Indeed, the conceptualization of space is
a critical area where science and Christianity have continually
intersected. As the historian Max Jammer has put it, "religious tradition exerted a powerful influence on physical theories of space
from the first to the eighteenth century."[1] Newton himself

---

1. Max Jammer, *Concepts of Space: The History of Theories of Space in Physics.*
Third, enlarged edition (New York: Dover, 1993), p. 28.

famously justified his vision of space as an infinite Euclidian void, not by recourse to scientific argument but by associating it with God. For the great seventeenth-century physicist space was nothing less than God's "sensorium", the universal and absolute "medium" through which an absolute deity could exercise his all-seeing eye, his all-powerful might.

But if for Newton and his contemporaries space had profound theological resonances, post-Newtonian physicists quickly stripped away the master's theistic frills leaving humanity adrift in a (literally) *despiritualized* void. This desanctified universe has been the official world picture of Western culture for the past three hundred years—the view that we are taught in school and that is promulgated in encyclopedias and the mainstream news.

Newton believed that the Euclidian view of space was the final word on the subject. But during the past century the nature of space has become one of the most fundamental topics in physics, as its practitioners have come to understand that this simple Euclidian picture is grossly inadequate. Physicists today comprehend space not as a passive Euclidian void, but as a highly dynamic membrane with a complex topology of its own. Beginning with Einstein's General Theory of Relativity physicists of the past century have built up a world picture in which space has become nothing less than the foundation of all reality—the ultimate underlying substrate from which everything else is fashioned. In these so-called 'hyperspace' theories everything that exists, including matter, is understood as a by-product of space itself curled up into patterns.

With modern science then we have reached a point where space has become the *primary* category of reality, with everything else being seen as a secondary manifestation of this foundational substrate. Physicist Paul Davies has summed up this vision by noting that according to these theories there is ultimately nothing but "structured nothingness."[2]

It is an extraordinary vision for any culture to have come to— reality as an enfolding of pure empty space. There is an almost zen-

---

2. Paul Davies. *Superforce: The Search for a Grand Unified Theory of Nature* (London: Unwin Paperbacks, 1986) p. 152.

like beauty here. But not without a price have we reached this point. As "the mathematicians have appropriated space," to use the apposite phrase of philosopher Henri Lefebvre, they have written out of our conception of reality any notion of spiritual space.[3] By this I mean any conception of a space in which a human spirit or soul might reside, for physicists' vision of 'structured nothingness' depicts a purely physical reality. In this sense the scientific world picture stands in stark contrast to the one which preceded it, that of medieval Christianity, for while modern science recognizes only a space for the physical body, the medieval Christian world picture incorporated spaces for both body and soul.

While it is true then that the modern scientific conception of space was originally developed with theological support, this vision has created in the end significant challenges for the Christian worldview. Indeed, I suggest, the nature of space represents a continuing dilemma for those who wish to find common ground between science and Christianity today.

My aim in this chapter is to follow the evolution of the Western conception of space from the Middle Ages to today, considering some of the theological and psychological upheavals that have been entrained along the way. The issue I want to primarily focus on is how we in the West made the transition from the dualistic cosmology of the Middle Ages, which encompassed spaces of both body and soul (a physical and a spiritual space), to the monistic cosmology of modern science, which recognizes only a physical space. Since we humans are intrinsically embedded in 'space' (however each era conceives of that term), our conceptions of space necessarily reflect our conceptions of who and what we are as human beings. The transition from the dualistic world picture of the Middle Ages to the monistic picture of seventeenth-century science was, I suggest, one of the most momentous cultural upheavals the West has experienced, and one that continues to send shockwaves through our society.

A Note: In this chapter I will be looking only at Western conceptions of space. That is not because I believe these conceptions

---

3. Henri Lefevbre, *The Production of Space* (Oxford: Blackwell, 1991), p. 2.

to be truer or more valid than any other cultures' conceptions. It is simply that I am a historian of Western science and this is what I study. *Every* culture has a conception of a wider spatial scheme in which its people believe humanity to be embedded; some of these conceptions are radically different to anything we in the West have ever conceived. These other world pictures are no less valid, and no less 'true', I believe, than our own. Even our scientific pictures should be seen as just that—as 'pictures' or models. As models, our scientific theories of space have proved immensely useful—they have helped us to map the cosmos with unprecedented accuracy and enabled us to send men to the moon—but like all models they have limited scope and power. There is much that is captured by other cultures' spatial schemes that our scientific pictures do not (and cannot) accommodate. Rather than dismissing these alternative spatial schemes, I believe we ought to take them seriously on their own terms. As I see it, coming to terms with these radically other spatial schemes and their attendant cosmologies is one of the primary challenges for the science and religion movement. By considering the implications of modern scientific views of space for the Christian world picture, I hope to shed some light on a set of issues that, as science becomes increasingly global, other cultures will also have to confront.

Medieval Space

One could begin a history of space anywhere. I choose to begin in the Middle Ages as this was the last time in the Western world that we had a profoundly *other* vision of a spatial scheme in which we are embedded. It is this vision that modern science would eventually overthrow.

Unlike the infinite (or quasi-infinite) vision pictured by contemporary science, the medieval cosmos was finite. The earth was at the center, surrounded by ten great concentric spheres which carried the sun, the moon, the planets and stars revolving around us. Beyond the sphere of the stars was the final sphere of the universe proper, what medievals, following Aristotle, called the 'primum mobile'. Technically, the primum mobile constituted the end of the physical universe—here, the medieval scholars believed that space and time came to a stop (another idea they inherited from

Aristotle). Critically, because physical space was seen to be finite, medieval minds could imagine that there was, so to speak, plenty of 'room' left 'beyond' the physical world for some other kind of space. This other space was metaphorically indicated on medieval maps of the cosmos, where beyond the outermost sphere of the primum mobile we usually find the label 'Heavenly Empyreum'. What lay 'beyond' physical space then was the *spiritual space* of God and the Christian soul (see Figure 12.4 in the next chapter).

At the end of *The Divine Comedy* Dante describes this transition. Having traversed the entire span of the medieval cosmos from the center of the earth through the successive celestial layers, Dante at the end of the poem pierces the shell of the primum mobile and bursting through the skin of the physical universe comes face to face with God. But here the poet is careful to stress that his description must be seen metaphorically: the Empyrean (that is Heaven), being a non-physical place, is forever beyond human modes of representation. Neither words nor images can capture this ineffable and irrevocably 'other' realm. The same philosophical point is also made by Giotto in his marvelous depiction of the *Last Judgment* in the Arena Chapel (Color Plate 12). At the very top of this fresco, hovering above the seried ranks of saints and angels in Heaven, Giotto painted two lone angels serenely suspended against a blue background. These winged figures are rolling back the picture plane as if it was so much wallpaper, revealing a glimpse of the true reality behind the image itself—two jeweled doors, the famous pearly gates of Heaven. Like Dante, Giotto's angels remind us that the realm of the Christian soul is in the end an *other* reality, a place that cannot be described or depicted by any human means.

This other realm, this spiritual realm, was for medieval thinkers the *primary* domain of reality. Indeed, they saw the physical realm as the *secondary* and rather pale reflection of the 'true' underlying spiritual reality. Spirit rather than matter was what took precedence in their worldview, spiritual space being for them the ultimate domain of the real. Just what it meant to have a 'place' outside physical space was a question that sorely exercised medieval minds—especially when one considered that the virtuous were promised resurrection in body as well as soul. Whatever the philosophical difficulties, all the great scholars of the age insisted on the reality of this non-physical domain. For them, physical space was simply not the *totality* of reality, but simply one half of a larger metaphysical whole.

The metaphysical dualism of matter and spirit that was so foundational to medieval thinking was mirrored in their cosmology by a dualism between the terrestrial and celestial realms. To medieval people terrestrial space and celestial space were two qualitatively different regions. Today when we have seen men walk on the moon and robot probes scuttling over the surface of Mars, we take it for granted that the celestial domain is essentially the same as the earthly one—that in both realms things are composed of the same basic substances and the same physical laws apply—but prior to the seventeenth century this was an almost heretical idea. Following the ancient Greeks, medieval natural philosophy held that in the terrestrial realm things were composed of the four basic elements—earth, air, fire, and water—but things in the celestial realm were believed to be composed of a mysterious fifth element, or quintessence, sometimes known as the ether. Everything in the terrestrial realm was subject to decay and death, it was mutable and mortal; but things in the celestial realm were believed to be eternal and immortal, subject neither to change nor decay. Although the terrestrial and celestial realms were both physical in essence, they were seen to be qualitatively distinct in their basic properties and characteristics.

Moreover, to medieval minds the celestial realm was not in itself homogeneous. As one ascended from the surface of the Earth, it was believed that each successive celestial layer became increasingly ethereal the closer one approached to God in the Empyrean 'above'. In effect celestial space exhibited a vector of grace, the closer one came to God the more 'pure' that region was seen to be. This grading was reflected in the various ranks of angels associated with each successive layer, the higher up the celestial hierarchy of planets the higher the rank of associated angel. Celestial space therefore served as a kind of transitional space between the purely material realm of Earth and the purely spiritual realm of Heaven— in essence, the celestial heavens of the planets and stars stood as a metaphor and pointer to the religious Heaven, the domain of God and the Christian soul. It is no accident that we use the same word for both realms. One of the great strengths of the medieval world picture was precisely this double parallel between the *metaphysical* dualism of body and soul, and the *cosmological* dualism of terrestrial and celestial space. The latter dualism was understood to be a reflection of the former, with the duality of the cosmos serving as a kind of guarantee for the dual nature of man.

But what if this cosmological dualism was wrong? What if the terrestrial and celestial realms were *not* fundamentally different? What if they formed one continuous unified domain? As long as Europeans continued to believe that celestial space was qualitatively distinct from terrestrial space, the realm of the planets and stars could continue to serve as a metaphor and pointer to the realm of the human soul. But if the distinction between earthly and celestial space was broken, what would be the ramifications for the whole medieval edifice?

The medieval distinction between terrestrial and celestial space would finally be shattered by the physics of Galileo and Newton, but long before that the seeds of this revolution could be found in the works of the Renaissance artists.

The Rise of Modern Science

Just such a challenge began to appear in the fifteenth century—though not until the seventeenth would its full implications be realized. The artistic reconceiving of space elaborated by the perspective painters of the fourteenth through sixteenth centuries would in fact pave the way for the momentous breakthroughs in physics and cosmology that we now recognize as the 'scientific revolution'. It is to art then that we must first turn in our efforts to understand the demise of the dualistic medieval vision of space.

As with medieval philosophy, so too early medieval art was primarily concerned with the spiritual realm of the Christian soul. Images were noticeably flat, with figures typically portrayed against flat gold or blue backgrounds, both iconically representing the ideal space of Heaven. If the backgrounds were flat, so were the figures—there is little or no sense of a third dimension. Proportions too were iconic: Christ was typically the largest figure in a scene, with angels and saints smaller than him, and ordinary humans smaller still. This was no childish ineptitude, but in keeping with a strict logic, for the aim here was not to convey the physical scale of bodies but to represent the greater spiritual hierarchy within which medieval minds placed all things. Giotto's *Last Judgment* is a paradigmatic representation of this spiritual hierarchy (see Color Plate 12). Notice how on the left hand side of the fresco the figures of the saved get progressively larger as they ascend toward Heaven. Note the size of the angels above, and of Christ, who is by far the largest figure. Consider now the puny size of the figures on the right hand side, the damned, who are bound for Hell. In the logic of medieval iconography, their stunted spiritual stature demands that they be the smallest figures in the scene. Early medieval painters were not attempting to represent physical reality, their focus was the spiritual realm, which was not subject to earthly conventions.

Giotto understood the great medieval cosmology of the soul yet in the early fourteenth century he more than anyone pioneered a new style of representation which focused on the physical realm. His *Last Judgment* occupies the back wall of the Arena Chapel, but the rest of the chapel is filled with images that consciously eschew the earlier medieval representational modes. On the two side walls and the front of the chapel Giotto painted a series of images telling the history of the Holy Family. What is immediately startling about these 'Christ Cycle' images is their three-dimensional quality. Consider Color Plate 13B, the Virgin Mary about to receive the Archangel Gabriel. In stark contrast to the flat iconic figures of early Christian imagery, here we have a woman of solid flesh and blood. It is as if Mary is really there in an actual room behind the picture plane. This three-dimensional illusionism is further enhanced by the addition of faux architectural details—the trompe l'oeil balconies on either side that appear to jut out from the picture plane into the space of the chapel itself. In this extraordinary rendition of Mary (Color Plate 13B), and the corresponding image of Gabriel (13A), a revolution is heralded—we see here the dawning of a new way of thinking about space.

Throughout the Arena Chapel Christ Cycle, Giotto strove for three-dimensional verisimilitude (what is often now called 'realism'). Figures here are solid and are anchored to the ground, as if by a real gravitational force. The flat blue and gold backgrounds of yore are replaced by attempts at genuine landscapes—there are mountains, trees, and carefully observed studies of animals. Buildings in particular are rendered with an unprecedented veracity. All this was in keeping with a new-found interest in the Western world—natural science.

After the hiatus of the so-called Dark Ages, Europeans had began to recover the science and mathematics of the ancient Greeks and during the thirteenth century the study of nature underwent a renaissance. The new artistic 'realism' reflected this emerging scientific interest, for in the careful attention to physical detail in the works of Giotto and his followers we see the results of serious empirical observation. In short, the revelations of the inner eye were being supplanted by the observations of the outer eye. Artistic attention was shifting away from the spiritual realm of the soul toward the physical realm of the body. But if these artists were inspired by a newly burgeoning science, equally their exercises were given credence by a novel theological development.

As medieval Europeans recovered Greek science one of the ancient thinkers they encountered was the mathematician and philosopher Pythagoras of Samos. If the science of modern physics has a spiritual mentor it is Pythagoras, for it is to this most enigmatic of the Greek sages that we trace the idea of a universe formed according to mathematical principles.[4] Today we call such principles 'laws of nature'. Pythagoras encapsulated his radical philosophy in the compact dictum 'All is number', and he believed that behind all physical forms were transcendent numerical archetypes, which he called the divine 'armonia' or mathematical 'harmonies' of the world. As early as the twelfth century we begin to see the re-emergence of a Pythagorean spirit in Western Europe, now recast into a Christian context.

Pythagoras had believed that numbers were literally gods, and he associated the numbers one through ten with the major gods of the Greek pantheon; late medieval thinkers took this pagan seed and refashioned it into the idea of the Judeo-Christian god as a mathematical creator. "The creation of number is the creation of things," wrote Thierry of Chartres in the twelfth century.[5] "God disposes everything in number, weight, and measure," Bishop Robert

---

4. Margaret Wertheim, *Pythagoras' Trousers* (New York: Norton, 1998).

5. Thierry of Chartres, quoted in N.M. Haring, 'The Creation and the Creator of the World According to Thierry of Chartres and Clarembalbus of Arras'. *Archives d'Histoire Doctrinale et Litterature du Moyen Age* (Paris: vol. XXII/1955), p. 196.

Grosseteste said in the thirteenth, and in the seventeenth century Galileo would famously declare that anyone who wanted to understand the "book of nature" must first grasp the language in which God had written it—mathematics.[6]

If God had written the book of nature in the language of mathematics, medieval Pythagoreans (following Plato) believed that the primary dialect He had used was Euclidian geometry. Now since God had crafted the world according to the principles of geometry, then surely that was the way artists *ought* to portray it, especially in religious imagery. So argued the Franciscan friar Roger Bacon, one of the first medieval champions of science and mathematics. In 1267 in a treatise to Pope Clement IV, Bacon proposed that the church encourage painters in the new three-dimensional style, what he called "geometric figuring" and which would later be known as perspectival representation. Not only would such artists truthfully be rendering God's creation, Bacon said, the new style would also serve a powerful propaganda purpose. The techniques of three-dimensional versimilitude would be so psychologically powerful, Bacon argued, that viewers would believe they were looking at the actual scenes depicted. They would believe, for example, that they were really seeing Christ raising Lazarus there in front of them. To use today's parlance, Bacon was suggesting that 'geometric figuring' could be a form of virtual reality. According to him, this medieval VR would have the power to convert unbelievers to the True Faith.

Within a decade of Bacon's treatise, work began on the Basilica of Assisi, the mother church of Bacon's order and the first major Christian church consciously filled with images in the new geometric style. Again Giotto was the master here. The visual revolution that he pioneered in Assisi and later in the Arena Chapel, and that would eventually be taken to such heights by the artists of the next two centuries, had the effect of retraining Europeans to see space in a new way—for the first time in history the frame of reality came to be seen as Euclidean.

Yale art historian Samuel Edgerton has argued that in this sense the perspective painters paved the way for the physicists of the

---

6. Robert Grosseteste, quoted in Alistair Cameron Crombie, *Robert Grosseteste and the Origins of Experimental Science 1100–1700* (Oxford: Clarendon, 1953), p. 102.

seventeenth century giving Europeans a visceral *experience* of physical space as a Euclidian arena.[7] Up until then most Western thinkers had pointedly rejected this conception of space. Historian Max Jammer has noted that indeed such a view was not "thought reasonable until the seventeenth century."[8] The embracing of this geometric vision of space is a particular idiosyncrasy of Western culture, for no other culture has seen their surrounding spatial scheme in anything like such a strict mathematical manner. From the point of view of the science and religion dialog it is germane to stress that one of the prime motivating forces behind this vision was the belief that God was a Euclidian creator. In fact theological arguments would continually be brought to bear on discussions about space throughout the sixteenth and seventeenth centuries.

Space the Same Everywhere

By the mid-sixteenth century Europeans were coming to accept that the space around them here on Earth was a Euclidian domain. But this realization raised an uneasy question: if terrestrial space is essentially Euclidian, then how far out does this space extend? Might it reach out to encompass the planets and stars? If not, then where did it end? The question, though not necessarily articulated in quite this form during the Renaissance, was of immense importance, because as we have seen the celestial realm was considered to be qualitatively different to the terrestrial realm, and this qualitative difference stood as a pointer to the central metaphysical dualism of body and soul. The new Euclidian vision of space raised the possibility that there were not *two* kinds of space but just *one*, encompassing both the Earth and the celestial bodies.

The first person to coherently suggest such a synthesis was a fifteenth-century cardinal of the Roman Catholic Church, Nicholas of Cusa. In Cusa's universe there were no crystal spheres, no limiting *primum mobile*, and no cosmic hierarchy of planets; instead there was an infinite space filled with countless

---

7. Samuel Y. Edgerton, *The Heritage of Giotto's Geometry: Art and Science on the Eve of the Scientific Revolution* (Ithaca: Cornell University Press, 1991).

8. Jammer, *Concepts of Space*, p. 26.

stars all substantially the same. Abolishing the medieval distinction between the 'base' Earth and the 'ethereal' heavens, Cusa proposed that the universe was essentially the same everywhere, with
the stars and planets also being solid material bodies like the Earth.
He even suggested that these other 'worlds' (as he called them) were
inhabited by other physical beings. Centuries later Cusa's concept
of cosmological homogeneity would become a mainstay of modern
science, for only if the universe is homogeneous—only if space is
the same everywhere—can we assume that the same physical laws
operating here on Earth also operate on the moon and Mars, or any
other celestial body.

Cusa's ideas were too daring for most of his contemporaries,
but in the sixteenth century the tectonic plates of the Western psyche begin to shift in this direction. Beginning with Copernicus
(who actually continued to believe in the medieval distinction
between terrestrial and celestial space), astronomers gradually
built up a picture of the cosmos which inexorably challenged the
old medieval worldview. By the mid-seventeenth century that
dualistic cosmology lay in tatters. Copernicus's sun-center system,
Kepler's elliptical planetary orbits, and Galileo's telescopic discoveries combined to shatter the crystal spheres, and to transform celestial space from the domain of angels into an arena of
prosaic physical study. One of the major achievements of the scientific revolution was indeed the conjoining of celestial and terrestrial space.

This unification was cemented by Isaac Newton, and in some
ways it remains his greatest legacy. In one of the great *tours de force*
in the history of science Newton showed that the same force of
gravity which operates here on Earth to make an apple fall to the
ground also operates in the celestial realm to keep the moon revolving around the Earth and the planets revolving around the sun.
Newton's law of gravity—a Pythagorean triumph if ever there was
one—demonstrated with compelling logic an essential continuity
between the terrestrial and celestial realms: if gravity operates
between celestial bodies then they too must be solid material bodies, for gravity is a force that arises between concrete lumps of matter. It is a little remarked on fact that the ephemerality of a mathematical equation is what finally clinched the argument for the
solidity of the planets and stars.

Newton's science shattered the distinction between celestial and terrestrial space; it also suggested (as Cusa had done two centuries earlier) that the physical universe might be infinite. Once astronomers abandoned the machinery of the crystal spheres there was no reason to believe that the physical cosmos had any limit whatever. Why should physical space not go on forever? By the end of the eighteenth century that view had indeed become scientific orthodoxy—and still is today.

The new cosmology had profound theological consequences, for with physical space extended to infinity there was literally no 'room' left for any other kind of space. With the medieval scheme one could imagine, even if strictly speaking only in a metaphorical sense, that there was plenty of room left for some other reality 'beyond' the physical realm, but with the physical realm now going on forever where could a spiritual realm possibly be? Of course one could still say, as liberal theologians often do, that the realm of the Christian spirit is simply beyond physical space and leave it enigmatically at that. In a strict sense the answer is still the same as in the medieval era. The difference is that when physical space was formally limited it was easy psychologically for people to accept the idea of a 'beyond'; once physical space was infinitized the very notion of what a 'beyond' might mean became extremely problematic. I do not intend to give the impression that this is an insurmountable theological problem; my purpose is only to draw attention to a serious psychological obstacle thrown up by modern cosmology. For better or worse, one of the major consequences of the scientific revolution was to write out of the Western world picture of reality any conception of spiritual space.

Newton himself was concerned about such atheistic tendencies within his cosmology and tried to rescue the situation by associating Euclidean space itself with God. Picking up on a tradition that originates with early Judaism, Newton saw space as the medium through which the deity's presence permeates the physical universe. But soon after his death, less religious men stripped these theological embellishments from the system and in doing so desanctified the world, leaving us with a purely physical account of reality.

What is at stake here is far from trivial. With their finite physical cosmology medieval Christians had no trouble imagining an expansive spiritual realm with its own complex geography—the tripartite geography of Heaven, Hell, and Purgatory that Dante lays out with such exquisite detail in *The Divine Comedy*. Once an infinite physical cosmology was articulated any such exercise in visualizing or mapping a spiritual domain became inherently problematic—one reason, I suspect, why Dante's book is still so beloved, even by those of us who are not Christians. With *The Divine Comedy* we have artistic genius underpinned by an untroubled belief in a geography of the soul: so viscerally does Dante conjure this spiritual landscape one can almost feel the mud beneath one's feet in the ditches of Malebolge, see the marbled terraces of Purgatory. The full weight of Dante's medieval faith in an architectonic spiritual space is brought to bear here: could any post-Newtonian author possibly compete? It is not that we moderns lack imagination or a sense of the fantastic—after all, we invented science fiction—what we lack is an uncomplicated faith in a 'beyond' to the physical domain and the psychological freedom to explore what such a meta-physical domain might be like.

Increasingly in the age of science we confront the dilemma that if you want to claim something is real you have to be able to triangulate its position in physical space. If you can't pinpoint its location on a physical map then more and more you invite the accusation that whatever it is is not real at all. Hence the liberal theological dilemma about Heaven. Where is it? What is it? How can it be made sense of in the light of scientific cosmology? Hell, like Purgatory, has largely been abandoned by liberal religious thinkers with little resistance, but Heaven—the domain of human salvation—is critical to Christian integrity.

Even in Newton's lifetime this physicalist attitude had begun to coalesce. For men such as the English philosopher Thomas Hobbes, and later French *philosophes* like Julien la Mettrie, the universe was a giant clockwork and Man simply "an atomic machine," to use la Mettrie's terse assessment. In their new rationalist vision, the soul became a childish delusion, a relic of a superstitious past that would have to be abandoned—along with Heaven and Hell, angels and demons, and ultimately God Himself.

How we see our spatial scheme necessarily impacts on how we see ourselves: for the medievals, with their dualistic spatial scheme, humans were necessarily dualistic creatures, but with the advent of a monistic world picture it has become increasingly difficult to argue for the reality of any kind of non-physical dimension to human existence. In discussions about science and religion it is often noted how corrosive mechanistic philosophy was to the religious idea of a human spirit; what is not generally recognized is how important a role our conception of space has played in this story. The mechanistic philosophy of nature was premised on a neutral, homogeneous, passive and infinite conception of space. The very qualities of Euclidian space that made it such a fruitful foundation for the evolution of mathematical physics are precisely the qualities that have become so problematic for those who wish to assert the reality of a spiritual plane of being.

The Rejection of Physicalism

The intellectual dilemma faced by liberal theologians and ministers trying to make sense of Heaven in the light of modern science is, I suggest, one reason why we are presently witnessing an effflourescence of fundamentalist modes of Christianity and New Age religions, as well as a surge of interest in indigenous and shamanistic religions. All these belief systems offer a concrete vision of a spiritual realm, an 'other' world beyond the physical plane. This is one reason also why popular culture is awash with visions of magical and supernatural phenomena. Turn on the television and it is teeming with programs about witches and vampires and supernatural beings: *Buffy the Vampire Slayer, Charmed, Angel, Sabrina the Teenage Witch*, to name a few. Over all this hovers the enigmatic cloud that is *The X-Files*. "The truth is out there," the show's opening credit sequence intones each week; if only we open our (inner?) eyes, the series implies, we will find that there is more to reality than physical science describes.

The success of *The X-Files*, the rise of Christian fundamentalism, the burgeoning belief in past lives, spirit channeling, and paranormal phenomena, can all be seen, I believe, as part of a wider response to the psychological vacuum created when the West adopted a purely physicalist account of reality. For better or worse, vast numbers of people are rejecting this purely physicalist world picture. They are not necessarily rejecting science itself, as is often said by science's champions, rather they want to believe in a spiritual world *as well*. In his insightful book *Technology as Symptom and Dream*, psychologist Robert Romanyshyn addresses this issue. Romanyshyn notes that in the age of science "any sense of the world as a reality of multiple levels simultaneously coexisting is the stuff of fancy and dream," yet it is just such a simultaneity that many people seem to be demanding.[9] For Romanyshyn this is hardly a surprise: when we try to push the 'magical' dimensions out of human life, he says, they do not disappear, but go underground and bubble up later in unexpected forms.

Like Romanyshyn, I do not believe it is psychologically stable to have a world picture that accommodates only physical phenomena. We need, I suggest, a cosmology of psyche as well as of soma— preferably one that does not disconnect them in a Cartesian dualistic way. I am not myself a religious person, at least not in a sense that most people of the monotheistic faiths might acknowledge, but what Romanyshyn calls "the flattening" of our world picture to "a single plane" of reality, also has secular consequences. Just as such a picture denies fundamental status to the Christian soul, so it denies status to the human psyche or self. In post-Newtonian cosmology only matter, and hence only the body, has a place, and indeed a 'reality'. Soul, spirit, psyche, self—all are ultimately denied in this purely physicalist account of the real.

Twentieth-Century Visions of Space

Can this problem be resolved within the context of physics itself? One of the most momentous scientific developments of the past century has been the articulation of a post-Euclidian view of space. In this understanding space has come to be seen not simply as the arena of reality—the passive and featureless medium through which matter moves—but as the very foundation of the physical world, the substrate from which everything else is constructed. As I noted at the start of this chapter, this is the new 'hyperspace' vision that physicists have been developing for the past few decades. Do hyperspace theories help us with the 'problem' of spirit? Might they be a useful theological resource? That

---

9. Robert Romanyshyn, *Technology as Symptom and Dream* (New York: Routledge, 1989), p. 181.

seems to be the implication in a number of recent books about physics and spirituality. Because matter is no longer primary in hyperspace theories, such theories are said to resolve many of the dilemmas raised by strictly materialistic views. I shall argue that hyperspace theories do not help here, and in some respects even compound the problem.

Let us look briefly at the science itself. Hyperspace theories trace their origins to Einstein's theories of special and general relativity. From the point of view of this discussion what is most important about special relativity is that with this theory Einstein showed how time could be understood as another dimension of space. A rather special dimension to be sure, but mathematically speaking, in special relativity, time becomes essentially just one dimension of the overall spatial manifold—which was now seen to have four rather than three dimensions. In the general theory of relativity, Einstein revealed something even more astonishing: by extending his earlier theory (to accommodate the case of accelerated motion) he showed that gravity could also be explained as a byproduct of the geometry, or shape, of space.

In Newtonian physics gravity had loomed as an essential mystery: Newton had attributed this vital cosmic force to God. The great triumph of general relativity (GR) is that it offers a mathematically precise, and now extremely well tested, account of gravity. According to GR the force that we experience as gravity is actually a byproduct of the curving of space around us. Here, space can be envisaged like a vast membrane, rather like the surface of a huge trampoline (only in four dimensions). Just as a bowling ball placed on a trampoline would warp the trampoline causing a depression around itself, so GR says that a celestial body like our earth 'warps' the membrane of space around itself causing a 'depression'. Such depressions are what we experience as the force of gravity. Just as a marble would roll down a depression created by our bowling ball on the trampoline, so crudely speaking the reason a stone falls to the ground is that it rolls down a depression in the cosmic spatial membrane. According to relativity theory, gravity is not something *separate* from space, but a byproduct of space's own structure.

Einstein's explanation of gravity was so esthetically pleasing that in the latter part of the century physicists began to dream that *all* the basic physical forces might be explained as byproducts of the warping of space. Physicists now recognize four fundamental forces: gravity, the electromagnetic force (which accounts for light, heat, radio waves and so on), and the two nuclear forces which are responsible for holding together the nuclei of atoms. In order to accommodate the other three forces physicists have found they have had to add into their equations a slew of extra dimensions. Today these 'hyperspace' theories suggest that we live in a ten- or eleven-dimensional universe. In these theories not only all four forces, but all particles as well become byproducts of the shape of space around us.

In this way of seeing, all structures—from the subatomic to the cosmological scale—arise from the intricate enfolding of an under-lying spatial manifold, which like a sheet of paper can be crinkled and contorted into complex forms. In effect, hyperspace theories paint a picture of the universe as a vast origami construction. Just as a piece of paper can be folded into the shape of a crane or a lotus blossom, so the membrane of space folds up upon itself giving rise to the wonderful diversity of physical structures that make up the universe today. Protons, petunias, and people, we all become crin-kles in hyperspace.

One of the most intriguing aspects of this picture is that matter loses its primary status—because it too now becomes a secondary phenomenon, an artifact of the local geometry of space. Some people have seen in this development a way out of the modern materi-alist dilemma, but such theories do not do the philosophical or the-ological work that many seem to be hoping they will. The problem is this: while hyperspace theories may well be called post-material-ist, they remain fundamentally *physicalist*. As with earlier scientific theories they account only for interactions between physical parti-cles and physical forces. Matter may no longer be primary, but that does not mean we have here an account of spirit or soul. Western culture has a long tradition of opposing matter and spirit, so it is perhaps a natural move within the context of such a culture to imagine that something not-material must *ipso facto* be spiritual. But perhaps that was always a false dichotomy. (Cyberspace is also the focus of a great deal of spiritual dreaming these days, because it is also a non-physical arena, but I doubt that many Christian the-ologians would accept the Net as a spiritual space.) By suggesting that there is something ontologically prior to matter hyperspace theories mark a philosophically important development in Western thinking, but they remain theories of the physical world alone, and in that sense are contiguous with their Newtonian predecessor.

In some ways hyperspace theories actually compound the problem, because in these theories reality is reduced fully and finally to a seamless monism—*everything* becomes just a byproduct of physical space. The very oneness that hyperspace theorists exalt (and which is in its own right so beautiful) means that there is no room within this vision for any kind of epistemic pluralism. Epistemic monism is the very point of such theories!

I want to stress here that this monism should not be seen as a failure on the part of the physics. Modern mathematically-based physics is extremely successful because its practitioners have restricted themselves to explaining interactions between physical particles and forces: historians of science have noted that it was just when physics became such a restricted field that it really started to take off. (In the Middle Ages, for example, people had tried to develop mathematical theories of sin and grace.) Physics in its modern mode was expressly developed to address itself to what Descartes called the *res extensa*— the extended realm of matter in motion. It was not designed to explain, or even to admit the existence of what the great French philosopher dubbed the *res cogitans*, the 'realm' of thoughts, feelings, emotions, and spiritual experience. No purely physical theory, no vision of physical space *per se*, can resolve the problem of the human spirit or soul. Descartes understood precisely this point when he insisted that *in addition* to the physical realm there must also be a non-physical domain.

With his dualism of the *res extensa* and the *res cogitans* Descartes tried to retain a kind of spatial dualism, but as we know his *res cogitans* was soon abandoned. And in truth it was always hard to see just what he had meant here. What exactly was his proposed 'realm' of mind? Where was it? Of what did it consist? These are dilemmas that continue to face those who wish to reconcile contemporary cosmology and Christianity. In the context of modern cosmology, what does one mean by a 'realm' of spirit (or even one of self)? As I noted earlier, the medievals with their dualistic world picture could easily accommodate a dualistic conception of human beings, and they accorded each aspect its own space, its own theater of action. As Descartes understood, the solution cannot be found within the equations of physics. The *res extensa* will always remain the space of matter in motion. That parsimony is the strength of this uniquely Western concept—and also its limitation.

If we believe that we are ultimately nothing but 'structured nothingness' then how can we be creatures of soul? How even can we be creatures of psyche? I am not a theologian or a psychoanalytic theorist and I do not presume to have answers here. My aim in this essay has not been to propose solutions but to clarify some of the questions. How we understand the spatial scheme in which we are embedded inevitably reflects on how we see ourselves as human beings; if we want a pluralistic conception of human being-ness, I suggest that in the long run we are going to need some conception of a more pluralistic spatial scheme. That does not mean I am advocating a return to metaphysical dualism, a concept I pointedly reject. Rather I am suggesting that we need a more pluralistic epistemology, one that recognizes that the 'space' which physics describes is not the totality of this complex puzzle we call 'reality'. What such a scheme might look like I cannot at present imagine, but it strikes me that this might be one place where we in the West may well have something to learn from other cultural traditions.

12

Images of Enlightenment: Slanted Truths

$\mathscr{C}$LIFFORD $\mathscr{N}$. $\mathscr{M}$ATTHEWS

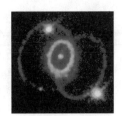

A mandala for consciousness includes the mythic elements of ouroboros, DNA, and yin-yang, combined to represent our creative activities in art, science, and religion that produce the metaphors, models, and myths by which we live.

Mandala, the Sanskrit word for circle, is defined in the *Random House Dictionary of the English Language* as:

> **1** a schematized representation of the cosmos, chiefly characterized by a concentric configuration of geometric shapes, each of which contains an image of a deity or an attribute of a deity; **2** (in Jungian psychology) a symbol representing the effort to reunify the self.

Most familiar to us are the colorful works of art on cloth or paper that we see as visual scriptures of Buddhism, illustrating the teachings arising from the Buddha's profound understanding of human nature. At the Parliament of the World's Religions in 1993, a most intriguing event was the construction in Chicago's Field Museum of the sand mandala of Kalachakra by Tibetan monks from the Namgyal Monastery of Dharamsala, India (see Figure 12.1). Colored grains of sand were patiently sifted into elaborate patterns and symbols rich in meanings that have been developed and handed down in unbroken lineage since the time of the Buddha over 2,500 years ago. Only in recent years has this ceremony of building and dismantling been performed outside Asia, thanks mainly to the initiative of the present Dalai Lama who sees Kalachakra—the Wheel of Time—as "a vehicle for attaining world peace." For a modern mandala (Common Ground, Chicago) see Figure 12.2.

Mandalas found in other cultures might include such western manifestations as Navajo sand paintings, Aztec stone calendars, and the stained glass windows of Gothic cathedrals. Contemplating these devotional artifacts of the past makes one aware how changed we are from our worshipping ancestors. However devout we may be, we have come to realize that science, rather than religion, is the shaping cultural force of our time, affecting the way we live, the way we see, the way we think. If indeed "scientists are the shamans and wizards, the wonder workers and myth-givers of today" as suggested by John Updike, can their revelations be expressed as a mandala, a visual embodiment of reason? Let's try, beginning by identifying key images and symbols that define certain critical periods in western intellectual history. Several sets of figures are displayed in the following pages, each accompanied by a collection of quotations and ruminations that lead step-by-step to the design of a mandala for science and, eventually, for the structure of human consciousness.

Divine Symmetry

Around the time of the Buddha's awakening, another path to enlightenment was opening up, this time based on a continuing examination of nature itself. Lovers of wisdom—philosophers—living on the islands and mainland of the eastern Mediterranean began to investigate nature's laws separately from any specific consideration of religion. Most influential was the introduction and development of mathematics by the Pythagorean brotherhood, true believers in the mathematical (and musical) harmony of nature. It took only 150 years for the startling announcement of Pythagoras—"All is number"—to become the legendary motto of Plato's Academy: "Let no one ignorant of mathematics enter here."

FIGURE 12.1 MANDALA OF KALACHAKRA

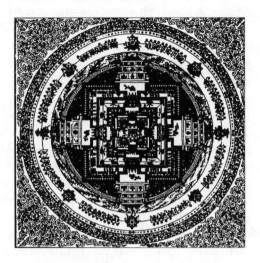

FIGURE 12.2 COMMON GROUND MANDALA

This mandala is a form of the sacred wheel. It is an ancient symbol of the diversity and convergence of the ways to truth. The spokes are the great spiritual paths. At the rim, the distance between the spokes is great, but at the center they meet. The rim end of the spoke represents the initial involvement of one's own tradition. The hub represents the deepest entry into that tradition. As we penetrate the mysteries of our own ways of walking, we move toward the center, and the distance that had separated us from one another diminishes. At the center, we discover common ground.

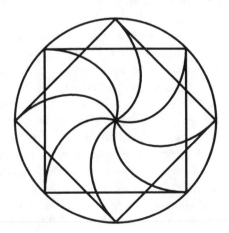

Once again, as in the far East, the circle and the sphere became dominant cosmic images. The cosmos was seen as spherical because the sphere is the most homogeneous of shapes: circular motion of its components most befitted reason and intelligence. The same argument was applied to the world around us consisting entirely of the four elements of Empedocles: earth, water, air and fire. For Plato and his star pupil Aristotle these elements just had to be directly related to the regular polyhedra beloved by the Pythagoreans for the beauty and simplicity of their symmetry. Only five such shapes can be constructed, as was proved later by Euclid. Each can be inscribed into a sphere so that their corners lie on the sphere's surface. Each can also circumscribe a sphere that touches the center of every face. The five Platonic solids can thus be regarded as approximations to the one figure possessing perfect symmetry—the sphere—just as our world, in Plato's view, is but a shadow of the true, underlying reality of things—the ideal. With his mystical appreciation of geometry, Plato saw fire in the tetrahedron, air in the octahedron, earth in the hexahedron (the cube), and water in the icosahedron. Each of these four polygons has surfaces consisting of triangles and squares. The fifth is different, however, being made up of pentagons. This quintessence was ascribed to a mysterious ether, the substance of the heavenly bodies above (see Figure 12.3). Down here on Earth, primary physical qualities such as heat, cold, moisture, and dryness must have resulted from particular combinations of the other four elements, an idea that was later adopted by practising alchemists, mostly Arabic, investigating transformations of matter.

Aristotle went on to teach that Earth was at the center of the cosmos, unmoved and unmoving, surrounded by concentric spheres of water, air, and fire that could interact with each other. Then came the heavenly spheres, crystalline and invisible, where the moon, Mercury, Venus, the sun, Mars, Jupiter, Saturn, and the firmament of fixed stars resided separately. Above these was the sphere of the *primum mobile*, the prime mover or driving force of the whole system, moving with infinite speed. Beyond lay a fiery outer sphere, the Empyrean, the unmoved mover that was the cause of all this activity. In medieval times the unmoved mover became God, perceived by some mystics as an intelligent sphere with center everywhere and circumference nowhere. For two thousand years belief in such a cosmos—absolute, divine, eternal—was central to western civilization (see Figure 12.4). Only when this

FIGURE 12.3

The five regular solids of Pythagoras and Plato, from Johannes Kepler,
Harmony of the World *(1619)*

FIGURE 12.4 COSMOS

*In medieval Christian cosmology, following Aristotle, Earth was at the
center of the universe, surrounded by the concentric crystal spheres of the
Sun, Moon, planets, and stars. Beyond the stars, and outside physical
space, was the heavenly Empyrean of God.*

heritage of classical Greece was challenged by observation and experiment could a new world come into being.

Human Designs

At the center of the School of Athens fresco in the Vatican we find Aristotle debating with a white-bearded Plato whom Raphael had portrayed with the features of Leonardo da Vinci (see Color Plate 14). This may have been to acknowledge the debt owed by the Renaissance not only to Aristotle but also to his mentor Plato, whose rediscovered manuscripts were being eagerly read by the intellectuals of Florence. What an honor for Leonardo! And for Plato too! Yet we know how different from each other these two geniuses really were, Plato the ultimate conservative who warned against "the prison house of sight" and indeed of all the senses, and Leonardo, whose unpublished notebooks contained the seeds of the future expressed in precise drawings and pregnant phrases such as the observation that "The eye, which is called the window of the soul, is the chief means whereby the understanding may most fully and abundantly appreciate the infinite works of nature."

We see Leonardo's images everywhere. In Chicago in 1993 I was fortunate enough to catch a wonderful stage performance of *The Notebooks of Leonardo da Vinci*. Conceived by Mary Zimmerman, every word of text and lyrics was taken from the writings of the master. Under her direction, eight actor/dancers in enchanting settings conveyed the boundless curiosity and intellectual passion of this incredibly versatile artist, architect, musician, scientist, inventor, and engineer who signed himself Leonardo da Vinci, disciple of experiment. It seems Leonardo himself was fond of spectacle and created many allegorical, theatrical entertainments for his patrons. I believe he would have applauded this special event.

As it happened I had just returned from a scientific conference in Trieste, Italy on the origin of life. Passing through the international airport in Rome named after Leonardo da Vinci I noticed in its lobby a larger-than-life three-dimensional wooden version of his well-known image of a human body enclosed in a square and circle. The original drawing in brown ink is, of course, only the size of this page. I saw it in all its modest power some years ago in Washington at the exhibition entitled *Circa 1492: Art in the Age of*

Exploration, where an enlarged copy also served as a striking poster for the show. Leonardo's remark that "Each man is an image of the world" may help to explain the universal appeal of this emblem combining the new humanism with neoplatonism. First propounded by Vitruvius, a scholarly architect in the Rome of Augustus Caesar, it aims to show that the human body is so proportioned that it can be incorporated into the perfect shapes of circle and square—Heaven and Earth—beloved of Pythagoras and Plato. Vitruvius managed an exact fit of the three components but only by distorting the human figure, which seems to me to be under considerable strain (see Figure 12.5). In Leonardo's more truthful version, however, based on close observation of actual torsos, we see that this perfect arrangement is not really possible. The outstretched body can fit exactly into either of the two shapes but not when the square is circumscribed by the circle. Using mind and hand and eye, Leonardo had inadvertently shown for the first time that the ideal symmetry of Plato was not demanded by nature (see Figure 12.6).

The Unexpected Universe

Investigating the world around us by theory, experiment, and observation soon became the hallmark of post-Leonardo Europe. Specific beliefs of Aristotle were first toppled by the achievements in astronomy and physics of Copernicus, Brahe, Kepler, Galileo, and Newton. More difficult, it seems, was the denial of the divine symmetry taught by Plato. "I undertake to prove that God, in creating the universe and regulating the order of the cosmos had in view the five regular bodies of geometry as known since the days of Pythagoras and Plato," wrote Kepler in the preface to his first book, *The Mystery of the Cosmos* (see Figure 12.3). Ironically, his attempts to make cosmological use of these symmetrical figures proved fruitless, and instead he became the reluctant iconoclast who showed that the planetary orbits were not circular but elliptical. For Galileo, that staunch Copernican, this oval pathway was unacceptable, given his view of nature as "a grand book written in the language of mathematics; its characters are triangles, circles and other geometrical figures." It remained for Newton to rationalize the seminal discoveries of his predecessors so that a dynamic open

FIGURE 12.5 HUMAN MEASUREMENT ACCORDING TO VITRUVIUS

FIGURE 12.6 LEONARDO'S FIGURE OF MAN, AFTER VITRUVIUS

universe could now replace the closed world of the ancients. Perhaps most revolutionary was the dawning realization of the significance of nature's asymmetry, for in the words of Richard Goodwin, "to strip humanity of its focal position in an eternal symmetry and to place it on a tiny circling globe carelessly lodged in endless space was not exile but liberation."

No wonder Sir Isaac Newton became the first hero-scientist, one who established the very style of modern physical science employing advanced mathematics to develop increasingly sophisticated concepts of matter and energy (see Figure 12.7). As described by Arthur Koestler in *The Sleepwalkers*, "In one of the most reckless and sweeping generalizations in the history of thought, Newton filled the entire space of the universe with interlocking forces of attraction issuing from all particles of matter and acting on all particles of matter, across the boundless abysses of darkness." Later, Charles Darwin's theory of evolution by natural selection made us aware for the first time that no living thing was created ready-made. Instead, all living forms have a family history and are related by common descent, "one of those half dozen shattering ideas that science has developed to overturn past hopes and assumptions, and to enlighten our current thoughts," according to Stephen Jay Gould (see Figure 12.8). Closer to our era, Albert Einstein's theories of relativity showed not only that matter and energy are equivalent but also that space and time are one and that curved spacetime can account for the presence of gravity, Newton's pervasive force which "dictates the motion of our planets, the rhythm of the tides, the fall of a stone, the float of an astronaut and the expansion of the universe." On the microcosmic scale—what is the world made of?— Max Planck's discovery that energy can exist as particles—quanta— as well as waves, enabled Niels Bohr and others to develop the fundamental ideas underlying another great generalization of science, that everything within and around us, down here and up there, consists of atoms of which a hundred or so varieties—our modern elements—are known. With admiration, we recall that the Ionian philosophers opposed by Plato and Aristotle had anticipated many of these ideas, particularly Democritus who believed that "Nothing exists but atoms and the void" and Heraclitus with his paradoxical thesis that "The only permanent thing in nature is change."

FIGURE 12.7

I do not know what I may appear to the world; but to myself I seem to have been only like a boy, playing on the seashore, and diverting myself now and then finding a smoother pebble or a prettier shell than the ordinary, while the great ocean of truth lay all undiscovered before me.
(Isaac Newton)

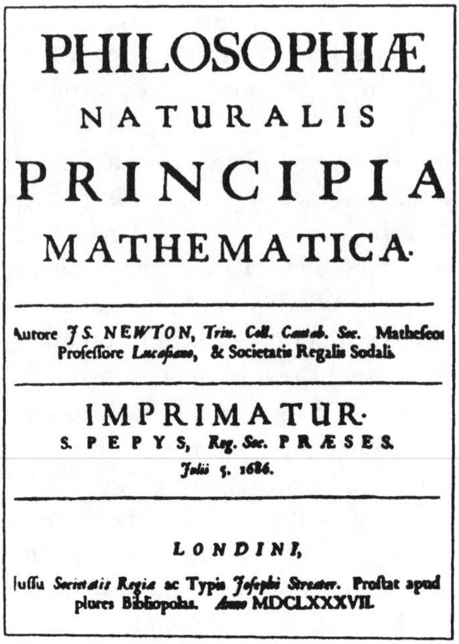

PHILOSOPHIÆ

NATURALIS

PRINCIPIA

MATHEMATICA.

Autore *J.S. NEWTON,* Trin. Coll. Cantab. Soc. Mathefeos Profeffore *Lucafiano,* & Societatis Regalis Sodali.

IMPRIMATUR·
S. PEPYS, *Reg. Soc.* PRÆSES.
Julii 5. 1686.

LONDINI,

Juffu *Societatis Regiæ* ac Typis *Jofephi Streater.* Proftat apud plures Bibliopolas. *Anno* MDCLXXXVII.

FIGURE 12.8

There is grandeur in this view of life, with its several powers, having been originally breathed by the Creator into a few forms or into one; and that, whilst this planet has gone cycling on according to the fixed laws of gravity, from so simple a beginning endless forms most beautiful and most wonderful have been and are being evolved.
(Charles Darwin)

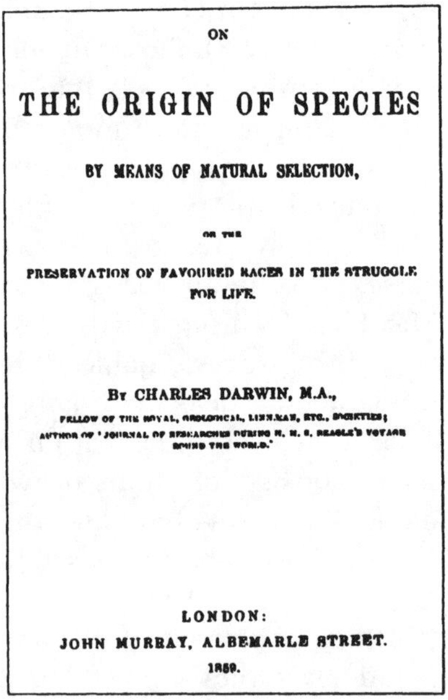

ON

THE ORIGIN OF SPECIES

BY MEANS OF NATURAL SELECTION,

OR THE

PRESERVATION OF FAVOURED RACES IN THE STRUGGLE
FOR LIFE.

By CHARLES DARWIN, M.A.,

FELLOW OF THE ROYAL, GEOLOGICAL, LINNÆAN, ETC., SOCIETIES;
AUTHOR OF ' JOURNAL OF RESEARCHES DURING H. M. S. BEAGLE'S VOYAGE
ROUND THE WORLD.'

LONDON:
JOHN MURRAY, ALBEMARLE STREET.
1859.

Broken Symmetry

Taken together, these wide-ranging discoveries concerning space, time, matter, energy, and life give us a world that is not a collection of things but a network of relations in which causality and determinism are replaced by probability and chance. We see, too, with Karl Popper, that "the cosmos bears the imprint of our mind" and that "all science is cosmology."

Consider the striking U-shaped symbol (Figure 12.9) designed by John Archibald Wheeler, who worked closely with Einstein and Bohr, and is still one of the most original theoretical physicists of our time. Starting small with the Big Bang and the synthesis of hydrogen atoms (upper right) the universe expands with the formation in galaxies of stars and planets, followed by the appearance of life. Observer participation eventually sets in (upper left) and in turn determines what we can say about even the earliest days of the Universe. No longer are we mere observers. Instead we take part in the defining of reality (see Figure 12.9).

The outcome is a universe perhaps best described as *participatory, transcendent, and open:* participatory as explained above, but also because "each one of us, and all of us, are truly and literally a little bit of stardust" as William Fowler noted when accepting a Nobel Prize in 1983 for his contributions to cosmochemistry; transcendent, in that we inhabit a continually emerging universe where every whole is more than the sum of its parts; and open, we sense, to possibilities "infinite in all directions," to use the title of Freeman Dyson's eloquent volume celebrating the diversity of our world and ourselves.

Most surprising is the continuing discovery in nature of principles of asymmetry operating at all levels of organization. As pointed out by John Barrow and Joseph Silk in *The Left Hand of Creation,* "One of the most extraordinary things about our universe is that although it often appears, at first sight, to be perfectly symmetric, closer examination invariably reveals that the symmetry is not quite exact. The universe is almost, but not quite uniform over its largest expanses; elementary particles are almost but not quite the same as those that are their mirror images; protons are almost but not quite, stable . . . We invariably find that tiny breaches in the perfect pattern we might have expected to find are the cogs of a glittering mechanism at the center of things, and are one of the rea-

FIGURE 12.9

The universe is a self-excited circuit. As it expands, cools, and develops, it gives rise to observer participancy. Observer participancy gives what we call tangible reality to the universe. (John Archibald Wheeler)

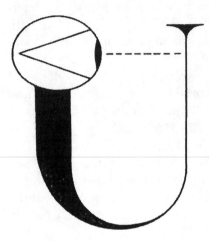

A true science of life must let infinity in . . . (Arthur Koestler)

*But infinities are only theoretical
     and terminate
        in the limit
          of the solitary
              I.*

(Roald Hoffman, from his poem To What End in The Metamict State*)*

FIGURE 12.10 THE ESSENTIAL TENSION

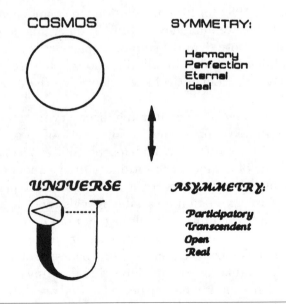

COSMOS

SYMMETRY:

Harmony
Perfection
Eternal
Ideal

UNIVERSE

ASYMMETRY:

Participatory
Transcendent
Open
Real

sons our very existence is possible . . . This tale of broken symmetries extends from the beginning of time to the here and now."

Broken symmetry, of course, implies the shadowy presence of symmetry. In our everyday encounters with art, science, and religion, it seems we equate symmetry with stability, and asymmetry with the ability to undergo change. Within us, then, there is an essential tension arising from our attempts, conscious or unconscious, to relate the asymmetric real universe we live in—participatory, transcendent, open—to an ideally symmetric cosmos ruled by principles of harmony, perfection, and the eternal (see Figure 12.10). To be or not to be, that is the question. Perhaps, as Vaclav Havel suggested on receiving the Philadephia Liberty Medal at Independence Hall in 1994, "the only real hope of people today is . . . a renewal of our certainty that we are rooted in the Earth and, at the same time, the cosmos. This awareness endows us with the capacity for self-transcendence."

Underlying Realities

Examining Wheeler's diagram of existence viewed as a self-synthesizing system makes us ask what special properties of matter, life and mind give rise to our unexpected universe? We can gain some insight into this question by considering those familiar symbols known as ouroboros, DNA, and yin-yang.

Ouroboros is defined in the new *Encyclopaedia Britannica* (15th Edition) as the "emblematic serpent of ancient Egypt and Greece, represented with its tail in its mouth, continually devouring itself and being reborn from itself. A Gnostic and alchemical symbol, ouroboros expresses the unity of all things, material and spiritual, which never disappear but perpetually change form in an eternal cycle of destruction and re-creation." Like Wheeler's figure, it is an entity self-generating and self-sustaining with built-in principles of self-organization. It represents our universe of change, of cycles rather than circles. It raises questions of beginnings and ends and leads us from the rational to the mystical, where, with Wittgenstein, we puzzle over "Not how the world is, but that it is." Ouroboros points to the connection between the microcosm of the atom, the macrocosm of the heavens, and everything in between.

"The spiral structure of DNA has become the most vivid image of science in the last years" observed Jacob Bronowski in *The Ascent of Man*. Deservedly, too, for according to J.D. Bernal "the double helix is the greatest and most comprehensive idea in all science." The unravelling of its molecular structure by James Watson and Francis Crick in 1953 immediately made rational much of biology, including the theory of evolution, by supplying for cells and genes a copying process that is almost, but not quite, perfect. Mistakes will happen, which is why we are here, together with so many other species. The double helix, then, would be a most appropriate symbol for life and its history on our planet.

"One Yin and one Yang go to make the Tao," says the *Book of Changes*, the *I-Ching*. It's significant that the yin-yang symbol pointing to the complementary forces of nature in ancient Chinese philosophy was adopted by Niels Bohr, the father of the atom, for his family coat-of-arms which was also graced by a legend in Latin meaning 'Opposites are complementary'. Seeing this profoundly simple design always makes me think of the left and right hemispheres of the brain, shown experimentally by neuroscientist Roger Sperry to be complementary spheres of consciousness, with linear thinking and analysis dominant in the left brain, spatial awareness and synthesis in the right. In his Nobel acceptance speech in 1981, Professor Sperry went on to propose that in our universe "although the causal forces at the lower quantal, atomic, molecular levels in the infrastructure continue to operate in full force as usual, they are enveloped, encompassed, overwhelmed, superseded, supervened and outclassed by the new causal properties that emerge in the whole." It would seem that the yin-yang representation could well stand for mind in all its creativity.

Overall, these universal symbols can be seen to parallel the domains of *cosmos, bios,* and *noos* which today we see as three stages of evolution, physico-chemical, biological and cultural (see Figure 12.11).

A Mandala for Science

Now we're in a position to construct a mandala combining the unidirectional loop of ouroboros, representing matter and mystery; the open-ended double helix of DNA, representing life and

FIGURE 12.11 UNIVERSAL ASYMMETRIC SYMBOLS

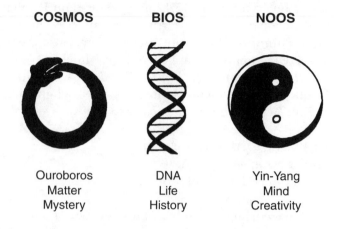

COSMOS	BIOS	NOOS
Ouroboros	DNA	Yin-Yang
Matter	Life	Mind
Mystery	History	Creativity

Two versions in English of the closing lines of the first stanza of the Tao Te Ching:

Yet mystery and manifestations
arise from the same source.
This source is called darkness.

Darkness within darkness.
The gateway to all understanding.
(Stephen Mitchell)

The core and the surface
Are essentially the same.
Words making them seem different
Only to express appearance.
If name is needed, wonder names
them both.
From wonder into wonder
Existence opens.
(Witter Bynner)

history; and the yin-yang circle of oneness, representing mind and creativity. Note that each of these pulsating symbols is asymmetric and that, to quote Freeman Dyson again, "Every time a symmetry is broken, new levels of diversity and creativity become possible. It may be that the nature of our universe and the nature of life are such that this process of diversification will have no end." Within this simple design we can see the emergence of the new sciences of chaos and complexity underlying our search for order.

For background we can use a square divided by color into four different sections (see Figure 12.12 and Color Plate 15) that might represent the elements of old—earth, water, air, fire—as well as the four quantum numbers that define today's atoms; also the four fundamental forces of nature we are currently trying hard to unify. Or the four nucleotide components of DNA and RNA. And for a motto I would choose the following sentence I was delighted to come across in Saul Bellow's novel, *Humboldt's Gift*:

We are free on earth because of cloudiness,
because of error,
because of marvelous limitation . . .

There is, indeed, an inevitable cloudiness about matter, as noted by Werner Heisenberg when he wrote that "by getting to smaller and smaller units we do not come to units that are fundamental or indivisible. We do reach a point where division has no meaning." He added further that "the common division of the world into subject and object, inner world and outer world, body and soul, is no longer valid." Concerning life's history and the need for error, we recall Lewis Thomas's conclusion that "the capacity to blunder is the real miracle of DNA. Without this special attribute, we would still be anaerobic bacteria . . ." And regarding creativity and our mind's limits, we hear Igor Stravinsky saying "Well, limits are precisely what I need and am looking for in everything I compose. The limits generate the form."

We see that there are no final truths and that "all science is tentative for ever" (Karl Popper). Acknowledging the award of a Nobel Prize in Physics in 1954 for his insight into the role of probability in atomic modelling, Max Born spoke for many when he concluded: "This loosening of thinking seems to me to be the greatest blessing which modern science has given us—for the belief in a single truth and in being the possessor thereof is the root cause of all the evil in the world."

Slanted Truths

Such remarks bring to mind the prescient words of Democritus, reiterated in our time by Jacques Monod, that "Everything existing

FIGURE 12.12 A MANDALA FOR SCIENCE

One aim of the physical sciences has been to give an exact picture of the material world. One achievement of physics in the twentieth century has been to prove that that aim is unattainable . . . There is no absolute knowledge. And those who claim it, whether scientists or dogmatists, open the door to tragedy. All information is imperfect. We have to treat it with humility. That is the human condition. (Jacob Bronowski, The Ascent of Man*)*

Imperfection, rather than perfection . . . is more in keeping with human nature. (Rita Levi-Montalcini, In Praise of Imperfection*)*

We are free on earth
because of cloudiness
because of error
because of marvelous limitation . . .
(Saul Bellow, Humboldt's Gift*)*

in the universe is the fruit of chance and necessity." Within these bounds, though, we are free . . . free to express our creativity, satisfy our curiosity and above all, experience community. In our evolving universe—participatory, transcendent, open—we come to terms daily with the eternal mystery of existence through our creative activities in art, science, and religion that produce the metaphors, models and myths by which we live, manifestations of what we might call 'slanted truths', following Emily Dickinson:

> Tell all the truth but tell it slant—
> Success in Circuit lies
> Too bright for our infirm Delight
> The Truth's superb surprise
> As Lightning to the Children eased by explanation kind
> The Truth must dazzle gradually
> Or every man be blind

Myths—stories illustrating some aspect of cosmic order—are seen by Joseph Campbell as secret openings "through which the inexhaustible energies of the cosmos pour into human cultural manifestations." Scientific models—simplified representations of a system or phenomenon—lead to advances in knowledge through our conjectures and attempted refutations, as suggested by Karl Popper. And we use metaphors, not only to bridge art and life, but also to enrich our myths and models. To quote Nietzsche "we possess nothing but the metaphors of things." Arrows and cycles, for example, are "eternal metaphors" illuminating the passage of time, as pointed out by Stephen Jay Gould. And whole civilizations are dominated by the metaphor of the family—God the Father—or by the metaphor of journeying, as in *The Way of Life* according to Laotzu and the Eight-fold Path of the Buddha.

Our imagination works in different ways in each of these slanted truths. Figure 12.13 lists their special characteristics that give rise to the world we live in, permeated by *design* from our art impulse, *technology* from our science search, and *ethics* from our religious imperatives.

Our mandala can then be seen to incorporate art and religion, as well as science, with each modality represented by the same tripartite core of mystery, history, and creativity. The background square with its four colors, however, will have become much more suggestive. For example, through art we might sense a world of form appearing as words (poetry, prose, drama), sound (music of all kinds), sight (painting, printing, film) and structure (sculpture, architecture). Or in science we could envision a universe of energy expressed through the concepts, mathematical or picto-

FIGURE 12.13 ASPECTS OF CONSCIOUSNESS: ART, SCIENCE, RELIGION

mode	ART	SCIENCE	RELIGION
method	METAPHOR	MODEL	MYTH
medium	FORM	ENERGY	LOVE
unit	IMAGE	NUMBER	WORD
impulse	CREATIVITY	CURIOSITY	COMMUNITY
quality	SENSUAL	INTELLECTUAL	SPIRITUAL
achievement	BEAUTY	TRUTH	GOODNESS
practical outcome	DESIGN	TECHNOLOGY	ETHICS

ONLY CONNECT!

rial, of physics, chemistry, geology, and biology. Or we may be reminded of devotional experiences achieved through ritual, prayer, worship, and meditation. Regarding the developing interaction between science and religion we could consider the four approaches defined by Ian Barbour—conflict, independence, dialogue, and integration—or the four quadrants of Ken Wilber based on intentional, behavioral, cultural, and social aspects of our existence.

All in all, our mandala would seem to be pointing to a new enlightenment in our time as we become aware of the interdependence of all being so clearly recognized by Buddha in his time. For a mantra reinforcing this new consciousness surely we can use those immortal words of E.M. Forster: *Only connect.*[1]

---

1. Earlier versions of this chapter were presented in 1999 as part of the Millennium Project of Nomad Central, Chicago, and as a Clampitt Lecture at Trinity United Methodist Church, Wilmette, Illinois.

Coda

AT HOME IN THE UNIVERSE

From wonder into wonder, existence opens. (Laotzu)

Science

- an endless search for unity in nature
- a continuing probe into the mystery of order
- a wandering dialogue with the unknown

is in our time achieving a new universality through the revelation that life may be an inherent property of matter arising by continuous processes of

- chemical evolution
- biological evolution
- cultural evolution

making possible today our re-entry into Nature, here on Earth and in the Cosmos as a whole.

In our evolving Universe

- participatory
- transcendent
- open

we come to terms daily with the ultimate mystery of existence through our creative activities in art, science, and religion that produce the metaphors, models, and myths by which we live. Above all, grateful for our being, we give and receive love.

Background Reading

Barbour, Ian. 2000. *When Science Meets Religion*. New York: Harper

Barrow, John, and Joseph Silk. 1983. *The Left Hand of Creation*. New York: Basic Books.

Bernal, John Desmond. 1971. *Science in History*. Cambridge, Massachusetts: MIT Press.

Brauer, Martin. 1997. *The Mandala: Sacred Circle in Tibetan Buddhism*. Boulder: Shambhala.

Campbell, Joseph. 1988. *The Power of Myth*. New York: Random House.

Davies, Paul. 1988. *The Cosmic Blueprint*. New York: Simon and Schuster.

Dawkins, Richard. 1986. *The Blind Watchmaker*. New York: Norton.

Dyson, Freeman. 1988. *Infinite in All Directions*. New York: Harper.

Eldredge, Niles. 2000. *The Triumph of Evolution*. New York: Freeman.

Ferris, Timothy. 1997. *The Whole Shebang. A State of the Universe(s) Report*. New York: Simon and Schuster.

Gleick, James. 1987. *Chaos: Making a New Science*. New York: Viking

Gould, Stephen Jay. 1987. *Time's Arrow, Time's Cycle*. Cambridge, Massachusetts: Harvard University Press.

Haught, John F. 1995. *Science and Religion: From Conflict to Conversation*. New York: Paulist Press.

Havel, Vaclav. 1997. *The Art of the Impossible*. New York: Knopf.

Heisenberg, Werner. 1971. *Physics and Beyond*. New York: Harper.

Hofstadter, Douglas. 1980. *Gödel, Escher, Bach*. New York: Vintage.

Kauffman, Stuart. 1995. *At Home in the Universe*. New York: Oxford University Press.

Koestler, Arthur. 1959. *The Sleepwalkers*. New York: Grossett and Dunlap

Kolb, Rocky. 1996. *Blind Watchers of the Skies*. New York: Addison Wesley.

Lakoff, George, and Mark Johnson. 1980. *Metaphors We Live By*. Chicago: University of Chicago Press.

Lloyd, G.E.R. 1970. *Early Greek Science: Thales to Aristotle*. London: Chatto and Windus

Matthews, Clifford N., and Roy Abraham Varghese, eds. 1995. *Cosmic Beginnings and Human Ends: Where Science and Religion Meet*. Chicago: Open Court.

Margenau, Henry, and Roy Abraham Varghese, eds. 1992. *Cosmos, Bios, Theos: Scientists Reflect on Science, God, and the Origins of the Universe, Life, and Homo sapiens*. Chicago: Open Court.

Margulis, Lynn, and Dorion Sagan. 1997. *Slanted Truths: Essays on Gaia, Symbiosis, and Evolution*. New York: Copernicus.

Monod, Jacques. 1971. *Chance and Necessity*. New York: Knopf

Popper, Karl R. 1971. *The Open Society and its Enemies*. Fifth edition. Princeton: Princeton University Press.

Rees, Martin. 1997. *Before the Beginning: Our Universe and Others.* New York: Simon and Schuster.

Smith, Huston. 1991. *The World's Religions.* New York: HarperCollins.

Swimme, Brian, and Thomas Berry. 1992. *The Universe Story.* New York: Harper.

Teasdale, Wayne. 1999. *The Mystic Heart.* Novato, California: New World Library.

Wheeler, John Archibald. 1992. *Geons, Black Holes, and Quantum Foam. New York: Norton.*

Whitehead, Alfred North. 1967 [1925]. *Science and the Modern World.* New York: Free Press.

Wilber, Ken. 2000. *A Brief History of Everything.* Boulder: Shambhala.

Wilson, Edward O. 1999. *Consilience: The Unity of Knowledge.* New York: Knopf.

PART II

The Emerging Alliance of Religion and Ecology

13

Beyond the Enlightenment Mentality

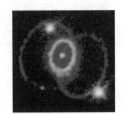

Tu Weiming

The Enlightenment heritage and its modernizing impact of democracy, free markets, and individualism, now possesses an almost universal appeal. But its disastrous consequences should encourage us to rethink and restructure it.

In my essay 'Challenges in Contemporary Spirituality', I, as a student of Asian and comparative religion, made the following observation:

> We need an ethic significantly different from the social Darwinian model of self-interest and competitiveness. We must go beyond the mentality that the promise of growth is limitless and the supply of energy is inexhaustible. The destructiveness of 'secular humanism' lies not in its secularity but in its anthropocentrism. While the recognition of the spirituality of matter helps us to appreciate human religiosity as a way of living the fulness of life in all its dimensions, the exclusive focus on humanity as the measure of all things or as endowed with the unquestioned authority of dominion over nature relegates the spiritual realm to irrelevance and reduces nature to an object of consumption. The human project has been so impoverished that the answer to "What is man that thou art mindful of him?" is either want or greed. The

crisis of modernity is not secularization *per se* but the inability to experience matter as the embodiment of spirit.[1]

My observation was occasioned by a powerful image: the celestial vision of the Earth, the stunningly beautiful blue planet as seen through the eyes of the astronauts. The image presents two significantly different realities. The unprecedented scientific and technological achievements that enable us not only to survey all boundaries of the good Earth but even to measure the thickness of the air we breathe is certainly an established fact. Yet a more compelling actuality is the realizationof how precious and precarious this lifeboat of ours is in the midst of the turbulent ocean of galaxies. This realization, heightened by a poetic sensitivity and infused by a religious sense of awe, impels us to recognize as professionals as well as concerned citizens of the world that we ourselves now belong to the category of the endangered species. This poignant recognition is deduced from the obvious fact that we have mercilessly polluted our own habitat.

We may gaze at the distant stars, but we are rooted here on Earth and have become acutely aware of its vulnerability and increasingly wary of its fragility. The imagined possibility of creating a new habitat for the human community on an unknown planet by massive emigration has lost much of its persuasive power even in science fiction. The practical difficulty of developing alternative sources of energy and the virtual impossibility of inventing radically different forms of life make us realize how unique is our life on Earth. As the horizon of our knowledge extends, we learn that there are limits to the speed and quantity of our economic growth, that natural resources are exhaustible, that the deterioration of our environment has disastrous consequences for the human community as a whole, that the serious loss of genes, species, and ecosystems is endangering the equilibrium of our life-support system, and that a minimum condition for continuous human survival requires the actual practice of sustainable life in highly industrialized societies. The painful acknowledgment that what we have been doing

---

1. In Steven Friesen, ed., *Local Knowledge, Ancient Wisdom* (Honolulu: East-West Center, 1991), pp. 2–3.

to nature in the last two centuries since the French Revolution, especially in the last four decades since the Second World War, has resulted in a course of self-destruction, has instilled in us a sense of urgency. Indeed, by poisoning the air we breathe and the water we drink, in short, by degrading our environment, we are recklessly reducing the livability of our habitat to a point of no return. The necessity of a basic reorientation of our thought with a view toward a fundamental restructuring of our style of life is glaringly clear.

Tools and methods specifically designed to reduce the magnitude of environmental degradation, such as recycling aluminum and applying pollution-control technology, are now readily available. The concern for halting the trend toward massive destruction of biodiversity has prompted new frontiers of research in ecological science. Furthermore, in economics, the emerging field of ecological economics has already recommended ways for using economic manipulations in favor of conservation. However, as Lawrence Hamilton poignantly reminds us, "they do not get at the cause of the problems."[2] Far-sighted ecologists, engineers, economists, and earth scientists, intent on developing a communal critical self-consciousness for 'saving spaceship Earth', have made an appeal to poets, priests, artists, and philosophers for their active participation in this intellectual and spiritual joint venture to make our habitat, our home, safe for generations to come. The felt need to focus our attention on ethics, values, and religions as ways of "caring for the planet and reducing its rate of impoverishment" is urgent. As we diagnostically and prognostically address issues pertaining to conserving biological diversity, the co-operation of schol-

---

2. I am grateful to Lawrence S. Hamilton of the Environmental and Policy Institute at the East-West Center. His commitment to bringing dimensions of human behavior and thought into the scientific discussion of biological diversity and his insistence that without the active participation of the humanists "the best attempts of natural scientists are destined to failure" was a source of inspiration for my reflection on the 'Enlightenment Mentality'. The unidentified quotations in this chapter are from his introduction to the projected volume referred to in note 7 below. Similar lines of thinking are further explored in my 'Core Values and the Possibility of a Fiduciary Global Community' in Katharine Tehranian and Majid Tehranian, eds., *Restructuring for World Peace on the Threshold of the Twenty-First Century* (Cresskill, NJ: Hampton Press), pp. 333–345.

ars in the natural sciences, social sciences, and humanities is necessary. In this chapter, I discuss the Enlightenment mentality so that we fully acknowledge the destructive power of these "transnational, transgenerational, and transideological" assaults on the environment. I hope to bring some understanding to a major paradoxas we reflect upon our human condition in a way scientifically disinterested and yet profoundly personal.

The Enlightenment mentality underlies the rise of the modern West as the most dynamic and transformative ideology in human history. Virtually all major spheres of interest characteristic of the modern age are indebted to or intertwined with this mentality: science and technology, industrial capitalism, market economy, democratic polity, mass communication, research universities, civil and military bureaucracies, and professional organizations. Furthermore, the values we cherish as definitions of modern consciousness, including liberty, equality, human rights, the dignity of the individual, respect for privacy, government for, by, and of the people, and due process of law are genetically, if not structurally, inseparable from the Enlightenment mentality. We have flourished in the spheres of interest and their attendant values occasioned by the advent of the modern West since the Enlightenment of the eighteenth century. They have made our lifeworld operative and meaningful.

We are so seasoned in the Enlightenment mentality that we assume that the reasonableness of its general ideological thrust is self-evident. The Enlightenment faith in progress, reason, and individualism may have lost some of its persuasive power in the modern West, but it remains a standard of inspiration for intellectual and spiritual leaders throughout the world. It is inconceivable that any modern project, including those in ecological sciences, does not subscribe to the theses that the human condition is improvable, that it is desirable to find rational means to solve the world's problems, and that the dignity of each person as an individual ought to be respected. Enlightenment as human awakening, as the discovery of the human potential for global transformation, and as the realization of the human desire to become the measure and master of all things is still the most influential moral discourse in the political culture of the modern age; for decades it has been the unquestioned assumption of the ruling minorities and cultural elites of the developing countries, as well as the highly industrialized nations.

A fair understanding of the Enlightenment mentality requires a frank discussion of the dark side of the modern West as well. The 'unbound Prometheus', symbolizing the runaway technology of development, may have been a spectacular achievement of human ingenuity in the early phases of industrial revolution. Despite impassioned reactions from the Romantic movement and insightful criticisms by the forefathers of the 'human sciences', the Enlightenment mentality fueled by the Faustian drive to explore, to know, to conquer, and to subdue persisted as the reigning ideology of the modern West.

By the late nineteenth century, the Enlightenment mentality, revealing itself as "knowledge is power" (Francis Bacon), the historical inevitability of human progress (Auguste Comte), or "the humanization of nature" (Karl Marx), had become an intellectual source for social Darwinian competitiveness. This competitive spirit, justified by a simpleminded reading of the principle of 'survival of the fittest', in turn provided a strong rationale for imperialism. To be sure, according to Max Weber, the rise of the modern West owes much to the Protestant work ethic which historically engendered the spirit of capitalism in Western Europe and North America. Nevertheless, modernization, as rationalization, is Enlightenment mentality to the core. Faith in progress, reason, and invidualism propelled the modern West to engulf the world in a restless march toward modernity. As the Western nations assumed the role of innovators, executors, and judges of the international rules of the game defined in terms of competition for wealth and power, the stage was set for growth, development, and exploitation. The unleashed juggernaut blatantly exhibited unbridled aggressiveness toward humanity, nature, and itself. This unprecedented destructive engine has for the first time in history made the viability of the human species problematical.

The realization that the human species may not be viable and that human life as lived in the last two centuries has explosive potential for destroying the entire life-support system has prompted some reflective and concerned minds in the natural sciences, social sciences, and humanities to join forces in a concerted effort to think through the issue in the broadest terms possible and to act immediately and concretely in order to bring about realizable incremental results.

The spirit of 'thinking globally and acting locally' enables us to put the *Problematik* at hand in proper perspective. Values espoused by the French Revolution, namely liberty, equality, and fraternity, as well as the aforementioned progress, reason, and individualism embedded in the Enlightenment mentality, are integral aspects of our heritage. We do well to recognize the persuasiveness of these values throughout the world and to affirm our commitment to them for giving meaning to our cherished way of life. The lamentable situation that these values are being realized only in Western Europe and North America must not be used as an excuse to relegate them to a culturally specific and thus parochial status. Notwithstanding the tremendous difficulty of spreading these values to other parts of the world, the potential for their universalizability is widely recognized. The most formidable defenders of these values are not necessarily found in Paris, London, or New York; they are more likely to be found in Beijing, Moscow, or New Delhi.

A brief look at what Talcott Parsons defined as the three inseparable dimensions of modernity two decades ago will help to sharpen our focus on the issue. Despite the acknowledgment that it has taken centuries for democracy to flourish in England, France, or the United States, and that the forms it has taken in these societies are still seriously flawed, democracy as a standard of inspiration has universal appeal. Moreover, the 'third wave of democracy' is a major transformative force in international politics. A more powerful dynamic can be seen working in the competitive markets. The disintegration of Communist Eastern Europe and the collapse of the Union of Soviet Socialist Republics clearly indicate the strength of democratic polity and market economy in defining the process of modernization. Although individualism, Parsons's third dimension of modernity, is less persuasive, it seems to symbolize an ethos underlying the entire value system of the modern West.[3]

While we are willing to grant that the modernization project as exemplified by the modern West is now the common heritage of

---

3. See Talcott Parsons, *The System of Modern Societies* (Englewood Cliffs: Prentice Hall, 1971), pp. 114ff.

humanity, we should not be blind to the serious contradictions inherent in the project and the explosive destructiveness embodied in the dynamics of the modern West. The legacy of the Enlightenment is pregnant with disorienting ambiguities. The values it espouses do not "cohere as an integrated value system recommending a coordinated ethical course of action."[4] The conflict between liberty and equality is often unresolvable. It may not be far-fetched to suggest. in grossly simplified terms, that while capitalist countries have embraced principles of liberty to organize their political life, Communist societies have articulated the rhetoric of equality to impose their ideological control. The matter is greatly complicated by the deliberate attempts of the capitalist countries to employ socialist measures, ostensibly to blunt the hard edges of free enterprise but, in reality, to save capitalism from collapsing since the end of the First World War.

Classical liberalism, as brilliantly developed by Friedrich von Hayek, has performed an invaluable service to elucidate the dangers of socialism as a "road to serfdom," but its own role and function in providing both theoretical and practical guidance to advanced capitalism are quite limited. The idea of a competitive market or free enterprise, in Adam Smith's sense, may have been both a motivational force and an ideological weapon in the modernizing process, but it has never been fully implemented as a political or economic institution. In fact, the enormous growth of the central government, not to mention the ubiquity of the military bureaucracy in all Western democracies has so fundamentally redefined the insights of the Enlightenment that self-interest, expansion, domination, manipulation, and control have supplanted seemingly innocuous values such as progress, reason, and individualism. A realistic appraisal of the Enlightenment mentality reveals many faces of the modern West to be incongruous with the image of the 'Age of Reason'. In the context of modern Western hegemonic discourse, progress means inequality, reason means self-interest, and individualism means greed. The American dream of owning a car and a house, earning a fair wage, and enjoying freedom of privacy, expression, religion, and travel, while reasonable in our sense

---

4. Tu Weiming, 'Intellectual Effervescence in China'. *Daedelus* 121 (Spring 1992), p. 257.

of what ordinary life entails, is lamentably unexportable as a modern demand from a global perspective.

An urgent task for the community of like-minded persons deeply concerned about ecological issues is to ensure that both ruling minorities and cultural elites in the modern West actively participate in this spiritual joint venture to rethink the Enlightenment heritage. The paradox is that we cannot afford to uncritically accept its inner logic in light of the unintended negative consequences it has engendered for the life-support system; nor can we reject its relevance, with all of the fruitful ambiguities it entails, to our intellectual self-definition, present and future. There is no easy way out. We do not have an 'either-or' choice. The possibility of a radically different ethic or a new value system separate from and independent of the Enlightenment mentality is neither realistic nor authentic. It may even appear to be either cynical or hypercritical. We need to explore the spiritual resources that may help us to broaden the scope of the Enlightenment project, deepen its moral sensitivity, and, if necessary, creatively transform its genetic constraints in order to fully realize its potential as a worldview for the human community as a whole.

A key to the success of this spiritual joint venture is to recognize the conspicuous absence of the idea of community, let alone the global community, in the Enlightenment project. Fraternity, a functional equivalent of community in the three cardinal virtues of the French Revolution, has received scant attention in modern Western economic, political, and social thought. The willingness to tolerate inequality, the faith in the salvific power of self-interest, and the unbridled affirmation of aggressive egoism have greatly poisoned the good will of progress, reason, and individualism. The first step in creating a new world order is to articulate a universal intent for the formation of a global community. This requires, at a minimum, the replacement of the principle of self-interest, no matter how broadly defined, with a new golden rule: 'do not do unto others what you would not want others to do unto you.' Since the new golden rule is stated in the negative, it will have to be augmented by a positive principle: 'in order to establish myself, I must help others to establish themselves; in order to enlarge myself, I have to help others to enlarge themselves.' An inclusive sense of community, based on the communal critical self-consciousness of reflective and concerned ecological minds, may emerge as a result.

The mobilization of three kinds of spiritual resources is necessary to ensure that this simple vision be grounded in the historicity of the cultural complexes informing our ways of life today. The first kind involves the ethicoreligious traditions of the modern West, notably Greek philosophy, Judaism, and Christianity. The very fact that they have been instrumental in giving birth to the Enlightenment mentality makes a compelling case that they reexamine their relationships to the rise of the modern West in order to create a new public sphere for the transvaluation of typical Western values. The dichotomizing of matter/spirit, body/mind, sacred/profane, man/nature, or creator/creature must be transcended to allow supreme values such as the sanctity of the Earth, the continuity of being, the beneficial interaction between the human community and nature, and the mutuality between humankind and Heaven to receive the saliency they deserve in philosophy and theology.

The Greek philosophical emphasis on rationality, the biblical image of man having "dominion over the fish of the sea, and over the fowl of the air, and over every living thing that moveth upon the Earth," and the so-called Protestant work ethic provided necessary, if not sufficient, sources for the Enlightenment mentality. However, the unintended negative consequences of the rise of the modern West have so undermined the sense of community implicit in the Hellenistic idea of the citizen, the Judaic idea of the covenant, and the Christian idea of universal love that it is morally imperative for these great traditions, which have maintained highly complex and tension-ridden relationships with the Enlightenment mentality, to formulate their critique of the blatant anthopocentrism inherent in the Enlightenment project.

The second kind of spiritual resources is derived from non-Western axial-age civilizations which include Hinduism, Jainism, and Buddhism in South and Southeast Asia, Confucianism and Taoism in East Asia, and Islam. These ethicoreligious traditions provide sophisticated and practicable resources in worldviews, rituals, institutions, styles of education, and patterns of human relatedness. They can help to develop styles of life, both as continuation of and alternative to the Western European and North American exemplification of the Enlightenment mentality. Industrial East Asia, under the influence of Confucian culture, has already developed a less adversarial, less individualistic, and less self-interested modern civilization. The co-existence of market economy with government leadership, democratic polity with meritocracy, and individual initiatives with group orientation has made this region economically and politically the most dynamic area of the world since the Second World War. The implications of the contribution of Confucian ethics to the rise of industrial East Asia for the possible emergence of Hindu, Jain, Buddhist, and Islamic forms of modernity are far-reaching. The westernization of Confucian Asia (including Japan, the two Koreas, mainland China, Hong Kong, Taiwan, Singapore, and Vietnam) may have forever altered its spiritual landscape, but its indigenous resources (including Mahayana Buddhism, Taoism, Shintoism, shamanism, and other folk religions) have the resiliency to resurface and make their presence known in a new synthesis. The caveat, of course, is that, East Asia having been humiliated and frustrated by the imperialist and colonial domination of the modern West for more than a century, the rise of industrial East Asia symbolizes the instrumental rationality of the Enlightenment heritage with a vengeance. Indeed, the mentality of Japan and the Four Mini-Dragons is characterized by mercantilism, commercialism, and international competitiveness. Surely the possibility of their developing a more humane and sustainable community should not be exaggerated—nor should it be undermined.

The third kind of spiritual resources involve the primal traditions: Native American, Hawaiian, Maori, and numerous tribal indigenous religious traditions. They have demonstrated with physical strength and aesthetic elegance that human life has been sustainable since the Neolithic age. The implications for practical living are far-reaching. Their style of human flourishing is not a figment of the mind but an experienced reality in our modern age.

A distinctive feature of primal traditions is a profound sense and experience of rootedness. Each indigenous religious tradition is embedded in a concrete place symbolizing a way of perceiving, a mode of thinking, a way of living, an attitude, and a worldview. Can we learn from Native Americans, Hawaiians, and others whom we often refer to as 'primal' peoples? Can they help us solve our ecological crisis?

Given the unintended disastrous consequences of the Enlightenment mentality, there are obvious lessons that the modern mindset can learn from indigenous religious traditions of primal peoples. A natural outcome of primal peoples' embeddedness in concrete locality is their intimate and detailed knowledge of their environment; indeed the demarcations between their human habitat and nature are muted. Implicit in this model of existence is the realization that mutuality and reciprocity between the anthropological world and the cosmos at large is both necessary and desirable. What we can learn from them, then, is a fundamental restructuring of our way of perceiving, thinking, and living; we are urgently in need of a new attitude and a new worldview. A critique of the Enlightenment mentality and its derivative modern mindset from primal consciousness as interpreted by the concerned and reflective citizens of the world could be thought-provoking.

An equally significant aspect of the primal way of living is the ritual of bonding in ordinary daily interaction. The density of kinship relations, the rich texture of interpersonal communication, the detailed and nuanced appreciation of the surrounding natural and cultural world, and the experienced connectedness with ancestors point to communities grounded in ethnicity, gender, language, land, and faith. The primordial ties are constitutive parts of their being and activity. In Huston Smith's characterization, what they exemplify is participation rather than control in motivation, empathic understanding rather than empiricist apprehension in epistemology, respect for the transcendent rather than domination over nature in worldview, and fulfillment rather than alienation in human experience.[5] As we begin to question the soundness or even sanity of some of our most cherished ways of thinking—such as regarding knowledge as power rather than wisdom, asserting the desirability of material progress despite its corrosive influence on our soul, and justifying the anthropocentric manipulation of nature even at the cost of destroying the life-support system—primal consciousness emerges as a source of inspiration.

---

5. Huston Smith, *The World's Religions* (New York: HarperCollins, 1991), pp. 365–383.

A scholar of world spirituality, Ewert Cousins, in response to the ecological crisis, poignantly remarks that, as we look toward the twenty-first century with all the ambiguities and perplexities we experience, Earth is our prophet and the indigenous peoples are our teachers.[6] Realistically, however, those of us who are seasoned in the Enlightenment mentality cannot abdicate the hermeneutic responsibility to interpret the meaning of the Earth's prophecy and to bring understanding to the primal peoples' message. The challenge is immense. For the prophecy and the message to be truly heard in the modern West, they may have to be mediated through dialogue with non-Western axial-age civilizations. This combined effort is necessary to enable primal consciousness to be fully present in our self-reflexivity as we address issues of globalization.

I am proposing that, as both beneficiaries and victims of the Enlightenment mentality, we show our fidelity to our common heritage by enriching it, transforming it, and restructuring it with all three kinds of spiritual resources still available to us for the sake of developing a truly ecumenical sense of global community. Our approaches, while divergent in their methodologies and different in their ethical and religious orientations, are all serious attempts to identify and tap the spiritual resources available in the human community for inspirational guides to find a way out of our predicament: the road to liberation may mislead us to the dark cave of an 'endangered species'. It may not be immodest to say that we are beginning to develop a fourth kind of spiritual resources from the core of the Enlightenment project itself. Our disciplined reflection, a communal act rather than an isolated struggle, is a first step toward the 'creative zone' envisioned by religious leaders and ethical teachers.[7]

---

6. See Ewert H. Cousins, 'Three Symbols for the Second Axial Period', In Steven Friesen, ed., *Local Knowledge, Ancient Wisdom*. Also see Cousins, *Christ of the Twenty-First Century* (Rockport: Element, 1992), pp. 105–131.

7. This chapter, originally written as an epilogue for a collection of papers on 'Relating Ethics, Culture, and Religion to the Conservation of Biological Diversity', edited by Lawrence S. Hamilton, was presented for discussion at the Fourth Conference on World Spirituality, sponsored by the Dialogue of Civilizations Project at the East-West Center in Honolulu, June 1992. It first appeared in Mary Evelyn Tucker and John A. Grim, eds., *Worldviews and Ecology* (Maryknoll: Orbis, 1994).

14

Living in a Universe: Native Cosmologies and the Environment

John A. Grim

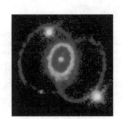

The cosmologies of Native Americans govern their view of their place in nature and fit with their productive activities. Traditional cosmologies have enabled native peoples to survive oppression and resist the continual challenge to their ways of life.

When the fish dam is put in, they have strict laws governing it. . . . families come in the morning, and each one takes from the trap that which belongs to them, as many salmon as they need, by dipping them out with a net that is made and used for this purpose; and they must not let a single one go to waste, but must care for all they take or suffer the penalty of the law, which was strictly enforced. . . . The whites have often said that the Indians ought not to be allowed to put in the fish dam and thereby obstruct the run of the salmon to their spawning ground, and it has been published in the papers that the fish dam ought to be torn out. . . . On the other hand, after the salmon cannery was established at Reck-woy, which is at the mouth of the river, the whites and the mixed-bloods commenced to fish for the cannery; the whites have laws that no one is allowed to let a net extend more than two-thirds the distance across the river, . . . Yet the whites set up one net from one side two-thirds across, and then just a few steps up another net from the other side, and which extends two-thirds across in distance. And in a distance of sixty yards, there will be from eight to ten nets, making so complete a network that hardly a salmon can pass. Will the whites preserve the salmon through all the ages, as the Klamath Indians have done, if they should survive so long? (Yurok elder, Che-na-wah Weitch-an-wah[1])

In this quotation from the Yurok elder, Lucy Thompson (Che-na-wah Weitch-an-wah), the political and ideological antagonisms between 'Indians' and 'whites' find material expression in the heated debate over native fish weirs and non-native nets. So also race, class, and economic questions lie behind the founding of a cannery after the turn of the century and its associations with 'whites and mixed bloods'. In her final remarks this Yurok elder raised ethical questions which expressed her doubts regarding the whites' practice of over-fishing with nets stretched to their legal limits. Underlying her ethical position is a cosmology in which fish dams serve as a material symbol representing human dependence on the renewal of life with the annual return of the salmon. This sustaining relation made present deeper mysteries for the Yurok that brought them to contemplate the interdependent whole of life.

Even as they took salmon life, these indigenous peoples acknowledged the need to set limits and to give thanks. In the Yurok tradition the fish dams, installed annually, were symbolically connected to the four-year world renewal cycle marked by the White Deer Skin Dance. Yurok cosmology and American Indian environmental thought more broadly considered sharpen the questions raised by Lucy Thompson. Religious cosmology, historical encounters, and ecological ethics are all part of the complex trajectory discussed here under the topic of Native American environmental issues.[2]

---

1. Lucy Thompson/Che-na-wah Weitch-an-wah, *To the American Indian: Reminiscences of a Yurok Woman* (Berkeley: Heyday Books, 1991), pp. 177–79. The Klamath River Indians refer to the Athapaskan-speaking Hupa, the Hokan-speaking Karok, and the Algonquian-speaking Yurok.

2. The terms 'American Indians', 'Native Americans', 'First Peoples' are used interchangeably here knowing that they are invented terms: there are no such peoples. Discussions of shared characteristics among the different native nations warrants a level of abstraction suggested by these terms. When discussing specific

In this chapter I plan to go beyond the romanticism of an 'eco-logical savage' or the arid historicism that tries to debunk the 'eco-logical Indian' as simply another human community that extin-guished species and altered the land. Both perspectives project ideological positions onto native peoples. They also fail to consider the religious and cosmological contexts of American Indian envi-ronmental thought and practice.

Living in a Universe: The Cosmology of Indigenous Religions

Indigenous peoples live in a universe.[3] This phrase highlights the cosmology-cum-economy system of many vital indigenous groups. There is a particular interaction between varied knowing systems among indigenous peoples and their ways of sustaining daily life that forms a seamless whole. Traditional indigenous elders do not see social, political and religious components as consciously sepa-rate. Often, however, the secular-sacred split of mainstream soci-eties has been imposed onto many Native North American peoples. In saying that indigenous peoples live in a universe the intention is not provocative as much as descriptive. It signals both theoretical and substantive issues that need to be grounded in particular, local case studies. For example, who are indigenous peoples? What types of ideological perspectives are embedded in the term 'indigenous'? How does one 'live' in a 'universe'? Can the local bioregion be con-sidered a 'universe'? Did American Indians interact with and alter their bioregions in a way that we have not understood? Did the First Peoples on the American continents actually conserve biodi-

---

rituals, life-ways, or symbol systems of a particular nation that people's name for themselves is the most appropriate term. In this latter sense these rituals, and the homelands of native peoples, are not simply 'texts'. These voices are more varied in their intentions than the literate, logocentric metaphor of texts indicates. 'Indigenous' refers to ethnic groups with clear cultural, linguistic, and kinship bonds who have been so marginalized by modern nation-states that their inherent dignity and coherence as societies are in danger of being lost.

3. This phrase, and the cosmology of religions approach, are directly borrowed from the geologian and cosmologist of religion Thomas Berry and from Brian Swimme. See Berry's *Dream of the Earth* (San Francisco: Sierra Club Books, 1988) and Swimme and Berry, *The Universe Story: From the Primordial Flaring Forth to the Ecozoic Era* (San Franscico: Harper, 1992).

versity or is this a contemporary concern which we project onto diverse native peoples? Do Native North American religions still relate to local bioregions? What types of environmental pressures have native peoples had to endure in their homelands?

In raising these questions we realize that specific indigenous communities have responded to environmental challenges from out of the diversity of their cosmologies, rituals, ethics, politics, subsistence, and local economic practices. Such an approach identifies cosmology not simply as narratives that provide an intellectual modeling of universe processes but as a realized cosmology, or functional cosmology. Two observations are made. First, from the perspective of the community of concern the narration of cosmologies transmits values both in the content and in the telling. Cosmological narratives do not necessarily seek to be comprehensive in describing the etiology of everything. Rather, they often inter-relate the origin and presence of places, actions, beings, and objects as central to the identity of a community. Second, cosmologies are a lived method of understanding, a synthetic knowing which draws together creation as it describes different creatures. In this understanding, the creative presence of mystery is embedded in the journey of a people through that creation rather than in an intellectual assemblage of doctrines.

Stories about the journey of the people or their emergence from earlier troubled times transmit the values that bind the collective soul of a people. Simply telling the cosmological stories is an act that gives expression to mystery. Spiritual meaning is thus implicated in both material techniques, such as fish dams and baskets, as well as ritual occasions set by the seasonal calendar. So also decision making, or ethics, is coded into diverse cultural stories of creation. Moreover, naming a new baby in an indigenous community brings together both an individual namer's revelatory vision experiences as well as the collective mythic memory of sacred names. Just as naming an individual or a place may evoke sacred kinship memories, those visionary experiences serve to alter, transform, and renew the very cosmologies that ground them.

Cosmologies provide cognitive grounding for thought about the world. The narrative telling may also initiate lengthy performance modes that bring the powers of the myth to current concerns. For the Tíboli people of Mindanao in the Philippines, narrating the creation story takes twelve days of ritualized activity. That cosmology also provided them with the context for resistance to a proposed hydro-electric dam on Lake Sebu in the 1980s. Cosmologies tell of the multiple relations between humans and the spiritual world, humans and the Earth, and humans to one another. This sequence of stories locates cultural religious life as intimately related to the powers of creation by using kinship terms, and ancestral memories directly related to local place-names and mythologies. Cosmologies often emphasize the processual mystery of creation as meaningful life unfolding in personal maturing life cycles, and recurring seasonal patterns and calendric events. Cosmologies tell of spiritual powers whose very naming simultaneously enfolds meaning into social roles, acts, and institutions.

As a method for the study of religion the cosmology of religions enquires into human relations with the most immediate experience of the cosmos, namely, the material reality of the Earth. In traditional North American Indian religions, the diversity of life in a local ecosystem, or bioregion, is often perceived as suffused with personhood and expressive of a creative, numinous power. This revitalizing power or 'Creative Spirit' manifests its own integral 'voice' to humans in dreams and visions which also transmits the capacity for transformation. Thus, cosmology of religions investigates human presence and interaction with the land and the larger observed world. It explores the communication of that mutual presence and interaction to human reflection in which individuals and communities come to know themselves. By means of cosmology individuals know themselves in the diversity of the world, celebrate themselves in the midst of fecund life, and place themselves within a coherent, meaningful world.

Cosmologies lead the human to deeper experiences of spiritual realms with other-than-human beings and of ancestors, both of whom are believed to co-exist within a coherent, differentiated cosmos. These spirit presences are immediately related to material existence as the 'voices' of nature that often spring creatively from local places and speak to individuals in dreams and visions. Such visions, as imaginative acts of individuals, are not separate from the natural world, rather these experiences are understood as implicated in the winds that communicate and in the fecund world that reveals its power to humans. Something of the cosmos in the human is believed to be capable of deep participatory awareness with the diverse patterning of life in the local region. Communities foster and contest such visions both by comparative evaluations with their ancestral mythic narratives as well as pragmatic assessments their terms of the efficacy of such visions for the people and in light of the performance of visionary knowledge. While this pragmatic assessment may be informal, such as in humor and teasing, even these seemingly casual exchanges arise from the creative interactions of cultural traditions concerning genetically coded activities such as breathing, eating, dreaming, maturing, and dying.

Native American Worldviews and Ecology

What has become clear in ethnographic studies is that people in indigenous societies transmit narratives and perform rituals that validate their view of the world. Indigenous cosmologies impregnate the local region with potential for meaning. This totalizing character of story was also embedded in the cosmologies of Western classical and medieval societies. The medieval Christian order of things was folded into the governance of the pre-European nation-states. Older European lifeways also modulated daily life by means of calendric rituals and life cycle stories, so as to experience transformation, identification, and participation in the power and meaning of local sacred space and time.

Beginning with the encounters with early modern Europeans, local indigenous peoples have been sharply challenged by increasingly secularized societies, autonomous individual decision-making, and rationalized consumption of the environment valued as private property. In the face of these ideological impositions of Amer-European values, indigenous societies have struggled to convey their own worldview values. Performed in rituals, these cosmologies place the time of an individual life in the space-time of a storied bioregion. Imaged in the lived experiences of visionary and dreaming life, cosmologies activate an intimate connection to the original energies of creation.

Functional Cosmology

One example of the manner in which cosmology[4] functions in indigenous interactions with local environments was articulated by the Cree trapper, Isaiah Awashish. The journalist Boyce Richardson gathered materials for a book on the substantive erosion of Cree/Eeyouch lifeways in northern Quebec caused by the massive hydro-electric projects of Hydro-Quebec, the provincially based Canadian multinational firm which produces electricity. His book *Strangers Devour the Land* is a personal, experiential account of his meetings and conversations with Cree people as he prepared films documenting indigenous life in both summer villages and winter hunting camps. He opens his work with a description of his encounters and conversations with the Cree elder, Isaiah Awashish. In one statement, translated by his son Philip, Isaiah Awashish described his life as a trapper in images whose cosmological significance is embedded in the local environment of his trap lines. He put it this way:

> Since I have been a trapper I have been able to see the future in a way that I really could not understand what it meant. Only after, when things happened, did I understand that I had seen it and had known it would happen. During the time I was in contact spiritually with the hunting spirit, what I could see was all about this [the disruptive effects on the land and the Cree people by Phase I of the James Bay hydroelectric project], what is happening now. A hunter must always watch his dreams, for from them he can tell where the animals are. He may see in his dreams a map of the land and on that land he can see where he will find animals. Now that I am coming to the end of my hunting life, now that my moccasins wear out every week or two because it takes me twice as much work to do as much as I used to do, the animals in my dreams are becoming smaller, so I know I am coming to the end.[5]

---

4. The academic lineage within the History of Religions in which cosmology has been primary would include: Friedrich Max Müller, *Introduction to the Science of Religion* (London, 1880); Edmund Husserl, *Idea of Phenomenology* (The Hague: Nijhoff, 1977); and Mircea Eliade, *Cosmos and History: The Myth of the Eternal Return* (New York: Garland, 1982). For "functional cosmology": see Berry, *Dream of the Earth*.

5. Boyce Richardson, *Strangers Devour the Land* (New York: Knopf, 1976), p. 9.

According to Isaiah Awashish, Cree cosmology is a participatory story with both theoretical suppositions and experiential perceptions. The Cree trapper appears to be spatially tenured to both land, animals, and hunting spirits. Cree trapping is also inexorably linked with time past, present, and future. This sense of time is culturally inscribed on the land just as it has been impressed on the trapper himself in the cultural calendar, in personal dreams, and in his experiences of the local landscape. What was revealed by the hunting spirit in past time is known in the events of present time. The causal sequence in this temporal interlude is different from causal knowledge in a western scientific perspective that focuses on proximate causes in a sequential chain. From the Cree perspective causality is multidimensional and proximity may not reveal the underlying motivations behind an event. The deeper meaning of the environmental devastation caused by the James Bay projects, for example, is assessed by Isaiah Awashish in relation to spiritual time. This is the revelatory calendar of the landscape embodied in the person of his hunting spirit

Space is mapped on the ground in the subsistence work of trapping and through the spiritual work of dreams. The map is a mutual exchange with the animals who reveal themselves, who give their bodies to the trapper or hunter. Animals are believed to return spiritually to the Keeper of the Game Animal and to be reborn and hunted again. Thus, animals may establish lifelong relationships with a hunter or trapper as 'friend', or 'lover'. This linkage of time and space with trapping is framed in the mythic dimension evoked by the hunting spirit. The hunting spirit is the spiritual matrix for knowing time and space, as well as a Cree metaphor for the experience of knowing itself. Epistemology is woven into trapping as a totalizing experience, a functional cosmology, whose synthetic dynamics bring the spiritually observant trapper into ways of knowing land, animals, people, spirits, and one's own life journey.

Trapping and hunting for the Cree have special linguistic characteristics which reveal intimacies of exchange between the hunted animal and the trapper or hunter. The language of Cree hunting classifies qualities of the animals hunted, echoes the domestic life of the Cree household in endearing terms used for slain animals, and resonates with the totalizing universe by establishing 'totemic' relationships with animals. The anthropologist Adrian Tanner observed that encounters with hunted animals "are framed as encounters with persons, and Cree interpretations use, as analogues, commonplace social mechanisms, such as coercion, sexuality and gift exchange."[6]

These three social mechanisms, coercion, sexuality, and gift exchange, are deeply embedded in the religious life of the Cree, or for that matter, of any people, prompting one to wonder if religion has not played a formative role in social organization as much as the reverse.[7] Rituals of coercion serve to locate and to fix the animal that will be hunted according to the known terrain of the dream map. Gift exchange thanks the animal for its sacrificial gift and ensures proper treatment of the animal and its bones so the species may be hunted another time.

Sexuality and social groupings according to Cree cosmology are also characteristics of the animals hunted and trapped. Just as rituals of coercion and thanks modulate hunters' relationships with animals, so also divining rituals frame the intimacies of association between the human hunter and the animal hunted. Cree hunting and trapping rites manipulate several types of relationships that the hunter can establish between himself and animals, for example, the placements of coercion rites on an axis of dominance or subordination. Equivalence is another social relationship that accords with rites expressing thanks to an animal as a friend and equal who returns again and again to give himself to the hunter or trapper. Intimate loving relationships may also be established between hunters and trappers and their animal victims which draw on the Cree language of sexuality.

In his discussions of this type of erotic relationship Adrian Tanner draws on the prior work of James Preston among the East Coast Cree of Hudson Bay. Tanner discusses this interesting relationship with animals, which is expressed in language analogous to human sexuality, saying that:

---

6. Adrian Tanner, *Bringing Home Animals: Religious Ideology and Mode of Production of the Mistassini Cree Hunters* (London: Hurst, 1979), p. 152.

7. Considered as a 'hidden history' of religion this topic was a central theme in Lawrence Sullivan's 1995–1996 American Lectures in the History of Religions titled 'Hidden Histories: Sensing Religion in American Experience'.

the victim can be represented as the female lover of the hunter. . . . By using material from hunting songs, myths, and accounts of divinatory dreams, [Preston] concludes that there is a love relationship between the hunter and his prey. In the case of the caribou this love is analogous to the sexual love between a man and his lover, or the love of a father for daughter, but in the case of a bear the love is analogous to the love a man has for his son or for his grandfather. In the case of bear hunting which [Preston] cites, however, the divinatory dream is about an old woman, for whom the dreamer feels very sad. According to Preston, the relationship to the beaver is also analogously sexual, but whereas the caribou gives itself to the hunter eagerly (analogous to sexual lust) the beaver gives itself to be killed with the more decorous attitude of generosity.[8]

The studies by Preston and Tanner deepen our appreciation of Isaiah Awashish's remarks quoted above. When this Cree trapper speaks of being "in contact spiritually with the hunting spirit" he draws together a range of analogous associations such as: a trapper's keen awareness of the bioregion, a dim awareness of future happenings, information about specific animal ways, and personal insights into his own life journey. It's not possible to separate out an environmental component or an epistemological constituent as dimensions of this elder's thought which have independent mental existence. In this sense the knowledge communicated by the hunting spirit does not establish an identity, or self, apart from the whole community or the whole landscape. Rather, relationships of dominance and subordination, of equivalence, or of erotic love, and the perspectives they bring to Cree environmental awareness, are meaningful patterns in Isaiah Awashish's remarks. They form the reflexive pathways for thinking about knowledge, self, and spiritual wisdom.

In human relations with spiritual beings, the pattern of dominance-subordination may be the prevalent model for knowing the local landscape, but in some relations with the natural world the Cree also establish homologous relationships of same to same.

---

8. Tanner, p. 138; for Preston see R.J. Preston, *Cree Narrative: Expressing the Personal Meanings of Events* (Ottawa: National Museum of Man, Mercury series. Canadian Ethnology Service, Paper No. 30), pp. 215–16, 230.

These types of connections establish meaningful epistemological values transmitted by Cree cosmology, namely, knowing as an act shared with many personal beings in the universe. Tanner ends his provocative study of Cree religious ideology and hunting by distinguishing the relationship of the hunter-trapper with the natural world as a way of knowing in which symbols and rituals are semantic tools with which the Cree knowingly manipulate their world. He writes:

> To the Cree a meaningfulness is apparently already given in particular items seen in nature, which we call symbols, and which are apparently parts of total systems, which lead to the conclusion that men do not so much express themselves by means of symbols when they perform rites, as attempt to perceive nature through symbols. For the purpose of this understanding rites mark the special occasions when this perception can take place. Thus rites, by focusing all attention on the oracular messages that come from nature, and which express themselves in the symbols, establish an external validity to religious thought as a form of reality within nature. This reality at the same time becomes the object of attempts to control it, and these attempts follow the pattern used in the realm of material production. For the Cree hunter the production of ideology is part of the process of economic production. But he produces it, at least in part, from his interpretations of religious symbolism. Like the symbolism itself, this aspect of ideology is not verbally explicit, and is not standardized in the form of exegesis. The symbols only offer a network of possibilities within which many ideological pathways and goals may be followed.[9]

Tanner skates across the Cree epistemological world cutting figures that suggest the material basis of Cree religious ideology as well as the embeddedness of this symbolic knowing in nature. Rituals as perception flow from out of deeper revelations within the natural world itself. Creatively narrating and presencing these patterns of revelation, expressed both in subsistence acts and in religious activities, is the central work of Cree cosmology. Rarely interpreted by the Cree themselves into verbal exposition the network of

---

9. Tanner, p. 214.

symbolic images and the performance modes of rituals, neverthe-less, give lived expression to these worldview values.

With the Cree we see that indigenous thought frames its critical modes within a "network of possibilities within which many ideo-logical pathways and goals may be followed." Indigenous Cree thought proposes that there is more than the materialist context with which many would circumscribe human mental and subsis-tence activities. What binds these realms of human thought and pragmatic activity together is a cosmology which is not always "verbally explicit" nor "standardized in the form of exegesis." Yet, among the possibilities for describing and experiencing functional cosmology are rituals and indigenous ecological practices that Native Americans have long considered paramount human acts of the body-mind.

Rituals as Establishing Human-Earth Relations

A major ritual of Native North American peoples is the preparation and use of tobacco in ceremonies associated with a sacred pipe. The antiquity of this culture-building practice is confirmed in the many archeological sites throughout the Americas in which tobacco paraphernalia appear. An anthropologist of South American cultures, Johannes Wilibert, discusses the ancient use of tobacco in these comments from his study, *Tobacco and Shamanism in South America* (1987):

> Prehistoric evidence for tobacco use in South America may go back some fifteen hundred years in the case of an assemblage of shaman's paraphernalia from Nino Korin, sixteen hundred years in a Nasca bur-ial . . . or even as far as three thousand years, in the case of tubular pipes from Marajo Island . . . and the lower Amazon . . . . But ritual tobacco is certainly much older on the continent than these dates sug-gest. Reaching back to the beginnings of lowland South American agri-culture some eight thousand years ago . . . and possibly even antedat-ing the domestication of food plants, the parent species of the hybrids *Nicotiana rustica* and *Nicotiana tabacum* may be the oldest cultigens in the Americas.[10]

---

10. From Johannes Wilbert, *Tobacco and Shamanism in South America* (New Haven: Yale University Press, 1987), p. xvii.

While ceremonial smoking of tobacco is not a pan-Indian ritual, where this rite is practiced it has especially pervaded indigenous religious life as the means for connecting the telluric world of matter with the atmospheric realm of spiritual power. Just as the smoke passes in and out of the human body, the smoke pervades the cosmological layers leading to ancient places where mythic ancestors became powerful. As a principle of communication and transaction with cosmic powers, tobacco has been used to mark transitions between cycles, stages, and roles in community lifeways. The cosmological significance of the pipe ceremony in the North American setting is related to the dividing and loading of the tobacco into the pipe bowl, and the burning of the tobacco as an offering that rises with the smoke. Ritualized gestures evoke mythic narratives establishing the continuity of the ritual with the ancestors.[11] These are performed as the pipe is used and passed among the participants. The abiding significance of the sacred pipe ceremony is such that it can be brought in a meaningful way into contemporary crises that involve both native and non-native peoples.

When the Anishinaabe of northern Wisconsin faced major environmental threats to their homelands from a variety of multinational mining companies, the pipe ceremony provided a ritual means for restating their traditional bonds with the land threatened by mining. This ritual also provided a context for the indigenous peoples of the Great Lakes region to think through possible linkages with non-native environmentalists.

One example occurred during a protest in Ladysmith, Wisconsin on 6th July, 1991. Traditional Anishinaabe-Chippewa and environmental activists had joined together in civil disobedience to protest a proposed open-pit copper mine planned by the Kennecott Copper Corporation backed by its parent organization, the British owned Rio Tinto Zinc (RTZ), the world's largest mining company.[12] At that demonstration an Anishinaabe elder prayed

---

11. Some sources on this subject are James R.Walker, *Lakota Belief and Ritual*, edited by Raymond J. DeMallie and Elaine A. Jahner (Lincoln: University of Nebraska Press, 1980) and Joseph Epes Brown, *Sacred Pipe: Black Elk's Account of the Seven Rites of the Oglala Sioux* (Norman: University of Oklahoma Press, 1953).

12. Al Gedicks in his work *The New Resource Wars: Native and Environmental Struggles Against Multinational Corporations* (Boston: South End Press, 1993), pp. 83–185) described this ongoing struggle into the early 1990s which challenged the

with the pipe before the civil disobedience and gave this talk after his spontaneous ritual prayer.

> I asked the spirits to acknowledge us, because we are a part of the movement that all humanity should be involved in, and that is the preservation of our land and our environment and all things that were given to us originally for the life of the human beings, and of the birds, and of fish, and of animals, and of vegetation. My people tell me from a long time ago that everything was created to be in balance, that one should not overpower the other, and that we should all live together in harmony, and that creation definitely has a purpose to be of great diversity. That's why we are of different races of people, that's why there are different animals and fish and birds. That's why there are different types of vegetation, because creation, life, was made to be a diverse life. And we need to preserve that. The earth upon which we stand is Mother Earth.
>
> And so when I performed the pipe ceremony this day I offered, to the spirit of the earth, the tobacco, and told the spirit that we are here today to protect this land. We are here today to protect all life that is a part of this land. Not only here in Ladysmith, Wisconsin but in the surrounding area, because my people say that everything is to be in balance in order for life to survive, in order for life to be good, in order for people to be happy and healthy, there must be balance in life. And that's why we are here today—to stop the destruction to Mother Earth, the removal of these things they want out of it, so that we can preserve life for ourselves and our children, and our children's children and the children yet to come.
>
> If it does not happen we will all cease to be. And there will be another *moosh-ka-nong* [destruction of the world as in primal times], what the Indian people talk about [in prophecies], another third creation will have to take place again.[13]

This statement of Eugene Begay, delivered after his pipe ceremony, shows how closely ritual is interwoven with cosmology,

---

mining of copper in Grant, just outside Ladysmith, Wisconsin. An update on the ability of the multinationals to push their mining agenda with state government help over local native and non-native opposition is available in Justine Smith, 'Custer Rides Again—This Time on the Exxon Valdez: Mining Issues in Wisconsin', in Jace Weaver, ed., *Defending Mother Earth: Native American Perspectives on Environmental Justice* (Maryknoll: Orbis, 1996).

13. Gedicks, *The New Resource Wars*, pp. 129–130.

worldview values, and actual community crises. One Anishinaabe value to which this elder makes references is 'balance' or *mino bimaatisiiwin*. Winona LaDuke, an Anishinaabe leader who directs the White Earth Recovery Project, co-chairs the Indigenous Women's Network, sits on the board of Greenpeace, and recently ran for vice-president on the Green party ticket writes that "the overall practice[s] of *mino bimaatisiiwin* imply a continuous inhabiting of place, an intimate understanding of the relationship between humans and the ecosystem, and the need to maintain the balance."[14]

This Anishinaabe interpretation of *mino bimaatsiiwin* is obviously different from scientific ecology or conservation. While this native value should not be reduced to another level of interpretation there are dialogic possibilities to be explored in these relationships between religion and science. This traditional value renews Anishinaabe ethical and spiritual relations between humans and their local bioregion. It images sacrificial associations that traditional Anishinaabe maintain with hunted animals and gathered plants and minerals. For the Anishinaabe the thanksgiving to these beings is a crucial ritual act for acknowledging their willingness to sacrifice themselves for human welfare. The pipe ritual provides the setting for a reciprocal offering to the spirits so as to think about the vital balance of life. Performative, imagistic, and narrative modes of knowing join in thanksgiving to the land and animals for revealing that which is sacred in life and death. Failure to reciprocate with ritual thanks, which is tantamount to rejecting the cosmogonic agreement to live in harmony with the land, may bring on the *moosh-ka-nong*, the destruction foretold in the mythic prophesies of the Anishinaabe.

The pipe ritual may be used in many settings just as diverse rituals among Native North Americans have been adapted to changed contemporary circumstances. Spontaneous ritualization and formal ritual not only bind groups together with shared worldview values but ritual also provides the means for individual passage across transitions in life, as well as into specialized roles. Ritual may allow for venting of repressed social energies followed by a reassertion of

---

14. Op. cit., p. xi.

established social relations. Ritual may also be the performative site in which change in society is first clearly expressed. The ritual concerns of the Anishinaabe pipe ceremony described above did not denounce all mining practices but celebrated the diversity of the local region. Rituals remind practitioners that the experience of seasonal cycles and calendric events affect animals, humans, and all life in the bioregion. The pipe ritual is a major performance system which orients participants towards both the diversity of creation and the balance needed within oneself to participate in that diversity. The pipe ritual renews a basic cosmological commitment among the Anishinaabe that accords with ecological practices seeking to sustain life for more than just humans.

Ecological Practices of Native Americans

Closely associated with ritual in Native American consciousness are practices undertaken, or activities forbidden, so that life in the bioregion could renew itself apart from human pressures. Historical examples are known such as the warnings given to the explorer David Thompson when he and his men came near congregated Salish village groups who were fishing at Kettle Falls in what is now Washington state. Welcomed to the area by the Okanagon and Colville peoples in the late eighteenth century, Thompson was told that he and his men must camp downriver from the fisheries and that they were not to use the river for toiletry or washing. This restriction was in place for all the people because the salmon, the symbol of life for these village peoples, were spawning in the river.[15] This example parallels the opening statement of this chapter in which the Yurok elder Lucy Thompson described inappropriate placements of nets for salmon runs in northern California.

A continuing ecological practice which has come under severe pressure recently is the self imposed restrictions practiced by the Gwichíin, a caribou hunting people of the Arctic. These Native North American people purposely refrain from crossing the mountains of their homeland to hunt in the calving grounds of the

---

15. See Richard Glover, *David Thompson's Narrative 1784–1812* (Toronto: Champlain Society, 1962), pp. xcviii, 335–358.

Porcupine Caribou herd. This area designated the Arctic National Wildlife Refuge is threatened by multinational oil development. It is estimated that the projected oil field could possibly sustain current United States usage of oil for six months; yet, the Gwich'in have sustained themselves for a thousand generations by means of their traditional ecological conservation. Gwich'in elders rightly ask, 'How will America survive the next fifty years, let alone the next thousand years, if their leaders keep acting like this?'

The ecological practices of another sub-Arctic group, the Koyukon, have been made well known by the work of Richard Nelson, especially in the book *Make Prayers to the Raven*. In that work Nelson describes Koyukon relations with their bioregion especially as they are regulated by *hutlaane*. *Hutlaane* are an assemblage of prohibitions that result in an ethical system for managing and protecting the bioregion from unlimited human exploitation. Based on restrictions set down in the Koyukon mythic stories of the primal period, or 'Distant Time', *hutlaane* are transmitted as wisdom teachings more than as stern moral prohibitions to restrict life. Thus, the constraints of *hutlaane* connect the Koyukon to their cosmology and to worldview values embedded in this peoples' reciprocal life with the bioregion.[16]

Resisting Limitless Consumption

The many ways in which mainstream America has understood Native American environmental thought reflect dominant agendas as much as they tell us about indigenous peoples. Thinking about these ways of knowing indigenous environmental concerns changes when we know that ecological knowledge is quite different among indigenous peoples. Indigenous environmental knowledge is not simply an antiquated cosmological system that has been carried into the present in hermetically sealed conceptual containers. Rather, indigenous communities have consistently drawn on their traditional environmental knowledge to fight for their survival both in the past and into the present.

---

16. See Richard K. Nelson, *Make Prayers to the Raven: A Koyukon View of the Northern Forest* (Chicago: University of Chicago Press, 1983).

The record of relations between dominant Euro-American communities and Native American nations has been uneven at best and genocidal at worst. To learn that story is to acknowledge both the historical past of mainstream America and to begin a healing of the larger cosmological vision of the North American continent. Native Americans have often been excluded from the history of mainstream America, yet they have never been absent from the actual life of the continent. Indigenous words, spiritual experiences, and visions have interacted with Euro-American names, spiritual beliefs, and dreams. What the different indigenous peoples have brought to this exchange from the beginning is their ancestral voice, the story of their journey, their intimate connection to the land as a living person. Now, many in the mainstream American nation-states, aware of augmented military power in an age of increasingly religiously motivated aggression, turn simultaneously in a search to know more intimately the First Peoples who were conquered militarily but refused to be spiritually overwhelmed.

As the American hemisphere faces a world increasingly global and ethnically diverse there is a growing awareness of diminished lands that are not developed, the resources they hold, and the indigenous peoples who often reside there. Concomitant with that awareness is a dim realization that central to the environmental knowledge of indigenous peoples is a mystical vision which cannot be simply appropriated by mainstream spiritual exploitation. It cannot be bought or faxed or emailed or taught in a weekend seminar. This communal, mystical vision of native peoples has been cultivated in kinship with the biodiversity of local regions and celebrated in cosmologies. It is not the case that native peoples have had no adverse impact on their bioregions: individuals anywhere may fall short of their societies' ethical norms. But it is the case that many native peoples intuit a different cosmological story than do mainstream societies. And that story resists accommodation to a dominant vision of limitless consumption.

15

Judaism and the Ecological Crisis

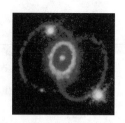

Mark X. Jacobs

The Jewish religious tradition has rules and practices which imply defense of the environment, but many of them have not yet been applied effectively.

Each of the world's religious communities must engage the ecological crisis through its own traditions and its own experience. Yet we find that in their beliefs about human relationship with creation, religious traditions around the world have much in common. As we in the West consider what our common Creator desires of us in relation to creation, those of us involved in the faith-based environmental movements find that the very task of seeking to bring our religious traditions, experiences, and intuitions to environmental issues takes us onto common ground.

Given that all humans share one Earth and that we must work together to protect and defend it, our goal should perhaps be to build a 'pan-religious' environmental movement—a joining together of religious communities in a common struggle for ecological sustainability and justice, an effort to bring all humankind together to forge right relationships with all creation. Yet a place to start is for each individual and each community to search within ourselves, our traditions, and our experiences for the basis from which we might understand and respond to both the particular circumstances we face and the circumstances humankind faces in relation to creation. We are still very much at the initial stage of all of this.

I offer here examples from three primary spheres of religious life through which the Jewish tradition has the potential to contribute to ecological healing: theology, ethics and law, and ritual. Alongside the examples, I also lift up the challenges we in the Jewish community face in mobilizing these offerings to protect and defend creation.

Jewish Theology: Creation and the Sabbath

The core belief of Judaism is that all that exists was created by a loving and just Creator and that humankind has a distinct role and distinct responsibilities in creation. *Genesis* describes human beings as having been created in the image of the Creator of Heaven and Earth, as having permission to exercise dominion over other creatures, and as being responsible for serving and protecting the mythical first ecosystem in which we lived: the Garden of Eden. Historically, many have interpreted the instruction in *Genesis* to have dominion over other creatures, and to subdue the Earth (*Genesis* 1:26, 28), as placing humankind at the top of a hierarchy of living forms and granting humankind permission to control other creatures for our own benefit. Jewish environmentalists tend to focus attention on the 'stewardship' tradition in *Genesis*—citing the second account of creation, wherein God instructs the human being 'to till and to tend', or 'to serve and to protect' the Garden of Eden (*Genesis* 2:15).

Many commentators throughout the ages have cautioned against the arrogant belief that all plants and animals were created for the benefit of humankind. The Talmud finds in the order of creation a cause for humility: "Why were human beings created last in the order of creation? So that they should not grow proud, for one can say to them, 'The gnat came before you in creation'."[1] Maimonides, a Jewish sage of twelfth-century Spain, wrote:

---

1. Babylonian Talmud, *Sanhedrin* 38a.

It should not be believed that all beings exist for the sake of the existence of humankind. On the contrary, all the other beings have been
intended for their own sakes and not for the sake of something else.
(*Guide for the Perplexed* 3:13. Translation by Shimo Pines.)

Perhaps we should understand the instruction to exercise
dominion in Genesis as having been granted to a human community still hunting and gathering, instructing early humans to clear
forest, plant crops, and domesticate animals so that humans might
more fully realize their potential for insight, creativity, love, and
justice.

Understanding the Creator's intent for humankind's role and
purpose within creation is vital as we develop a vision for
humankind's ideal relationship with the natural world. Yet, we
must confront the reality that today humankind has *de facto*
dominion over Earth and all its creatures. Given the pervasiveness
and scale of our activities and influences, we presently have no
other choice but to actively manage nature for its own well-being.
Humankind must now have a self-conscious relationship with
most of Earth's ecosystems—and even Earth's planetary systems,
such as climate—in order to maintain their integrity and stability.
Even the planet's remaining wild places require active human
management of wildlife populations to retain ecological balance.
We find ourselves today deeply bound in the tension embodied in
Genesis; effective stewardship of creation requires that we exercise
dominion.

In addition to the challenge of understanding what the original
intent of 'dominion' might have been, or what it might mean today,
we are also challenged in an exploration of Jewish theology by the
model of nature in traditional Jewish sources, which understands
God as having created a static 'order of creation' with fixed species.
The Bible thus prohibits the mixing of species (*Leviticus* 19:19),
and commentators instruct humans to prevent the extinction of
species.[2] Though Judaism's traditional concern for the integrity of
the created order contributes to an ecological ethic, it does not

---

2. For example, Nachmanides wrote in thirteenth-century Spain: "Torah does
not permit a killing that would uproot a species, even if it permitted the killing [of
individuals] in that species" (commentary to *Deuteronomy* 22:6).

account for the dynamism of ecosystems or the evolution of species as we now understand them. As we develop a Jewish environmental ethic, we must adapt Judaism's traditional concern for the integrity of a static creation to the ever-changing and evolving world in which we live.

Giving the Earth a Rest

The account of creation in *Genesis* finishes with an idea and practice that many Jewish environmentalists celebrate as embodying essential wisdom of the Jewish tradition with respect to the human relationship with Creator and creation: the Sabbath. Every seventh day, Jews observe *Shabbat*, 'a remembrance of creation', a cessation from work, and a time spent in communion with Creator, creation, family, and community. As a cessation from work and all active interference in the natural world, *Shabbat* is a practice in restraint and humility. It is a practice deeply rooted in a vision of justice: all Jews, regardless of economic station, and all of their domestic animals, are commanded to rest. In this age of ceaseless production and consumption, *Shabbat* seems an essential practice for ecological and social well-being as we search to strike a healthy balance between creative work and rest, between changing and embracing the world around us, between doing and being, being creating and communing.

The weekly Sabbath is mirrored by the sabbatical year, the *Shmita. Leviticus* instructs that "the land shall keep a Sabbath to the Eternal. Six years you shall sow your field, and six years you shall prune your vineyard and gather in its fruit; but the seventh year shall be a Sabbath of solemn rest for the land, a Sabbath for the Eternal" (Leviticus 25:2–4). During *shmita*, the land is to lie fallow—a practice central to sustaining its fertility. The sabbatical year rests on the Biblical premise that the land belongs to God; humans are tenants who must obey the given commandments in order to remain in the land. Other commandments include tithing a tenth of all produce for the priestly classes and abstaining from harvesting the corners of fields so that the land can sustain the poor among the people.

Although the traditions of Shabbat and the sabbatical year are among the building blocks of a Jewish environmental ethic, they also present and highlight challenges in creating and implementing such an ethic. Jewish environmentalists who aspire for the Sabbath to serve as an ecologically helpful practice are faced with the actual effect Sabbath observance has on most of its adherents. Even among those who strictly observe its restraints, such as not travelling or actively using electricity, Shabbat often is not consciously practiced in a manner that inspires either ecological humility or increased awareness of nature. With timers and other automated devices, the Sabbath can indeed do just the opposite; it can embody in the extreme our capacity to control our environment. The clock can now tell us when *Shabbat* begins and ends; we no longer need to go outside to observe the setting sun or the emerging stars. Technological innovations can mute the ecological potential of the Sabbath.

The ecological dimension of the sabbatical year, in turn, has been erased by legal innovation. Since the Talmudic period, rabbis have allowed the sale of land to non-Jews during the sabbatical year to reduce the economic hardship of taking land out of production for a year. In an early confrontation in Jewish history between economics and religious obligation (or as we might view it today, economy and ecology), economic activity prevailed. While this allowance may have emerged at a time of severe economic hardship, when taking land out of production for a year would have meant tremendous human suffering, the allowance still is practiced almost universally today at a time when land degradation is clearly undermining both ecological health and long-term economic and food security.

We look to theological principles and the observances and behavior they inspire as a grounding for a religiously based environmental ethic. Yet, the principles of God's ownership of creation and limitations on human use of natural resources derived from it have not necessarily constrained human activity when technologies or legal rationales for circumventing such restraints have been available. Today, we must seek ways to translate the theological principles of creation and God's ownership into concrete ecologically-protective practices. Fortunately, there are precedents in the Jewish legal and ethical traditions for guiding the ecologically relevant behavior of individuals, institutions, and communities based on principles of justice and righteousness.

Jewish Ethics and Law: Preventing Harm, Curbing Waste

As most of the 'normal' activities and behavior patterns of modern living are implicated in some way in the environmental crisis, creating sustainable societies and ways of living requires that we pay attention to the minutiae of our behavior and strive to bring our behavior into alignment with ecological principles and values. The application of broad values to the details of daily life has long been a concern of Judaism. From the intricacies of dietary laws to the regulation of commerce, from the ethics of routine speech to the ethical treatment of animals, the Jewish legal and ethical tradition has sought to apply religious values and virtues to virtually every arena of human life and interaction. Quite a number of Jewish laws are directly relevant to environmental issues and may serve as a model for the application of broad principles and values to specific circumstances. However, Jewish laws generally address circumstances that arose before the modern era, and often have not been applied to contemporary circumstances, though they might be.

For example, the Talmud imposes numerous restrictions on a wide range of commercial activities present in the first centuries of the Common Era, such as milling, tanning, construction, laundering, and trading. Jewish laws and regulations sought to minimize the exposure of people to the nuisances and effluents that were considered harmful to human health or well-being at the time, including smoke, noxious odors, and noise.[3] The law requires industrial and commercial facilities to be located away from residential areas in such a manner that neither wind nor water bring harmful effluents into residential areas. Interestingly, though Jewish law allows a person to voluntarily agree to sustain economic losses caused by an industrial plant (such as a reduction in the value of property) in exchange for monetary compensation, this is not allowed if one's health will be damaged.[4]

---

3. Meir Tamari, 'Environmental Issues and the Public Good', in Tamari, *With All Your Possessions: Jewish Ethics and Economic Life* (New York: The Free Press, 1987), pp. 278–306.

4. Meir Tamari, *In the Marketplace: Jewish Business Ethics* (Jerusalem: Targun and Feldheim, 1991), p. 141.

These and other laws are based on the Biblical principle of pre-venting harm. *Deuteronomy* 22:8 instructs that "When you build a new house, you shall make a fence for your roof, so that you do not bring blood guilt on your house if anyone should fall from it." The Jewish legal tradition derives from this commandment many specific requirements to take all reasonable measures to prevent harm to human health that could arise from one's property, broadly defined.

The questions of how rigorously we should prevent harm, and who is responsible for preventing harm, are central to numerous environmental issues. Many Jewish environmentalists argue that the religious obligation to prevent harm applies to the thorough testing of all potentially harmful chemicals or bio-technologies before they are approved for commercial use. And they argue that this obligation requires us to take all reasonable actions to reduce greenhouse gas emissions to prevent harm to future generations, even if we do not know with certainty the effects of global warming.

Concerning these and other issues, there are many questions requiring further ethical exploration. What do we do in cases where we are radically uncertain of the potentially negative future effects of a certain technology or action? What degree of certainty that harm will not be caused is required before proceeding with an action? What potential harm is it permissible to impose on future genera-tions to obtain known benefits to people alive today—and what level of risk is permissible for what gain? Who is responsible for the removal and abatement of environmental hazards to human health if those hazards were not recognized as such when they were placed into the environment? Is the community responsible for assisting workers or business owners who suffer economic dislocation as a result of the regulation of a product or service? The Jewish tradition offers an under-utilized framework for considering such issues.

Bal Tashchit and Sumptuary Laws

In addition to laws concerning public and commercial behavior, Jewish tradition addresses private ethics and virtues. Judaism rec-ognizes and honors human nature. Its thrust is to embrace sensu-ality, sexuality, and appetite, and to channel these fundamental aspects of human nature and life into holy expression. A tradition of moderation, Judaism seeks to understand and affirm human nature and need while controlling human want. Distinguishing human need from human want has long challenged Judaism, as it challenges all who seek to envision and build a sustainable way of living on Earth.

Following are two of many examples of traditional Jewish restraints on private behavior and their seemingly self-evident applications to contemporary environmental issues. *Deuteronomy* 20:19 prohibits cutting down the fruit trees of one's enemy in a time of war. From this commandment, the rabbis derived the principle of Do Not Destroy (*Bal Tashchit*), a broad-based prohibition against needless destruction and waste. This is applied by the Talmud to such things as not burning a lamp more brightly than necessary to avoid the needless consumption of oil. In a modern context, and particularly in light of air pollution and global warming, Do Not Destroy would seem to have clear applications to the conservation of electricity, gasoline, and other fuels.

In the Middle Ages, rabbis imposed sumptuary laws in many communities limiting the lavishness of and maximum expenditure for such things as daily attire and wedding celebrations.[5] The reason: to protect poor people from feeling embarrassed about the modesty of their attire and their life-cycle celebrations, and to prevent those who could not afford luxuries from spending money they did not have due to social pressure. The relevance of such laws to a society plagued by competitive conspicuous consumption seems clear—for the benefit of both poor people and the environment.

Despite obvious environmental relevance, neither the practice of *Bal Tashchit* (Do Not Waste) nor sumptuary laws have been extended or mobilized to apply to environmental protection. The reasons for this are largely sociological. First, the Jewish community shares with most others a general ignorance about the nature and severity of environmental issues and the effects of our individual behavior on the environment. In addition, both the experience of being a minority in larger societies for almost 2,000 years as well as the separation of economic and religious life in the contemporary West have resulted in a dissociation between Jewish tradition

---

5. Salo Baron, *The Jewish Community*, Volume II, Chapter 16, Section 2, 'Sumptuary Laws'.

and routine economic behavior. Participation in the market—whether as producers, consumers, traders, or investors—is not widely seen in the Jewish community today as being subject to religious principles. An exception is keeping kosher, which is conventionally understood as purely ritualistic and not a matter of ethics.

Jewish ethical and legal traditions could be extended and mobilized to address environmental degradation and create an environmental ethic that applies to the minutiae of economic activity and daily behavior. Yet, in order to realize this contribution, the Jewish community needs to undertake a new exploration and conversation of Talmudic scope—assembling a broad diversity of expertise and perspective to understand and analyze the ethical and religious implications of the full spectrum of contemporary economic and environmental behavior and actions.

Jewish Ritual: The Agricultural Roots of Festivals

The Jewish calendar is rooted in the rhythms of nature and the agricultural cycle of ancient Israel. Passover, *Sukkot* (Tabernacles), and *Shavuot* (Pentecost) have roots in ancient harvest festivals. The connection that the Jewish people maintain to their agricultural roots through these festivals provides a distinctively Jewish link with nature. Indeed, many Jewish environmental programs are timed to occur with the observance of these festivals.

Yet, these festivals are linked to the specific agricultural and natural cycles of the Land of Israel—creating an ever-present tension for a global religious community with roots in a particular land. In most of the world, the Jewish festivals occur in seasons that do not quite match those of Israel. The ecological disconnect that accompanies celebration of the festivals in the Diaspora has contributed to an increasingly historicized, spiritualized, and even psychologized celebration of them. The ecological context no longer has much meaning for Diaspora Jews. This has contributed to an overall delinking of Jewish religious life from nature.

Diaspora Jewish environmentalists are seeking to change this by giving greater attention to the agricultural roots of *Sukkot* (the fall harvest festival), Passover (in addition to the celebration of the exodus, it is called in the Bible "the festival of spring"), and *Tu B'Shvat* (the New Year of the Trees). Many communities are finding ways to connect to local ecosystems and farms. Yet, beneath the surface of such efforts a question lurks: does living a faithful Jewish life that is connected to one's environment require living in the Land of Israel?

This tension is destined to remain, as Diaspora Jewish communities recover and renew the ecological traditions and dimensions of Judaism. Given current demographic trends, millions of Jews will likely continue to live outside of the Land of Israel for the foreseeable future. And given the severity of environmental challenges that Israel already faces, it is clear that this narrow strip of land on the eastern shore of the Mediterranean does not have the capacity to sustain the entire world Jewish community. Thus, Jewish communities around the world seeking to revitalize the Earth-based rituals of Judaism will continue to face the irony that though contemporary Jews have a direct connection to an ancient agricultural society (a precious and rare thing among modern peoples), adapting those traditions to new continents and ecosystems in a manner that maintains their integrity, wholeness, and potential effectiveness is a profound challenge—and it raises fundamental questions about the nature and future of Jewish peoplehood.

Teshuva: Repentance, Return, Renewal

The practice of beginning again, of 'wiping the slate clean' of all of one's transgressions, is a central component of Jewish life. The most serious period of the Jewish calendar is the time leading up to *Yom Kippur*, the Day of Atonement, during which one practices *teshuva*. *Teshuva* is usually translated as 'repentance', yet a closer translation would be 'return'. Jews 'do *teshuva*' for both individual and collective wrong-doing, for sins against other humans and for sins against God. Teshuva requires effecting all possible rectifications and providing compensation for any harm experienced or losses incurred as a results of one's actions. Jewish tradition teaches that through teshuva, prayer, and charity/justice (*tzedakah*) we can nullify God's decree against us for our sins.

Today we have before us many tasks of 'ecological *teshuva*'— restoring ecosystems, cleaning up industrial pollution, reversing global warming, and restoring the purity of lakes, rivers, and oceans. Yet, much ecological damage cannot be reversed. We can repent in our hearts and we can resolve to do better, but we cannot nullify the decree that has resulted from our actions. Extinct species cannot be brought back. Lives lost and shortened cannot be restored. Cultures extinguished as a consequence of ecosystem destruction cannot be revived. The Jewish sages warned of this over a thousand years ago:

> When God created the first human being, God led Adam around the Garden of Eden and said, "Look at my works! See how beautiful they are, how excellent. For your sake I created them all. See to it that you do not spoil or destroy my world. For if you do, there will be no one else to repair it after you. And what is worse, you will bring death even to righteous people in the future." (*Ecclesiastes Rabbah* 7:13)

There are sins that cannot be reversed—and innocents in future generations may well suffer if such sins are committed. There's no justification for this truth in Judaism—just a recognition that we, through our error, can and do impose pain on future generations. Such a recognition calls for vigilant responsibility—and a solemn awareness that repentance cannot be made a substitute for responsibility.

True to the literal meaning of *teshuva* (return), ecological *teshuva* indeed requires a return—to ecological balance and a harmonious relationship between humankind and creation. Yet, we must effect ecological *teshuva* in a manner that does not send us searching to return to an earlier, more simple time. We cannot sufficiently address ecological challenges by doing so—even if it were possible. In order to be successful, we must fully engage the human spirit and the wisdom of the human community in confronting circumstances as they are now. We must imagine new ways of living and we must establish new social arrangements.

Religious traditions such as Judaism can help guide us as we confront urgent ecological problems, but they do not provide easy, simple solutions. Neither theological formulations nor ethical principles create clear resolutions to complex challenges and circumstances. Yet Judaism's principles and values can guide the assessment of circumstances and illuminate the moral, spiritual, and ethical questions at the heart of these challenges. The intricate Jewish legal and ethical traditions also can nurture the hope that we can indeed create an environmental ethic that applies to the minutiae of our lives. Judaism may provide some helpful models for such an effort.

A Jewish engagement with the ecological crisis provides an opportunity for the enduring values of Judaism to guide humankind toward a sustainable future. Exploring the environmental crisis through the lens of Judaism links our struggle today with the Jewish struggle for justice and search for meaning across civilizations, continents, and millennia. Such an effort also provides an opportunity for the Jewish people to find new meaning in ancient texts and observances, to deepen our spirituality, to extend our principles and values to new circumstances, and to re-evaluate our beliefs based on an ever-growing understanding of the nature of life and creation. In partnership with the world's other religious traditions, we can move forward into a new era of human civilization in a manner that builds on the enduring values, hard-won wisdom, and visions of righteousness and holiness that are the common inheritance of humankind.

16

Christianity and Ecological Awareness

Stephen Bede Scharper

As the world's most widespread religion, Christianity has the potential to make both cosmological and sociological contributions to the advent of a new age of environmental awareness.

To understand the Christian mystical sensibility, and its relevance to an ecological perspective, it's helpful to turn to the beginning of its liturgical year, which Christians call Advent. This season is the liturgical prelude to Christmas, celebrated December 25th, a time when Christians prepare to welcome Jesus Christ once again into their personal and collective histories. It's a time when the Christian imagination turns to epiphanies, manifestations of the divine in our midst.

Like the Israelites who once followed a wisp of cloud by day and a pillar of fire by night in their desert quest for the Promised Land, Christians in this season are guided by the gleam of a dazzling star, a cosmic sign of the Spirit, sparkling over Bethlehem. The Nativity, heralded by the heavens, is seen not just as a terrestrial event, but as a universal occurrence, for, as the great framer of Christian theology, St. Paul, wrote to the Christian community in Rome, creation groans with travail until it is assuaged by the redemptive power of the Creator (*The Holy Bible, Romans* 8: 21–22). The birth of Jesus is thus at once both a human and cosmic narrative.

In the Christian story, the star served as docent for the Magi, the wise men from the East, who brought gold, frankincense, and myrrh—symbols of royalty, divinity, and death—to the infant Jesus, whom Christians believe to be the savior of the world.

Christianity now has a special opportunity to give gifts in return—in that child's name—to the world at large, as collectively we confront one of the globe's severest trials—the wholesale trammeling of the planet's ecosystems by human feet and hands—and their technological extensions.

Ironically, the greatest gift Christianity brings to the environmental movement is not an object or an idea, but persons.

For Christianity, Jesus is of course The Pivotal Person. His curriculum vitae, however, is rather truncated by today's professional and academic standards. Born to an unwed mother, he never published a single thought, and probably never traveled more than 100 miles from his home in first-century Palestine.

He grew up in a modest Jewish household and matured to become a teacher of enormous power, who, according to his followers, healed the sick, made the lame walk, and opened the eyes of the blind. Like other Jewish teachers, He preached universal love and nonviolence, and proclaimed the contemporary reign of God.

He also excoriated those who used their power to sully rather than celebrate the human spirit, and taught forgiveness as a habit of being. In his early thirties, he was arrested, tortured, and executed as a political criminal by the extended fist of the Roman Empire.

As the second millennium dawned, Christians worldwide have been celebrating his two-thousandth birthday.

This one person inspired many persons, to such an extent that today Christianity is the world's most populous faith, with approximately two billion adherents. According to a recent study, titular Christians comprise 84.9 percent of the population of North America, 92.7 percent of Latin America, 46.6 percent of Africa, 83 percent of Oceania, and 8.3 percent of Asia.

There are some, such as deep ecologists, who tend to minimize or look askance at the role of people in the planet's ecosystems, and hence might be critical of this critical mass. People, after all, they argue, are the source of the eco-crisis. The fewer people inhabiting the planet, Christian or otherwise, they aver, the better off the planet's ecosystems will be. While overpopulation is indeed a serious environmental threat, as is the level of consumption by those in the northern nations, might not this galaxy of believers be seen also as a potential asset? Who else other than humans, for example, will clean up our ecological mess? As mathematical cosmologist Brian Swimme has observed, blue whales, snail darters, and spotted owls are neither culpable for, nor capable of the clean up of, the pollution that we as a human family have produced. As the world's most populous religion, Christianity, by dint of its size alone, as well as the cultural, political, and economic power of its titular adherents, can be, indeed, must be, a major force for positive human-Earth relations if we are to achieve an ecologically vital future.

Cosmological and Sociological Gifts

In addition to persons, however, Christianity also brings symbolic and sociological offerings to place at the feet of the expanding environmental movement. Yet, when talking about Christianity in general terms, it is helpful to recall James Joyce's definition of the Catholic Church: "Here comes everybody!" The pioneering Irish author's quip denotes the huge swath of diversity in the Christian community.[1] My laconic comments here will thus necessarily be unable to do justice to the wide variety of Christian perspectives on the environment.[2]

Cosmological Contributions

The symbolic aspect of Christianity involves its scripture, imagery, liturgy, and, perhaps most importantly, its cosmology—the story of the provenance and progression of the universe and the human role within it.

---

1. For helpful, accessible overviews of Christianity in general, see Oxtoby 1999 and Cox 1993.
2. For a comprehensive overview of Christian responses, see Hessel and Ruether 2000.

The Christian world is a graced one, proclaimed "good" by the divine, according to *Genesis*, the opening book of the Bible, long before humans ever stood erect to behold the evening sky. Thus, one thing all Christian ecological thinkers acknowledge is that in Scripture "the Earth is the Lord's," no one else's. Despite the famous article by cultural historian Lynn White (1967) which claimed that Christian anthropocentrism gave rise to the ecological crisis, Christians maintain that we are mere transients on a land that we never have and never will hold title to. The world remains unabandoned by the Creator, who has never relinquished his claim to creation.

From this root claim, however, ecological thinking has grown many branches, a few of which are highlighted below.

STEWARDSHIP

A cornerstone of much Christian ecological reflection is steward-ship. Building on the Hebrew understanding in Deuteronomy and Leviticus, stewardship claims that "the Earth is the Lord's." God has never relinquished title to the planet, and we will be answerable to God for how we tread upon or trample the Earth. Theologians such as Douglas John Hall of Canada, Calvin de Witt of the Au Sable Institute in the U.S., and Morris Daneel of the Earthkeepers build on this notion in their writings and ministry. While this model places sanguine restrictions on humanity's treatment of the non-human world, it has, for some, too much of a land-manager connotation to be ultimately effective in healing the human-Earth relationship.

ECOFEMINISM

Noting parallels between the oppression of women and the oppres-sion of nature, ecofeminists strive to move from a cultural para-digm of patriarchy to one of mutuality. Constructing a critical the-ological response to sexism and structural inequality, Rosemary Radford Ruether (1992), Sally McFague (2000) and Vandana Shiva (1993) to name but a few, are claiming that any ecological practice that does not take seriously the oppression of women is deeply flawed. Moreover, they argue that new models of God, such as mother, lover and friend, or biological systems such as the co-operative model of the Gaia theory, can help lead us to a more sustainable way of relating to the Earth.

PROCESS THEOLOGY

Inspired by the work of philosopher Alfred North Whitehead, process theology has attempted to blend an emerging understanding of the divine with a new understanding of the role of the human in light of environmental destruction. John B. Cobb Jr. and his students Jay McDaniel and Catherine Keller have tried to remain faithful to the Christian tradition while integrating discoveries from quantum physics and advanced molecular biology. Eschewing a deeply individualistic concept of the human agent found in various strands of the Enlightenment, process theology has put forward the concept of person-in-community. Moreover, it proposes an 'ecological' rather than a 'mechanistic' model of nature which perceives the human more as a participant with, rather than master over, the natural world. In addition, process theologians have come to critique consumerism or rather 'economism', as the reigning imaginative construct of our increasingly globalized society.

ENVIRONMENTAL RACISM

With the reading assistance of the social sciences, church groups, especially in the United States, are realizing that the placement of toxic waste dumps and poison-belching incinerators in poor neighborhoods of Black and Hispanic citizens is deliberate. They make the connection between economic and racial oppression and ecological degradation (Westra and Wenz 1995). Here there is a clear nexus between social justice and environmental sustainability.

LIBERATION THEOLOGY

Like those who explore environmental racism, liberation theologians, especially from Latin America, are drawing parallels between marginalized persons and devastated ecosystems. A pioneer in this venture is Leonardo Boff, the twice-silenced Brazilian liberation theologian. Boff has drawn a cogent connection between environmental and human rights concerns, focusing on indigenous cultures of the Amazon rainforest where pre-literate societies are being razed along with the rainforest. Liberation theologians such as Boff and fellow Brazilian Ivone Gebara base their critique of modernity on a highly sophisticated analysis of development and underdevelopment. They argue that the church, when confronted with oppression, cannot remain neutral. It is summoned to take sides on behalf of the vulnerable. When these threatened elements happen to be ecosystems, they argue, the church must also come to their defense.

NEW COSMOLOGY

Geologian Thomas Berry and mathematical cosmologist Brian Swimme, building on the insights of Pierre Teilhard de Chardin, aver that the universe has a psycho-spiritual dimension as well as a physical dimension. Consequently, they claim that the universe is a communion of subjects not a collection of objects. From this premise they launch an inspired critique of consumerism as a false cosmology, arguing that we undergo a soul loss when we cut ourselves off from the larger unfolding of the universe for the sake of shopping malls, land rovers, and stock portfolios. For Berry, in particular, the present generation is called to the "Great Work" (Berry 2000) of healing the human-Earth relationship and finding a new way to relate to our home.

As the variety of the above approaches suggests, an ecological Christian ethic will not be dropped down, deus ex machina, as a monolith from the heavens. It will be a framework built out of the richness of these perspectives and the lived practice and reflection of the sundry communities. This biodiversity of perspectives is therefore as sanguine as it is necessary.

Sociological Contributions

Christianity, of course, in addition to its cosmological imagination, has a political, professional voice. When it has used its institutional status and influence to advance the cause of human rights and social justice, it has been a forceful source of social change.

SOCIAL JUSTICE AND HUMAN RIGHTS CONCERNS

At their 1971 Synod, the world's Roman Catholic bishops pronounced one of the most challenging, and some would say prophetic, sentences in modern church social teaching: "Action on behalf of justice," they wrote, "is a constitutive dimension of the preaching of the gospel" (quoted in Walsh and Davies 1984). In other words, if the church is not engaged in the quest for spcial justice, it is not fulfilling its mission.

Behind this watershed proclamation lay over a hundred years of important church teaching, but, perhaps more importantly, church activism in the cause of social justice. In the post–World War II period these movements included the Catholic Action movement, the Civil Rights movement of Martin Luther King Jr., the anti-apartheid movement spearheaded by Bishop Desmond Tutu in South Africa, and the U.S. Sanctuary Movement, inspired by Presbyterian minister John Fife and Quaker rancher Jim Corbett, which gave aid to Central American refugees fleeing to the United States. One of the most important features of church social action has been the witness of the Latin American church which embraced the ideals and practice of liberation theology. Utilizing small faith communities and espousing a preferential option for the poor, the Latin American church from the late 1960s through the 1980s spoke out often against human rights abuses, social injustice, economic exploitation and military dictatorships. These movements represent the basis for contemporary Christian environmental social action.

ENVIRONMENTAL JUSTICE

The church today is involved in a myriad of environmental initiatives, from the World Council of Churches participation in the Climate Change Initiative, emanating from their Justice, Peace, and Integrity of Creation program to the Ecojustice Working Group of the National Council of Churches in the United States and the National Religious Partnership for the Environment based in New York, as well as myriad grassroots Christian environmental groups worldwide. One of the most encompassing of these has been the Jubilee Initiative, an international, ecumenical three-year program that has focused on debt cancellation for nations of the south, redistribution of wealth, and an ecological Sabbath for the land (Mihevc 2000).

ECOMINISTRY

In addition to such advocacy, ecoministry has also emerged, especially among Roman Catholic religious women. Sister Miriam Therese McGillis, for example, and Sister Paula Gonzalez are leaders of an ecoministry movement which advances community-supported agriculture and earth literacy education and promotes eco-audits of congregational properties. Other creative Earth-based ministries include the Earthkeeping Project of M.L. Daneel, founder of the Zimbabwean Institute of Religious Research and Ecological Conservation and the Association of African Earthkeeping Churches, a movement of 100 African Independent Churches which works with indigenous cultures to preserve forests, preserve wildlife, and protect water resources.

Gifts and Challenges

One of the greatest assets Christianity brings to our environmental situation is a cosmologically rich and theologically vibrant tradition which has reflected critically on the momentous social crises of the past two millennia. Out of this engaged diversity, one controverted but nonetheless perduring theme has been the church's commitment to social justice. In recent decades, by attempting to read the Bible through the prisms of the poor, the churches have taken a radical step in defense of those (human and non-human) who have been pushed to the margins of our world.

A second gift the churches bring is a history of implementing their vision of a socially just world. Church action on behalf of the environment has generated extensive networks, new organizational skills, resources, social analysis and strategic action which are now part of a larger historical trajectory and possibility for social change.

With these gifts in hand, the Christian churches must grapple with three significant challenges.

ANTHROPOCENTRISM

Part of the Christian tradition has emphasized salvation to the exclusion of all other material reality. Thus one challenge is to move from an anthropocentrism to an anthropo-harmonic approach to environmental issues. The anthropo-harmonic approach sees humans as mutually constitutive with non-human nature and is a perspective that may assist us in moving away from an exclusive, excessively humanistic point of view.

WORLD RENUNCIATION

There's a deep strain within Christianity that is more world-renouncing than world-affirming. Amalgamated with the notion of original sin, this Christian attitude tends to obscure the 'original blessing', to use Matthew Fox's phrase, with which the Earth was originally endowed. The Christian challenge here involves perceiving creation as inherently good, the place in which our salvation is to be worked out

In facing these important challenges for the future, the cosmological and sociological traditions of Christianity can indeed be viewed as 'gifts' that Christians bear in this time of ecological advent—a time of hopeful waiting for a new star that will lead ultimately to a celebration of God's dream for the Earth.

References

Cox, Harvey. 1993. Christianity. In Arvind Sharma, ed., *Our Religions* (San Francisco: HarperCollins), pp. 357–424.

Hessel, Dieter, and Rosemary Radford Ruether. 2000. *Christianity and Ecology*. Cambridge: Harvard University Center for the Study of World Religions Publications.

McFague, Sallie. 2000. *Abundant Life*. Minneapolis: Fortress.

Mihevc, John, ed. 2000. *Sacred Earth, Sacred Community: Jubilee, Ecology, and Aboriginal Peoples*. Toronto: Canadian Ecumenical Jubilee Initiative.

Oxtoby, Williard G. 1996. The Christianity Tradition. In Williard G. Oxtoby, ed., *World Religions: Western Traditions* (New York: Oxford University Press), pp. 198–350.

Ruether, Rosemary Radford. 1992. *Gaia and God: An Ecofeminist Theology of Earth Healing*. San Francisco: HarperCollins.

Shiva, Vandana, and Maria Miles. 1993. *Ecofeminism*. London: Zed Books.

Walsh, Michael, and Brian Davies. 1984. *Proclaiming Peace and Justice: Documents from John XXIII–John Paul II*. Mystic: XXIII Publications.

Westra, Laura and Peter S. Wenz. 1995. *Faces of Environmental Racism: Confronting Issues of Global Justice*. Lanham: Rowman and Littlefield.

White, Lynn, Jr. 1967. The Historical Roots of Our Ecological Crisis. *Science* 155, pp. 1203–07.

17

Jainism and Ecology

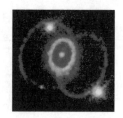

CHRISTOPHER KEY CHAPPLE

The Jaina religion holds a unique biological view of reality, attributing life to the elements as well as to organisms. With some reservations, Jainism has the potential to become a powerful force in defense of the environment.

The Jaina religion, currently practiced by around four million persons in India and several hundred thousand scattered across the globe, in many ways provides a worldview that seems ready-made for the issue of ecological concern. Jainism posits a living universe, uncreated, and eternal. Its essential philosophy is voluntarist, emphasizing that one's individual, self-generated karma determines one's present and future reality. Its core ethics requires the careful practice of nonviolence to all forms of life, which purifies one's soul (*jiva*) through dispelling negative karmic influences. In light of the contemporary diminishment of biodiversity through the world, Jainism might offer a unique perspective, due to its careful description of the immense complexity and diversity of life forms.

From an ecological point of view, the Jaina definition of life holds particular interest. It extends far beyond the standard dictionary usage of "that property of plants and animals which makes it possible for them to take in food, get energy from it, grow, adapt themselves to their surroundings, and reproduce their kind; it is

the quality that distinguished a living animal or plant from inorganic matter or a dead organism."[1] In this definition, life is confined to organisms such as plants, animals, and bacteria. By contrast, the Jaina definition of life requires the presence of
consciousness, energy, and bliss, and ascribes these qualities not
only to plants, animals, and micro-organisms, but also to the elements of earth, water, fire, and air. Much of what would be considered non-living in the western definition pulses with life, according
to Jainism.

This worldview began with the teachings that informed the religious development of Mahavira, the great Jaina leader who lived
during the same period as the Buddha, around the fourth century
B.C.E. Mahavira himself is said to have arrived at his definition of
life through direct observation:

> Thoroughly knowing the earth-bodies and water-bodies, and fire-bod-
> ies and wind-bodies, the lichens, seeds, and sprouts, he comprehended
> that they are, if narrowly inspected, imbued with life.[2]

The earliest known Jaina text, the *Acaranga Sutra*, lists in detail
different forms of life and advocates various techniques for their
protection. It states that "All breathing, existing, living, sentient
creatures should not be slain, nor treated with violence, nor
abused, nor tormented, nor driven away. This is the pure,
unchangeable, eternal law" (*Acaranga Sutra* I.4.1). The *Acaranga
Sutra* discusses avoiding harm not only to animals, but also to
plants, by not touching them, and to the bodies that dwell in the
earth, the water, the fire, and the air. For instance, Jaina monks and
nuns must not stamp upon the earth, or swim in water, or light or
extinguish fires, or thrash their arms in the air.

In the later philosophical tradition, Umasvati's *Tattvartha Sutra*
(around 100 C.E.), states that the universe is brimming with souls
weighted by karmic material (*dravya*), many of which hold the
potential for freeing themselves from all karmic residue and attaining spiritual liberation (*kevala*). These souls constantly change and

---

1. *Webster's New World Dictionary* (New York: Prentice Hall, 1994), p. 846.
2. Acaranga Sutra I:8.I.11–12. Trans. Hermann Jacobi. *Jaina Sutras: Part I. The
Akaranga Sutra. The Kalpa Sutra* (New York: Dover, 1968). First edition, 1884.

take new shape due to the fettering presence of karma, described as sticky and colorful. By first accepting this view of reality and then carefully abiding by the five major vows (nonviolence, truthfulness, not stealing, sexual restraint, and nonpossession), the Jaina aspirant moves toward the ultimate goal of untrammeled spirituality. At the pinnacle of this achievement, all karmas disperse and the perfected one (*siddha*) dwells eternally in omniscient (*sarvajna*) solitude (*kevala*).

Umasvati explains how careful action will help ensure one's rebirth in a higher realm. Violent action might thrust one down into one of seven infernal regions or hells; auspicious action might elevate a person to one of the eight heavenly regions. The highest spiritual action can only be undertaken in the middle realm, Earth or *Jambudvipa*, by human beings. If effective, one's meditation and careful observance of nonviolence might release one into a state of perfection, the *siddha loka*, where one dwells eternally experiencing energy, consciousness, and bliss, while retaining one's sense of individuality, symbolically represented by ascent to the summit of one's own mountain peak.

A Jaina Perspective on Biodiversity

The Jainas were careful to observe and describe the many life forms that they hoped to spare. They catalogued them according to the number of senses they possess. Earth bodies, plants, and micro-organisims (*nigodha*) are said to possess the sense of touch. Earthworms and mollusks are said to add taste to touch. Crawling insects add the sense of smell. Moths, bees, and flies add sight. At the highest realm Jainas place animals that can hear and those that can hear and think, including reptiles, birds, and mammals. Santi Suri, a Jaina writer of the eleventh century, summarizes this assessment of different life forms in the *Jiva Vicara Prakaranam*, a text of 50 verses. He makes clear that all forms of life, from clods of earth to human beings, have "life, breath, bodily strength, and the sense of touch."[3] Hence, all must be protected.

---

3. Santi Suri. *Jiva Vicara Prakaranam along with Pathaka Ratnakara's Commentary.* Edited by Muni Ratna-Prabha Vijaya. Trans. Jayant P. Thaker (Madras: Jain Mission Society, 1950), p. 163.

The issue of biodiversity holds particular interest when viewed from a Jaina perspective. The Jainas claim that according to Umasvati's *Tattvartha Sutra*, 8,400,000 different species of life forms exist.[4] These beings are part of a beginningless round of birth, life, death, and rebirth. Each living being houses a life force or *jiva* that occupies and enlivens the host environment. When the body dies, the *jiva* seeks out a new site depending upon the proclivities of karma generated and accrued during the previous lifetime. Depending upon one's actions, one can either ascend to a heavenly realm, take rebirth as a human or animal or elemental or microbial form, or descend into one of the hells, as a suffering human being or a particular animal, depending upon the offense committed.

Jainism posits a cosmological view that at first glance seems similar to that put forth in Ptolemy's theory of the spheres and Dante's *Divine Comedy*. At the base of this cosmos can be found various regions of hell. In the central realm is the surface of the planet, on which reside the five elements, living beings, and humans. Above this realm extends a sequence of heavenly worlds. At the pinnacle of this cosmos exists a domain of liberated beings who have risen above the vicissitudes of repeated birth in the lower, middle, and higher realms. In spatial orientation and its theory of moral consequences, it seems to evoke Dante's system of Hell, Purgatory, and Heaven. Depending on one's actions, one earns a berth in one of the three domains. In later Jaina literature, various authors describe the living world with a great deal of care and precision.

Santi Suri's *Jiva Vicara Prakaranam* lists types of life and their frequency of appearance and cites an approximate lifespan for each. For instance, he states that hardened rock can survive as a distinct life form for 22,000 years; "water-bodied souls" for 7,000 years; wind bodies for 3,000 years; trees for 10,000 years, and fire for three days and three nights (*Jiva Vicara Prakaranam*, p. 34). Each of these forms demonstrates four characteristics: life, breath, bodily strength, and the sense of touch (p. 163). Moving from the elements to descriptions of plants, he lists various plant genres,

---

4. Umasvati, *That Which Is (Tattvartha Sutra): A Classic Jain Manual for Understanding the True Nature of Reality*. Trans. Nathmal Tatia (San Francisco: Harper Collins, 1994), p. 53.

with precise detail given for plants with fragrance, hard fruits, soft fruits, bulbous roots, thorns, smooth leaves, creepers, and so forth. Santi Suri includes passages that urge one to restrict the use of specific plants, with special attention paid to determining avoidance of undue harm to plants that harbor the potential for even greater production of life forms.

He then describes two sensed beings, possessing touch and taste, which are said to live twelve years and include conches, cowries, gandolo worms, leeches, earthworms, timber worms, intestinal worms, red water insects, white wood ants, among others (p. 66). Three sensed beings live for 49 days and include centipedes, bedbugs, lice, black ants, white ants, crab-lice, and various other kinds of insects (pp. 69–70). These beings add the sense of smelling. Four sensed beings, which add the sense of sight, live for six months (p. 144) and include scorpions, cattle-bugs, drones, bees, locusts, flies, gnats, mosquitoes, moths, spiders, and grasshoppers (p. 71). At the top of this continuum reside the five-sensed beings, which add the sense of hearing and can be grouped into those who are deemed "mindless" and those who are considered to be sentient. This last group includes the denizens of Hell, gods, and humans. Various lifespans are cited for five sensed beings, which Santi Suri describes in great detail: land-going, aquatic, sky-moving, and so forth. The detailed lists by Santi Suri and his later commentators present a comprehensive overview of life forms as seen through the prism of Jainism.

Environmental Resonances and Social Activism

Unlike Aristotle, who described the reality of things in a rather dispassionate manner, the Jaina worldview cannot be separated from the notion that the world contains feelings and that the Earth feels and responds in kind to human presence. Not only do animals possess cognitive faculties including memories and emotions, the very world that surrounds us can feel our presence. From the water we drink to the air we inhale, to the chair that supports us, to the light that illumines our studies, all these entities feel us through the sense of touch, though we might often take for granted their caress and support and sustenance. According to the Jaina tradition, humans, as living, sensate, thinking beings, have been given the special task and opportunity to cultivate increasingly rarefied states of awareness and ethical behavior, to acknowledge that we live in a universe suffused with living, breathing, conscious beings that warrant our recognition and respect.

Various authors within the Western biological, philosophical, and psychological disciplines have similarly argued for the possibility that animals possess cognition and that the world itself cannot be separated from our cognition of it. Few have committed themselves to the very radical Jaina notion that the elements possess consciousness, though some environmental thinkers such as Christopher Stone has argued for the legal standing of trees. For Jainas, the living realities suffuse what in pre-contemporary physics would be considered inert. Each *jiva* is said to contain consciousness, energy, and bliss. Earth, water, fire, air bodies, which comprise material objects such as wood or umbrellas or drops of water or flickers of flame or gusts of wind all contain *jiva* or individual bodies of life force.

The Jainas were quite assertive in making their minority religious views known in areas of India where they gained ascendancy. Many of the southern kingdoms of Karnataka offered protection and patronage to the Jainas, who won several concessions regarding public laws designed to encourage vegetarianism and discourage hunting.[5] Jainism exerted profound influence throughout this region from 100 to 1300 C.E. In the northern kingdoms of Gujarat, it experienced a golden era when Kumarapala (who reigned 1143–75) converted to Jainism. He encouraged the extensive building of temples, and under the tutelage of the Jaina teacher Hemacandra (1089–1172) became vegetarian.[6] He enacted legislation that reflected Jaina religious precepts regarding the sanctity of all life. In the north central area of India, Jincandrasuri II (1541–1613), the fourth and last of the Dadagurus of the Svetamabara Khartar Gacch of Jaina monks, traveled to Lahore in 1591 where he greatly influenced the Mughal Emperor Akbar the

---

5. Basker Anand Saletore, *Medieval Jainism with Special Reference to the Vijayangara Empire* (Bombay: Karnatak, 1938).

6. John E. Cort, 'Who Is a King? Jain Narratives of Kingship in Medieval Western India'. In John E. Cort, ed., *Open Boundaries: Jain Communities and Cultures in Indian History* (Albany: State University of New York Press, 1998), p. 100.

Great. Akbar protected Jain places of pilgrimage and ordered non-interference with Jaina ceremonies. Most remarkably, he forbade the slaughter of animals for one week each year.[7] The Jainas tirelessly campaigned against animal sacrifice, which is now illegal in most states of India. Gandhi, the best-known leader of modern India, was deeply influenced by the Jaina commitment to nonviolence and adapted it in his campaign for India's political independence from Britain.

It might seem logical for Jainas to become active in India's burgeoning environmental movement. The Jainas have been great protectors of life within India. They have inspired legislation to protect animals over the course of centuries, and have been influential in the modern government of India. Though the great struggles to ban ritual slaughter of animals and to free India from colonial rule have largely been won, Jainism is well equipped to face the new challenges faced by India as it continues to pursue a course of rapid industrialization.

Within the past decade, India has faced terrible air pollution. By some estimates its capital city, New Delhi, ranks as one of the five dirtiest cities in the world. India also grapples with development issues such as the Narmada Dam project that threatens to dislocate hundreds of thousands of peasants and submerge vast areas of wild lands. Not only do these problems threaten the life of the air, the earth, and the water, they also can cause great harm to animals and humans. The Jaina worldview, as we have seen, perceives inherent value in all of these life forms. Hence, the Jaina ethic of nonviolence would seem to prompt some response to these issues on the part of the Jainas. Furthermore, the Jaina history of activism on social issues such as animal slaughter might provide a model that could be followed in developing an eco-friendly platform.

The Jaina community has undertaken some steps toward including environmental issues within its religious discourse. L.M. Singhvi, a noted jurist and Member of Parliament, published a small book titled *Jain Declaration on Nature* in 1990.[8] It quotes

---

7. Lawrence Babb, *Absent Lord: Ascetics and Kings in a Jain Ritual Culture* (Berkeley: University of California Press, 1996), p. 124.

8. L.M. Singhvi, *The Jain Declaration on Nature* (London: The Jain Sacred Literature Trust, 1990).

Mahavira's warning that observant Jainas must be respectful of the elements and vegetation: "One who neglects or disregards the existence of earth, air, fire, water, and vegetation disregards his own existence which is entwined with them" (*Jain Declaration*, p. 7). Singhvi himself writes that "Life is viewed as a gift of togetherness, accommodation, and assistance in a universe teeming with interdependent constituents" (ibid.). Stating that there are countless souls constantly changing and interchanging life forms, he goes on to note that "Even metals and stones . . . should not be dealt with recklessly" (p. 11).

Several Jaina organizations have taken up the cause of environmentalism, regarding it as a logical extension of their personal observance of nonviolence (*ahimsa*). The Shrimad Rajchandra Kendra near Ahmedabad announced in 1990 plans to operate a news service to "supply information on different Jain environmental projects and on ecology issues generally to the 450 Jain newsletters and magazines in India as well as abroad."[9] Reforestation projects have been underway at various Jaina pilgrimage sites, such as Palitana in Gujarat, Ellora in Maharashtra, and Sametshirkhar and Pavapuri in Bihar. At Jain Vishva Bharati in Rajasthan, a fully accredited university, the Ahimsa Department offers a specialization in ecology. In December 1995, the department co-sponsored a conference entitled 'Living in Harmony with Nature: Survival into the Third Millennium'. Topics included the environmental crisis, ecological degradation, and unrestrained consumerism. These activities at various Jaina organizations reflect some ways in which the ethics of the tradition has been newly interpreted to reflect ecological concerns.

Scholars of Jainism in the West have looked to Jainism as providing a worldview that speaks to the issue of environmental degradation. Michael Tobias has produced a video, *Ahimsa*,[10] that presents an Earth-friendly view of Jainism, as does his companion volume, *Life Force: The World of Jainism*.[11] Tobias has proclaimed that "Jains are an important challenge and inspiration to all envi-

---

9. *Ahimsa Quarterly Magazine* (1991), p. 5.
10. Santa Monica: JMT Productions, 1989.
11. Michael Tobias, *Life Force: The World of Jainism* (Berkeley: Jain Humanities Press, 1991).

ronmentalists."[12] In my own writing, I have suggested how the ethical precepts of Jainism might be re-interpreted in an eco-friendly manner and have noted some parallels between the Jaina theory of life and the Gaia theory of James Lovelock, which has inspired many thinkers to see the Earth as an organic, living reality.[13] In the forthcoming volume *Jainism and Ecology*, being published by Harvard University's Center for the Study of World Religions, twelve scholars of Jainism speculate on how the Jaina theory of life and the practices of nonviolence can become important tools for cultivating ecological sensitivity.

Tensions between Jainism and Ecology

At first glance, the Jaina tradition might seem to be inherently ecologically-friendly. It emphasizes nonviolence. It values all forms of life in their immense diversity, not merely in the abstract but in minute detail. It requires its adherents to engage only in certain types of livelihood, presumably based on the principle of *ahimsa*. However, if we look at both the ultimate intention of the Jaina faith as well as the actual consequences of some Jaina businesses, we might detect a need for in-depth critical analysis and reflection. First it must be noted that the observance of *ahimsa* must be regarded as ancillary to the goal of final liberation or *kevala*. Although the resultant lifestyle for monks and nuns resembles or approximates an environmentally-friendly ideal, its pursuit focuses on personal spiritual advancement. In a sense, the holistic vision of interrelated life is no more than an eco-friendly by-product.

In terms of the lifestyle of the Jaina layperson, certain practices such as vegetarianism, periodic fasting, and eschewal of militarism might also be seen as eco-friendly. However, some professions adopted by the Jainas due to their religious commitment to harm only one-sensed beings might in fact be environmentally disastrous, such as strip-mining for granite or marble, unless habitat restoration accompanies the mining process. Likewise, how many

---

12. Michael Tobias, *World War III: Population and the Biosphere at the End of the Millennium* (Santa Fe: Bear and Company, 1994), p. 435.

13. Christopher Key Chapple, *Nonviolence to Animals, Earth, and Self in Asian Traditions* (Albany: State University of New York Press, 1993).

Jaina industries contribute to air pollution or forest destruction or result in water pollution? The development of a Jaina ecological business ethic would require extensive reflection and restructuring, a tradition well known within the Jaina community, but in this instance, requiring an additional level of scrutiny that might not seem readily apparent. Nonetheless, the Jaina community, despite their relatively small numbers, is extremely influential in the world of Indian business, law, and politics. If Jains speak with a united voice on environmental issues, their impact can be quite profound.

A Universe Teeming with Life

The worldview of the Jainas might be considered to be a bio-cosmology. The Jainas perceive a universe teeming with life. Though Jainism arose in a time when biological extinctions were not known, the Jaina commitment to protecting life in all its forms equips its members with a sensitivity to the fragility of life that can appreciate the urgency of the loss of biodiversity. Due to their perception of the 'livingness' of the world, Jainas hold an affinity for the ideals of the environmental movement. The Jaina observance of nonviolence, as practiced by monks, nuns, and laypeople, has provided a model for a way of life that respects all living beings, including eco-systems. The Jainas are well-suited to reconsider their traditions in an ecological light, particularly because of their successful advocacy against meat-eating and animal sacrifice, as well as their success at developing businesses that avoid overt violence. Through a rethinking of contemporary industrial practices, and concerted advocacy of environmental awareness through religious teachings and the secular media, the Jaina tradition might help reverse the increased threat to biodiversity faced not only in India but throughout the world.

18

Green Buddhism

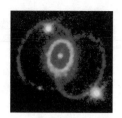

STEPHANIE KAZA

The new Buddhist environmentalism draws upon traditional Buddhist concepts such as non-harming, compassion, mindfulness, and interdependence.

During its 2,500-year history, Buddhism has evolved across a wide range of physical and cultural geographies. From the Theravada traditions in tropical South and Southeast Asia, to the Mahayana schools in temperate and climatically diverse China and Japan, to the Vajrayana lineages in mountainous Tibet, the Buddhist teachings have been received, modified, and elaborated in many ecological contexts. Across this history the range of Buddhist understandings about nature and human-nature relations has been based on different teachings, texts, and cultural views. These have not been consistent by any means; in fact, some views directly contradict each other.

Scholars debate whether or not Buddhist philosophies of nature led to any recognizable ecological awareness among early Buddhists. Most members of early Buddhist societies, including many monks, preferred the comforts of village life over the threats of the wild. Only forest ascetics chose the hermitage path with its immersion in wild nature. The word 'nature' itself has many different meanings in various Asian languages. Concepts and attitudes toward nature vary across time and place as well. Indian Buddhist literature, for example, shows relatively little respect for wild nature, preferring tamed nature instead; Japanese Buddhism reveres the wild but engages it symbolically through highly developed art forms.

Even with these distinctions, Buddhist texts do contain many references to the natural world, both as inspiration for teachings and as source for ethical behavior. For those exploring Buddhist teachings in the context of the environmental crisis, Buddhist traditions are potential sources for philosophical and behavioral guidelines towards nature. From the earliest guidelines for forest monks to the hermitage songs of Milarepa, from the Jataka tales of compassion to Zen teachings on mountains and rivers, the inheritance is rich and diverse.

Early Buddhist Views of Nature

Buddhism developed as a major world religion in the fifth century B.C.E. in north India, where the historical Buddha lived and taught. At the time the region was undergoing some amount of ecological upheaval through growth of urban centers and political centralization. Previously uninhabited forests were cleared for agricultural expansion and town development. Wild areas that were home to rhinos, elephants, tigers, and large snakes, were seen as filled with threats but also available as marginal land. The Buddha and his followers took advantage of some of these lands but mostly adapted their teaching and retreat times to accommodate the farming seasons and to draw on local community support.

In the canonical story of the Buddha there are many references to nature, especially trees. The Buddha was born under a tree and spent many years wandering in the forests and mountains of India in pursuit of spiritual understanding. His enlightenment experience took place at the foot of a bodhi tree, and for many years after he taught in shaded groves to large gatherings of monks and lay people. According to the story, the Buddha vowed not to move from the tree until he gained some understanding of the source of human suffering.

After six days and nights of sitting in meditation, in a state of great concentration, he perceived all his previous lives in a continuous cycle of birth and death, and then saw the vast universe of birth and death for all beings. From this he gained understanding of the law of cause and effect or *karma* and the universal existence of suffering due to impermanence. This was the First Noble Truth. Then he realized the driving force behind birth and death—craving or attachment to existence: the Second Noble Truth. As the Buddha came to see that all phenomena—all of nature—arise from complex sets of causes and conditions, he realized that liberation from suffering lay in this very insight—the law of mutual causality or dependent origination (in Sanskrit *pratityasamutpada*, in Pali *paticca samuppada*). This was the Third Noble Truth: the path to release from suffering. He further laid out a prescription for practice in the Fourth Noble Truth of the Eight-fold Path. He named right livelihood, right practice, and right speech, among others, as methods for achieving release from suffering.

The Buddha's profound appreciation for the universal existence of suffering engendered a great compassionate response, expressed in the form of sharing his teachings with others. Compassion (*karuna*) and loving kindness (*metta*) for all beings arises directly from this understanding of the nature of suffering. Early Buddhism was strongly influenced by the Hindu and Jain principle of *ahimsa* or nonharming. Buddhist teachings urged monks not to harm any living thing; killing animals for food was against the monastic code. The classic Jataka Tales of India recount the many former lives of the Buddha as an animal or tree when he showed great compassion to others who were suffering. Over 500 tales have been handed down from the oral tradition, ranging from simple animal fables to fragments of heroic epics. It is said that the verses and stories were told by the Buddha himself as a way of commenting on particular life situations challenging his students. In each of the tales the Buddha-to-be sets a strong moral example of compassion for plants and animals in his many lifetimes before his rebirth as the Buddha.[1]

The *Agganna Sutta* from the Pali Canon of early Buddhist teachings relates the Buddhist counterpart of a creation story in which

---

1. One collection is by Ethel Beswick: *Jataka Tales: Birth Stories of the Buddha* (London: Murray, 1956).

human activities clearly affect their environment. The original beings are described as self-luminous, subsisting on bliss and freely traveling through space. At that time it is said that the Earth was covered with a flavorful substance much like butter which caused the arising of greed. The more the beings ate of the butter, the more solid their bodies became. Difference of form appeared and the more beautiful ones developed conceit and looked down on the others. Self-growing rice appeared on the Earth to replace the butter and before long, people began hoarding and then stealing food. As people erred in their ways, the richness of the Earth declined. The point of the sutta is to show that environmental health is bound up with human morality.[2] Several other suttas also spell out the environmental impacts of greed, hate, and ignorance, showing how these three poisons produce both internal and external pollution. In contrast, the practice of generosity, compassion, and wisdom can reverse such environmental decline and produce health and purity.

The early monastic code, the Vinaya, contained a number of guidelines for caring for the environment.[3] Monks were not to travel during the rainy season for fear of killing the worms and insects that come to the surface in wet weather. Similarly, monks were not to dig in the ground or drink unstrained water. Even wild animals were to be treated with kindness. Plants too were not to be injured carelessly but respected for all that they give to people. Buddhists adopted a reverential attitude toward large trees, carrying on the Indian tradition regarding *vanaspati* or 'lords of the forest'. Some of these huge trees were thought to be former Buddhas; protecting trees and preserving open lands were considered meritorious deeds. The Buddha constantly urged his followers to choose natural habitats to engage in meditation, free from the influence of everyday human activity.

---

2. Described in detail in P.D. Ryan, *Buddhism and the Natural World: Toward a Meaningful Myth* (Birmingham: Windhorse, 1998).

3. See, for example, Lily de Silva, 'Early Buddhist Attitudes toward Nature' in *Dharma Rain: Sources of Buddhist Environmentalism* (Boston: Shambhala, 2000).

Northern Views: The Mahayana Tradition

As Indian Buddhism developed into many strands of philosophy and practice, teachings were carried north to China. Each sect emphasized particular texts, principles, and practices, each with varying degrees of application to environmental concerns. The Hua-Yen school of Buddhism which developed in seventh-century China, placed particular emphasis on the law of interdependence or mutual causality. Ecological understanding of natural systems fits very well within the Buddhist description of interdependence.[4] Throughout many cultural forms of Buddhism, nature is perceived as relational, each phenomenon dependent on a multitude of causes and conditions. These causes include not only physical and biological factors but also historical and cultural factors, in other words human values and forms of thought.

The Hua Yen Avatamsaka Sutra developed a teaching metaphor, the Jewel Net of Indra, to communicate the infinite complexity of the multicausal universe. This cosmic net contains a multifaceted jewel at each of its nodes, with each jewel reflecting all the others. If any of the jewels become cloudy (toxic or polluted), they reflect the others less clearly. To extend the metaphor, tugs on any of the net lines, e.g. through loss of species or habitat, affect all the other lines. Likewise, if clouded jewels are cleared up (rivers cleaned, wetlands restored), life across the net is enhanced. Because the net of interdependence includes not only the actions of all beings but also their thoughts, the intention of the actor becomes a critical factor in determining what happens. This, then, provides both a principle of explanation for the way things are, and a path for positive action.

The law of interdependence suggests a powerful corollary, sometimes noted as 'emptiness of separate self'. If all phenomena

---

4. See for example, Francis H. Cook, 'The Jewel Net of Indra', in J. Baird Callicott and Roger T. Ames, eds., *Nature in Asian Traditions of Thought* (Albany: State University of New York Press, 1989), pp. 213–230; Bill Devall, 'Ecocentric Sangha', in Alan Hunt-Badiner, ed., *Dharma Gaia* (Berkeley: Parallax, 1990), pp. 155–164; Paul O. Ingram, 'Nature's Jeweled Net: Kukai's Ecological Buddhism. *The Pacific World* 6 (1990), pp. 50–64; Joanna Macy, *Mutual Causality in Buddhism and General Systems Theory: the Dharma of Natural Systems* (Albany: State University of New York Press, 1991).

are dependent on interacting causes and conditions, nothing exists by itself, autonomous and self-supporting. This Buddhist understanding and experience of self directly contradicts the traditional western sense of self as a discrete individual. Philosopher Alan Watts called this assumption of separateness the 'skin-encapsulated ego'—the very delusion that Buddhist practices seek to cut through. Interpreting the Hua Yen metaphor, modern American poet Gary Snyder suggests that the empty nature of self provides a link to "wild mind," or access to the energetic forces that determine the nature of life.[5] These forces act outside of human influence, setting the historical, ecological, and even cosmological context for all life.

T'ien-t'ai monks in eighth-century China believed in a universal Buddha nature that dwelled in all forms of life. Sentient (animal) and non-sentient (plant) beings and even the Earth itself were seen as capable of achieving enlightenment. This concept of Buddha-nature is closely related to Chinese views of *chi* or moving energy, ever changing, taking new form. Thus their views of nature reflect a dynamic sense of flow and interconnection between all beings, with Buddha-nature arising and changing constantly.

Northern or Mahayana schools also came to emphasize the path of the bodhisattva, one who vows to serve others until all the world's suffering is extinguished. Where earlier Theravada schools emphasized achieving enlightenment and leaving the world of suffering, the northern schools influenced by Confucian social codes, placed great value on service to others. Tibetan schools reinforced this vow by encouraging people to treat all sentient beings as possibly having been their mother in a former life. Bodhisattva acts of service are thus personally motivated, creating a foundation for a kind of virtue ethic. This directly applies to relations with plants and animals as well as people, encouraging environmental protection and kindness as important to enlightenment.

As Zen Buddhism became established in Japan, monastic temples were often built in mountainous or forested places. The strong tradition of haiku and other classic verse forms cultivated a sense of oneness with nature, whether insect or landform. Dogen, founder of the Soto sect of Zen, spoke of mountains and waters as

---

5. Gary Snyder, *A Place in Space* (Washington, DC: Counterpoint, 1995).

sutras themselves, the very evidence of the Dharma arising.[6] He taught a method of direct knowing, experiencing this dharma of nature with no separation. The goal of meditation was nondualistic understanding, complete communion or transmission between two beings. Dogen showed how much of human suffering described in the First Noble Truth generates from egoistic views based in dualistic understanding. Enlightenment is then the breakthrough or liberation from these views to experience the self and myriad beings as one energetic event.

Modern Buddhist Ecological Views

Buddhist environmental teachers and writers at the turn of the century are currently emphasizing five primary arenas of practice and philosophy which support an environmental view: interdependence, compassion, mindfulness, nondualistic views, and detachment from self. At the heart of the Buddha's path is reflective inquiry into the nature of reality. Some experience interdependence in its more ecstatic forms of communion with plants and animals or sacred places. But engaging interdependence in today's environmental context also means undertaking rigorous examination of conditioned beliefs and thought patterns regarding the natural world. This may include such challenges as objectification of plants and animals, stereotyping of environmentalists, dualistic thinking of enemyism, the impacts of materialism, and environmental racism.

The law of interdependence is based on an understanding of the nature of the many relations at play in a situation. This may mean, for example, assessing who's who in an environmental conflict from a context of historical and geographical causes and conditions. Such investigation includes learning about ecological relationships under siege as well as observing the distribution of power across the human political relationships.

The practice of *ahimsa* or non-harming arises naturally from a true experience of compassion. The basic Buddhist precepts or eth-

---

6. See 'Mountains and Waters Sutra' in Kazuaki Tanahashi, ed., *Moon in a Dewdrop: Writings of Zen Master Dogen* (San Francisco: North Point, 1985), pp. 97–107.

ical guidelines rely fundamentally on non-harming or reducing the suffering of others. The first precept, 'not killing', has been applied to ethical dilemmas around food, land use, pesticides, pollution, and cultural economic invasion. The second precept, 'not stealing', suggests examining the implications of global trade and corporate exploitation of resources. 'Not lying' brings up issues in advertising and consumerism. 'Not engaging in abusive relations' covers a broad realm of cruelty and disrespect for nonhuman others. Vietnamese Zen teacher Thich Nhat Hanh interprets the precept prohibiting drugs and alcohol to include the toxic addictions of television, video games, and junk magazines. Non-harming extends to all beings—not merely to those who are useful or irritating to humans. It also applies to environmental oppression of plants, animals, rivers, rocks, and mountains as well as to human oppression based on race, class, or gender discrimination. This green Buddhist teaching is congruent with many schools of ecophilosophy which respect the intrinsic value and capacity for experience of each being.

Mindfulness practice, a natural support to Buddhist environmentalism, is being taught in a range of contexts. The basic teachings of the *Satipatthana Sutta* or the mindfulness text, cultivate awareness of breath, body, feelings, and mind. Walking and sitting meditation are used to generate a sense of centered presence and alertness to where one actually is. Such mindfulness generates appreciation and respect toward the natural world, with practices related to food and eating, time and place, and personal well-being. Those practicing mindfulness are encouraged to slow down, consider their actions carefully, and make every effort not to cause suffering to others, including plants and animals.

Most political battles play out as confrontations between apparent enemies: loggers versus spotted owl defenders, housewives versus toxic polluters, birdlovers versus pesticide producers. From a Buddhist perspective, this kind of dualistic hatred destroys spiritual equanimity, thus, it is much better to work from an inclusive perspective, offering kindness to all parties involved, even while setting firm moral boundaries against harmful actions. A Buddhist orientation to nondualism can help to stabilize a volatile situation and establish new grounds for negotiation. Buddhist texts emphasize a strong relationship between intention, action, and karmic effects of an action. If an environmental campaign is undertaken out of spite, revenge, or rage, that emotional tone will carry forth into all the ripening of the fruits of that action (and likely cause a similar reaction in response). However, if an action is grounded in understanding that the other party is also part of Indra's Jewel Net, then things unfold with less antagonism.

Perhaps the most significant teaching of the Dharma relevant to Buddhist activism is the practice of detachment from the ego-generating self. Thus, a Buddhist approach to environmental activism would be nonheroic, not motivated primarily by the need for ego identity or satisfaction. Strong intention with less orientation to the self relieves the activist from focusing so strongly on results. One does what is necessary in the situation, not bound by the need for it to reinforce one's ideas or to turn out a certain way. Small 'b' Buddhists have been able to act as bridge-builders in hostile or reactive situations by toning down the need for personal recognition. Cautioning against the self-serving ego, Buddhist teachers emphasize the power of *kalyana mitta*, or spiritual friendship—acting together in mutual support to help others practice the Dharma and take care of this world.

The Buddhist path of liberation includes the practice of physical, emotional, and mental awareness. Such practice can increase appreciation for the natural world; it can also reveal cultural assumptions about privilege, comfort, consumption, and the abuse of nature. Scholar Alan Sponberg suggests that a Buddhist environmental ethic is a virtue ethic, based fundamentally on development of consciousness and a sense of responsibility to act compassionately for the benefit of all forms of life.[7] Through the practice of green virtue ethics, modern teachers encourage students to be environmentally accountable for all of their actions, from eating food to using a car to buying new clothes. Through following the fundamental precepts, environmentally-oriented Buddhists can practice moderation and restraint, simplifying needs and desires to reduce suffering for others.

---

7. Alan Sponberg, 'Green Buddhism and the Hierarchy of Compassion', in Mary Evelyn Tucker and Duncan Ryuken Williams, eds., *Buddhism and Ecology: The Interconnectedness of Dharma and Deeds* (Cambridge: Harvard University Press, 1997), pp. 351–376.

Recent History of Buddhism and Ecology

In the last few decades, Buddhists around the world have responded creatively to environmental problems, drawing on principles of Buddhist philosophy and practice. Forest monks in Thailand lead meditation walks around polluted areas; Tibetans collaborate with western NGOs to expose recent environmental destruction in Tibet. American Buddhists have worked on issues of consumerism, wilderness protection, and animal rights. One of the earliest voices for Buddhist environmentalism was Gary Snyder, North American Zen student and poet, who illuminated connections between Buddhist training and ecological activism. In the 1950s and 1960s, members of the Beat generation and Sixties counterculture explored these links further, certain that spiritual leadership was necessary to halt planetwide ecological destruction.

In the 1970s the environmental movement swelled, and Buddhist centers became well established in the West. Some retreat centers confronted ecological issues head on. Zen Mountain Monastery in New York faced off with the Department of Environmental Conservation over a beaver dam and forestry issues. Green Gulch Zen Center in northern California worked out water use agreements with its farming neighbors and the Golden Gate National Recreation Area. At a time when vegetarianism was not such a popular choice, most Buddhist centers refrained from meat-eating, often with awareness of the associated environmental problems. Several Buddhist centers made some effort to grow their own organic food.[8]

By the 1980s Buddhist leaders were explicitly addressing the ecocrisis and incorporating ecological awareness into their teaching. In the 1989 Nobel Peace Prize acceptance speech, His Holiness the Dalai Lama proposed making Tibet an international ecological reserve. Vietnamese peace activist and Zen monk Thich Nhat Han spoke of 'interbeing' using ecological examples. Zen teachers Robert Aitken in Hawaii and Daido Loori in New York examined

---

8. For a detailed study of two Buddhist centers see Stephanie Kaza, 'American Buddhist Response to the Land: Ecological Practice at Two West Coast Retreat Centers', in Mary Evelyn Tucker and Duncan Ryuken Williams, eds., *Buddhism and Ecology: The Interconnectedness of Dharma and Deeds* (Cambridge: Harvard University Press, 1997), pp. 219–248.

the Buddhist precepts from an environmental perspective. Joanna Macy creatively synthesized elements of Buddhism and deep ecology, challenging people to take their insights into direct action. The Buddhist Peace Fellowship, founded in 1978, gave prominence to environmental concerns on its activist agenda.

In Thailand, village priests took the initiative to perform ritual ordination of significant trees as a symbolic gesture of solidarity with threatened forests. Other monks got involved with activist efforts to question economic development and its environmental impacts. Plastic bags, toxic lakes, and nuclear reactors were targeted by Buddhist leaders as detrimental influences on people's physical and spiritual health. Similarly, in Tibet and Burma, Buddhist environmentalists drew attention to oil pipelines, hunting of endangered species, and threats to unique habitats.

In the western world, the Buddhism and Ecology theme was picked up by Buddhist publications, conferences, and retreat centers. Buddhist Peace Fellowship produced a substantial packet and poster for Earth Day 1990. The first popular anthology of Buddhism and ecology writings, *Dharma Gaia*, was published by Parallax Press that same year, following the more scholarly collection, *Nature in Asian Traditions of Thought*. World Wide Fund for Nature brought out a series of books on five world religions, including *Buddhism and Ecology*. Buddhist magazines such as *Tricycle, Shambhala Sun, Inquiring Mind, Turning Wheel, and Mountain Record* devoted whole issues to the question of environmental practice.

In 1990 Middlebury College in Vermont hosted a conference on Spirit and Nature where the Dalai Lama stressed his commitment to protection of the environment. At the 1993 Parliament of the World's Religions in Chicago, when Buddhists gathered with Hindus, Muslims, pagans, Jews, Jains, and Christians from all over the world, a top agenda item was the role of religion in responding to the environmental crisis. Parallel interest in the academic community culminated in ten major conferences at Harvard University, with the intention of defining a new field of Religion and Ecology. The first of these conferences, convened by Mary Evelyn Tucker and John Grim in 1996, focused on Buddhism and Ecology.[9]

---

9. The papers were published in Tucker and Williams, *Buddhism and Ecology*.

For the most part, the academic community did not address the practice of Buddhist environmentalism. This was explored by socially engaged Buddhist teachers such as Thich Nhat Hanh, Bernie Glassman, the Dalai Lama, Sulak Sivaraksa, Christopher Titmuss, John Daido Loori, and Philip Kapleau. Joanna Macy developed a transformative model of experiential teaching designed to cultivate motivation, presence, and authenticity. Her methods were strongly based in Buddhist meditation techniques and the Buddhist law of co-dependent arising. Working with John Seed, Buddhist Australian rainforest activist, she developed a ritual 'Council of All Beings' to engage people's attention and imagination on behalf of all beings. Thousands of councils have now taken place in Australia, New Zealand, the United States, Germany, Russia, and other parts of the western world.

Buddhist Environmental Activism

Examples of green Buddhism on the front lines are still relatively rare. They reflect three major types of activism which characterize environmentalism today: 1) holding actions of resistance; 2) structural analysis and alternatives; and 3) cultural transformation. Holding actions aim to stop or reduce destructive activity, buying time for more affective long-term strategies. In northern California, a small group of 'Ecosattvas' has been protesting the logging of old growth redwood groves, supported by the Humboldt County eco-sangha, Buddhist Peace Fellowship, and Green Gulch Zen Center. For one demonstration, they created a large prayer flag covered with human handprints to serve as a testimony of solidarity for those participating in the resistance actions. Later, several Ecosattvas made a pilgrimage into the heart of the Headwaters Forest, carrying a Tibetan treasure vase with gifts and prayers on behalf of the redwoods.

Moved by the suffering of animals in research cages, factory farms, and export trade stores, two Zen students in the San Francisco area formed a Buddhists' animal rights group. Drawing on principles of non-harming, they educated Buddhists about the plight of monkeys, beef cattle, and endangered parrots. One of them has continued this work in Europe, focusing on the cruelty in large-scale hog farming. Addressing the dangers of nuclear waste, a study group under Joanna Macy's leadership protested the storage of nuclear waste below ground. As an alternative they developed a vision of 'nuclear guardianship' for storage containers above ground based in Buddhist spiritual practices. In a parallel action, Zen student and artist Mayumi Oda helped to organize Plutonium-Free Future and the Rainbow Serpents to stop shipments of deadly plutonium to Japan.

The second type of activism, structural analysis and the creation of alternative visions, has also engaged modern Buddhists. In 1997 the Soka Gakkai-affiliated group, Boston Research Center for the 21st Century, held a series of workshops addressing the People's Earth Charter, an internationally-negotiated set of ethical guidelines for human-Earth relations. The Center published a booklet of Buddhist views on the Charter's principles to stimulate discussion before adoption by the United Nations. Members of the International Network of Engaged Buddhists and Buddhist Peace Fellowship called the 'Think Sangha' have undertaken structural analysis of global consumerism. Collaborating between the United States and southeast Asia, they have held conferences in Thailand on 'Alternatives to Consumerism', pressing for moderation and lifestyle simplification. One of the boldest structural alternatives is the Dalai Lama's proposal that the entire province of Tibet be declared an ecological reserve.

Scholars have offered structural analyses using Buddhist principles to shed light on environmental problems. Rita Gross, Buddhist feminist scholar, laid out a Buddhist framework for considering global population issues. Stephanie Kaza has compared ecofeminist principles of activism with Buddhist philosophy, showing compatabilities between the two. Through Buddhist-Christian dialogue, Jay McDaniel has developed spiritual arguments for compassionate treatment of animals as a serious human responsibility. Sociologist Bill Devall integrated Buddhist principles into his elaboration of Arne Naess's Deep Ecology philosophy urging simplification of needs and wants. Joanna Macy draws on Buddhist philosophy and practices to analyze the paralyzing states of grief, despair, and fear that prevent people from acting on behalf of the environment.

The third type of activism, transforming culture, is barely underway and sometimes meets with resistance. Two Buddhist cen-

ters in rural northern California, Green Gulch Zen Center and
Spirit Rock, already demonstrate a serious commitment to the
environment through vegetarian food practices, land and water
stewardship efforts, and ceremonies which include the natural
world. In the Sierra foothills, Gary Snyder has been a leader in
establishing the Yuba River Institute, a bioregional watershed
organization working in co-operation with the Bureau of Land
Management. Members have done survey work, controlled burns,
and creek restoration projects engaging the local community in the
process. Snyder models the level of commitment necessary to rein-
habit a place and build community that might eventually span generations. Zen Mountain Center in Southern California is beginning
similar work, carrying out resource management practices such as
thinning for fire breaks, restoring degraded forest, and limiting
human access to some preserve areas. Applying Buddhist principles in an urban setting, Zen teacher Bernard Glassman has developed environmentally-oriented small businesses which employ
local street people, sending products to socially responsible companies such as Ben and Jerry's.

Several Buddhist centers have developed lecture series, classes,
and retreats based on environmental themes. Zen Mountain
Monastery in the Catskills of New York state offers 'Mountains and
Rivers' retreats based on the center's commitment to environmental conservation. These feature backpacking, canoeing, nature photography, and haiku as gateways to Buddhist insight. Ring of Bone
Zendo at Kitkitdizze, Gary Snyder's community, offers backpacking
sesshins in the Sierra Nevada. Green Gulch Zen Center co-hosts a
'Voice of the Watershed' series with Muir Woods National
Monument, with talks and walks across the landscape of the two
valleys. Manzanita Village in southern California includes deep
ecology practices, gardening, and nature observation as part of
their mindfulness retreats.

Most of these examples represent social change agents working
within Buddhist or non-Buddhist institutions to promote environmental interests. Alongside organizational initiatives, individual
Buddhists are taking small steps to align their actions with their
Buddhist practice. Many people, Buddhists included, are turning to
vegetarianism and veganism as more compassionate choices for
animals and ecosystems. Others are committing to eating only

organically grown food, in order to support pesticide-free soil and healthy farming. Thich Nhat Hanh has strongly encouraged his students to examine their consumption habits, not only around food and alcohol, but also television, music, books, and magazines. His radical stance is echoed by Sulak Sivaraksa in Thailand, who insists the western standard of consumption is untenable if extended throughout the world. Some Buddhists have joined support groups for reducing credit card debt, giving up car dependence, and creating work co-operatives. For many students, environmental awareness and personal change flow naturally from a Buddhist practice commitment.

Buddhism and the Environmental Crisis

How might Buddhism and ecology affect the larger environmental movement and how might it influence western Buddhism in general? Will Buddhist environmentalism turn out to be more environmental than Buddhist? The answers to these questions must be largely speculative, since green Buddhism is just gaining a footing. It is possible that this fledgling voice will be drowned out in the brownlash against environmentalists, or in western resistance to engaged Buddhism. Environmental disasters of survival proportions may overwhelm anyone's capacity to act effectively. The synergistic combination of millennialism and economic collapse may flatten green Buddhism as well as many other constructive initiatives.

But if one takes a more hopeful view, it seems possible to imagine that green Buddhism will grow and take hold in the minds and hearts of young people who are creating the future. Perhaps some day there will be Ecosattva chapters across the world affiliated with various practice centers. Perhaps Buddhist eco-activists will be sought out for their spiritual stability and compassion in the face of extremely destructive forces. Buddhist centers might become models of ecological sustainability, showing other religious institutions ways to encourage ecological culture. More Buddhist teachers may become informed about environmental issues and raise these concerns in their teachings, calling for moderation and restraint.

That being said, Buddhism is not the only or necessarily the best path for dealing with the environmental crisis. Moral leadership

and community organizing from all religious traditions are needed
to stop the downward spiral of planetary ecological devastation.
Committed practitioners of nonharming can inspire others who are
trying to resist destructive practices. Ecologically-articulate
Buddhists can advance inter-religious dialogue to meet the challenges of global warming, overconsumption, and other systemic
ills. Drawing on a Buddhist perspective, academics, policy analysts,
and poets can bring fresh insights to once-intractable problems.

What happens next lies in the hands of those who are nurturing
this wave of enthusiasm for green Buddhism into the next century.
Religious leaders, teachers, and scholars as well as the younger
generations, full of energy and passion for protecting the home
they love, will determine the shape of Buddhism and ecology in the
future. As the rate of environmental destruction continues to accel-
erate, many forms of dialogue and activism are sorely needed.
Buddhism and its environmentally-supportive teachings have
much to offer the assaulted world. Like other world religions, this
ancient tradition is being called to transform once again and offer
its wisdom teachings in yet another context.

Bibliography

Batchelor, Martine and Brown, Kerry, eds. 1992. *Buddhism and Ecology*.
London: Cassell.

Callicott, J. Baird and Ames, Roger T., eds. 1989. *Nature in Asian Traditions
of Thought*. Albany: State University of New York Press.

Chapple, Christopher Key. 1993. *Nonviolence to Animals, Earth, and Self in
Asian Traditions*. Albany: State University of New York Press.

Habito, Reuben L.F. 1993. *Healing Breath: Zen Spirituality for a Wounded
Earth*. Maryknoll: Orbis.

Hanh, Thich Nhat. 1993. *Love in Action*. Berkeley: Parallax.

Hunt-Badiner, Alan, ed. 1990. *Dharma Gaia*. Berkeley: Parallax.

Kapleau, Philip. 1982. *To Cherish All Life: A Buddhist Case for Becoming
Vegetarian*. San Francisco: Harper and Row.

Kaza, Stephanie, and Kenneth Kraft. 2000. *Dharma Rain: Sources of
Buddhist Environmentalism*. Boston: Shambhala.

Macy, Joanna. 1991a. *Mutual Causality in Buddhism and General Systems
Theory: The Dharma of Natural Systems*. Albany: State University of
New York Press.

———. 1991b. *World as Lover, World as Self*. Berkeley: Parallax.

Macy, Joanna, and Molly Young Brown. 1998. *Coming Back to Life: Practices to Reconnect Our Lives, Our World.* Gabriola Island, British Columbia: New Society.

Schmidthausen, Lambert. 1997. The Early Buddhist Tradition and Ecological Ethics. *Journal of Buddhist Ethics* 4, pp. 1–42.

Queen, Christopher, ed. 2000. *Engaged Buddhism in the West.* Cambridge, Massachusetts: Wisdom.

Seed, John, Joanna Macy, Pat Fleming, and Arne Naess. 1988. *Thinking Like a Mountain: Towards a Council of All Beings.* Philadelphia: New Society.

Sivaraksa, Sulak. 1992. *Seeds of Peace.* Berkeley: Parallax.

———, ed. 1999. *Socially-Engaged Buddhism for the New Millennium.* Bangkok: Suksit Siam.

Snyder, Gary. 1990. *The Practice of the Wild.* San Francisco: North Point.

———. 1995. *A Place in Space.* Washington, D.C.: Counterpoint.

Tucker, Mary Evelyn, and Duncan Ryuken Williams, eds. 1997. *Buddhism and Ecology: The Interconnectedness of Dharma and Deeds.* Cambridge, Massachusetts: Harvard University Press.

19

Confucian Ethics and the Ecocrisis

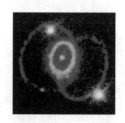

$\mathcal{M}$ARY $\mathcal{E}$VELYN $\mathcal{T}$UCKER

*Confucian concerns for personal
self-cultivation, educational efficacy,
political morality, and ecological cosmology
may contribute to a more sustainable
future for the Earth community.*

It is becoming increasingly clear that we are living in a period of enormous change and upheaval, especially due to the environmental crisis which is threatening life systems on the planet in drastic and often unexpected ways. From resource depletion to population explosion, from pollution excess to biodiversity decrease, we are straddling a precarious moment in human history. Indeed, the human community has never before faced such a challenge in terms of sustaining life and livelihood on the planet. As the scientist Brian Swimme has stated, "We are making macrophase changes on the planet with microphase wisdom." The cultural historian Thomas Berry has raised the question of whether or not the human is a viable species. In this vein he notes we have developed ethics for homicide and suicide, but not for biocide and ecocide. In other words, the moral restraints formulated by a comprehensive environmental ethics are still not in place. Hence we continue to destroy ecosystems and species at a staggering rate. We need not elaborate all the particulars of this destruction, as the statistics are well known. The scale, complexity, and urgency of the environmental crisis are, however, of such magnitude as to require radical rethinking of worldviews and ethics in order to halt this mindless destruction.

There are currently three significant movements in this direction. The first includes efforts to describe the broad sweep of the epic of evolution and to articulate the role of the human in this process. The second is enunciated by Tu Weiming in his call to move beyond the Enlightenment project and draw on the spiritual resources of the world's religions. The third is the collaborative work on formulating an Earth Charter and a Global Ethics to be brought to the United Nations. This paper on Confucian ethics can be situated in both the second and third categories. Our thesis is that the spiritual dynamics of self-cultivation in the moral political philosophy and the ecological cosmology of Confucian tradition are important resources for overcoming our present alienation from one another and from the Earth itself. We will briefly discuss the three movements mentioned above, and then outline the role of the potential contributions of Confucianism.

The Epic of Evolution

Those involved in developing the epic of evolution include Pierre Teilhard de Chardin, Thomas Berry, Brian Swimme, Eric Chaisson, E.O. Wilson, Ursula Goodenough, and Loyal Rue. In their book *The Universe Story*, Berry and Swimme note that we need to situate humankind amidst some five billion years of Earth's evolution and against the backdrop of some 13 billion years of cosmic evolution. This provides a sufficiently comprehensive worldview against which to formulate an ethics of ecological sustainability and biological integrity to counteract the forces of massive environmental destruction. By reorienting ourselves to this vast sweep of time and space, we have new grounds for an appropriate anthropocosmic perspective beyond simply anthropocentric preoccupations. It is here, for example, that the Confucian virtue of humaneness takes on particular significance, for it is a virtue that is understood to have both cosmic and personal dimensions. Thus, self-cultivation links the individual to others and to nature as a whole, identifying the microcosm and the macrocosm.

Beyond the Enlightenment Mentality

Harvard professor Tu Weiming contributes a second important dimension to this discussion in his efforts to move beyond the negative effects of the Enlightenment. Tu calls our attention to the unintended consequences of the Enlightenment project in its frequently unrestrained promotion of rationality, individuality, science, and technology. The objectification of knowledge as power has become a driving force behind viewing the material world as simply a collection of resources to be exploited. Tu suggests that we need to critique the Enlightenment mentality while nonetheless drawing on the positive aspects of the Enlightenment legacy. For example, we have inherited the Enlightenment ideas of liberty and equality, which emphasize the importance of the individual and of democratic systems.

On the other hand, the idea of fraternity may need rethinking in the West in light of communitarian and environmental ethics. How we understand fraternity may be key to our survival as a species and as a planet. Most traditional religions have been anthropocentric and divine-centered; postmodernists have been largely human-centered and politically oriented; communitarian ethicists have likewise been socially focused. All of these perspectives are not fully adequate to the challenges we face. Our devotion to individual liberty, human equality, and justice has blinded us to other broader possibilities of being communal. As Thomas Berry has observed, we have become autistic in relation to the natural world.

Yet several projects may offset these tendencies. One is Tu Weiming's proposal to bring forth the traditional wisdom of the world's religions for contemporary concerns. This needs to be done with a sufficient sensitivity to the broader cosmological context in which religions arise. In this vein we might observe that Mircea Eliade, who established the History of Religion program at the University of Chicago, was attempting to do precisely this in his efforts to link religious symbols with natural processes such as the fluctuation of day and night, the agricultural cycles, and seasonal rhythms. Similarly, over a three-year period, Tu Weiming convened a series of conferences at the East-West Center in Hawaii on the Dialogue of Civilizations, focusing on religious interactions. Scholars and practitioners came together to explore the resources of these traditions for contemporary concerns. In this same vein, a number of people are recognizing the value of the Confucian tradition in that it does not have a metaphysics of radical transcendence. Rather, it embraces a profound sense of the recovery of relational resonances between humans and the natural world. It is based on a sophisticated understanding of macrocosmic and microcosmic relations. In short, it promotes correlative thinking in which the personal and the cosmic dimensions are continually interrelated.

Another such project is the conference and book series on 'Religions of the World and Ecology' at the Center for the Study of World Religions at Harvard University. From 1996 to 1998, eleven major conferences were held at Harvard, examining the resources of the world's religions to meet the environmental challenge.[1]

The Earth Charter and Global Ethics

Under the auspices of the Earth Council in Costa Rica and with the leadership of Steven Rockefeller, over the last several years an Earth Charter has been written by an international drafting committee. This Charter will be brought to the United Nations General Assembly for adoption by the year 2002. This is a formidable task in an age which celebrates diversity, multiculturalism, and radical particularity. Whether the human species can agree upon a unifying framework of global ethics for a sustainable future remains to be seen. This process may require three dimensions to be fully effective. One is a sufficiently broad cosmological, evolutionary context; second is the means of deepening human-Earth relations through enhancing patterns of interaction with the natural world; and third is a concreteness or embodiment of eco-justice perspectives in laws and institutions. The first calls for the overcoming of the dualism of matter and spirit, the second requires new modes of self-cultivation in relation to Heaven, Earth, and humans, and the

---

1. These conferences were organized by John Grim and Mary Evelyn Tucker, who also serve as series editors for the books being published by the Center and Harvard University Press. See Mary Evelyn Tucker and John Berthrong, eds., *Confucianism and Ecology: The Interrelation of Heaven, Earth, and Humans* (1998).

third elicits the formation of a global ethics, covenants, laws, and institutions to embody this more embracing worldview. The overall aim is to set forth parameters and goals for establishing sustainable life and livelihoods for future generations. With this context in mind we turn now to explore the resources of the Confucian tradition in relation to contemporary efforts to forge a comprehensive and inclusive global ethics.

Overview of the Confucian Tradition

The acknowledged founder of the Confucian tradition was the sage-teacher K'ung Futzu (551–479 B.C.E.) whose name was latinized by Jesuit missionaries as Confucius. Born into a time of rapid social change, Confucius devoted his life to re-establishing order through rectification of the individual and the state. This involved a program embracing moral, political, and religious components. As a creative transmitter of earlier Chinese traditions, Confucius is said, according to legend, to have compiled the Five Classics, namely, the Books of *History, Poetry, Changes, Rites,* and the *Spring and Autumn Annals.*

The principal teachings of Confucius, as contained in the Analects, emphasize the practice of moral virtues, especially humaneness or love (*jen*) and filiality (*hsiao*). These were exemplified by the 'noble person' (*chun tzu*) particularly within the five relations, namely, between parent and child, ruler and minister, husband and wife, older and younger siblings, and friend and friend.

Confucian thought was further developed in the writings of Mencius (372–289 B.C.E.) and Hsün tzu (298–238 B.C.E.). As a political philosophy, it was utilized during the Han period (206 B.C.E.–220 C.E.) especially with the thought of Tung Chung-shu (179–104 B.C.E.). The tradition culminated in a Neo-Confucian revival in the eleventh and twelfth centuries which resulted in a new synthesis of the earlier teachings. The major Neo-Confucian thinker, Chu Hsi (1130–1200), designated four texts as containing the central ideas of Confucian thought. Called the Four Books, they consisted of two chapters from the *Book of Rites,* namely *The Great Learning* and *The Doctrine of the Mean,* and the *Analects and Mencius. He elevated these to a position of prime importance over the* five classics mentioned earlier. These texts and Chu Hsi's commentaries on them became, in 1315, the basis of the Chinese civil examination system which endured for nearly six hundred years until 1905.

Chu Hsi's synthesis of Neo-Confucianism was recorded in his classic anthology, *Reflections on Things at Hand*. In this work, Chu provided, for the first time, a comprehensive metaphysical basis for Confucian thought and practice. In response to the Buddhists' metaphysics of emptiness and their perceived tendency towards withdrawal from the world in meditative practices, Chu formulated a this-worldly spirituality based on a balance of religious reverence, ethical practice, scholarly investigation, and political participation.

Unlike the Buddhists who saw the attachment to the world of change as the source of suffering, Chu Hsi and the Neo-Confucians after him affirmed change as the source of transformation in both the cosmos and the person. Thus Confucian spiritual discipline involved cultivating one's moral nature so as to bring it into harmony with the larger pattern of change in the cosmos. Each moral virtue had its cosmological component. For example, the central virtue of humaneness was seen as that which was the source of fecundity and growth in both the individual and the cosmos. By practicing humaneness, one could effect the 'transformation of things' in oneself, in society, and in the cosmos. In so doing, one's deeper identity with reality was recognized as 'forming one body with all things'.

To realize this identification, a rigorous spiritual practice was needed. This involved a development of poles present in earlier Confucian thought, namely, a balancing of religious reverence with an ethical integrity manifested in daily life. For Chu Hsi and later Neo-Confucians such spiritual practice was a central concern. Thus interior meditation became known as 'quiet sitting', 'abiding in reverence', or 'rectifying the mind'. Moral self-discipline was known as 'making the will sincere', 'controlling the desires', and 'investigating principle'. Through conscientious spiritual effort one could become a 'noble person' who was thus able to participate in society and politics most effectively. While in the earlier Confucian view the ruler was the prime moral leader of the society, in Neo-Confucian thought this duty was extended to all people, with a particular responsibility placed on teachers and government officials. While ritual was primary in the earlier view, spiritual discipline became more significant in Neo-Confucian practice. In both, major emphasis was placed on mutual respect in basic human relations.[2]

Neo-Confucian thought and practice spread to Korea, Japan, and Vietnam where it had a profound effect on those cultures. Since 1949, the government of the People's Republic of China has repudiated the Confucian heritage. However, the Confucian tradition is currently being re-examined on the mainland, often relying on new publications of Western scholars, especially Tu Weiming, Julia Ching, and William Theodore de Bary. Furthermore, as Tu Weiming has noted, we may be entering a third epoch of Confucian humanism in terms of its revival in both East Asia and the West.

The Confucian tradition is one which may make a significant contribution to a shared global ethic because of its broad anthropocosmic vision and its deep commitment to self-cultivation as a means of affecting the larger social-political-natural order. This is a tradition which affirms the goodness of human nature and values the importance of education. At the same time, it is committed to social harmony and political stability. These are two primary goals of the Confucian tradition, namely, fostering the moral and intellectual growth of the individual while trying to create appropriate familial structures and stable political institutions. The effort of Confucianism is constantly to balance self and society, the individual and the community. When Confucianism is judged by certain standards (especially contemporary Western democratic principles), it appears not always to be able to live up to its goals of achieving an effective balance at different points in Chinese history.

We acknowledge, then, the historical failures of Confucianism (like every religious tradition) to achieve its highest aims. Yet at the same time, we recognize the significant achievement of Confucianism in perpetuating the stability and longevity of Chinese culture as well as in contributing to the cultural identity of East Asia as a whole. The Confucian influence on Korea, Japan, and Vietnam needs to be underscored in this respect. The Confucian tradition has played a central role in shaping the social, cultural,

---

2. The above six paragraphs appeared in a slightly different form in 'An Ecological Cosmology' in Christopher Chapple, ed., *Ecological Prospects* (Albany: State University of New York Press, 1994).

and political institutions of a large number of the world's people, both historically and at present. Indeed, it has been a defining influence in directing the destiny of China, one of the world's oldest continuing civilizations.

Confucianism was often seen as an authoritarian political system, a hierarchical social system, and a repressive family system. While the tradition has been used for personal and political control, this is a distortion of its central teachings. Moreover, while the role of women in Confucian societies has not been seen as 'liberated' by contemporary standards, this has been true for women in most pre-modern societies around the world. We will draw on the positive aspects of the Confucian tradition to address the question of its potential contributions to a more just and sustainable world order. For it is the universal principles and aspirations of the world's religions that need to be brought to bear on the constructive formation of a global ethics undergirding an equitable system of global governance. From many quarters such a call for a global ethics is emerging—for example, from Hans Küng's Global Ethics Foundation, Baird Callicott's work on environmental ethics, the drafting of an Earth Charter, and the long-term commitments of Global Education Associates to an Earth Covenant.

Working Toward a Shared Global Ethic

PEACE AND ECOLOGICAL SECURITY

> When things are investigated, knowledge is extended; when knowledge is extended, the will becomes sincere; when the will is sincere, the mind is rectified; when the mind is rectified, the personal life is cultivated; when the personal life is cultivated, the family will be regulated; when the family is regulated, the state will be in order; and when the state is in order, there will be peace throughout the world. From the Son of Heaven [Emperor] down to the common people, all must regard cultivation of the personal life as the root or foundation. (*The Great Learning*[3])

---

3. Chan, Wing-tsit, trans., *A Source Book in Chinese Philosophy* (Princeton: Princeton University Press, 1963), pp. 86–87.

Confucianism has a profound commitment to establishing a peaceful order through the transformation and self-cultivation of the individual. *The Great Learning* indicates in a series of eight graduated steps that when one wishes to establish a peaceful society, one must first regulate oneself, then one's family, and finally the state. The text speaks of the need for understanding roots and branches in order to affect the interconnected network of individual, family, society, and country. Thus, carefully prioritizing and acting in a reflective manner means that peaceful ends will be realized more readily. Again, while this is an ideal goal, the image of concentric circles spreading outward like ripples in a pond calls to mind the ability of the individual to influence change from oneself outwards.

This model is central to all Confucian ethics and would be a major contribution to a larger global ethics. It might be called the concentric-circle model of ethics, in which peace and ecological security rest on the dynamic interplay between the individual and the key communities in which s/he is imbedded. This is not a dependency model, but rather a responsibility model which reflects the recognition of personal self-cultivation as the key to a peaceful society. This cultivation rests especially on the sincerity of will, which means avoiding self-deception and being watchful over oneself when alone. A rigorous reliance on moral individuals is the backbone of regulated families, stable societies, and peaceful nations.

The picture of individuals who are self-reflective yet contributing to and nurtured by communities is quintessentially Confucian. East Asian societies with these values have been described as 'group-oriented societies'; the underlying implication of this terminology is often that such societies are somehow inferior to the highly individualistic societies of the West. However, it is precisely this group orientation which emphasizes the development of the person in relationship to others that is needed in today's world. This model encourages responsibilities to and co-operation with the larger social and political order, which is lacking in societies that place individual freedom unconditionally above public responsibility. Hence we have great difficulty in the contemporary West to establish the grounds for a common good.

A peaceful and ecologically secure society is impossible without a minimal commitment to a communitarian sensibility, common aspirations, and shared ethical imperatives. It would seem that this is one of the most important contributions Confucianism can make to a shared global ethic. In short, peace and ecological security are impossible without a greater sense of common good and shared destiny—of both humans and the Earth. These links need to be forged by an ethic of concentric circles, where the individual has the security of being connected to interlocking communities and at the same time has the affirmation that his or her development as an individual will add to the flourishing of the entire community. In our times it is essential that the notion of community include not only humans but the Earth as well. This communitarian consciousness is the basis of a lasting peace.

For the Confucians to achieve this communitarian ideal it meant that economic profit needed to be subordinated to humaneness and righteousness (equity and distributive justice). That was the first principle of Mencius. In addition, for Mencius humane government meant government for the people, not only of and by the people. Rulers needed to put the public good and the common future above private gain and short-term interests.

ECOLOGICAL SUSTAINABILITY

Only those who are absolutely sincere can fully develop their nature. If they can fully develop their nature, they can then fully develop the nature of others. If they can fully develop the nature of others, they can then fully develop the nature of things. If they can fully develop the nature of things, they can then assist in the transforming and nourishing process of Heaven and Earth. If they can assist in the transforming and nourishing process of Heaven and Earth, they can thus form a trinity with Heaven and Earth. (*The Doctrine of the Mean*[4])

The Way of Heaven and Earth may be completely described in one sentence: they are without any doubleness and so they produce things in an unfathomable way. The Way of Heaven and Earth is extensive, deep, high, brilliant, infinite, and lasting. The heaven now before us is only this bright, shining mass; but when viewed in its unlimited extent, the sun, moon, stars, and constellations are suspended in it and all things

---

4. Chan, Wing-tsit, *op. cit.*, pp. 107–08.

are covered by it. The Earth before us is but a handful of soil; but in its breadth and depth, it sustains mountains like Hua and Yueh without feeling their weight, contains the rivers and seas without letting them leak away, and sustains all things. The mountain before us is only a fistful of straw; but in all the vastness of its size, grass and trees grow upon it, birds and beasts dwell on it, and stores of precious things [minerals] are discovered in it. The water before us is but a spoonful of liquid, but in all its unfathomable depth, the monsters, dragons, fishes, and turtles are produced in them, and wealth becomes abundant because of it [as a result of transportation]. (*The Doctrine of the Mean*[5])

As Tu Weiming has observed, Confucianism has a profoundly anthropocosmic sensibility, for Confucian cosmology situates the human within the dynamic, organic processes of nature, not above or controlling those processes. The aim of Confucian self-cultivation and social-political philosophy is to achieve harmony of humans with themselves, with one another, and with the cosmos itself. It is the human who completes Heaven and Earth and forms a triad with them. As *The Doctrine of the Mean* notes, it is the human who can assist in the transforming and nourishing process of Heaven and Earth.

For Confucians the Earth is seen as abundantly fecund, rich with resources and resilient with seasonal change. Of course, there are passages which acknowledge ecological problems, such as one in Mencius describing deforestation on Ox Mountain. However there is an abiding sense that the concentric community in which the human is embedded includes the natural and cosmic orders. Indeed, harmony in these communities depends on the ability of the human to establish and maintain a balance between the human and natural worlds. Numerous ritual structures and patterns of correspondence were set up to insure this connection, especially in Han Confucian thought.

Moreover, Confucian societies affirmed that ecological harmony was not merely a matter of reciprocal relations of humans and the Earth as a means of self-cultivation. Rather, ecological sustainability depended on proper cultivation of the land itself. For the government to promote agriculture and sericulture was essential. To build appropriate technological assistance for these endeavors was

---

5. Chan, Wing-tsit, *op. cit.*, p. 109.

all-consuming. Huge irrigation projects and massive public works were undertaken, including dikes and canals, and storage granaries and roads for transporting goods. All of this implied that ecological sustainability was primary. Confucian texts, especially Mencius, speak frequently of practical learning to assist agriculture and to insure the good of the commoners.

THE NATURALISTIC COSMOLOGY OF CONFUCIANISM

As an example of the intellectual resources of Confucianism, a more detailed discussion follows of some of its key ideas regarding cosmology and ethics. Chinese naturalism as a primary ingredient of Confucianism is characterized by an organic holism and a dynamic vitalism. The organic holism of Confucianism refers to the fact that the universe is viewed as a vast integrated unit, not discrete mechanistic parts. Nature is seen as unified, interconnected, and interpenetrating, constantly relating microcosm and macrocosm. This interconnectedness is already present in the early Confucian tradition, in the *I Ching*, and in the Han correspondences of the elements with seasons, directions, colors, and even virtues. Cheng Chung-ying has described the organic naturalism of Confucian cosmology as characterized by "natural naturalization" and "human immanentization" in contrast to the emphasis on rationality and transcendence in Western thought.[6]

This sense of naturalism and holism is distinguished by the view that there is no Creator God; rather, the universe is considered to be a self-generating, organismic process.[7] Confucians are traditionally concerned less with theories of origin or with concepts of a personal God than with what they perceive to be the ongoing reality of this self-generating, inter-related universe. This interconnected quality has been described by Tu Weiming as a "continuity of being."[8] This implies a kind of great chain of being, in continual

---

6. Cheng Chung-ying, *New Dimensions of Confucian and Neo-Confucian Philosophy* (Albany: State University of New York Press, 1991), p. 4.

7. Frederick F. Mote, *Intellectual Foundations of China* (New York: Knopf, 1971), pp. 17–18.

8. See 'The Continuity of Being: Chinese Visions of Nature', in Mary Evelyn Tucker and John Berthrong, eds., *Confucianism and Ecology: The Interrelation of Heaven, Earth, and Humans* (Cambridge: Center for the Study of World Religions and Harvard University Press, 1998).

process and transformation, linking inorganic, organic, and human life forms. For the Confucians this linkage is a reality because all life is constituted of *ch'i*, the material force or psycho-physical element of the universe. *Ch'i* is the unifying element of the cosmos and creates the basis for a profound reciprocity between humans and the natural world.

A second important characteristic of Confucian cosmology is its quality of dynamic vitalism inherent in *ch'i* (material force). Material force as the substance of life is the basis for the continuing process of change and transformation in the universe. The term *sheng sheng* (production and reproduction) is used in Confucian texts to illustrate the ongoing creativity and renewal of nature. Furthermore, it constitutes a sophisticated awareness that change is the basis for the interaction and continuation of the web of life systems—mineral, vegetable, animal, and human. And finally it celebrates transformation as the clearest expression of the creative processes of life with which humans should harmonize their own actions. In essence, human beings are urged to "model themselves on the ceaseless vitality of the cosmic processes."[9] This approach is an important key to Confucian thought, for a sense of holism, vitalism, and harmonizing with change provides the metaphysical basis on which an integrated morality can be developed. The extended discussions of the relationship of *li* (principle) to *ch'i* (material force) in Neo-Confucianism can be seen as part of the effort to articulate continuity and order in the midst of change. *Li* is the pattern amidst flux which provides a means of establishing harmony.

Clearly, this cosmological understanding of the universe as organic holism and dynamic vitalism is essential for the effective formation of an environmental ethics. Without this understanding of the interconnectedness of natural processes, it will be difficult to generate the appropriate sense of respect for nature not simply as a resource but as the source of life itself.

---

9. Tu Weiming, *Confucian Thought: Selfhood as Creative Transformation*, p. 39. Professor Tu notes: "For this reference in the *Chou I*, see *A Concordance to Yi-Ching*, Harvard Yenching Institute Sinological Index Series Supplement no. 10 (reprint; Taipei: Chinese Materials and Research Aids Service Center, Inc., 1966), 1/l."

Confucian Values for Global Ethics

To summarize some of the values of Confucianism which can contribute to the formation of a global ethics, we list the following principles.

1. Moral and spiritual self-cultivation can positively affect the larger social and political order.
2. A concentric-circle mode of ethics based on communitarian sensibilities needs to be fostered.
3. Economic profit needs to be subordinated to humaneness and righteousness (equity and distributive justice).
4. Humane government means government for the people, not only of and by the people.
5. Leaders need to put the public good and the common future above private gain and short-term interests.
6. Mutual responsibilities in human relations need to be valued as significantly as individual freedom.
7. Humans need to see themselves as part of nature, thus harmonizing with, not controlling, natural processes.[10]

10. A longer version of this chapter will be published in Melissa Merkling and Patricia Mische, eds., *Toward a Global Civilization? The Contribution of Religions* (New York: Peter Lang).

PART III

Science and Religion: Resource and Challenge for Each Other

20

A Hindu View on Science and the Spiritual Vision

$\mathscr{V}$ARAHARAJA $\mathscr{V}$. $\mathscr{R}$AMAN

While science is a collective enterprise which uses well-calibrated instruments to probe the phenomenal world, the spiritual quest is a personal investigation using prayer and other exercises to directly apprehend spiritual reality.

As self-aware beings, we wonder about the world around us, and we are mystified no less by this fleeting flicker of human experience that comes and goes like a brief glint of light in the inconceivable stretch of eternity.

Religions are multi-faceted. They have their sages and saints, their rites and rituals, their fasting and feasting, their celebrations and sacraments, their symbols and ethical framework. Every religion also has a vision of the beyond. This is at its core, and constitutes its spiritual dimension. It is through the spiritual dimension that one seeks to make the cosmic connection which is what the religious experience is all about. Let's look at some aspects of the spiritual dimension of Hinduism.

Hindu Scriptures

Since very remote times, India has been a land where the spiritual quest has flourished in a grand way. As Swami Vivekananda, the eloquent nineteenth-century exponent of Hinduism put it, India is the land where "arose the doctrines of the immortality of the soul, the existence of a super-immanent God in nature and in man, where the eternal Himalayas, rising tier above tier, look as it were into the very mysteries of heaven." There in the distant past, sages meditated serenely on the banks of sacred rivers, and acquired spiritual insights which they articulated in sublime Sanskrit meters. These came to be called the Vedas: treasure-chests of spiritual knowledge, which have served as the scriptural pillars of the Hindu world for more than three millennia.

Vedic hymns are grand and complex poetic visions. They personify the primordial principles of fire, water, and air that sustain life as gods and deities. They speak of the Creator as "the only One, bearing the names of different deities" (*Rig Veda* X: 83). They extol the One God for His multiple manifestations: "Millions are in Thy million. Thou art a billion in Thyself" (*Atharva Veda* XIII:4). They express the view that beneath and beyond the brute forces that are apparent at the perceived levels, there is a subtle order, an eternal law (*rita*) which "caused to shine what shone not, and lighted up the dawns" (*Rig Veda* VI:39). In the fair form of *rita* are many splendid beauties (*Rig Veda* IV: 23.9). There is the recognition that beneath it all is a guiding intelligence and a silent harmony.

The Vedas are scientific in their wonderment, and yet imbued with a sense of reverence which is deeply religious. They are religious again when they incorporate supernatural elements in their cosmogony, but here and there they also express a skeptical caution which is scientific at its core. Thus, a hymn of Creation (*Rig Veda* X: 129) closes with the lines:

> Who really knows, and who can swear,
> How Creation arose, when or where!
> Even Gods came after Creation's day,
> Who really knows, who can say
>
> When and how did Creation start?
> Did He do it? Or, did He not?

Only He up there knows, maybe;
Perhaps not, not even He.[1]

Later Hindu writings, especially the Upanishads and the Brahmasûtras
which embody some of the doctrinal foundations of the Hindu tradition, are also amalgams of science and spirituality—for they speak precisely in causative terms about the phenomenal world, they propound
their theories of cosmology, physiology, and psychology, but they never
falter in their insistence on an undergirding spiritual substratum (*brahman*) in which this ephemeral world of experience is imbued.
Brahman, declares the Taittirîya Upanishad, is the origin of everything
and unto which everything ultimately returns (3.1).

Science, Religion, and Spirituality

The link between the Hindu religious perspective and science lies
in that both are ardent quests. The greatest minds of the ages have
striven to explain the wonders of nature and of the universe. Why
does the sun rise and set, the moon wax and wane? How do stars
shine? What makes the rainbow multihued? Such are the questions
explored by science. There are other puzzles that intrigue the
human mind: why did Man and mind come to be? What should be
our role towards one another and towards the world of Nature?
How should we envision our Creator? These are some of the questions that traditional religions have answered. And finally, there is
the mystery of mysteries: human consciousness, this subtle splendor that seems to light up the cold expanse of silent space. For all
the light or beauty, the grandeur and majesty of the universe are
reflected only in the human spirit. There would be no equations for
elliptical orbits, no reckoning of space or time if there was only
mute matter and no measuring mind in the cosmos. It is on the
nature of this experiencing entity that Hindu spirituality probed
and proclaimed.

What is propounded is not regarded as theology or philosophy
or metaphysics. Rather, it is affirmed as the discovery of something
grand and glorious beneath and beyond our perceptually acquired
impressions of the phenomenal world.

---

1. The translations in this chapter are my own.

This recognition is very different from the scientific description of the world. It has naught to do with gravitation or electromagnetism, with leptons or hadrons. Rather, it is like the revelation that there is a higher dimensional reality to which our normal modes of perception are not attuned. It is a dimension of reality that is as real to the spiritual aspirant as Hilbert space and Lie groups are to the mathematician. What is prayer or meditation if not efforts to communicate with that loftier realm of Reality?

The Hindu spiritual view also underscores the relative nature of the intellectual mode. It reminds us that the thinking mind and critical analysis reveal but one aspect of Reality: its phenomenal component. Spiritual awareness enables one to see that while the logical-rational mode is necessary for comprehension and fruitful in the manipulation of sensorilly perceived phenomena, it is utterly ineffective, and may even be a detriment, in the discernment of the transcendental realm.

This point must be emphasized in discussions on the relationship between science and religion. When die-hard materialists categorically declare that there is *nihil ultra*, nothing beyond gross matter, they ignore the fact that there is more to human experience than the causal and the spatio-temporally localizable. How can one ignore intangible entities like thought and value, meaning and aesthetic delight which cannot be reduced to quarks and gluons and the standard model?

The spiritual Reality proclaimed by Hindu seers goes even beyond that. Insubstantial ideas and concepts, in so far as they are associated with the human body, may still be regarded as physical too. In the Hindu framework, the spiritual undercurrent of the physical universe goes beyond human presence on our planet.

Now, one may ask, on what basis can this be affirmed with certainty? To answer this, let us consider a corresponding question in the world of science: on what basis does one declare that there are planets like Neptune and Pluto, that there are microbes and chromosomes? We need instruments like the telescope and the microscope to unravel aspects of gross physical reality that are not immediately perceivable. The instruments will have to be well calibrated, their lenses must be cleaned and polished too. Furthermore, the observer must be trained in their handling. So too, say the spiritual masters, in order to acquire the vision with which one can gain awareness of spiritual Reality, one needs to develop and sharpen one's other potentials. This is the goal of spiritual initiation and exercises.

Differences between Spirituality and Science

Unlike science, the revelation of spiritual reality is not the result of collective activity. After initiation, each seeker has to choose his or her own path, and will come upon varying glimpses of the beyond, which is kaleidoscopic in its multi-splendor. A verse in the *Atharva Veda* (IV: 16.8) says:

> Into the Supreme do all converge
> From the Supreme do all diverge.
> It is of our land, and of aliens too.
> It is divine and human too.

It is this insight that prompted a Vedic seer to declare (*Rig Veda* I:164): "The one essence, the wise call by many names." When such a view is extended to the global arena, it opens up our hearts and minds to the diversity that is much valued in our own times. It leads to the much-needed enlightenment that not only tolerates but also respects and validates all religious modes and cultural traditions for their respective practitioners.

The goal of science is to *describe* and *explain* the phenomenal world, whereas the goal of the spiritual quest is to *apprehend* its inner essence even as one experiences aesthetic delight from art and music. The brochure in the museum may tell us which paintings are in which halls, but the joy to be derived from the art is of an altogether different category. Spiritual vision is based on anubhava which refers to intense personal experience. The author of a verse in Yajur declares

> I have known this Mighty Being
> Effulgent as the Sun beyond darkness.

This knowledge does not arise from experiments with external tools.

Objectivity and Interconnectedness

Science's concern is with objectivity. Galilean-Newtonian science seeks to know how the world would function whether or not the human mind happens to be in it. It is, in a sense, a rebellion against the subjectivist and anthropocentric world views of ancient science. It is based on the conviction that the observing mind can not only study the course and contents of the phenomenal world, but can gain a true understanding of it, by keeping itself away from whatever transpires. It is not unlike studying child behavior using a TV camera rather than by direct observation which is sure to affect that behavior and thus distort the matter observed.

Long before Descartes distinguished what he called the *res extensa* from *res cogitans*, Hindu philosophers had propounded the dichotomy between *prakriti* (mindless Nature) and *purusha* (the experiencing principle). One might say in the terminology of the Hindu world framework that science is a serious and systematic attempt to fathom the intricacies of *prakriti* without a *purusha*. But it is good to remember that such a *prakriti* is as useless and irrelevant as encyclopedias in the bottom of the sea. In other words, the universe prior to the emergence of the human (or similar) minds would have been a wasteful wilderness, where chunks of matter arise, whirl around, and get transformed in routine rhythms for eons and boring eons.

Admirable and productive as it is, a purely objective apprehension of the world cannot be reached even in principle, since science is based on concepts which arise in the human mind. Science is condemned to explore and explain only from within the confines of the human cerebrum and cerebellum. In science, what one means by objectivity is that descriptions ought to be independent of the specific human minds which articulate them. Scientific propositions demand criteria of universality which are based on independent experimentation, logical modes, and communicability. Scientific objectivity is thus essentially collective subjectivity.

Hindu spirituality grants such collective subjectivity, but regards it as illusory. By this we mean two things. First, the physical phenomenal world, such as it appears, is a consequence of the constraints and characteristics of the human mind. Secondly, and more importantly, even the experience of individuality, of the I-ness that takes us through life's journey, is a grand illusion. It is important to be clear about this notion of mâyâ or illusion which is a tenet of Hindu spirituality. What it means is not only that one of the characteristics of the human brain is to respond to external reality in convenient projections which, however, are as useful as, but not more real than, maps to guide us through a territory; but also that the brain-generated separateness that we experience is a veil that covers a cosmic interconnectedness.

A second difficulty with objectivity arises from our probes into the microcosm. Quantum physics has brought into focus the intrinsic intertwining of subject and object, of the observer and the observed. It has, in effect, revealed that there are levels of Reality. At the macroscopic level of objects at our normal scales of experience and the astronomical, a bifurcation between subject and object is not only useful but indispensable for a coherent description of the world. At the microcosmic level, however, such distinctions become impossible in practice and in principle. No electron can be observed without impinging on its intrinsic state. Deep down in the world of atoms and fundamental particles, at the level of the ultimate bricks of the material universe, there is a nebulous overlapping of entities that cannot be resolved into utterly independent units. Everything seems to be inextricably connected to everything else.

The thesis of Hindu spirituality is that there is yet another level of Reality at which all is fused into a universal one. The awareness and experience of this ultimate interconnectedness of all conscious minds (*purushas*) with the inert world (*prakriti*) has been attested by mystics in various traditions.

This recognition need not, indeed should not, undervalue the relative relevance of the ordinarily experienced levels of reality. If this happens, zest for life, search for solutions to everyday problems, and the joys of terrestrial existence will be ignored. What is to be understood is that the substratum of *physical* reality can be grasped only through concepts, mathematics, and instruments, leading to logically coherent and exploitable results; which accounts for the stupendous successes of science. On the other hand, that of the *spiritual* domain is to be apprehended through prayer, and other spiritual exercises, leading to intensely personal ecstatic experiences, which accounts for the importance of religion.

It is failure to recognize this intrinsic difference between, and the relative values of, the two realms that leads to the never-ending debates between science and religion.

Individual and Supreme Spirit

The human body is a frail and puny entity, confined to a mere planetary speck in the awesome stretches of an expanding universe. But it is not insignificant in cosmic history. There is in each of us the magic of experience and feeling, the glory of art and music, the excitement of love and the ennobling of ideals. Encased in us is also a probing mind that can unveil the ultimate nature of this wondrous world, reach the very ends of the universe through thought and reckoning, mathematize the microcosm, and reflect on it all. The human sprit is the capacity for self-awareness, for joyful interaction, for religious ecstasy, and yes, for being touched by awe in the face of the *mysterium tremendum*.

There is splendor in the perceived world, pattern in its functioning, and joy in its contemplation. If all this is part of the human experience, then even prior to the advent of *Homo sapiens*, there must have been a *purusha* of vastly superior order, spanning the cosmic stretches of space and time. This then is the Hindu vision of *brahman*, the undergirding cosmic principle. It says in the *Brihadâranyaka Upanishad* (I: 4.10):

> Brahman was in the beginning.
> It knew itself only as "I am brahman."
> Therefore it became all.

From this perspective, we are, one and all, miniature lights that have emanated from the cosmic effulgence, destined for the terrestrial experience for a brief span, only to re-merge into that from which we have sprung. The quintessence of Hindu spirituality is contained in the phrase, *tat tvam asi:* That thou art. And whoever realizes this, the seers declare, becomes one with it, attains spiritual fulfillment.

This perspective recognizes our transience and finitude as individual entities, but incorporates us into the Infinity that encompasses us. It does not rule out the possibility of other manifestations of brahman, carbon or silicon based, elsewhere amidst the stellar billions. It regards religious expressions as robust echoes of the Universal spirit; like volcanic outbursts, they reveal hidden potencies of immensely greater magnitude. Hindu spirituality recognizes the role of matter and the limits of the mind, but it sees sublime spirit at the core of it all.

Spiritual Insights and Science: Traditional and Modern Approaches

From the Hindu perspective, then, science and spirituality are both quests, but of very different levels of Reality. It is not surprising that in classical India, scientific inquirers investigated matter and motion, astronomers charted the skies, medical men looked for remedies, artisans created, philosophers argued, and everyone went about their business, but the spiritual seekers would have nothing of all this. These were the saints and sages to whom the populace went, not to learn physics and cosmology, not for proofs and justifications, but to experience, however vicariously, a little of the spiritual bliss the seers radiated.

However, ever since the advent of modern science in the Indian intellectual framework, largely as a result of European intrusions and influences, Hindu thinkers have also been adopting the apologetic approach of Western theology whose goal is not only to reason out and elucidate religious doctrines, but also to defend it against the onslaughts of modern science. After all, philosophers and theologians, in their admiration for the results and coherence of scientific methodology, and in their veneration of, not to say addiction to, rationality and scientific consistency, have always tried to establish the deeper elements of religious insights in the framework of the positive sciences.

In my view, attempts to add weight and credence to spiritual truths by hanging on to the coat-tails of current science are not only unnecessary, but may even backfire, given that the scientist's world view is subject to continual modification. The mystical visions apprehended by the human spirit go beyond the facts and figures, the charts and formulas that are accumulated by empirical observation and analysis of the physical world.

The contribution of ancient Hindu spirituality lies not in the revelation of any esoteric truth about the quantum world, but rather in helping us understand that the logical-rational approach serves us well in comprehending one level of Reality as the spiritual-mystical does in apprehending another. For a wholesome journey through the human experience one is as important and enriching as the other.

Religion in the Twenty-First Century

Though it would be more idealistic than factual, more naive than insightful, to declare that all religions preach essentially the same thing, it would be fair to say that there are certain core principles, on both the ethical and spiritual planes, which are common to all religions. One of the goals of a conference like the Parliament of the World's Religions is to seek out from the doctrinal and scriptural sources of the various religions some commonly binding principles, and formulate from them a trans-denominational credo.

To achieve this, there must be mutual respect among the cults, creeds, and sects that give meaning and purpose to people all over the planet. This respect can only be inspired by enlightened religious leadership. Religious leaders must realize that the presumption and proclamation that one's own system is the only true one for all of humanity and that those of others, being wrong or evil, need to be silenced, transformed, or destroyed, will only lead to belligerent confrontations with potential for more anger and hatred than love and compassion. More urgent than bridges between science and religion is understanding among the religions of the world.

The universal credo, while cherishing and deeply adhering to one's own religion, and even proclaiming it to be the sole guiding light for oneself, could also resolve to treat with respect the belief systems of others as long as they cause no harm or hurt. That, I like to think, will be the direction that religions will take in the new century.

âkâsâd patitantôyam
yadâ gachchadi sâgaram
sarvadéva namaskâra
srî késavam pradigachchdi

As waters raining from the skies
All return to the self-same sea,
So prostrations to different gods
Reach back to the same divinity.

21

Buddhism—an Ally of Science?

Pinit Ratanakul

*Buddhism is allied with science because of
its belief in an orderly universe accessible to
human knowledge, its spirit of open enquiry,
and its lack of any reliance on divine revelation.
While science focuses on the physical world,
Buddhism investigates the inner life.*

It's not difficult to consider whether science is an ally or enemy of Buddhism, for there are close analogies between Buddhist truths and some discoveries in modern science. An obvious analogy is the fundamental Buddhist belief that existence is orderly (*itippapccayata*) and that man can discover that order, inherent in the structure of physical reality, for himself. This natural order is understood as the law of cause and effect which states the conditionality of all phenomena (*paticcasamupapada*)—*that* all phenomena are mutually conditioned as cause and effect of one another.

Causation in Buddhism is therefore not strictly deterministic nor completely indeterministic, for it refers to the conditioned state of being or the inter-related and dependent relationship of all phenomena. The present paradigm shift of modern science from the Newtonian mechanical model, which dissected the universe into separate parts, to a holistic model, which emphasizes the inter-relationship of all levels of reality, accords with the Buddhist

338

world-view, which sees the universe as a process—a complex of causal relationships.

Not being based on revelation, Buddhism has no divine commandments to be obeyed. Buddhism has a free and open spirit of inquiry and encourages the search for truth in an objective way. This religion therefore invites reasoned criticism and objective analysis of its truth to be verified by personal experience. The Buddhist system of meditation is offered as a means of such verification by enabling the meditator to discover truth by himself, or in Buddhist words, to see truth 'face to face'. Perhaps it's this free and open spirit of inquiry, along with the emphasis on verifiable truth, that have attracted many intellectuals and scientists to Buddhism. Einstein himself wrote that if there is any religion which is acceptable to the modern scientific mind it is Buddhism.

The Buddhist method of inquiry leads to the adoption of tolerance as a principal value for the seeker of truth. This spirit of tolerance enables Buddhism to be open to the discovery of truth by other means. In fact there are many similarities between Buddhist concepts and scientific discoveries particularly with regard to the evolution of the universe and life, the nature of physical reality and the dynamic relationship between space and time. The scientific revolution therefore has not called Buddhist beliefs into question to the same extent as it has other religious traditions.

Most modern scientific discoveries provide reasonable ground for the truths of Buddhism, yet Buddhism departs from science in the kind of truth it searches for. While scientific discoveries help unlock the mystery of physical reality, Buddhist investigation shows that the realm of moral and spiritual phenomena is open to human discovery, in which the self-existent law of cause and effect operates as in the physical world. Inherent in the cosmic order are different causal laws varying according to their spheres of operation. These laws are physical laws (*utuniyama*) in the material domain, biological laws in the domain of living beings, psychological laws (*cittaniyama*) and the moral and spiritual laws (*dhanunaniyama*) in the realm of morality.

In the moral sphere Buddhism lays great emphasis on the law of karma or moral retribution. This law states a correlation between action and its accompanying consequences—one reaps as one sows. The knowledge of this moral law enables us to discover the cause of suffering and the release from suffering. The root cause is one's own ignorance (*avija*) of the true nature of existence conjoined with dispositions of hatred (*dosa*) and greed (*lobha*) from which arise other human evils. It should be clear that Buddhism is not concerned with the search for truth for its own sake, like pure science, but with the kind of truth that can have a practical effect on the release from suffering and in the transformation of man. Of course, similarly applied science also strives to lessen human suffering and to transform the external aspects of human life. But science as science can do nothing to change the human heart nor to release it from the suffering caused by human moral failure.

How Science Can Learn from Buddhism

Buddhism commends science as a promoter of knowledge and a benefactor of mankind. It is obvious that science has greatly increased our understanding of life and the world while applied science, technology, has provided the means for better living, for example, the cure of diseases, and the gaining of comfort and convenience. No one can deny these benefits. But these benefits in many cases have been outweighted by the unintended perils science has introduced. Some practitioners of modern science hold an optimistic belief that all human ills can be eliminated and all human problems solved. But this optimism is unrealistic. Despite scientific progress human life will continue to be imperfect, darkened always by the shadows of grief, disappointment, and uncertainty.

It is here that Buddhism can help the scientist. It can remind the scientist that scientific knowledge is not the only knowledge man needs and that scientific explanation cannot at all deal with questions about the spiritual and moral life of man. Just as the great religions recognize that they do not have absolute truth about ultimate reality, so science should be made humble about its ability to attain the whole truth. Buddhism can also help engender mindfulness in the scientist, to make him aware of the fact that science is not an end in itself. Therefore he has to be concerned with the effects of his discovery, which may be harmful to the environment and to human life. Such concern for future effects is rather weak among many present-day scientists. Without this concern science will be, not a benefactor to mankind, as it has claimed, but a destroyer. Certainly it cannot then be an ally to Buddhism.

Buddhism, which has long studied the psyche and has gained greater knowledge about the nature of the mind and the craft of the heart can, perhaps, contribute to the modern quest for understanding the psychosomatic unity of man and the working of the mind, as well as to the development of techniques and practices that help relieve anxiety and transform destructive emotions into positive ones. This aspect of Buddhism is useful for psychologists and psychiatrists in the treatment of psychosomatic sickness, neuroses, and mental disorder in their patients. Buddhist psychotherapy can restore calm and inner harmony in men and women living in our turbulent and disturbed world, without the use of 'tranquilizing tablets'.

On the intellectual side, Buddhism does not accept the view of scientific materialism which reduces all phenomena, including the mental, to the physical and thereby makes the mind a by-product of matter (the brain). Buddhism objects to this outlook on the ground that it rejects the relationship between man and transcendent reality, or in Buddhist terminology, the Unconditioned which lies beyond finite conditioned existence. This relationship with transcendent reality is the *summum bonum* of all religions. Without it, total release from suffering and inner transformation are impossible. Buddhism, like many modern scientists, is aware of the complexity of different levels of existence and their interaction, and therefore rejects any simplistic reductionism, especially that which would eliminate human moral and spiritual freedom.

How Buddhism Can Learn from Science

Modern scientific findings do not contradict the truths of Buddhism, which were discovered some 2,500 years ago. To the contrary, the contemporary scientific stress on wholism, the interconnectedness and mutual influence of all planes of reality, and the insubstantiality of matter are all implicit in Buddhist teaching.

Most scientists today agree that they have discovered indeterminism in the cosmic order including life itself, evidence from quantum physics, thermodynamics, and Neo-Darwinian evolution theory. If this discovery is accepted as scientific truth, then

Buddhism may have to modify the way it talks about physical laws, to allow room for the amount of indeterminacy in physical reality. Such a modification has no adverse effect on fundamental Buddhist teaching, which is concerned with suffering and the release from it, and which has always taught that there is human freedom in an open universe.

On the other hand a scientific outlook can assist the Buddhist in weeding out the pre-Buddhist magico-animistic elements which have become entwined with Buddhist teaching and may tend to distract the Buddhist from following the Buddhist path to wisdom and compassion. A scientific outlook is therefore considered necessary, not only for a truly moral and religious life but also for the continual self-examination which such a life demands.

For the Buddhist, science reinforces the Buddhist belief in the importance of critical investigation and personal experience in morality and religion. The Buddhist also commends science for its ability to expand our knowledge of physical reality. But when scientists trespass on the domain of morality and religion, they necessarily fail to provide adequate explanations, for science alone is not competent to deal with value questions. The Buddhist therefore rejects the claim made by some sociobiologists that genetics directs human morality. Moral and spiritual growth in man is not merely a matter of genes but of freely following moral and spiritual laws. However, the Buddhist admits that in the realm of physical reality scientific discovery needs to be taken seriously by every religion, for its theories form the the basis of modern knowledge. Every religion has to adapt itself to the accepted knowledge of its time if the religion is to remain living, able to communicate meaningfully to the modern mind which finds it more and more difficult to believe in dogma unsupported by reason and personal experience. Buddhism, throughout its long history, has shown an incredible ability to reinterpret and to adapt itself to different cultures and new historical circumstances. Today this adaptability has been shown in the current dialogue between Buddhism and modern science taking place in the East and West dialogue which gives witness that Buddhism is more an ally than an enemy. The positive interaction and co-operation between science and Buddhism will help mankind in its search for an understanding of reality and for release from human suffering.

22

Being Human: A Personal and Mostly Catholic Perspective

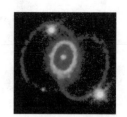

$\mathscr{I}$NGRID $\mathscr{S}$HAFER

The dialogue of religion and science tends toward an understanding of humanity as manifestation of ever more advanced consciousness.

On a flight from Dallas to Miami I found myself seated next to Professor Harbans Lal, Chairman of Pharmacology at the University of North Texas Health Science Center, whose research emphasis is the human brain. Professor Lal is a Sikh and it turned out that we were both on the way to the World Parliament of Religions.

We spent much of the flight discussing the phenomenon of individual and cosmic consciousness, and the possibility of a nonlocal connection of consciousness with someone at the point of death. He commented that he was troubled by what he considered the excessive emphasis in the Parliament Program on ethics, and planned to say so. I showed him a passage from Whitehead's *Science and the Modern World* which I happened to have in my purse in which Whitehead expressed a parallel concern, noting that "Conduct is a by-product of religion—an inevitable by-product, but

not the main point. . . . The insistence upon rules of conduct marks
the ebb of religious fervor." Whitehead continues:

> Religion is the vision of something which stands beyond, behind, and
> within, the passing flux of immediate things; something which is real,
> and yet waiting to be realized; something which is a remote possibility;
> and yet the greatest of present facts; something that gives meaning to
> all that passes, and yet eludes apprehension; something whose posses-
> sion is the final good, and yet is beyond all reach; something which is
> the ultimate ideal, and the hopeless quest. (Whitehead 1977, p. 191)

On the long flight from Miami to Capetown I continued to ponder
the issue of the tension between religion as social activism and religion as spirituality, a tension that clearly transcends individual religious traditions and is relevant both to the question concerning the
meaning of being human and the science-religion syzygy. Andrew
Greeley, for example, sociologist and Catholic priest, is quite critical of the tendency of certain groups in the church to put the horse
of action before the cart of faith and nuanced deliberation. On the
other hand, there is a danger in any attempt to sever conduct from
consciousness (and conscience). Religion is both, as Leonard
Swidler's definition of religion as "an explanation of the ultimate
meaning of life, and how to live accordingly" implies. Still, even as
I teach a course on Global Ethics over the Internet to U.S. military
personnel in different parts of the world and design the Global
Ethics website for the Global Dialogue Institute, I believe that the
appropriate initial 'space' for a meeting of science and religion is in
the internal region of spirituality and consciousness more than the
external arena of ecological, political, and social activism that
might eventually flow from that primary encounter.

Whitehead: Reality as Emergence

Around 1955, when I was sixteen, in my native Austria, I won a
crossword puzzle construction contest conducted by the Amerika
Institut, a U.S. government-sponsored organization to introduce
the United States to the people of post-war Europe (and, presumably, other parts of the world). They published my crossword puzzle and sent me a box of German translations of American fiction.

I wrote back, thanking them for the prize, but wondering why they were sending books in German (and fiction!) when I had so little access to serious works written in English. After all, their crossword puzzle contest involved designing a puzzle in English! I didn't really expect a response but thought I'd give it a try. A few weeks later a second box arrived, filled with assorted books in English, including a slim paperback of Alfred North Whitehead's *Science and the Modern World*. I started reading and found myself utterly captivated, not because Whitehead's philosophic understanding of the cosmos as configurations of evolving processes was new to me but precisely because for the first time in years I felt no longer quite alone. My chance prize had introduced me to someone who seemed to share my primal intuition of reality as process and my fascination with religion, science, and poetry—not as enemies but as valid complementary paths into the mystery of meaning.

At the time I had discovered my Catholic roots and could not comprehend why being a woman kept me from the study of theology and priestly ordination. But faith for me was not a matter of scientific truth. It was a quest for the transcendent, a path of unconditional love for everyone and everything, a soaring of spirit. It never even occurred to me to read Genesis or the story of Noah's Ark as literal truth, and I am still surprised when my students do so today. Long before I was in first grade, my father would take me on outings to gather butterfly eggs to place into muslin covered jars with appropriate vegetation, and I would watch pinhead-size eggs turn into caterpillars and caterpillars into cocoons and seemingly dead cocoons open up to release wondrous winged creatures of color and light. But I was also fascinated by geometry and calculus, poured over my aunt's zoology text books, painted portraits, wrote poetry, and devoured Cicero, Goethe, Undset, and assorted English poets from Donne to Shelley and T.S. Eliot. No wonder I fell in love with Whitehead. In his analysis of *Prometheus Unbound* (Whitehead 1977, p. 85) I even sensed echoes of the crystal pyramid of my vision.

Today, 75 years after his Lowell Lectures were first published, I can only read Whitehead on the relationship of religion and science and wonder why his notions have not more radically informed the intervening conversation. Whitehead wrote:

> When we consider what religion is for mankind, and what science is, it
> is no exaggeration to say that the future course of history depends upon
> the decision of this generation as to the relation between them. We
> have here the two strongest general forces . . . which influence men,
> and they seem to be set one against the other—the force of our reli-
> gious intuitions, and the force of our impulse to accurate observation
> and logical deduction. (p. 180)

Whitehead goes on to note that viewed from the large-scale perspective, religion and science have been in conflict from the beginning but they have also both continued to change, adapt, and grow
(p. 183) precisely in and through the kinds of challenges that force
us to overcome the inertia of complacent attachment to one set of
doctrines or the other. While we should keep from "mutual anath-
emas," we should not despair, for "[t]he clash is a sign that there are
wider truths and finer perspectives within which a reconciliation of
a deeper religion and a more subtle science will be found" (p. 184).
"A clash of doctrines," Whitehead continues, "is not a disaster—it
is an opportunity" (p. 185). He goes on to observe that the traditional ideas we inherit are never static. "They are transformed by
the urge of critical reason, by the vivid evidence of emotional experience, and by the cold certainties of scientific perception. . . . You
cannot permanently enclose the same life in the same mould" (p.
187). In the sciences, new theories that modify old ideas are interpreted as a triumph (p. 188), and, Whitehead argues, "Religion will
not regain its old power until it can face change in the same spirit
as does science. Its principles may be eternal, but the expression of
those principles requires continual development" (p. 188).

From Teilhard to the Vatican Observatory

It is in this spirit that the Catholic Church has not only—very belat-
edly—exonerated Galileo, but now supports one of the most
renowned astronomical institutes in the world, the Vatican
Observatory, with locations in Rome and Tucson, Arizona, an ideal
location for observational astronomy. I was touched when I visited
the Vatican Observatory website and discovered the following
translation of the text on a plaque to mark the spot where the
Arizona observatory is located:

This new tower for studying the stars has been erected during the XV year of the reign of John Paul II on this peaceful site so fit for such studies, and it has been equipped with a new large mirror for detecting the faintest glimmers of light from distant objects. May whoever searches here night and day the far reaches of space use it joyfully with the help of God.

This—along with the Pope's recent endorsement of the theory of evolution—seemed an excellent example of the ability of a religious institution to adapt in response to genuine scientific challenges, cautiously, gradually, too slowly maybe for many, but adapt nevertheless. Even more importantly, this seemed a major step in the direction of fruitful cultural, religious, and ideological dialogue and crosspollination, indicative of the vision of the human future by the Jesuit paleontologist and mystic Teilhard de Chardin—a vision that survived its condemnation by the Vatican and is becoming ever more convincing as the Internet connects even the most distant regions on earth. A half-century ago Teilhard presented evidence for "the relentless progression of the life force to a higher complexity and a higher consciousness, and hopefully to the nobler one which he calls the Omega point—that is, the point of an all-encompassing consideration of one man for the other" (Berman). He conjectured that the spherical shape of the Earth combined with exponential growth of populations and proliferation of communication—including "those astonishing electronic machines (the starting point and hope of the young science of cybernetics) . . ." (Teilhard de Chardin 1960, p. 109) would lead to the convergence of previously diverging cultures. He argued that global consciousness would precipitate creative unions which would intensify and focus individuality and diversity. He used the metaphors of sexual love and radioactivity: by merging in the generative core of their being, creative nuclei release new energy, a process which engenders greater complexity which precipitates a chain reaction of further creative unions (Teilhard de Chardin 1960b, p. 262).

Teilhard spent some 16 years of his life in China (between 1924 and 1946, with periodic interruptions), and his 'first Peking period' (1932–1938) was the time when many of his most original notions germinated. Thus he wrote in a letter of 3rd July 1933: "I have the obscure feeling that something stirs and grows within me; as if, during this period of complete liberty, the true 'me' continues to free itself of the world of conventions" (Cuénot 1965, p. 213). The imagery is clearly birth-imagery. China appears to have been the catalyst for the emergence of Teilhard's mature thought from the pupa stage. His vision of cosmogenesis establishes a bridge between the mind-matter dualism of the West, with its static, transcendent "'God model', where an independent and superordinate principle determines order and value in the world while remaining aloof from it," (Ames and Rosemont 1998, p. 31) and the Chinese "commitment to the processional, transformative, and always provisional nature of experience," a sense of dynamic immanence that "renders the 'ten thousand things' [or, perhaps better, 'events'] . . ." which make up the world, including the human world, at once continuous one with another, and at the same time, unique" (*ibid.*).

The geographic location of the Vatican Observatory is a region I knew to be of deep spiritual significance for Native American populations and I was delighted by this sharing of 'sacred space'. I saw this not only as a weaving together of science and religion but an example of Teilhard's creative synthesis of native ways with a formerly hostile religion as well as the most advanced scientific and technological tools. On a personal level, my father was an agnostic, but among the most powerful religious experiences of my childhood were the hours we spent peering into the heavens on clear nights. More recently, Chris Corbally, S.J., one of the astronomers at the Tucson facility, helped me recapture that same wondrous mixture of awe and cosmic 'belongingness' that had marked my initial imaginative journeys into space

My very paradigm of hope was discussed in a Parliament Symposium on Native American Religious Freedom with Professor Huston Smith as an example of the "dangers of organized religion partnering with science" because constructing telescopes on Mount Graham is interpreted as a profanation of what the Apache people consider a sacred place. Apparently, the forces of what Teilhard considered "dissipating tangential energies which delay and obstruct the evolution of the mind and society until it can again be redirected back into the main radial channel" (Berman) have not yet been quite overcome.

Toward Cosmic Consciousness

However, this in no way invalidates the thrust of my main argument that the dialogue of religion and science tends in the direction of an understanding of humanity as manifestation of ever more advanced consciousness culminating in the emergence of what Teilhard calls the Noosphere. Teilhard is not alone. Charles Laughlin, John McManus, and Eugene d'Aquili assert that the "transcendent desire" (Laughlin, McManus, and d'Aquili 1993, p. 162) which leads to mystic experiences can be explained in terms of neurophysiology, and credit Paul Ricoeur's category of "philosophical reflection" (p. 164) with allowing the rational integration of knowledge gained during a numinous experience into a cycle of meaning that can be shared. Physicist Fred Alan Wolf argues that "modern physics, particularly quantum mechanics or quantum physics . . . provides a theoretical basis for understanding the mind's basic functions: intuition, feeling, sensation, and thought" (Wolf 1984, p. 12). In a chapter on the "physics of love" he posits fear and love as structural elements of matter, as the particles of "annihilation-fear" we call fermions and the particles of "condensation-love" (cf. Teilhard's "convergence") we call photons—or particles of light. "We are all," Wolf writes, "beings of light the lowliest to the highest among us, from the slugs to the astronauts" (p. 145).

Despite the resistance to the very notion of consciousness of sociobiologists during much of the twentieth century, the study of consciousness—including self-consciousness—is becoming acceptable again, not only in reference to humans but also in reference to the higher animals. Donald R. Griffin, for example, writes (1984) that we cannot legitimately defend a human monopoly on conscious thinking. Earlier he had already pointed out that neurophysiologists have found a continuity of structures and functions in neurons and synapses among animals and humans which would lead one to assume a parallel continuity of mental experiences among higher animals (Griffin 1976). Gordon G. Gallup argues that chimpanzees and orangutans have 'minds' because they clearly have a sense of self (Gallup n.d.).

Teilhard's Noogenesis

As we consider the multi-million-year biogenetic process which produced *Homo sapiens*, the noogenetic aspect of evolution leaps into focus the way a pattern hidden to those who are caught up in it on Earth becomes clear from the elevated vantage point of a jet or earth-orbiting satellite. We are Mind-in-the-Making. Before us opens the terrifying and fascinating vista not only of evolution but of biological and cultural evolution with deliberate human input as well as the evolution of evolution. As far as we know, humans are the only animals that can become aware of their adaptive behavior, and hence have the potential of consciously affecting it. We now have the chance not only to locate the chromosomal bases of certain birth defects or potential illnesses, we have the opportunity to discover the genes and memes that give rise to intellectual, creative, and moral excellence. We are called upon to co-invent ourselves both physiologically and culturally and not give in to what Harvey Cox called the greatest sin—sloth. Contemporary science adds poignant significance to the words of the humanist Count Pico della Mirandola, speaking with the Creator's voice:

> We have made you a creature neither of heaven nor of earth, neither mortal nor immortal, in order that you may, as the free and proud shaper of your own being, fashion yourself in the form you may prefer. It will be in your power to descend to the lower, brutish forms of life; you will be able, through your own decision, to rise again to the superior orders whose life is divine.

Teilhard believed that human beings are charged by God with helping spiritualize matter and 'build the earth' by collaborating with the inherent divine purpose. In *The Heart of Matter*, he speaks of "a suddenly launched current of love [that] spreads over the entire surface and depth of the world" (Cited in Tresmontant 1959, p. 86) and in *The Divine Milieu*, echoing Paul, he writes that "By virtue of the creation and still more of the Incarnation, nothing here below on earth is profane to him who knows how to see. On the contrary, everything is sacred to the men who can distinguish that portion of the chosen being which is subject to Christ's drawing power in the process of consummation" (1960a, p. 66). Teilhard's spirituality was integrated into his fascination with investigating the processes of nature, and he spent most of his life battling the dualistic under-standing of spirituality which pervaded much of the Catholic cul-ture prior to the Second Vatican Council.[1]

Karl Rahner's Evolutionary Christology

The most renowned Catholic theologian to integrate evolution and Christology was Karl Rahner, a major contributor to the Second Vatican Council. In the 1960s he developed a theory of incarnation which is fundamentally consistent with evolution. The Scotists had argued that human personality consists in the capacity for inde-pendence (or lack of capacity for dependence). This potential is fully realized in the hypostatic union when Christ's human nature is fully oriented to God. In *Foundations of Christian Faith*, Rahner defines God's interventions in the world as "the becoming histori-cal and becoming concrete in that 'intervention' in which God as the transcendental ground of the world has from the outset embed-ded himself in this world as its self-communicating ground" (p. 87). In 'Christology Within an Evolutionary View', he tells us to

> take into consideration the known history of the cosmos as it has been investigated and described by the modern natural sciences: this history is seen more and more as one homogeneous history of matter, life and man. This one history does not exclude differences of nature but on the contrary includes them in its concept, since history is precisely not the permanence of the same but rather the becoming of something entirely new and not merely of something other. (p. 166)

For Rahner the premier sign that spirit and matter are not dualis-tically opposed is the human being: "the self-transcendence of

---

1. The Second Vatican Council, the largest and first truly ecumenical council in the history of the Catholic Church, with some 3,000 participants drawn from all over the globe, was called by Pope John XXIII to promote "peace and unity of all humankind," and was in session 1962–1965. It opened the Church to the modern world and radically changed the traditional official attitudes toward non-Catholic Christianity, non-Christian religions, and Catholics who called for freedom of thought and conscience. Self-segregation, condemnation, and proselytizing gave way to constructive dialogue with the secular world and other denominations or religions.

living matter" and the manifestation of the "yesterday which natural history develops towards man, continues in him as his history,
is conserved and surpassed in him and hence reaches its proper
goal with and in the history of the human spirit" (p. 168). He even
argues that, "the Incarnation appears as the necessary and permanent beginning of the divinization of the world as a whole" (p.
161).

The Second Axial Period

Ewert Cousins interprets Teilhard's vision as one of the indicators
that the present age represents a radical quantum leap of consciousness—the Second Axial Period (Cousins 1992, pp. 7–10)—
which will transform individual consciousness into global consciousness—a global consciousness envisioned not as simple,
homogenized or empty obliteration of individuality but as fruition
of the person in and through mutuality.

The process of creative collaborating with others from all over
the world may itself take on some of the characteristics of a religious act, an invitation to look at things a certain way, to celebrate
differences while rejoicing in convergence (*not* conformity), to
undergo what Lawrence Sullivan calls an 'initiation', a sort of
Lonerganian appropriation/conversion. Thus, while the Internet,
World Wide Web, interreligious and intercultural dialogue, the various ongoing global ethics projects, and the World Parliament of
Religions do not unilaterally propagate certain specific, already
existing faiths or ideologies, they all are rooted in the newly emerging master paradigm of dialogue and interconnectivity, and that
paradigm is bound to affect the way people understand their various worlds, including their religious doctrines and rituals. In fact,
the process of engaging in these kinds of integrating activities has
itself the potential of becoming the catalyst of a genuine change in
the way humans understand themselves, one another, the world,
and ultimate reality.

The key term at the edge of the twenty-first century is INTER—
a word that assumes a 'both-and' ontology and alludes to the
processes of life-giving, growth-enhancing exchange—in other
words: the primacy of love! To embrace pluralism constructively is
a metaphysical commitment, a stepping out of one's cozy cave of

familiar certainties and modes of functioning into the larger arena of competing paradigms and values. At this point participants in the dialogue become more than transmitters of information, facilitators of the exchange of ideas. They become agents of change, Socratic midwives, co-creators who de-familiarize the familiar and encourage their fellow-seekers to break through their respective pupa shells without leaving them newly-hatched and unprotected in a void, their old assurances and criteria for judgment gone, and nothing to take their place. All those involved are drawn into the ongoing conversation on an existential level, and all are at once learners and teachers, mutually responsible for themselves and others.

For Teilhard the concept of evolution was not only a theological category but also a principle of interpretation which allowed him to develop a Christian paradigm of the universe as process of becoming, and specifically as the coming not "of the decline of God in our minds and our hearts" but as "an undreamed-of renaissance of God in the universe, in the form of love-energy, produced as the fruit of, and within, a matter that has become for us the home and the expression of an evolutionary convergence" (Teilhard 1963, p. 280)—up through countless organisms, up through humanity, up through the Christ Logos toward the Omega Point of ultimate unification.

From *Homo sapiens* and *Homo faber* to *Homo communicator* and *Homo religiosus*

The present age, often called the 'information age' challenges us to consider a modified model of what it means to be human, a model that involves the 'sapiens' as well as the 'faber': the model of the human being as communicator, as a life form specifically designed to allow information exchange to become incarnated in a rational, self-conscious person who exists not in isolation but in constant dialogue with other persons, an individual node in the vast web of the exchange, merging, and emergence of ideas, past, present, and future. It is highly significant that the development of an accessible and nuanced written language ushered in the major transitions in Western civilizations from Plato's Academy and the scriptoria of the Irish monks or Charlemagne's court to movable type and finally the Internet and World Wide Web. In addition to the written language, indexing is essential. Without indexing, information cannot be readily retrieved and utilized.

Information exchange is fundamental to the roots of humanity, both biologically and culturally. Fertilization is a process of exchanging, decoding, and applying information, and the four nucleotides arranged like letters along the DNA 'backbone' in the cell nucleus provide the program that will convert chemicals into living cells (*via* proteins) and control the functions of these cells. I am not a microbiologist, and the technical details boggle my mind but even as a lay person I can understand such terms as 'genetic alphabet' and 'messenger ribonucleic acid' (mRNA). Scientists have known for almost a century that genetic material a. has a stable structure; b. can serve as model for self-replication; c. contains an information code that can be expressed; and d. is capable of change and variation. This means that we have known for at least a century that our biological foundation is as information-based as our cultural projection. The Genome project is simply our attempt to index genetic information in order to make it useful in the practical sphere.

In order to persist through time and have a sense of identity, communities must be constituted of individuals who are engaged in information exchange and are capable of passing on the essential elements of what makes their community this-and-no-other community to the next generation. Richard Dawkins coined the term 'memes' for those remembered images and cultural building blocks, these bits of information generally encoded in documents and texts, to complement the 'genes' of evolutionary biology. In fact, the link of human nature and speech/information exchange is ancient. Mythically, in the Judeo-Christian tradition, this idea is expressed in such images or stories as God revealed/concealed as the four letters of the Tetragrammaton, as Adam 'naming' the inhabitants of Eden, as the importance of the Holy Scrolls in Judaism, as the kabbalistic speculations concerning the symbolism of letters and numbers, and in the definition of Christ as the divine LOGOS, the 'Word' of God. Language, story and metaphor are essential to our sense of self. In cyberspace we have a chance to weave poems and stories on the loom of the web as we invent *midrashim* on the meaning of the broken tablets and haltingly enter each other's worlds, and imperceptively change—and are changed in the process of dialogue. Cyberspace becomes the perfect matrix, the womb/loom that can incubate/weave the emergent religions of the future and help us construct our multiple 'Ways' appropriate to the dawning Age of Dialogue of what Karl Jaspers, Ewert Cousins, and others have called the Second Axial Period.

PRAYER

Let us give thanks for chaos and logos and
explicate, implicate, and superimplicate orders;
for black holes, bright galaxies, and nonlocal connections;
for crystals and continents;
for the emergence of mind and memes from matter;
for Lucy's skull and Mary Leakey's
footprints in volcanic ash; for Thales' water,
Heraclitus' fire, and Pythagorean music of the spheres
that choreographs
the elementary particle dance of Heisenberg's
fundamental symmetries;
for Aristotle's taxonomy and Bacon's idols;
for the Indian zero, algebra, and algorithms; for the
oscillations of the Yin and the Yang; for
acupuncture, Su Sung's astronomical clock, and
Huang Tao P'i's textile technology; for Arabic
alchemists on the Old Silk Road and Ibn Sina's
Canon of Medicine;
for Euclid and Newton and Einstein's space-time;
for Leonardo's bio-art and Rembrandt's
meditative merging of darkness and light;
for Kepler's snowflake and Kekule's dream;
for Mendel's monastery peas and the genetic
Tetragrammaton on the spiral staircase of life;
for fractals, ferns, and fall foliage; for
caterpillars and cocoons; for the infant's first
cry; for Pachelbel's canon; for stained glass
windows, Leeuwenhoek's microscope, and the Galileo
probe; for Sheldrake's morphogenetic fields
of archetypal information exchange and Teilhard's

noogenetic vision of the emergent higher consciousness;
for the World Wide Web to help us become aware
of ourselves as co-creators of cosmic interconnectedness;
and most of all, let us give thanks for the twin passions
which make us fully human—the meaning-making
yearning to transcend the boundaries of time and space by
learning and by loving.

References

Ames, Roger T., and Henry Rosemont, Jr. 1998. *The Analects of Confucius: A Philosophical Translation*. New York: Ballantine.

Cousins Ewert. 1992. *Christ of the 21st Century*. Rockport, Massachusetts: Element.

Cuénot, Claude. 1965. *Teilhard de Chardin: A Biographical Sketch*. Baltimore: Helicon.

Gallup, Gordon G. n.d. Toward a Comparative Psychology of Mind. In Roger L. Mellgren, ed., *Animal Cognition and Behavior* (Amsterdam, NY: North-Holland Publishing).

Griffin, Donald R. 1976. *The Questions of Animal Awareness: Evolutionary Continuity of Mental Experience*. New York: Rockefeller University Press.

———. 1984. *Animal Thinking*. Cambridge, Massachusetts: Harvard University Press.

Laughlin, Charles D., Jr., John McManus, and Eugene G. d'Aquili. Mature Contemplation. *Zygon: Journal of Religion and Science* 28:2 (June 1993).

Rahner, Karl. 1966. Christology within an Evolutionary View of the World. *Theological Investigations: Volume 5* (Baltimore: Helicon), pp. 157–192.

———. 1978. *Foundations of Christian Faith*. New York: Crossroads.

Teilhard de Chardin, Pierre. 1960a. *The Divine Milieu*. San Francisco: Harper and Row.

———. 1960b. *The Phenomenon of Man*. San Francisco: Harper and Row.

———. 1963. *The Activation of Energy*. New York: Harcourt Brace Jovanovich.

Tresmontant, Claude. 1959. *Pierre Teilhard de Chardin: His Thought*. Baltimore: Helicon.

Whitehead, Alfred North. 1977 [1925]. *Science and the Modern World*. Boston: The Free Press.

Wolf, Fred Alan. 1984. *Star Wave: Mind, Consciousness, and Quantum Physics*. New York: Macmillan.

23

Science and Religion as World-Builders

PHILIP HEFNER

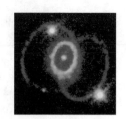

Science and religion are both ways of world-building—constructing worldviews in which people can make sense of their place in the universe story. Science and religion need each other if the worldviews they create are to be satisfactory.

Anthropologists have written a great deal about religion as a fundamental element of human life, in which people 'put their world together'. I like this term even though it is an awkward one. Putting our world together is what I also call worldview-construction or world-building. Individuals put their worlds together, but communities and entire societies are also engaged in world-building.

As we go about our lives, we live in what a poet has called, a "buzzing whirl." The philosopher, Holmes Rolston refers to the same thing as an endless "milieu of events." In this buzzing whirl or endless milieu of events, we are aware of a kaleidoscope of things: other people, friends and foes, noises, sights, nature around us, moral challenges, language, music, weather, food, health, disease, death, our own feelings, the need to work, and on and on. Instinctively, we try to make sense of this buzzing whirl. We attempt to weave our desires, our obligations, our relationships with other people, our social placement, the ideologies that we have absorbed—all into some kind of viable, workable whole. We do this unconsciously, instinctively, and we also occasionally do it self-consciously and rationally.

I focus on this quintessential human concern in my portrayal of religion, because I think that it is religion's central concern, its core. There are other things in human life besides the search for meaning, and there is more to religion, of course, but surely this search is at the heart of it. 'Meaning' and 'meaningfulness' are terms that call attention to the sense in which we stand in a relationship to the buzz and whirl of our lives. There is some kind of 'fit' or 'coherence' between us and whatever it is that we encounter in life. The question why things 'matter', what their 'significance' is, arises in this context. When we speak about the meaning and meaningfulness of a thing, we also, at least implicitly, describe its significance for us.

'Meaning' and 'meaningfulness' have both objective and subjective dimensions. No matter how appealing we find the so-called postmodern perspectives, we believe that what we perceive as meaning and meaningfulness characterize the very nature of the things we know. Thus, there is an objective pole to our perceptions of meaning and meaningfulness. At the same time, we call our perceptions and descriptions adequate or inadequate, thus referring to the subjective pole. We seek meaning and we seek coherence when we ask how we belong or do not belong to the whirl, the milieu of events, that is our daily life.

Religion is about this activity of meaning-formation, which is synonymous with world-building. The rituals, dogmas, moral codes, personal devotional habits, and all religious behaviors are part of this world-building, and they are bearers of the personal and communal meanings that constitute world-building. Not every religion engages in world-building in the same way, but they all have an approach to this task. The so-called 'orthodoxic' religions, such as Christianity in general and Protestant Christianity in particular, may put a particular premium on self-conscious doctrines in the world-building process, whereas so-called 'orthopraxic' religions, such as Buddhism or Judaism may put the priority on ritual or moral behaviors—but world-building is a preoccupation in either type of religion.

Where Science and Religion Meet

Science is both a method of exploring the world and a body of knowledge about the world. It is a way of thinking and an activity, but it is also the assembly of all the facts and theories that science has brought together as knowledge of the world. Both of these aspects of science—method and knowledge—are significant for the activity of world-building, and it is in this activity that science and religion meet each other at the deepest level.

It is oftentimes very difficult to distinguish between science and religion in the enterprise of world-building. The Christian theologian Paul Tillich has insisted that science and religion both grow out of the primordial human propensity to seek knowledge and truth. This propensity is far older than our perception of any difference between science and religion. Since it is natural for religion to want to know how the world operates, it is also natural for religion to be concerned with exploring the world and gaining knowledge about it. Since the natural and social world is at the center of scientific concern, scientists have a very deep interest in discovering meaning in the processes that they explore; this deep interest includes a sensitivity to behavior that is harmonious with what they learn in their explorations of the world, especially moral behavior. They are also very often struck by the awesomeness and mystery of what they study. Scientists are often depicted as persons who treat the world they explore in ruthlessly manipulative, dominating ways. It is just as true to say that scientists approach the world as lovers, seeking to woo nature into revealing herself.

When we view religion and science in these perspectives, then it is not surprising that they are sometimes difficult to separate into watertight compartments. The scientist whose deep regard for nature includes a dimension of moral responsibility and awe is not far from religion. The religious believer who seeks to understand the world because it has a deep significance, even rooted in God, in the case of theistic religions, and who wishes to live harmoniously with this nature—that religious believer is not far from science.

We can hardly overestimate the significance of this insight: that the scientific and the religious propensities were one before they became two different activities; their fundamental unity precedes their current separateness. No matter how much science has changed in the last five hundred years, and no matter how tempestuously science and religion fight against each other at times, the unity that Tillich speaks of is ineradicable. This unity is clearly visible in the concern of many scientists today that evolution be understood as an epic of creation, and also in the concern of many theologians and other religious believers that scientific knowledge be integrated into religious belief and behavior.

Scientific Knowledge as Material for World-Building

Perhaps the most obvious impact of science upon our world-building is the body of knowledge that it produces. The theory of the universe's origins in what we call the Big Bang; the biological interrelatedness of all living things on Earth, together with theories about the origins of life; genetic science, which depicts the ways in which our lives are conditioned by our genetic make-up—these kinds of knowledge are inescapable as elements of the way we look at the world. Consequently, these elements of scientific knowledge cannot be ignored as we engage in world-building. If we believe that this world is the creation of a God, about whom we learn in our sacred scriptures, then our world-building must somehow bring our beliefs about God and our scientific knowledge into the same frame of meaning. And if meaning has, as I have suggested, something to do with our relationship to the world and our belonging within it, then our world-building must place us within the world of Big Bang cosmology, cell biology, and genetics, must clarify our 'fit' within this world. Our world-building must help us to understand how cosmology, cell biology, and genetics are related to our own sense of self, who we are, and how our community life is to be structured, both in terms of our religious communities and our secular communities.

World-building is tied very closely to the actual experiences of life. Science, together with science-based technology, intersects human life not only in the intellectual realm, with its knowledge about the world, but also in the existential, affective realm where it engenders experiences that are in themselves new to human life.

From their origins, human beings have been conditioned to be alert to the large and sudden challenges that come their way, producing immediate consequences: the pounce of a tiger in the jungle, the stampede of elephants, lightning and thunder, avalanches, warfare. Our sensory systems are not suited to notice the very small, the microscopic challenges that may have no immediate consequences for us, but which may threaten us over the long haul: smoking tobacco and ingesting other slow-acting toxic substances, polluting waterways upstream from their irrigation functions, polluting the air, handling radioactive substances, and the like. It is science that enables us to be aware of these minute, long-term effects. Awareness of these subtle consequences engenders a range of new experiences that must be integrated into our interpretation of life and our assessment of behaviors, even moral behaviors.

Science, when linked to certain technologies, enables us to intervene in natural processes in ways that were unimaginable even a generation ago. This is apparent in the practice of medicine, particularly as it pertains to the beginning and ending of life. It's a new experience for us to be obliged to decide when a loved one must die after having been kept alive by medical interventions for weeks, months, or even years. It's a new experience for us to become aware that the baby in a mother's womb has lethal genetic defects and therefore might be aborted. It is also new to us that science-based *in vitro* fertilization technology can give babies to women who are otherwise not able to bear children.

Since birth and death are themes of great significance to all religions, these new experiences must be understood, interpreted, and morally engaged by religious believers as they attempt to put their worlds together in the world-building activity.

Science's Challenge to Religious World-Building

I have said that religion and science encounter each other most significantly in the human effort to put the world together in a viable, meaningful way. It is as partners, or even as siblings, in this world-building process that religion and science find their kinship, and it is here that they challenge each other, sometimes to the point of open hostility. Here I will focus only on science's challenge to religion.

The challenge science offers to religion in the process of world-building comes at precisely the three points I have mentioned: the points of contact between science and religion in the world-building process.

The basic human desire for knowledge and truth lies at the heart of the primordial unity of science and religion. The closeness that is engendered by this original unity is also the closeness that breeds conflict. The reasons for this conflict are too complex to analyze here, but we can sketch them briefly. First, science has come to a point where its methods of seeking knowledge and truth differ substantially from those of religion. Second, the use of language and concepts in the two quests for truth also differ in important ways, and each has a tendency to misunderstand the use of language by the other. Third, both science and religion have been co-opted by societal and cultural forces whose differing, even conflicting, interests tend to accentuate the conflict between science and religion. The outcome of these sources of conflict is that the primordial unity I spoke of is often scarcely recognizable nowadays.

The religions of the world accept, as normative, articulations of wisdom about the world that are millennia old. Even though much of this wisdom is profoundly relevant to life today, its form is for the most part archaic. This puts it, at least *prima facie*, at odds with scientific knowledge, whose articulations are continually presented in new and current forms.

Communication between archaic forms and current ones is difficult at best, even for those persons who understand that archaic forms are not necessarily to be understood literally. Unfortunately, most religious believers today, as well as most scientists consider ancient religious formulations to be literally intended. Fundamentalists, of course, in both science and religion, hold this literalism to be the norm, and so do other conservative religious adherents. Until both scientists and religious believers gain more awareness of the uses of language, and the differences between scientific and religious language, we will experience great difficulty in integrating scientific knowledge into the process of religious world-building.

There's another sense in which scientific knowledge poses a challenge for all attempts at finding meaning in natural processes, not simply for religious attempts. Scientific theories of chance, indeterminacy, blind evolution, and heat death, to name only a few, actually oppose any coherence that finds meaning in specifically human life. These themes are at the center of efforts by religious thinkers to put the world together, but they are difficult to harmonize with many of the findings of science.

The new experience engendered by science and technology accentuates the manner in which religion is rooted in ancient formulations that in turn mirror ancient experience. If we focus for a moment on religions that believe in a God, theistic religions, we observe how difficult it is to relate new forms of experience and scientific-technological reality to the work of God's creation. Genetic engineering, for example, is not related in any positive way to the work of God by most theistic thinkers. Furthermore, moral codes that grow out of ancient times are very difficult to correlate to contemporary experience as it is shaped by science and technology. Most of the dilemmas surrounding reproductive science and technology are rooted in experiences that ancient men and women simply had no possibility of knowing. The same can be said of medical practices that pertain to the end of life.

Religion is faced, therefore, with formidable challenges when it seeks to engage science and include science in its efforts at world-building. It is little wonder that many of us think that traditional religious thought will have to undergo deep transformation if we are to engage science in our world-building. It is also little wonder that many voices in the secular world, and among scientists themselves, are seeking ways of world-building that offer an alternative to traditional religion.

Why Science and Religion Need Each Other

Although the challenges of science to religious world-building are daunting to many religious people, the resources that science offers religion in the world-building process are impressive.

Science offers resources of vitality and credibility that cannot be overlooked in any attempt at world-building. The reasons why science poses difficulties to world-building are the very grounds of its being a resource for the effort of constructing meaningful worldviews. When worldviews face up to the issues of indeterminacy and heat death, for example, they also gain vigor, vitality, and the ability to engage their adherents more vividly.

For theistic religions, attention to the new experiences that science and technology engender is a way to encounter the new modes in which God is working in the world, and a way of opening up avenues for human reflection upon the work of God.

Religion needs science for its world-building, if its interpretations are to be credible and possess a sense of actual reality. Science needs religion, because unless its knowledge is incorporated into credible world-building, science forfeits its standing as a humanistic enterprise, and is left isolated as an anti-human methodology and body of knowledge.

Loyal Rue, in his book, *Everybody's Story* (SUNY Press, 1999), states the issues that I have raised here. He lays bare the challenge to classical religious narratives: they are increasingly shown to be, on the one hand, so tied to the archaic circumstances of their origin that they possess little credibility for people in the twenty-first century, and on the other hand inadequate to interpret and ground human life in the face of what Rue and Gerald Barney have called "the global problematique," by which they mean the current crisis of human solidarity and the lack of a planetary ethic.

Rue understands this situation to pose a near-lethal challenge to traditional religion. He proposes that the evolutionary epic, which is the grand narrative of evolutionary theory, cosmic, biological, and cultural, become a new myth that functions religiously to interpret human life and ground the behaviors of human solidarity and planetary responsibility.

I agree with Rue's posing of the challenge. I differ from him in my conviction that the situation he describes so incisively is not only a challenge but also a resource for religion and an occasion for its renewal. Humanity is indeed challenged to reinterpret and refigure its traditional religious myths—unless it does so, they cannot be a vital resource for human life in the twenty-first century. At the same time, traditional religion possesses resources that simply cannot be accessed elsewhere at the deep level that can sustain the broad reach of entire societies and civilizations—the reach that includes all economic and social classes, all levels of education and occupations, through all the phases of the life cycle of individuals and groups. The kind of science-based mythic construction that Rue recommends will serve many people, including intellectuals and others who are attuned to science-based thinking—admittedly a group that is counted in the millions. However, the mythic refiguring of human existence works at a psychic depth and aesthetic and moral breadth that require the experience and resources of traditional religion.

The challenge of science to religion is also a resource for religion. The current inadequacy of religion is its potential. Religion's search for knowledge and truth requires the vitality of science and its creations.

On Convergence

JIM KENNEY

How in the world is science to meet and greet religion? And how can such encounters give way to dialogue and co-operation? Can the two disciplines really ever meet? Can they somehow converge? That is, of course, the terrain mapped out in this book. And perhaps a tentative answer to such questions lies in a revisit to Cape Town and the ground of the present encounter.

The key to understanding this volume's animating dynamic is to place the encounter between science and religion in the context of the encounter between and among the religions themselves. Each of the essays in this book approaches the engagement of science with religion from a unique point of view or with a particular persuasion. It should, however, be understood that the symposium from which they emerged, the gathering that sought a "home in the universe" for a myriad of different scientific perspectives was itself at home in a powerfully unusual setting. More than 7,000 people—representing scientists as well as the range of the world's religious, spiritual, and cultural traditions and communities—had gathered in Cape Town to celebrate, reflect, deliberate, argue, confer, collaborate, and even occasionally agree about the past, present, and future of a world in the throes of a powerful paradigm shift.

It was a very special moment when scientists and religionists (and the many who fell somehow into both camps) came together in the celebratory, confrontational, and transformational atmosphere of a Parliament of the World's Religions. It was simply amazing to gather in a setting where strange and unlikely and joyful encounters were everywhere, where theologians strove to balance their enthusiasm for the universal with the intellectual demands of the particular, and where differences became topographical features, cast in sharp relief against the breathtaking sweep of newly discovered common ground.

On the Sacred Wheel

As I reflect on the exhilarating meeting of science and religion at the 1999 Parliament of the World's Religions, I recall a powerful image from the Indian tradition. Originally intended as a way of opening minds and hearts to the convergence of the worldís religious teachings, the Hindu story of the sacred wheel can serve today as an evocative illustration of an even more inclusive dynamic—the convergence of the full range of human ways of knowing. And so it lends itself well to a conversation about the meeting of science with religion.

Imagine a great wheel whose immense and beautifully carved spokes converge in a tiny glistening hub. In the center of the hub, there is only the brilliant blue of empty sky. In the Hindu tradition, the sacred wheel is a symbol of the richly variegated human quest. Each of the spokes is uniquely shaped and decorated and each symbolizes one of the countless paths to understanding. The rim of the wheel—the outside—represents the most superficial level of involvement in and understanding of one's own tradition or way. It's the level of greatest disparity between the paths. But the hub is the center from which each spoke emerges and the point at which all come together. It represents the common source and the deepest level of each and every way of understanding. It's the point of unity and the source of promise (see Figure 12.2).

And as I stand on the outer end, say, of the Christian spoke and gaze across at my Buddhist counterpart, I cannot begin to understand her beliefs and practices. From my vantage point, her way seems strange, if not bizarre. Alternately, let's imagine that I stand at the rim end of the spoke that is the way of science and gaze across at some person of religious faith. It's possible that my puzzlement is even more sharply drawn (as likely is hers, contemplating me). How could anyone—I might wonder, from my not-so-lofty vantage as a scientific novice (a 'rim dweller')—countenance a world moved by divine whimsy rather than by the cold precision of mechanical determinism?

And yet, as I begin to move along my own spoke and toward the center, slowly at first and then with more confidence, the distance that had separated me from that other, from all the others, begins to diminish. As I venture more deeply into my own tradition, learning something of its symbolic language and hidden dimensions, I find that the other's symbols begin to seem somehow kindred to my own. Suddenly it's clear that our paths are convergent; they share a common center. Just as the wagon wheel needs both its circles, the rim and the hub, so the symbolic wheel, the human religious/spiritual/philosophical heritage, requires the diversity, the color, the pageantry, and variety of the outer circle as well as the unity of the inner. But it is convergence, 'inclining to a center', that makes a wheel a wheel.

And as one moves 'along a spoke' and 'toward the center', one begins to apprehend the necessity and the power of encounter and dialogue with the other. As the distance between the spokes diminishes, as their convergence becomes more apparent, it becomes increasingly urgent to reach out and engage the other way of knowing.

The great Jewish thinker Martin Buber, author of *I and Thou*, one of the seminal books of our age, once recalled his first experience of what he called "feeling the other side." On a farm in the German countryside, he was absorbed in the simple task of brushing and currying an old horse. As her breathing changed in response to the strokes, Buber suddenly felt as though he had changed places with the animal. Although his own arms continued their rhythmic movement, he now began to feel the currying as if he were the recipient. In a sense, he 'became' the horse and shared its experience. In that moment, the vision of interfaith encounter that would shape so much of Buber's life and work began to emerge. "Dialogue," he would later write, "I call it experiencing the other side." And that was indeed the spirit of the 1999 Parliament in Cape Town, the spirit that enfolded the gathered religious and spiritual communities and that animated *At Home in the Universe*.

On Shifting Paradigms

Several years ago, in a similar mood, I wrote the Introduction to the summary volume from the first Parliament Symposium on Science and Religion. *Cosmic Beginnings and Human Ends: Where*

Science and Religion Meet, edited by Clifford N. Matthews and Roy Abraham Varghese, grew out of the 1993 Parliament held in Chicago. At that time I reflected on a growing certainty that ours is an age of shifting paradigms, of the wholesale transformation of our most fundamental values and assumptions about the universe, the planet, the human condition, and ourselves.

And indeed today, on every side and in virtually every discipline one can hear voices articulating those new ways of thinking, new models and modes of understanding, all informed by a shared appreciation of the interdependence of all life and a new convergence of ways of knowing. In the Introduction to *Cosmic Beginnings and Human Ends*, I wrote:

> A good friend once asked me, "How many people do you think lived through the Renaissance?" I've never forgotten his question. He wasn't inquiring about population figures, but about the essence of the time. How many people knew then that they were living in an age of revolution? How many woke each morning eager to find out 'how the Renaissance is coming along'? How many simply went about their daily tasks 'blissfully' unaware of the new world taking shape around them? Who responded to the opportunity and the challenge? Who exulted?
>
> Like the Copernican ferment, the modern stirring that can already be felt in so many disciplines and areas of experience is in a sense a reflection of developments in our understanding of the physical world. Put as simply as possible, it derives in part from increasing evidence of the radical interdependence of the elements of existence, elements which were once believed to be only occasionally interconnected.

I remember that I wrote those words because I felt such enthusiasm for the convergence that seemed underway and for the vital role to be played by the emerging understanding of interdependence. At the same time, I was deeply concerned about the critical challenges facing the world at the threshold of a new century— building cultures of peace, creating structures of economic and social justice, and establishing ecological sustainability. And as I write today, the enthusiasm and concern are no less. The issues remain crystalline in their clarity.

And it may well be that a paradigm shift—a new understanding of interdependence and a cultural transformation of the first order—is in fact now stirring. If so, it may be to a degree self-empowering (with the all but irresistible energy of the proverbial "idea whose time has come"). Paradoxically, however, it will certainly demand the enthusiastic advocacy and the thoughtful choices of concerned and informed members of the world community if it is to be fully realized. Visions of alternative futures must first be widely shared, understood, and opted for before they can be achieved. Alternative, paradigm-transforming visions must engage the key sectors of human culture and understanding. And that was what made the *At Home in the Universe* symposium so very unusual, focused and, finally, transformative.

That perception is clearly borne out in the essays assembled here.

On Convergence

The three sections of the 1999 Parliament Symposium At Home in the Universe present an elegant and persuasive framework for thinking about the future course of the religion-science conversation and about the dynamics of global transformation. They comprised: I. The Universe Story: Science at the New Millennium; II. The Emerging Alliance of Religion and Ecology; III. Science and Religion: Resource and Challenge for Each Other in the Coming Millennium

The Universe Story, put together by Clifford Matthews, a scientist deeply involved in research on the origin of life, offers a range of perspectives on what may be the most powerfully evocative mythic structure of our time. Grounded in interdisciplinary evolutionary thinking, as in the work of Thomas Berry, Brian Swimme, and others, this developmental re-telling of the cosmic creation tale creates a wonderful new platform for dynamic, interactive encounter and exchange between science and religion. At a critical time in Earth/Human history, this new telling of the story of the emergence of the cosmos may yet offer the most coherent and widely sharable mythos to ground a new path to a sustainable future. The link between the scientific and the spiritual that is forged in these presentations represents a vital contribution to an essential new conversation.

The Emerging Alliance of Religion and Ecology is arguably the most potent structure-transformative model on the modern horizon. The remarkable work done by Mary Evelyn Tucker and John

Grim, through the Forum on Religion and Ecology, has established a new library and a new normative reference for the dialogue between religion and science in regard to what is likely the most critical issue of our age. The presenters at the symposium and the authors here represented call our attention not only to critical issues but also to powerful new ways of engaging those issues.

The final section, organized by Philip Hefner for the Zygon Center for Religion and Science and the Institute on Religion in an Age of Science, brings it all together, in a sense, by posing the topic or question: Science and Religion: Resource and Challenge for Each Other? The new dialogue demands new vocabulary, new structures, new interactive modes, and new jntimacy between two formerly estranged partners; and the contributors to this section make major contributions to that effort.

On Pluralism

Something is clearly in the wind. Convergence—whether grounded in the new story, in the religion-ecology nexus, or in the larger structure of the science-religion resource/challenge rubric—is clearly here to stay. Worlds are converging. Science and religion are indeed meeting in this third millennium. And somehow their meeting informs and is informed by the meeting of the world's religions. In other words, it's altogether appropriate that such an extraordinary meeting should take place in such an extraordinary setting.

So lately I've been thinking about pluralism. At the same time, I've been thinking about exclusivism, which are positions on the same continuum. All three have to do with one's relationship to other ways of thinking. Usually the terms are used in a religious context, but they also clearly apply to our current discussion. Exclusivists, of course, believe that their own beliefs are so very true that all other belief systems must be wrong, and dreadfully so. They are to be found just as often in the camp of the 'scientists' as in that of the 'religionists'.

Inclusivists are more generous. An inclusivist might hold, for example, that, although your orientation is not fully correct, it's 'right enough' to give you a reasonable chance at 'salvation', 'enlightenment', 'heaven', or just plain 'correctness'. You might just be included under the canopy of the truer faith or philosophy.

Exclusivism and inclusivism are belief systems. They postulate 'truths' and calculate outcomes. One either accepts their inferences and conclusions or not. Pluralism, however, is an entirely different sort of intellectual model, not a belief system at all. Pluralism is, instead, a philosophical/spiritual hypothesis. It works like this. As one's horizon of encounter and experience broadens, one is likely to be forced to confront the insight, the acumen, the wisdom, and/or the simple genuineness of at least one other way of knowing the universe. As a consequence, one may begin to search for a way to understand how that wisdom or genuineness can be acknowledged and embraced without compromising one's commitment to one's own tradition. It's the challenge of convergent models for understanding. It holds the key to the creative engagement of science with religion.

I was once teaching a class on the religions of China when a woman raised her hand, stood up and turned to face the group. "I'm 77 years old," she said, "and I've just gotten back from a trip to China. Well, I met some of these 'Taoists' he's been telling us about and I want you to know . . . they're perfectly nice people!"

She wanted to share a moment of awakening; something new had entered her world. In this case, it was the simple good news that Taoists were nice people; but something larger had in fact taken place. China had given her a first 'pluralist moment', the first nagging awareness that 'niceness', and insight, and wisdom come in a variety of religious and cultural packages. She was already on her way to shaping her very own pluralist view of a richly diverse world. Let's hope it catches on.

Let's hope as well that encounter, exchange, dialogue, and cooperative common action between the world's religious and scientific communities will emerge as an essential, even animating, ingredient of the movement toward a peaceful, just, and sustainable future. We're on track. It could just happen.

This Book's Story

CLIFFORD *N.* MATTHEWS

At the Parliament of the World's Religions held in Cape Town from the 1st to the 8th of December, 1999, over seven thousand people from around the world—scientists, teachers, scholars, believers, and practitioners—came together to experience astonishing spiritual and cultural variety, to exchange insights, to share wisdom, to celebrate their unique religious identities, in short: to be amazed, delighted, and inspired. At the same time, participants were challenged to respond to the critical issues facing the global community, while seeking the moral and ethical convergence that leads to shared commitment and action.

The 1999 Parliament was a celebration of hope and a vision of possible futures. It also gave powerful testimony to the good hearts and good will of the many thousands of people, from every part of the world and from almost every religious and spiritual tradition, who believed that this gathering could indeed be the harbinger of a new day dawning.

It was not the intention of those who gathered in Cape Town to create a new religion or to diminish the precious uniqueness of any path. Instead, they came together to demonstrate that the religious and spiritual communities of Cape Town, of South Africa, and of the larger world can and should encounter one another in a spirit of dialogue and co-operation, seeking to discover new ways to rise to the challenges and the opportunities of life at the threshold of a new century. And they came with the realization that as each of us reaches out to the sacred in her or his own way, somehow, we are no longer strangers to one another.

The above remarks, based on the opening paragraphs of the Summary Report of the Council for the Parliament of the World's Religions, suggests what a wonderful gathering it was, taking place in such colorful surroundings, nestled against Table Mountain not far from the Cape of Good Hope! With the help of many volunteers, the logistics, involving a shuttle-bus service between half a dozen meeting venues and numerous hotels a mile or two apart, worked remarkably well, giving us all a chance to experience Cape Town as a vibrant and upbeat city that clearly welcomed our presence.

Jim Kenney, Dirk Ficca, Travis Rejman, and the International Planning Committee deserve the highest praise for putting together the incredibly rich and varied programs we were offered during those unforgettable days, ranging from the opening parade through the city following the Mayor's official welcome, to the eloquent plenary speech by Nelson Mandela thanking religious communities for their steadfast anti-apartheid achievements, and finally to the closing ceremony with the Dalai Lama and the dynamic Taiko drummers from Japan.

Interspersed with these events were innumerable intellectual, artistic, and spiritual offerings, including our four-day symposium focused on the developing dialogue between science and religion. Entitled *At Home in the Universe*, the symposium held at the University of Cape Town was divided into three parts: I. The Universe Story: Science at the New Millennium; II. The Emerging Alliance of Religion and Ecology; and III. Science and Religion: Resource and Challenge for Each Other in the Coming Millennium.

I. *The Universe Story: Science at the New Millennium*, organized by Clifford Matthews, began on Thursday, 2nd December with *Origins*, a whole-day consideration of current ideas on the origin and evolution of matter, life, and mind.

MORNING SESSION: 10:00 a.m.–12:00 noon. Eric Carlson, Adler Planetarium and Astronomical Museum, Chicago, *Our Universe in Space and Time*; Clifford Matthews, University of Illinois at Chicago, *The Origin of Life on Earth*.

AFTERNOON SESSION: 2:00–4:00 p.m. Elisabet Sahtouris, Living Systems Design, *Earthdance: Living Systems in*

Evolution; Matt Cartmill, Duke University, *The Appearance of Humankind*.

AFTERNOON SESSION: 4:00–6:00 p.m. Ronald Clarke, University of the Witwatersrand, *Searching for our Ancestors*; Terrence Deacon, Boston University, *The Co-evolution of Language and the Brain*.

Friday, 3rd December. *The Universe Story* continued with *Questions Arising?*, concerning cultural evolution, consciousness, and creativity.

MORNING SESSION: 10:00 a.m. to 12:00 noon. George Johnson, *New York Times*, *Science and Faith*; George Ellis, University of Cape Town, *Cosmology and Religion*.

AFTERNOON SESSION: 2:00–4:00 p.m. Margaret Wertheim, producer of the Public Television documentary on *Faith and Reason, Space and Spirit*; Clifford Matthews, University of Illinois at Chicago, *Images of Enlightenment: Slanted Truths*.

PANEL DISCUSSION: 4:00–5:30 p.m. *Cosmic Beginnings and Human Ends: Where Do We Come From? What Are We? Where Are We Going?*

By a happy coincidence, these ideas were reinforced visually during the week of the Parliament by the presence of a fascinating photo and text exhibit, *A Walk Through Time: From Stardust to Us*. Brought to the Parliament by the California-based Foundation for Global Community, the exhibit (about half a mile in length) laid out the five-billion-year history of the Earth as a Walk in which each step represented two million years.

II. *The Emerging Alliance of Religion and Ecology*, on 4th December, was organized by Mary Evelyn Tucker for the Forum on Religion and Ecology to highlight the important roles religions play in constructing moral frameworks underlying human interactions with the environment. Brief opening statements by panelists with different religious backgrounds were followed by moderated panel discussions.

MORNING SESSION: 10:00 a.m.–12:00 noon. Chair and Discussant: John Grim, Bucknell University. Judaism: Mark Jacobs, Coalition on the Environment and Jewish Life; Christianity: Stephen Scharper, University of Toronto; Islam: Nargis Virani, Harvard University.

AFTERNOON SESSION: 2:00–3:30 p.m. Chair and Discussant: Mary Evelyn Tucker, Bucknell University. Hinduism: Vasudha Narayanan, University of Florida; Jainism: Christopher Chapple, Loyola Marymount University; Buddhism: Kenneth Kraft, Lehigh University.

AFTERNOON SESSION: 4:00–5:30 p.m. Chair and Discussant: Mary Evelyn Tucker, Bucknell University. Confucianism: Tu Weiming, Harvard University; Indigenous Traditions: Teresia Hinga, De Paul University.

III. *Science and Religion: Resource and Challenge for Each Other in the Coming Millennium*, on 5th December, was organized by Philip Hefner for the Zygon Center for Religion and Science and the Institute on Religion in an Age of Science.

MORNING SESSION (PLENARY): 10:00 a.m.–12:00 noon. *Resources and Challenges*. Solomon Katz, anthropologist, University of Pennsylvania (Jewish), *A Scientist's Questions for the Millennium*; V.V. Raman, physics, Rochester Institute of Technology (Hindu*)*, *Science and the Spiritual Vision*; Hamam Hadi, medicine, University of Gadjah Mada, Indonesia (Muslim), *Religion as Resource for Science*. Pinit Ratanakul, religious studies, Mahidol University, Bangkok (Buddhist), *Religion and Science in Buddhist Perspective*; Viggo Mortensen, theology, Aarhus University, Denmark (Christian), *A Model for Dialogue*.

AFTERNOON SESSION: 1:30–2:15 p.m. (concurrent seminars). *Methods and Issues of Dialogue between Science and Religion*. Satoto, medicine, Diponegro University Research Institute, Indonesia (Muslim), *Integrating Scientific and Religious Paradigms for Understanding the World*; Philip Hefner, theologian, Lutheran School of Theology at Chicago (Christian), *A Christian Theologian's Questions for the Millennium*; Ghulam-Haider Aasi, religious studies, American College of Islam, Chicago (Muslim), *Science and the Qu'ran*.

AFTERNOON SESSION: 2:30–3:15 p.m. (concurrent seminars). *Methods and Issues of Dialogue between Science and Religion*. Norbert Samuelson, religious studies, Arizona State University (Jewish), *Minds, Emotions, and Human Beings: A Jewish Perspective*; Ingrid Shafer, philosophy, University of the Arts and Sciences of Oklahoma (Roman Catholic), *What Does It Mean to be Human?*

PANEL AND GROUP DISCUSSION: 3:30–5:30 p.m. *The Religion and Science Dialogue as a Gift to the Parliament and to the World* (with special reference to the *Call to Guiding Institutions* issued at the Parliament). Leaders: Ursula Goodenough, biology, Washington University, St. Louis (religious naturalist); Karl Peters, philosophy, religious studies, Rollins College (Unitarian-Universalist); William Lesher, church leader and pastor, New World International Foundation (Christian); Andrea Ng'weshemi, chaplain, University of Dar-es-Salaam (Christian).

The significance of this symposium for the Parliament as a whole can hardly be exaggerated in view of the enormous impact of modern science on all aspects of twentieth-century life, particularly religion. It is our hope that the presentations were of value not only in terms of the relation of science to religion—and hence of ethics to technology—but also for the light they shed on both the nature of science and the science of nature.

At the previous Parliament held in Chicago in 1993, Clifford Matthews and Jim Kenney organized a successful week-long symposium entitled *Cosmic Beginnings and Human Ends*. The resulting volume of Proceedings, using the same title with the sub-title *Where Science and Religion Meet*, was edited by Clifford Matthews and Roy Varghese (Open Court, 1995). It was awarded the Templeton Prize in 1995 as an outstanding book at the science-religion interface. Enthusiastic feedback from our symposium efforts in Cape Town encouraged us to put together the volume now in your hands, once again appropriately published by Open Court, with its longstanding connection reaching right back to the original Parliament held in 1893 at the Columbian Exposition in Chicago.

Most of our symposium presenters were able to contribute papers, aiming to capture in print the substance of their stimulating presentations. Three papers have also been included by authors who were unable to be present in Cape Town: Sir Martin Rees, Phillip Tobias, and Stephanie Kaza. A more comprehensive collection of papers from Part III will be included in a special issue of *Zygon: Journal of Religion and Science.*

Our symposium was entitled *At Home in the Universe*, but we found there were already two excellent science books available with that title, one by John Archibald Wheeler (American Institute of Physics, 1994) and the other by Stuart Kauffman (Oxford, 1995), as well as other books with very similar titles. After much thought and discussion, we eventually came up with a title which accurately communicates the purpose of the book and draws attention to the coming together in our time of the sciences and of the world's religions. *When Worlds Converge: What Science and Religion Tell Us about the Story of the Universe and Our Place in It* sounds right to us and, we hope, to you!

About the Authors

ERIC CARLSON is Astronomer Emeritus at the Adler Planetarium and Astronomical Museum in Chicago, where he served as Senior Astronomer for 28 years. He authored scripts for many of the planetarium's Sky Shows including 'Is There Life on Mars?' and the perennial 'Star of Bethlehem', developed a far-ranging program of astronomy courses for the general public, and now shares his vision of the Universe in frequent color slide programs in Chicago and across the country. Prior to his career in astronomy he studied with Huston Smith at Washington University and for several years at the Divinity School of the University of Chicago with special interest in world religions. He attended the 1993 Parliament of the World's Religions and is currently a consultant for a plan to build a planetarium in Bethlehem and for a Sky Show on the cosmology of the Pawnee Indians. He recently returned from India where he participated in the Synthesis Dialogues with the Dalai Lama.

SIR MARTIN REES is Royal Society Research Professor at Cambridge University and holds the honorary title of Astronomer Royal. After early researches in the U.K. and the U.S. he became a professor first at Sussex University and then at Cambridge, where he was also, for nine years, Director of the Institute of Astronomy. He has held his present post since 1992. With his numerous collaborators, he has contributed many ideas to our current understanding of galaxies, quasars, black holes, and the evolution of the universe. He has held visiting positions at leading centers in the U.S. and elsewhere and is an honorary member of the National Academies of the U.S. and Russia and of the Pontifical Academy of

Sciences as well as several other foreign academies. His awards include the Balzan International Prize, the Franklin Institute's Bower Award for Science, and the Gruber Foundation Cosmology Prize. He is actively involved in science policy, overseas as well as in the U.K. and is a former president of the British Association for the Advancement of Science. In addition to his extensive researches, Martin Rees lectures and writes frequently for general audiences. His books include *Gravity's Fatal Attraction: Black Holes in the Universe* (co-authored with Mitchell Begelman), *Before the Beginning: Our Universe and Others*, *Just Six Numbers*, and *Our Cosmic Habitat*.

CLIFFORD N. MATTHEWS was born in Hong Kong in 1921 and received his early education there. College years at Hong Kong University were interrupted by the outbreak of war and his subsequent experience as a prisoner-of-war in Hong Kong and Japan. After the war he completed his undergraduate studies in England at the University of London (B.Sc. 1950) and then moved to the United States for graduate work in chemistry at Yale University (Ph.D. 1955). Following several years in industry, mostly at Monsanto carrying out fundamental chemical research, he became Professor of Chemistry at the University of Illinois at Chicago in 1969, becoming emeritus in 1992. Here his continuing research on cosmochemistry and the origin of life led him to use the unifying theme of universal evolution in all his teaching efforts. In Chicago Professor Matthews regularly offered a minicourse—*Milky Way to DNA*—at the Adler Planetarium and in 1993 he organized a symposium on *Cosmic Beginnings and Human Ends* for the Parliament of the World's Religions. In 1999 he participated in the Synthesis Dialogues with the Dalai Lama in Dharamsala, India. In all these activities on and off campus his major aim has been to add breadth and perspective to the specialized programs demanded of undergraduate and graduate science majors and to convey to students of the humanities and professional schools, and to the general public, something of the excitement and significance of science as the shaping cultural activity of our time.

ELISABET SAHTOURIS is an internationally known American-Greek evolution biologist and futurist, author, speaker and consultant on living Systems Design. She has taught at the University of Massachusetts and M.I.T., was a science writer for the *Horizon/Nova* TV series and a United Nations consultant on indigenous peoples, and is a member of the United Religions initiative. Elisabet's current focus is on evolutionary biology as a model for organizational change. Her recent books are *Biology Revisioned* (co-authored with Willis Harman), *A Walk Through Time: From Stardust to Us* and *EarthDance: Living Systems in Evolution*.

MATT CARTMILL was born in Los Angeles, California in 1943 and graduated from Pomona College in 1964. After completing his Ph.D. work at the University of Chicago in 1969, he went to Duke University to teach anatomy in the School of Medicine, where he is currently Professor of Biological Anthropology and Anatomy. Dr. Cartmill has published over a hundred scholarly and popular works on the evolution and functional anatomy of people and other primates and on the history and philosophy of evolutionary biology. He is the author of the anatomy textbook *Human Structure* (with W.L. Hylander and J. Shafland) and of *A View to a Death in the Morning*, a history of Western ideas about hunting, human origins, and the animal-human boundary. The recipient of numerous awards for his research, writing, and teaching, Dr. Cartmill is the former Editor-in-Chief of the *International Journal of Primatology* and the *American Journal of Physical Anthropology*. In 1996 he was elected President of the American Association of Physical Anthropologists.

RONALD J. CLARKE, an academic researcher at the Institute for Anthropology and Human Genetics at J.W. Goethe University, Frankfurt, Germany, and Deputy Director of the Sterkfontein Research Unit of the University of the Witwatersrand, was born in England in 1944 and studied at London University (B.Sc. 1972) and in Johannesburg at the University of the Witwatersrand (Ph.D. 1977) after serving for six years (1963–1969) as archaeological and paleontological assistant to L.S.B. Leakey in Nairobi, Kenya. His subsequent wide experience in southern Africa included teaching human evolution and primatology, designing and installing museum exhibits and carrying out excavations in the Sterkfontein Caves, twenty years of research culminating in the recent discovery of a complete hominid skeleton perhaps 3.33 million years old.

PHILIP V. TOBIAS is Professor Emeritus at the University of the Witwatersrand, Johannesburg, where he has served as Chair of the Department of Anatomy for 32 years, and A.D. White Professor-at-Large of Cornell University. He was born in Durban, Natal, in 1925 and obtained a medical doctorate, Ph.D. and D.Sc. at the University of the Witwatersrand. He has carried out researches on mammalian chromosomes; human biology of the living peoples of Southern Africa, especially the Kalahari San (Bushmen); secular trends in growth; somatotypes; hominid evolution, especially the study of South and East African Fossils; and the history and philosophy of anatomy, anthropology, and biology. He is Director of the Sterkfontein Research Unit and has conducted researches at this famous hominid site since 1966, being responsible for the recovery from it of some 600 hominid fossils. His published works run to more than a thousand items including 40 books and monographs and over 90 chapters in books. He has received 16 honorary doctorates, the Balzan International Prize, L.S.B. Leakey Prize, Huxley Memorial Medal, Wood Jones Medal, Hrdlicka Medal, Charles Darwin Lifetime Achievement Award, Carmel Award of Merit, and many other honors. In 1992 he received the Order of Meritorious Service from President F.W. de Klerk and in 1999 the Order of the Southern Cross from President Nelson Mandela. He is a Commander of the Order of Merit of both France (1998) and Italy (2000).

TERRENCE DEACON, Professor of Biological Anthropology at Boston University, conducts research there and at McLean Hospital at Harvard Medical School. In addition to his neuroscience research on brain evolution and development, he has played a significant role in the innovation of neural transplantation techniques for the treatment of human brain disorders. Fresh answers to long-standing questions of human origins and consciousness are proposed in his 1997 book *The Symbolic Species: The Co-Evolution of Language and the Brain*.

GEORGE JOHNSON writes regularly for the *New York Times* on scientific subjects and their philosophical implications. Since 1995 he has lived in Santa Fe, New Mexico, where he is co-director of the Santa Fe Science Writing Workshop. Previously he was staff editor for six years on *The Week in Review* section of the Sunday edition of the *New York Times*. A special interest in ultimate questions concerning the nature of matter, life, and mind is revealed by his books, *Machinery of the Mind: Inside the New Science of Artificial Intelligence* (1986); *In the Palace of Memory: How We Build the Worlds Inside Our Head* (1991); *Fire in the Mind: Science, Faith, and the Search for Order* (1995); and most recently, *Strange Beauty: Murray Gell-Mann and the Revolution in Twentieth-century Physics*.

GEORGE F.R. ELLIS was born in Johannesburg in 1939 and studied at the University of Cape Town (B.Sc. 1961) and Cambridge University (Ph.D. 1964). He returned to UCT as Professor of Applied Mathematics in 1974, becoming Distinguished Professor in the Faculty of Science in 1999. His international career in teaching and research (with extended visits to Cambridge, Trieste, and many other academic centers) has led to the publication of over 200 scientific papers, mainly on relativity theory and cosmology, as well as ten influential books including *The Large-Scale Structure of Space and Time* (with S.W. Hawking) and *Before the Beginning*. Other titles such as *Low-Income Housing Policy in South Africa* (with D. Dewar) and *On the Moral Nature of the Universe: Cosmology, Theology, and Ethics* (with N. Murphy) reflect his concern as a Quaker with the topics of race and poverty. Professor Ellis was awarded the Gold Medal of the South African Association for the Advancement of Science in 1993, and in 1999 was presented with the Star of South Africa Medal by President Nelson Mandela.

MARGARET WERTHEIM is a science writer and commentator now living in Los Angeles. She is the author of *The Pearly Gates of Cyberspace: A History of Space from Dante to the Internet*, and *Pythagoras' Trousers*, a history of the relationship between physics, religion, and women. She writes about science and society for many publication including *New Scientist*, *The Sciences*, *The Guardian*, the *Times Literary Supplement*, the *Australian's Review of Books*, *Salon*, and *L.A. Weekly*. She is a columnist for *The Age* newspaper in Melbourne, and has written ten television science documentaries. *Pythagoras' Trousers* was a winner of the Templeton Science and Religion Book Prize in 1996, and in that year she was the J.K. Russell Visiting Fellow at the Center for

Theology and the Natural Sciences in Berkeley. She is a Research Associate at the American Museum of Natural History in New York and a fellow of the Los Angeles Institute for the Humanities. Margaret lectures frequently about science and religion at colleges and universities across the U.S. exemplifying her belief that "the scientific community has a social and moral responsibility not to speak just to each other, but to make serious efforts to reach the general public."

TU WEIMING is Professor of Chinese History and Philosophy at Harvard University and a fellow of the American Academy of Arts and Sciences. He has taught at Princeton University and the University of California at Berkeley and has lectured at Peking University, Taiwan University, the Chinese University of Hong Kong, and the University of Paris. He is currently the Director of the Harvard Yenching Institute. His research interests are Confucian thought, Chinese intellectual history, Asian philosophy, and comparative religion. Among his many books are *Confucian Thought: Selfhood as Creative Transformation* (1985) and *Way, Learning, and Politics: Essays on the Chinese Intellectual* (1989). Among many books he has edited are *China in Transformation* (1994) and *The Living Tree: The Changing Meaning of Being Chinese Today* (1995).

JOHN A. GRIM is Professor in the Department of Religion at Bucknell University. As a historian of religions, John undertakes annual field studies in American Indian lifeways among the Apsaalooke/Crow peoples of Montana and the Swy-ahl-puh/Salish peoples of the Columbia River Plateau in eastern Washington. He published *The Shaman: Patterns of Religious Healing among the Ojibway Indians* (University of Oklahoma Press), a study of Anishinaabe/Ojibway healing practitioners. With his wife, Mary Evelyn Tucker, he has co-edited *Worldviews and Ecology*, a book discussing perspectives on the environmental crisis from world religions and contemporary philosophy. Mary Evelyn and John are currently organizing the series of twelve conferences on Religions of the World and Ecology held at Harvard University's Center for the Study of World Religions. John is President of the American Teilhard Association.

MARK X. JACOBS serves as Executive Director of the Coalition on the Environment and Jewish Life (COEJL), a collaboration of 29 national American Jewish organizations and 13 regional affiliates. Jacobs took leave from a doctoral program at the University of Michigan to work with COEJL, the Jewish member of the National Religious Partnership for the Environment. Jacobs has been a leading figure in the development of a Jewish movement for environmental protection. He has written a wide variety of resources for Jewish activists and educators, and his columns appear regularly in the Anglo-Jewish press. Born in Bethal, South Africa, Jacobs now resides in New York City.

STEPHEN BEDE SCHARPER, who holds a Ph.D. in Religious Studies from McGill University, has taught Religious Ethics and the Environment at McGill, the University of Notre Dame, and the University of Toronto. He is author of Redeeming the Time: A Political Theology of the Environment (1997) and with his wife Hilary Cunningham, The Green Bible (1993). Formerly an editor with Orbis Books and Twenty-Third Publications, he has served as President of the Religious Education Association of the United States and Canada. He is Assistant Professor with the Department for the Study of Religion and the Institute for Environmental Studies at the University of Toronto.

CHRISTOPHER KEY CHAPPLE is Professor of Theological Studies and Director of Asian and Pacific Studies at Loyola Marymount University where he teaches Religions of India and Comparative Theology. He has published several books, including *Karma and Creativity: Nonviolence to Animals, Earth, and Self in Asian Traditions*; a co-translation of Patanjali's *Yoga Sutra*, and several edited collections of essays, including *Ecological Prospects: Scientific, Aesthetic, and Religious Perspectives*.

STEPHANIE KAZA is Associate Professor of Environmental Studies at the University of Vermont, where she teaches Religion and Ecology, Ecofeminism, Radical Environmentalism, Environmental Philosophy, and Nature Writing. She is a long-time Soto Zen practitioner affiliated with Green Gulch Zen Center in California. Her book, *The Attentive Heart: Conversations with Trees* (1993), is a collection of meditative deep-ecology essays on West Coast trees. She has also co-edited with Kenneth Kraft a collection of classic and modern texts exploring Buddhist foundations for ecological work, entitled *Dharma Rain: Sources of Buddhist Environmentalism* (2000).

MARY EVELYN TUCKER is Professor of Religion at Bucknell University in Lewisburg, Pennsylvania, where she teaches courses in World Religions, Asian Religions, and Religion and Ecology. She has published *Moral and Spiritual Cultivation in Japanese Neo-Confucianism* (SUNY, 1989). She co-edited *Worldviews and Ecology* (1994) with John A. Grim, *Buddhism and Ecology* (1997) with Duncan Williams, *Confucianism and Ecology: The Interrelation of Heaven, Earth, and Humans* (1998) with John Berthrong, and *Hinduism and Ecology* (forthcoming) with Christopher Key Chapple. She and John Grim directed the series of twelve conferences on Religions of the World and Ecology at Harvard's Center for the Study of World Religions. They are also editors for Orbis Books' series on Ecology and Justice.

VARADARAJA V. RAMAN holds a B.S. in Physics; an M.S. in Applied Mathematics (both from the University of Calcutta); and a Ph.D. in Theoretical Physics (from the University of Paris). He has published numerous papers on the historical and philosophical aspects of science and its impact on culture and society. He has authored five books on Indian culture and religion. He is Emeritus Professor after serving as Professor of Physics and Humanities at Rochester Institute of Technology, and has been active in science-religion dialogues for more than a decade.

PINIT RATANAKUL is Chair of the Religious Studies Department and Director of the Human Resources Center, Mahidol University, Bangkok. He is a leading scholar of religion in Southeast Asia. He received his doctoral education at Yale and is now establishing a major project at Mahidol University, relating religion and science to Thai culture and society.

INGRID SHAFER, a native of Austria, is Professor of Philosophy and Religion, as well as Mary Jo Ragan Professor of Interdisciplinary

Studies at the University of Science and Arts of Oklahoma, where she has taught since 1968. She also teaches an online graduate course in Global Ethics at the University of Oklahoma. In addition to four books, including *Eros and the Womanliness of God* and *The Incarnate Imagination*, Shafer has published more than 50 articles, book chapters, and poems. She has lectured in Africa, Asia, Europe, and the United States. She is a member of the Jewish-Christian-Muslim International Scholars Annual Trialogue and has co-edited a volume of papers (forthcoming from Ashgate Publishing) on human rights and democracy, presented in February 2000 in Jakarta.

PHILIP HEFNER is Professor of Systematic Theology at the Lutheran School of Theology at Chicago, Director of the Zygon Center for Religion and Science, and Editor-in-Chief of *Zygon: Journal of Religon and Science*. He has published widely on themes in theology and in religion and science. His most recent book is *The Human Factor: Evolution, Culture, Religion*. He has been active in ecumenical Christian circles, representing his own church, the Evangelical Lutheran Church in America, in which he is ordained. Professor Hefner served on the co-ordinating committee which drew up the 1998 church fellowship agreements between three Reformed churches and the Lutheran Church.

JIM KENNEY is co-founder and Executive Director of Common Ground, an adult educational organization and study center in greater Chicago which offers a wide range of programs focusing on the great cultural, philosophical, and spiritual traditions of the world. As Program Chair for the Parliament of the World's Religions, he was responsible for planning and organizing the many events that took place in Chicago in 1993 and in Cape Town in 1999. He is now Global Director of the Council for the Parliament of the World's Religions and a Trustee of the International Initiative for Peace Council. He is co-editor, with Ron Miller, of *The Fireball and the Lotus: Emerging Spirituality from Ancient Roots*.

Index